S0-BAU-136

Separatism, the Allies, and the Mafia

Separatism, the Allies, and the Mafia

The Struggle for Sicilian Independence, 1943–1948

Monte S. Finkelstein

Lehigh
University
Press

Bethlehem: Lehigh University Press
London: Associated University Presses

© 1998 by Associated University Presses, Inc.

All rights reserved. Authorization to photocopy items for internal or personal use, or the internal or personal use of specific clients, is granted by the copyright owner, provided that a base fee of $10.00, plus eight cents per page, per copy is paid directly to the Copyright Clearance Center, 222 Rosewood Drive, Danvers, Massachusetts 01923. [0-934223-51-3/98 $10.00+8¢ pp, pc.]

Associated University Presses
440 Forsgate Drive
Cranbury, NJ 08512

Associated University Presses
16 Barter Street
London WC1A 2AH, England

Associated University Presses
P.O. Box 338, Port Credit
Mississauga, Ontario
Canada L5G 4L8

The paper used in this publication meets the requirements of the American National Standard for Permanence of Paper for Printed Library Materials Z39.48-1984.

Library of Congress Cataloging-in-Publicatio Data

Finkelstein, Monte S., 1950–
    Separatism, the allies and the mafia : the struggle for Scilian independence, 1943–1948 / Monte S. Finkelstein.
        p.   cm.
    Includes bibliographical references and index.
    ISBN 0-934223-51-3 (alk. paper)
    1. Autonomy and independence movements—Italy—Sicily. 2. Sicily (Italy)—Politics and government—1870–1945. 3. Sicily (Italy)—Politics and government—1945– 4. Italy—History—Allied occupation, 1943–1947. 5. Mafia—Italy—Sicily. I. Title.
DG869.2.F56 1998
945.091—dc21
                                                                98-13534
                                                                CIP

PRINTED IN THE UNITED STATES OF AMERICA

Contents

Preface

Introduction   13
 1. Sicily from Mussolini to Badoglio   18
 2. The Birth of the Separatist Movement   36
 3. The Struggle Begins   53
 4. Separatism and Its Enemies   69
 5. On the Rise   93
 6. At the Height   106
 7. In the Balance   126
 8. The Radical Phase   137
 9. Decline   150
10. The State Acts   163
11. The End   175
Epilogue   186

Notes   196
Bibliography   267
Index   277

Preface

REGIONALISM has played a crucial role in shaping Italian history. Today, 125 years after the *Risorgimento,* unity is again threatened by calls for separatism or federalism. The popularity of Umberto Bossi and the Northern League is a reflection of the more materially advanced north's desire to rid itself of southern Italy's social and economic ills. Rather than being dismissed as an impractical idealist, or threatened with imprisonment for his views, Bossi has become a preeminent politician on the national level.

Fifty years ago, Andrea Finocchiaro Aprile met a quite different fate. As head of the Sicilian separatist movement, Finocchiaro Aprile called for Sicilian independence within a federal state. But, instead of gaining the status of a rather serious national leader, Finocchiaro Aprile and his followers were reviled as betrayers of the *Risorgimento,* and traitors to the nation. Instead of attaining the pinnacle of political power, Finocchiaro Aprile was imprisoned by the Italian state, and his movement dismantled.

The separatist movement of 1943–1948 represented the climax of regionalism in Sicily. It expressed the frustrations of one of the poorest regions of Italy, which felt it could prosper only by freeing itself from an abusive national government. It is a cruel irony that the strongest calls for federalism now emanate from the most prosperous provinces of Italy. The complaints may have a different twist, but the parallels between Bossi's Northern League and Finocchiaro Aprile's separatist movement are striking. Both show that Italian unification is not yet complete.

The Sicilian separatist movement had its roots in a long-standing historical tradition dating back to the Middle Ages, and its modern expression placed the island at the center stage of the Italian political scene from 1943 until 1946. This book examines the movement's origins, its leaders and followers, the actions in which separatists engaged in their attempt to establish a free Sicily, the factors that led to the movement's demise, and its legacy.

The separatist movement did not operate in a vacuum. Its fate was linked to the policies of the United States and Great Britain, and to the Sicilian mafia. To understand the successes and failures of the movement, its relationship with those forces must be examined.

No complete study of the Sicilian separatist movement has been published in any language. During the last forty years, memoirs and popular treatments of the subject have appeared that provide useful but often misleading information. Much of the previous work sensationalized the events of the period or assumed a journalistic tone. Legends and exaggerations have been spun based on hearsay, unfounded speculation, and ideological imperatives. My purpose has been both to clarify the record and to add to it by relying heavily on documentary evidence located in archives in the United States, Great Britain, and Italy. Much of this documentation has never before been used. To obtain a complete picture of the times, I have also reviewed and incorporated separatist and non-separatist memoirs, books, speeches, pamphlets, and newspapers.

Of the areas researched for this book, the mafia presented the most difficulties. The origins, character, and organization of the mafia have been analyzed in many scholarly and popular works, but the prevailing view remains the one derived from Hollywood, from embellished memoirs of former mafiosi, or from the transcripts of criminal proceedings. The mafia's survival in the face of constant prosecution has further added to its mystique. Much of its history remains obscured because the mafiosi of the past held more tightly to the code of *omertà*. To decide what the mafia was in 1943, I relied on the most recent scholarly works and published documentary sources. American archival sources, however, were the key to uncovering the mafia's role during the separatist period. The diplomatic dispatches sent by the American Consul in Palermo, Alfred T. Nester, to Washington, D.C., were especially helpful. Nester had good ties with leading mafiosi, as well as an excellent network of informers. The Office of Strategic Services also had sources which provided much detailed information on the mafia. The OSS material essentially came from two locations: the National Archives in Washington, D.C., and the Central Intelligence Agency. In 1983, the CIA declassified a number of papers relating to the separatist movement and the Sicilian mafia following a request made under the auspices of the Freedom of Information Act. The material arrived in 1984 without a file, entry, or box designation, and there was no explanation as to why OSS documents were contained in CIA archives. These papers, as well as those from the National Archives and other locations, helped to shed new light on the rebirth of the mafia after the war and its association with the Italian government. Not surprisingly, little data on the mafia came from Italian archival records, because such information would prove embarrassing to an

Italian state which constantly proclaims its antagonism toward the organization.

As I was told repeatedly by a variety of agencies, many records concerning this period have been destroyed or lost, or remain classified. I am still waiting for replies to some requests years after they were first made, and without constant recourse to the Freedom of Information Act, much of the information in this book would not have seen the light of day.

Many people shared in the making of this book. First and foremost, I would like to thank my former major professor, friend, and mentor, Dr. Philip V. Cannistraro for all of his assistance. When I was a graduate student at Florida State University, Dr. Cannistraro introduced me to Italian history and culture. In spite of my sometimes off beat choice of research topics, Dr. Cannistraro always encouraged my work and, when I was at the lowest point of my career, he urged me to continue my studies. Many years ago he suggested that I write my dissertation on the separatist movement, a project that he had planned to do himself. Over the years he has given freely of his time, energy, and most of all, his patience. Without his advice and encouragement, this book would never have been completed.

Unfortunately, I cannot remember the names of all the staff members who assisted me during my research in archives and libraries in Italy, the United States, and Great Britain. There are several people who deserve special mention. Mario Missori, formerly of the Archivio Centrale dello Stato in Rome, helped me navigate the Archivio during my first research trip to Rome and directed me to many collections which I would never have found on my own. At the Archivio Storico del Ministero degli Affari Esteri, Professor Pietro Pastorelli and his staff provided invaluable assistance in locating obscure records. James Miller provided my introduction to the collections in the National Archives in both Washington, D.C., and Suitland, Maryland, and has given me helpful advice throughout the years. John Taylor of the National Archives went out of his way to offer support, direction, and information every time I worked in Washington, D.C.

At Tallahassee Community College, a number of people helped in preparing this book. My closest friend and colleague, Mark Goldman, knows this work almost as well as I do, because he has read every draft. He provided much in the way of editorial and critical advice. My fellow historians, Dr. Frank Baglione, Dr. Will Benedicks, Dr. Carol Miller, and Dr. David Mock, also read the manuscript at various times and provided advice and encouragement. Tammy Kinsey deserves a special mention for teaching me how to use a computer, helping to edit my work, and for doing much of my typing under trying conditions. Debra Ilic Moran typed many of my letters to archives and colleagues. Carol Chenoweth and Jeannie Lawhon of the college library hunted down many obscure books through the interlibrary loan department and put up with my constant requests for technical assistance in the final stages of preparation. A special thanks goes to Ms. Kit Turner for having read and edited one of my earliest manuscripts.

Finally, I would like to thank a number of individuals who throughout the years have provided advice and encouragement: the late Professor Renzo De Felice of the University of Rome, the late Professor A. William Salomone of the University of Rochester, Professors Elena Aga Rossi of the University of Aquila, Francesco Renda, Lamberto Mercuri, Denis Mack Smith of Oxford University, and Maria Pia Rinaldi. The Finkelsteins of Columbia, Maryland assisted me by providing free lodging every time I journeyed to Washington, D.C. A special note of appreciation goes to Dr. Charles Killinger of Valencia Community College with whom I have spent countless hours commiserating about our respective projects.

* * *

Both my wife, Leah, and daughter Celia, deserve a very special thanks. They accompanied me on numerous car trips to Washington and New York and did not complain when I did research during what were supposed to be family vacations. My wife especially has shared in both my joy and agony over this project, and has given me the freedom to work when necessary. Without her love and encouragement, I could never have finished this book.

Introduction

APPEARING for the first time as a clandestine organization during World War II, the Sicilian separatist movement sought to create an independent Sicilian nation. It soon became one of the most critical and potentially dangerous problems in postwar Italian politics. Stimulated in part by Allied policy, separatists exploited the crisis conditions on the island and played upon the deep-rooted Sicilian resistance to centralized authority. Supported by the large landowners and the mafia, separatists constituted a real threat to Italian unity. From 1943 until late 1944, when the Italian government was most vulnerable and island conditions most unstable, the movement followed moderate, legal policies. In hindsight, this was a grievous mistake. The separatists' restraint in these years cost them their best opportunity for success. The consolidation of the Italian government, the Allied refusal to grant them recognition, the desertion of the mafia, and increasing pressure by anti-separatist forces, drove separatist leaders to adopt more radical tactics, including the formation of an armed force. In late 1945, following an unsuccessful campaign for foreign assistance and the separatists' failure to launch an uprising, the Italian government mounted a vigorous offensive against the movement. In October 1945, the separatist leader Andrea Finocchiaro Aprile was arrested, and within months, the separatist army succumbed to relentless government pressure. After May 1946, when the Italian state granted Sicily regional autonomy, Sicilian separatism disappeared as a viable political force.

Separated from Italy by the straits of Messina, Sicily occupies a strategic position at the crossroads of Europe, Africa and the Middle East. It is the largest island in the Mediterranean, measuring some nine thousand square miles. Its terrain reveals stark contrasts of high mountains, hills, deep ravines, plains, and forests. Once a rich agricultural center, the island has remained a predominantly rural society. In 1943, most of Sicily's four million inhabitants lived and worked in an agricultural setting. Only three major urban centers—Palermo, Catania, and Messina—existed.

Separatism has been a traditional Sicilian response to external authority. Invaded and conquered repeatedly by foreigners since ancient times, Sicily has nevertheless produced a unique regional identity.[1]

This patriotic consciousness, combined with harsh exploitation, has resulted in an intense popular sentiment for self-government. The thirst for independence became more pronounced after the eleventh and twelfth centuries, when Sicily boasted a brilliant and prosperous civilization under the Normans and Hohenstauffens, and served as a pivotal center of the Mediterranean world. Later, when other foreign powers controlled the island and exploited its resources, Sicilians often rose in revolt. In 1282 the famous "Sicilian Vespers" struck out against the Angevins. In the eighteenth century they rebelled several times against the Bourbons. Later, in the Napoleonic period, British authorities who occupied the island encouraged separatist sentiments.[2] The revolutions of 1820 and 1848 had separatist undertones, and during the Italian *Risorgimento*, Sicilians showed little enthusiasm for unity within an Italian kingdom.[3] Indeed, separatists regarded the 1860 plebiscite that joined the island to the mainland as a fraud.

Since unification, Sicilians have protested bitterly that the central government treated them like colonial subjects rather than equal citizens of the Italian nation. Sicilian politicians and Italian reformers accused the government of forming an alliance with the island's large landowners and northern industrial capitalists, resulting in the persistence of an essentially pre-capitalist, traditional agrarian society. This situation created a permanent depression on the island and forced millions of poor and unemployed Sicilians to emigrate.

In this perspective, the Sicilian separatist movement is a manifestation of the larger "southern question" that has plagued Italian politics since unification. This problem has been characterized by massive economic underdevelopment, chronic poverty, dismal social conditions, extreme illiteracy, and the lack of a modern socioeconomic infrastructure. In the half-century following the creation of the Kingdom of Italy, the domestic programs of the central government did little to alleviate these conditions, and southerners felt neglected and abused by a state controlled by the more prosperous northern Italians. Southerners protested that their economic and social stagnation resulted not from their own weakness, but rather from a deliberate policy of the Italian government to keep them in a state of economic subservience to the north.[4]

Sicilian protests have often been met with brutal repression. During the peasant uprisings of the Fasci Siciliani in the 1890s, the government subjected Sicily to harsh military occupation. Italian administrative personnel were sent to crush dissension, not to introduce a program of social and economic reform.[5]

The separatist movement of 1943 arose in reaction to Fascist policies, under which the exploitation of the island reached its height and further widened the chasm between Sicily and the mainland. Fascism represented the worst excesses of state centralization, and left Sicily seething with popular discontent. When the Allies invaded in July 1943, the island was left defenseless, and was heavily damaged by military operations. Sicilians seized on the moment of liberation from Fascism as an opportunity to free themselves from Italian hegemony.

It was once estimated that at least ten percent of the Sicilian population adhered to the separatist movement. Separatist sentiment cut across all ideological and class lines, and many who supported it did so for narrow and often contradictory reasons. The broad base of support hindered the development of a well-defined platform. On the contrary, the movement was held together by a policy of compromise which assumed that only after independence was achieved would fundamental social and economic issues be addressed. The movement derived its leadership from the large landowners, the middle class—many of whom were lawyers and former politicians—and most importantly, the chiefs of the island's mafia.

The mafia that re-emerged following the Allied invasion of Sicily in July 1943 was a traditional organization that used illegal methods falling within the confines of Sicilian custom and culture.[6] Its development was rooted in Sicily's historical experiences and its feudal socioeconomic structure. Contrary to popular opinion, the island mafia was not then, and probably never was, a tightly knit criminal association controlled by a single "godfather."[7] It was, instead, a loosely coordinated federation whose operations took place on a local level. Members of this group, mafiosi, followed a strict code of behavior while "traditional bonds of honor, kinship, and instrumental friendship" held the organization together.[8]

To establish and maintain their reputations, mafiosi employed violence, but their power derived not so much from the fear they instilled as from their socioeconomic and political influence. In a society that valued individualism, honor, silence, personalized and measured violence, and disdain for authority, mafiosi appeared to personify the best elements of Sicilian culture. They were "men of honor" who defended Sicilian traditions from dangerous outside influences. In many cases, they enjoyed the respect of their fellow islanders because they represented justice and order in a place where many viewed government as intrusive and oppressive. As defenders of Sicilian values, mafiosi often supported popular movements as long as they did not threaten their preeminent position. They also mediated local disputes, offered protection to local elites, indulged in a wide range of illegal activities, and dominated the island's economic structure by forming a tentative alliance with large landowners. By influencing and controlling the local political scene, mafia leaders insulated themselves from prosecution by the state.

The elitist, conservative, and personality-based nature of the Italian political system provided fertile soil in which the mafia thrived. In return for electoral support, maintaining the status quo, and stifling disorder, mafiosi received patronage, economic power, and immunity from persecution. No Italian leader dared challenge the mafia, and over time, it and the government became parasitic partners, each feeding off the other while exploiting the Sicilian people.[9]

Because mafia chiefs and landowners helped to guide it, the separatist movement came under attack as an instrument through which the island's reactionary classes sought to retain their traditional powers and privileges against the threat of modernization. These groups had held power on the island for centuries, and were reluctant to accept the consequences of entrance into the modern industrial world, a move that would have eventually destroyed their unique status. Separatist leaders propagandized for independence through nostalgic references to Sicily's glorious medieval culture, when the world had not yet entered the age of technology.

Although the island's elites had worked in conjunction with the national government to exploit the lower classes, the peasants and workers had their own reasons to support separatism. The peasants wanted changes in the structure of land ownership, but they also wanted to preserve their traditional social values against the potentially dangerous influences of modernization. In this sense they were the unnatural allies of the landowners. The workers, after having witnessed the exploitation and disappearance of local industry in favor of those in the north, wanted an industrial rebirth on the island. Independence seemed a better alternative than continued exploitation by the north. Yet, the support for separatism by both these groups proved only temporary, because they found outlets for reform in other political factions.

Like Fascism, the separatist movement represented a conservative revolution. Like Fascism, separatism emerged out of a postwar crisis and proposed an extreme solution to solve Sicily's historical ills. The revolution that the separatist leadership envisioned aimed at preserving traditional Sicilian culture, and despite the unwieldy character of the movement, Finocchiaro Aprile managed to hold his followers together for almost three years by following a moderate, centrist course, often arranging compromises with political elites and recalcitrant followers. He always spoke in broad, abstract terms that many applauded but few understood. He realized that the separatist movement, like Mussolini's Fascism, was too heterogeneous for consistent ideological positions.

Similarly, separatism, like Fascism, was dominated by one man, Andrea Finocchiaro Aprile, and like Mussolini he never fully controlled his followers. Separatist leaders such as Lucio Tasca, Antonio Canepa, and Antonino Varvaro held differing goals and often worked to increase their own influence. At any time during the separatist period, Lucio Tasca could have easily challenged Finocchiaro Aprile for leadership. He was perhaps the most powerful separatist because of his close ties to the mafia and other conservative groups. Tasca also proved to be a skillful politician. In 1944, he recognized that the survival of Sicily's traditional social arrangement depended on whether some compromise could be reached with the Italian government. For this reason he acted as the intermediary in secret talks between those government officials, mafia leaders, and separatists who had decided to accept autonomy rather than independence. That compromise cleared the way for the state to take decisive action against Finocchiaro Aprile and his intransigent followers. The mafia's defection spelled the end of the separatist movement.

1

Sicily from Mussolini to Badoglio

SICILY UNDER FASCISM

Mᴜssᴏʟɪɴɪ, like other Italian leaders, promised Sicilians much but delivered little. In 1937 he boasted that he would make Sicily one of the most productive regions in the world and labeled it the "geographic center of the empire." Yet the Fascist regime did almost nothing to improve conditions on the island, and it never won widespread acceptance. Fascist neglect helped plant the seeds of the separatist movement.[1]

In Sicily, as in much of the Italian south, Fascism penetrated slowly and much later than it did in the north. Before Mussolini's seizure of power, Sicily suffered less from the effects of Blackshirt *squadrismo* than most other regions, and Sicilian participation in the March on Rome was minimal. Only after October 1922 did Fascism gain substantial strength on the island; but local Fascists remained more nationalistic than anything else. Fascist organizations never had large followings, continually failed to carry out the national program, and never resolved crippling internal conflicts.[2]

Mussolini's rise to power caused neither regret nor excitement among Sicilians, and most islanders passively accepted the passing of power from the liberal state to a stronger regime. To a people accustomed to a minimal amount of democracy, Fascism promised little in the way of political change.[3]

After the Fascist seizure of power in October 1922, Sicilians rushed to join the governing party. The island's conservative groups saw the new regime as a bulwark for their traditional privileges, and many sought the party's protection and patronage. Landowners were especially enthusiastic, becoming Fascism's most ardent supporters. They viewed the establishment of a totalitarian state as a way of preserving their long-established dominance, while ending their troublesome alliance with the mafia. Until the late 1930s, ties between landowners and the government were the basis for Fascism's hold over the island.[4]

18

Opposition to Mussolini's state remained strong in Sicily throughout the Fascist period. Significantly, the first sign of anti-Fascism had its roots in an intense monarchical attachment. The Soldino Movement first appeared in May 1923, when in Messina and other cities, monarchists sewed emblems onto the lapels of their jackets. These little coins or "soldini" displayed the king's image and represented an effort to call the monarch's attention to the Italian internal situation. A month later, prodded by the appearance of the Soldino Movement, Mussolini made his first visit to the island and attempted to increase popular support by promising to rebuild Messina, much of which was still in ruins as a result of an earthquake in 1908.[5]

Political opposition to the regime received a major blow when Sicilian elder statesman Vittorio Emanuele Orlando, who mistakenly believed that Fascism was headed down the path of moderation and legitimacy, joined a common candidate list with the Fascists in the 1924 elections. The ticket won a decisive victory, crippling the opposition parties on the island and strengthening Mussolini's ability to change Italy's laws.[6] By 1925, Fascists controlled all the positions of power in Palermo, and a year later Mussolini declared his dictatorship.

After having consolidated his position, Mussolini sought to stamp out all resistance to the regime. The greatest potential source of opposition in Sicily was the mafia, and Mussolini acted forcefully to eliminate it. Originally, mafia chieftains had supported Mussolini. Mafiosi saw Mussolini and Fascism as instruments through which they could maintain their preeminent position in Sicily. It is not surprising, therefore, that mafiosi were among Mussolini's earliest and warmest followers. But, following a visit to the island in 1924, Mussolini sensed that the mafia represented a threat to his policies of centralization. He proceeded to relieve mafiosi of their arms, and destroyed their ability to control local elections. By doing so, he ended the mafia's traditional alliance with the island's politicians.[7]

Cesare Mori's appointment as prefect of Palermo in 1925 marked the beginning of a strenuous anti-mafia campaign. His crackdown brought into public view the authoritarian nature of the Fascist police state. Using torture, arbitrary arrests, and secret trials, Mori carried out a rather ineffective campaign to dismantle the organization's chain of command and end the mafia's hold over the islanders.[8] Mori had only limited success against major figures, and concentrated on less powerful leaders.

Despite Mussolini's claims that Mori's campaign was a success, it achieved little of long-term benefit. Mori neither completely destroyed nor seriously weakened the mafia's structure. Though Mori imprisoned or exiled to other countries some of the more powerful figures, many maintained contact with their island associates. Indeed, his campaign came to an end when he challenged "respectable" mafiosi who occupied high administrative offices. Although forced underground during the Fascist regime, the mafia's quick recovery in the post-invasion period can be partially traced to Mori's failure to eliminate the social and economic conditions under which it had flourished.[9]

While Mori indulged in his fruitless campaign, Mussolini made plans to modernize and incorporate Sicilian agriculture into his national program. This attempt at agrarian reform proved equally unsuccessful, because the Fascist dictator failed to consider Sicily's conditions. Rather than promote crop diversification, Mussolini urged Sicilians to plant wheat and participate in his "battle for grain." His policy of autarchy ruined any chance for Sicily to revive itself through an influx of foreign capital. Although some marginal lands were reclaimed, he actually weakened Sicily's agricultural economy.[10]

The support of the island's large landowners for the regime was contingent upon Mussolini's reluctance to attack their interests. By the late thirties, however, Mussolini had concluded that their traditional farming methods deprived the nation of food. The need for increased production led him to plan the restructuring of the island's agricultural system. On 20 July 1939, Mussolini met with the leading Sicilian Fascists and announced a scheme for a revolutionary economic step—the liquidation of the *latifondi,* or landed estates. He wanted to divide large estates and create small landholdings on which peasants would live. Villages would be established, with streets and water provided. He believed that these changes would make Sicily one of the most productive regions in Italy and enable the country to support twice its population.[11] In October of the following year, Mussolini announced the start of the program, but the war terminated his efforts.

Mussolini's policies did little to gain the allegiance of Sicilians. Opposition to the regime had been sustained by Mussolini's centralizing tendencies, the attempted abolition of the *latifondi,* and the forced delivery of food to government warehouses. Most importantly, however, Fascism had imposed an unwanted war on Sicily, and after 1940 brought German troops to the island. Mussolini continued to distrust Sicilians, and for security reasons, in August 1941, he ordered all islanders who served in an administrative capacity transferred to the mainland.[12] For Sicilians, the Fascist regime represented the culmination of eighty years of exploitation by the Italian state.

Unlike such movements in the rest of Italy, the Sicilian resistance never had an opportunity to mount an intense armed struggle against the Fascists. Some acts of sabotage did, however, take place prior to the invasion, most notably against the Gerbini airport in Catania. Only in the last days of the Allied invasion did sporadic encounters occur between German troops and the island population.[13]

Future leaders of the separatist movement, like Lucio Tasca in Palermo and Stefano La Motta in Nicosia, controlled anti-Fascist organizations.[14] These particular groups were never strong or unified, but undoubtedly served to plant the roots of the separatist organizations that appeared in 1942 and 1943 under the leadership of the same two men.

FROM ANTI-FASCISM TO RESISTANCE: THE CASE OF ANTONIO CANEPA

Antonio Canepa was one of the foremost leaders of the Sicilian resistance. Born on 25 October 1908 into one of the wealthiest families in Palermo, Canepa received a degree in jurisprudence from the University of Palermo in 1930. In April 1932 he joined the Fascist Party, though he did not truly support the regime. Indeed, in the summer of 1933, Canepa and some followers planned a surprise attack against the Republic of San Marino in order to demonstrate the existence of an anti-Fascist resistance in Italy. The conspirators planned to converge on the republic, occupy its police and military stations, and force pro-Fascist officials there to release the treasury, which would be used to finance the anti-Fascist struggle. They also planned to seize a radio station and broadcast news of their takeover. Before any action could be taken, however, Fascist authorities learned of the plot and arrested Canepa and his co-conspirators. As punishment, Canepa was sent to a home for the mentally ill, from which he was freed in November 1934.[15]

Following his release, Canepa decided to undermine the system from within. In 1937 he wrote *Sistema della dottrina del fascismo* (The System of Fascist Doctrine), and a year later penned *L'Organizzazione del partito nazionale Fascista* (The Organization of the National Fascist Party). In the earlier text, Canepa sought to dispel official doubts as to his loyalty, while hoping that his readers would "read between the lines and in the notes of the work" so that they would "know how many anti-Fascists there are in the world." Censors failed to grasp the real nature of Canepa's work, and in light of his literary contributions, Canepa gained a teaching position in the history of Fascist Doctrine at the University of Palermo and Catania. He also worked at the Institute of Fascist Culture in Palermo.[16]

In the pre-invasion period, Canepa organized the first local clandestine centers of Giustizia e Libertà (Justice and Liberty), one of the most important anti-Fascist organizations. He found his most fervent supporters among university students, some of whom would join him in the separatist cause.

Canepa also established contacts with the British Secret Service. He constructed a system of "observers" to feed the British information regarding a possible Italian invasion of Malta, and might have made as many as three trips to London.[17]

As he lay the groundwork for an active resistance, Canepa continued his literary assault upon the Fascist state. He exploited student discontent with the government by attacking the draft and Fascist injustices to Sicily. In 1942 he circulated a work lambasting Fascist rule, *Vent'anni di malgoverno fascista* (Twenty Years of Fascist Misgovernment) and a pro-separatist tract titled *La Sicilia ai siciliani!* (Sicily to the Sicilians!). To escape the censors, Canepa assumed the pseudonym "Mario Turri," which he retained until his death in June 1945.

Prior to the Allied landings, Canepa also masterminded armed attacks against the Fascists and Nazis. Because of the large German presence and the widespread expectation of an imminent invasion, Canepa and his followers had to limit their campaign to small acts of sabotage, such as raids on trains near Messina and munitions dumps at Catania. In June 1943, Canepa coordinated, and his followers carried out a strike against the Gerbini airport which rendered the base useless.[18]

THE ALLIED INVASION

On 10 July 1943, American and British troops landed in Sicily. The offensive surprised neither the Italian High Command nor German army officials in Rome. Attempts by the Allied High Command to deceive the Axis forces about the invasion site failed miserably, but promises of a more lenient and democratic government softened popular resistance.[19] Though this propaganda eased the invasion, it laid the groundwork for future problems. Sicilians anticipated an immediate improvement in their lives under American-British rule. When the occupying powers failed to satisfy these expectations, morale deteriorated and the population became susceptible to separatism's promises of a better life.

The invasion of Sicily opened the second front in Europe. Superior Allied forces guaranteed the operation's success, although the actions of Italian and German troops on the island also aided the invaders. The Italian detachments were not front-line soldiers, and disliked their German allies. Many Italian units surrendered en masse. With their lines broken, the Germans, although willing to fight, retreated quickly before the British.[20]

The Sicilian campaign took only thirty-eight days and ended with an Allied victory. The Americans and British suffered approximately 20,000 casualties, as compared to 28,000 for the Germans and 7,000 for the Italians. While the Allies captured over 100,000 Italians, an estimated 50,000 Germans escaped, many with their equipment intact.[21]

AMERICAN INTELLIGENCE AGENCIES AND THE MAFIA

The relative ease with which the Allies took control of Sicily, and the support given them by the local population, aroused speculation that the invaders had been helped by the mafia in the United States and its Sicilian counterpart. This assumption was partially correct. While there is no archival evidence of cooperation between the two underworld organizations, there is proof that both lent support to American military forces on their respective shores.

Connections between American Naval Intelligence and high-level mafia leaders in the United States had been established long before the Sicilian invasion. In what the Federal Bureau of Investigation itself labeled "an amazing and fantastic case," Naval Intelligence officials did in fact establish ties with and use Charles "Lucky" Luciano as an informant.[22]

In 1942, government authorities were concerned about sabotage by enemy agents as well as "possible assistance given to submarines by fishing boats departing from ports." To defend against such dangers, the rackets division of the District Attorney's office in New York City and the local Office of Naval Intelligence began to collaborate. Following several discussions, officials of both agencies decided that "some underworld characters might be of assistance with the problems confronting Naval Intelligence." They decided to "set up a flow of information from the underworld to combat the possibility [of sabotage]." It was suggested that contacts be made with the attorneys of underworld figures to obtain the information. Eventually, a network linked Naval Intelligence, the District Attorney's office, Luciano and his lawyer Moses Polakoff, and other gangsters such as Joe "Socks" Lanza.[23]

Luciano was already in prison in New York, but arrangements were made so that he could talk with his lawyer. Several meetings were held between Luciano and his attorney "in order to discuss matters which were of interest to Naval Intelligence." Mob figures such as Meyer Lansky, Frank Costello, Joe "Socks" Lanza and a host of relatives visited the underworld figure. One FBI informant reported having heard rumors that officials from the OSS and the War Department had also contacted Luciano at Great Meadows Prison.[24] While it is unclear how effective or crucial Luciano's influence was in stopping sabotage, authorities noted that strikes on the docks stopped immediately after Luciano's attorney contacted underworld figures who had influence over the longshoremen and their unions.[25]

The plan to invade Sicily brought to light the inadequacies of the American intelligence services. In their first stages of intelligence-gathering, agencies relied upon visitors to Sicily and new immigrants. After exhausting these sources, Naval Intelligence officials decided to collect information "from all available sources in the New York area," including Luciano and his underworld cohorts.[26] Naval officials believed that the imprisoned mobster had a great deal of influence within the Italian-American community in New York.[27] Though still in prison, Luciano again became a primary conduit of information.

Of special interest to intelligence officials were Sicilian-born Italians who could provide "information concerning conditions in Sicily which would be helpful to our armed forces preparing intelligence for the campaign."[28] Naval Intelligence told Luciano's attorney what was required. The result was that "large numbers of informants" constantly appeared at Naval Intelligence headquarters in New York City. The number of informants that appeared directly because of Luciano's influence could not be accurately gauged, but the officer in charge of the operation believed that "the greater part of the intelligence developed in the Sicilian campaign was directly responsible to the number of Sicilians that emanated from the Charles 'Lucky' Luciano contact."[29] Another naval official viewed Luciano's assistance in a different way. "It is impossible to substantiate from available records," he wrote, "that any information was furnished by LUCIANO or any of his associates, or if any was furnished, that it was of value in the successful prosecution of the Italian campaign."[30]

Luciano was evidently willing to do more than simply supply information to Naval Intelligence. At one point, a plan was formulated to release him from prison and send him to Sicily. Intelligence officials, however, rejected this scheme, and Luciano remained incarcerated.[31]

Luciano's assistance reinforced the positive attitude toward the Sicilian mafia held by American officials, who characterized its members as having a strong sense of "chivalry and justice;" one 1942 report even credited the mafia with having killed many German officers on the island.[32] As the invasion progressed, OSS agents gained the allegiance of many Sicilians who wanted to fight Fascism. These recruits willingly carried out acts of sabotage and murder, and OSS agents considered them "devoid of any moral scruples." More important were the OSS connections with the Party of Action and the mafia. Only five individuals knew of these arrangements, and no formal policy regarding this alliance existed.

The Party of Action, formed in January 1943 as an outgrowth of Giustizia e Libertà had few ties to the other anti-Fascist groups on the mainland, and had no apparent connection with either the mafia or the separatists. The local organization attracted the attention of the OSS because it was free from British influence and had a "better element directing its activities." OSS agents understood that neither Vincenzo Purpura, the Party of Action's local leader, nor the party platform supported separatism, but simply wanted better representation for Sicily in a united Italy.[33]

Concern over British policy was largely responsible for convincing OSS agents to attach themselves to the Party of Action and the mafia. These alliances were a means to further thwart the British, whom the OSS believed had infiltrated every organization and who aimed to guide and influence all political activities in Sicily. American forces were unwilling to accept British intelligence, and therefore sought out alternative sources of information.[34]

Suspicion of British influence prevented any collaboration between the OSS and Andrea Finocchiaro Aprile's newly formed separatist movement, which demanded independence for the island. The OSS acknowledged Finocchiaro Aprile as the leader of the separatists, but agents surmised that the British were sponsoring the movement as part of a plan to gain control of the Mediterranean. Based on these assumptions, OSS agents dismissed the separatist movement as a source of information or as a political movement they could use to further American interests.[35]

OSS agents acknowledged the mafia as both a political organization that could support American policies and a group that could be used to crush any elements opposing the occupation forces. They divided mafia elements into two branches: the upper, including intellectuals and professionals, and the lower, containing those willing to do "strong-arm work." They also regarded the mafia as the only organization capable of suppressing the black market and influencing the peasants.[36]

OSS agents held meetings with the leaders of both the mafia and Party of Action, and reported that "a bargain had been struck that they will be doing as we direct or suggest." The OSS considered the agreement unbreakable. In return, the two groups pledged to have nothing to do with any other intelligence organization, although OSS agents promised nothing in return for their loyalty. While OSS agents seemed to believe that mafiosi would cooperate with them fully, they neverthe-less organized a "complicated network of informants" on the island to watch over the mafia and the separatist movement. At the same time they warned both groups of confederates against backing any move-ment that sponsored Sicily's separation from the Italian state, stressing that such a movement would involve the island in a struggle for control of the Mediterranean.[37]

The Party of Action benefited little from its cooperation with the OSS, but for the mafia, the help given the Americans was the first step in its dramatic recovery from Fascist suppression. By serving as informants and "strong-arm elements" for the Americans, the mafia started to recover the power, lost under Mussolini, to control the is-land's political situation. Mafiosi also gained the opportunity to take control of the black market, eliminate enemies, and participate in the Allied administration of the island. Within months, the mafia had rees-tablished itself as the strongest political and social force in Sicily.

Ironically, the separatist movement also reaped benefits from the mafia-OSS cooperation. Because of the mafia's collaboration, little was done to stifle the separatist movement, with which certain mafia ele-ments soon aligned. American officials might have hoped that the pres-ence of pro-American mafia elements in Finocchiaro Aprile's movement would undercut British influence. As much as any other factor, this explains American tolerance towards separatism over the next two years.

SICILY UNDER ALLIED MILITARY GOVERNMENT

The Allied invasion of Sicily provoked the crisis of the Fascist re-gime, leading directly to the 25 July 1943 meeting of the Fascist Grand Council that ousted Mussolini. King Victor Emmanuel III replaced Mussolini with Marshal Pietro Badoglio, who created a new govern-ment in which almost all the major cabinet positions were assigned to military officers. These events caused little change in Sicily's local administration, in which many known Fascists retained office, a fact the population resented.[38]

Opposition to Badoglio's rule came from anti-Fascist groups based in Milan and Rome. They objected to Badoglio's ties to the Fascist regime and his reluctance to sign an alliance with the Allies. These groups had existed as underground resistance forces before Musso-lini's fall, and they coalesced during the first months of Badoglio's regime to form the Committee of National Liberation in September 1943. During the first forty-five days of his administration, Badoglio negotiated an armistice with the Allies, but was constantly thwarted in his efforts to create a strong regime by the anti-Fascist forces, who demanded a fully democratic government.[39]

Following the announcement of the armistice on 8 September 1943, German troops invaded Italy. Immediately, the king and Badoglio fled to Brindisi, which became the capital of the so-called "Kingdom of the South," which included Sardinia and all the provinces south of Salerno and Bari. The northern part of Italy fell under the domination of Hitler, who allowed Mussolini to organize the Repubblica Sociale Italiana, the Italian Social Republic, better known as the Republic of Salò.[40]

Events on the mainland had little effect on Sicilians, who were pre-occupied with their immediate survival. From the local point of view, the invasion had merely placed the island under the control of another foreign power. Unlike those of the past, however, these rulers were supposed to bring a reign of plenty and a democratic government. In their pre-invasion propaganda the Allies had made unrealistic prom-ises, and Sicilian enthusiasm for the new rulers waned as the pledges remained unfulfilled.

After the invasion, Sicily fell under the jurisdiction of the Allied Military Government of Occupied Territory (AMG). Its development had begun early in the war but had been slowed by questions concern-ing the role of civilians in military government, the extent to which the conquered territory should be rehabilitated, and which governmental agencies should have control. The invasion and occupation of North Africa provided the Allied powers some practical experience in civil administration, but little of this expertise could be incorporated into their plans for Sicily. Sicily provided a different case from that of North Africa in that it would be the first enemy territory to be conquered and occupied.[41]

AMG's organization and goals made it clear that civil affairs and the rehabilitation of conquered areas and their populations were second-ary to military needs. Military officials staffed and controlled AMG. Those personnel at the lower levels were specially trained for their civil-affairs tasks, but AMG's main objectives were to assure the secu-rity of the occupation forces and maintain lines of communication. Military attitudes concerning the civil administration of occupied terri-tory were very clear:

> The Army is not a welfare organization. It is a military machine whose mission is to defeat the enemy on the field of battle. Its interest and activities in military government and civil affairs administration are incidental to the accomplishment of the military mission. Nevertheless, these activities are

of paramount importance as any lack of a condition of social stability in an occupied area would be prejudicial to the success of the military effort.[42]

Given this stance, AMG officials received little cooperation from military authorities, some of whom were unaware of its purpose. From the beginning, therefore, military policy and a lack of inter-agency cooperation greatly limited AMG's ability to restore order.[43]

AMG guidelines prohibited local party leaders and organizations from having any role in determining the policies of the administration.[44] Yet, its highest administrative officials had little experience in civil affairs. General Sir Harold Alexander served as Sicily's military governor. Major General Lord Rennel of Rodd was the Chief Civil Affairs Officer. Lord Rennel's main responsibility was to advise Alexander on all military questions relating to Sicily. The highest-ranking American, Brigadier General Frank S. McSherry, served as Deputy Chief Civil Affairs Officer and Rennel's assistant. Local administration fell to the Civil Affairs Officers (CAOs) who were stationed in important cities and towns.[45] In the chaos that followed the invasion, many CAOs found themselves isolated, and made decisions without conforming to any strict policy. Since many of them lacked an understanding of the Fascist system, they often relied on local opinion or the advice of ecclesiastical officials.[46] This often led to the retention of former Fascists in administrative positions because of their usefulness, or the appointment of popular local personalities. Indeed, although AMG's primary political interest was the end of the Fascist regime, the defascistization process was disorganized.[47] The CAOs' lack of understanding of the Sicilian situation, the overwhelming number of problems, and an unworkable, and in some cases uncooperative, military bureaucracy complicated their tasks. In many cases, therefore, inequities between regions developed.

Mistrust between American and British officials also hampered AMG's operation. The two powers proved to be at odds concerning the administration of conquered territories, especially those with strategic or historic importance, such as Sicily. Nothing in their previous colonial experiences had prepared the Americans or the British for the Sicilian situation, and each sought to control AMG.[48]

As late as April 1943, President Roosevelt felt that AMG should emphasize the American character of the occupation in order to take full advantage of "certain valuable political and psychological factors" and prepare the way for cooperation from the civilian population. Among those circumstances were the pro-American sympathies that derived from the presence of several million Italian-Americans in the United States, many of whom were of Sicilian origin. This "political" fact of life formed the basis for the American interest in dominating the military administration and helped to determine American policy toward Italy. Roosevelt felt that the votes of these Italian-Americans, many of whom had fears concerning Sicily's fate, could be significant in the 1944 elections.[49]

The British desire to dominate AMG stemmed from its historical interest in the Mediterranean. English strategists had long-standing concerns about the naval situation in the area, and were adamant about controlling AMG. Indeed, American officials complained that the British deliberately kept information about the area from them, and sought to "infiltrate" British agencies with their own people.[50] In April 1943, Winston Churchill asserted that England should be the senior partner because of its special regional interest, but after Roosevelt applied pressure, he withdrew the request. Two months later, British military leaders again advocated British seniority, but just prior to the invasion they agreed to an equal partnership. Despite this arrangement, the British dominated the military government's hierarchy, a situation that deeply annoyed Charles Poletti, the American Civil Affairs Officer in Palermo. Months after the landing, Poletti criticized AMG headquarters in Palermo as an ineffective body and laid most of the blame on Rennel. "Major General Rennel," he wrote, "had better abandon military government and devote himself to grouse shooting. . . . He knows nothing of governmental administration. . . . General Rennel is the main cause of AMGOT HQ ineffectiveness. The leader sets the pace and it has been a wobbling shuffle."[51] For their part, the British disliked Poletti and suspected that he was one of the chief American instigators of the separatist movement.

If the possibility of a separatist seizure of power ever existed, the chances for success were highest during AMG's administration. In the wake of the invasion, a series of seemingly insurmountable problems beset Sicily. Banditry, a recurrent phenomenon of the Italian *mezzogiorno,* struck the Sicilian countryside with such unparalleled fierceness that even some police officials finally understood its social and economic roots. Michele Iantaffi, one of the island's highest public-security officials, described the causes of the chaotic situation this way:

> . . . the aerial bombardment which led to the evacuation of many homes; the whirling rise of the cost of living; the almost total paralysis in all activities, including the sulphur workers, inadequate communications, hardships of every kind; and above all the numerous escapes from prison by many of the most dangerous persons together with the collapse of the army at the moment of the occupation, and the consequent abandonment of great quantities of arms.[52]

Spiritually and physically devastated by the war, Sicily's economic and social stability had collapsed.[53] AMG's policies compounded the difficulties. At first, many Sicilians believed that AMG had liberated them from "twenty years of slavery," but the initial euphoria dissipated when AMG officials were unable to restore normality to areas under their control. The issuance of proclamations, the attempt to control food supplies, and the implied destruction of Fascism did little to relieve the gravity of the situation.[54] Sicilians, Poletti wrote, "could not understand why all of the resources and facilities of the Allies should not be placed at their disposal, now that they were the 49th state of the Union or part of the British empire."[55] To many, it seemed that the Allies were more concerned with propaganda bulletins than with concrete improvements. Statements that promised a quick end to Sicilian suffering totally ignored reality. In August, Lord Rennel reported "a substantial change" in public sentiment:

> From being and adopting the attitude of whipped dogs or fawning puppies immediately after the landing of the Allied troops, the Sicilians of all classes have reacted. They seem to me again to be becoming thinking, emotional and definite human beings . . .[56] the first fine flush of enthusiasm and friendly reception of the Allied troops is over. The Sicilian has remained friendly and generally has accepted the consequences of the invasion with fair grace. But he is already complaining that food is not available, that railways and telecommunications do not work, and that a new administration has not replaced the old one.[57]

Only the presence of a friendly population permitted AMG to make headway. In fact, in the later stages of the Allied occupation, Sicilians complained that the Fascist and German authorities had always maintained efficient transportation facilities for commercial purposes.[58]

While many difficulties plagued the Allied government, none were more vexing or serious than the inability of the occupation forces to supply enough food to the public market place, destroy the widespread black market, and lower the prices of necessities. The ineffectiveness of AMG aroused considerable discontent, and antagonism toward the Allies was easily transferred to the newly established Italian government. As early as November 1943, Sicilians complained that they were being maltreated and ignored by the Badoglio regime.[59]

Pre-invasion estimates of food supplies on the island had indicated that Sicily was self-sufficient and could produce enough foodstuffs for its basic needs.[60] AMG regulations called for the release of military supplies only in the most dire circumstances. This policy compounded an already difficult situation. In July, AMG officials conceded that food had already become the most pressing problem and that despite food price controls, much of the produce was sold on the black market. In an effort to curb the illicit marketplace, the Allies continued the *amassi,* a system of food collection established during the Fascist regime. This arrangement required growers to send a quota of grain and other products to collection points. Excess foodstuffs would be sold on the open market at a set, affordable price. Unfortunately, the *amassi* were understaffed and the prices offered the grower were too low to encourage compliance.[61]

The *amassi* system stimulated the expansion of the black market, while alienating many who saw it as a symbol of the Fascist era. While there might have been enough food on the island, farmers hoarded it in the hope that *amassi* prices would rise to a profitable level. When they did not, growers sold their produce on the black market, where they could reap large profits. As a result, some basic provisions, especially grain, were obtainable only at the black market.[62] In November 1943, when the food shortage became critical, the Allies reduced the amount of grain that a producer could retain, and warned hoarders that they would be unable to obtain ration cards if they failed to deliver their crops to the open market.

The black market and its exorbitant prices frustrated Allied efforts to feed the population, and contributed to a growing sentiment that authorities were ignoring the plight of Sicilians. With prices rising, only the upper classes could afford to feed themselves. The working classes, the unemployed, and those on fixed incomes experienced great hardship. By 1944, food prices were higher than they had been in the last year of the Fascist regime. By March 1944, ten months after the Allies had promised Sicilians democracy and relief, the OSS admitted that the misery of the masses was on the rise.[63]

Sicilians did not wait complacently while the Allies mismanaged the situation. Protests broke out in parts of the island, although most were relatively peaceful. All political factions were forced to focus on the food issue, but none provided a solution.[64]

Burdens other than the food problem pushed Sicilians to the point of hopelessness. Housing, transportation, and jobs were all in short supply.[65] A constant flow of civilians from town to town caused a further breakdown in stability. The Allies, however, persisted in their determination not to deal with these problems until the end of the war.

As the crisis deepened, Sicilians turned increasingly toward illegal, but traditional, methods to survive. Armed bands, some led by men who would later join the separatist army, began to plunder the countryside.[66] Enriched by the illicit grain trade, these bands recruited demobilized soldiers who had returned to Sicily. Some members belonged to the island's most respected families. Supplied with weapons left behind by the retreating Germans, these groups continued to terrorize the countryside even after the island had been returned to Italian jurisdiction. Many Sicilians understood that these bands were neither tied to political movements nor meant to embarrass the Allies, but were an outgrowth of the island's terrible economic conditions.[67] On the other hand, the Italian government regarded these cliques as an organized threat to the state, theorizing that they operated in concert with other anti-government forces, and attributing to them partial blame for the island's terrible conditions. The inability of Italian security forces to disperse these groups led to fear of violent revolution in Sicily.[68]

After several months of Allied rule, Sicilians felt less secure about public safety than they had under Fascism. Islanders doubted the ability of police agencies to secure order, and began to call for harsher punishments, including the death penalty.[69] Radical, and sometimes desperate, measures became acceptable solutions to the problems of 1943 and 1944. Within this context, separatism would find its breeding ground.

SICILY AND ITALY

AMG was never meant to be a long-term governing body. The Allied powers wanted to return Sicily to Italy as quickly as possible in order to "demonstrate that AMG operates only where and when needed."[70] As early as October 1943, the transfer of territory was discussed. Nothing happened because Badoglio and the Allies felt that the Italian government was not yet strong enough. Practical problems concerning administration, legal questions on the Allied side, and discussion over how much influence the Allied powers should retain in areas returned to Badoglio further delayed the transfer. Yet, the shift in jurisdiction was inevitable since the Allies viewed it as a way to demonstrate their support for Badoglio, and give his administration a measure of legitimacy. On 11 February 1944, the Badoglio government received control over Sicily and all liberated territory south of the provinces of Salerno, Potenza, and Bari.[71] In Sicily, Badoglio could rely on the prefects who had affirmed their desire for national unity prior to the official transfer, and called for the cooperation of all political parties. The prefects also asked that full administrative autonomy be given the island, but rejected any suggestion that they swear allegiance to the king.[72] In their own fashion, they reflected the disgust that many Sicilians felt toward the Italian monarchy.

In reality, the Allied powers had no intention of giving Badoglio absolute control over the island. A secret agreement which detailed the rights and prerogatives of the Allies limited his powers. To retain a measure of influence and enforce the conditions of the armistice, the Allies established the Allied Control Commission (ACC).[73] Although Badoglio controlled the island, the ACC played a major role in local affairs and influenced high-level decisions.

Poletti thought the transfer of power a mistake, because he considered the new government incompetent. He believed that it would undo AMG's achievements, and argued that Sicilians did not want either Badoglio or the king. He expected demonstrations against both once political freedom was restored. Poletti supported a plebiscite, which he believed would result in a vote against the current government, but for unity with Italy.[74] Other officials believed that the departure of AMG would benefit the separatists. "There would be riots and disorder," one official predicted. "Sicilians might attempt a revolt and declaration of independence, hoping to obtain Allied support for such a move."[75]

Response to the transfer was mixed. Some Sicilians saw the shift as a sign that the Allies were no longer interested in the island's problems, and many met the transaction with a sense of apathy, being more concerned for their living conditions. Some islanders actually wanted AMG to remain in control of the island for an indefinite period. Former members of the pre-Fascist Chamber of Deputies objected to the move and pleaded with Poletti to delay the turnover until the king and Badoglio had been removed. Anti-separatist politicians welcomed the action and believed that the transfer represented the death blow to the separatist movement. Separatists did all they could to prevent the exchange of territory and the departure of American troops from the island. There were no significant displays of pro-government support, and the Allies felt no need to promote Sicilian loyalty to the government.[76]

Once in control of Sicily, Badoglio began to search for a high commissioner. All local political groups agreed that a Sicilian should be appointed, and separatists threatened passive resistance if Badoglio chose either a non-Sicilian or a military figure.[77]

The separatists' first choice for the position was Giovanni Guarino Amella, whom the OSS regarded as a co-leader of the movement. Separatists presented Amella's name to Poletti, along with a request for the formation of an advisory committee with representation from all political parties. Separatists hoped that Amella would control the commission regardless of its composition. Poletti ignored separatist suggestions, however, because he had already given his support to Francesco Musotto.[78]

Along with Musotto, General Giuseppe Castellano emerged as a front-runner for the position. Castellano had helped negotiate the armistice of 3 September, but some Sicilians considered him an "arrogant Fascist and brutal character." Though the OSS believed both men to be unpopular, Musotto originally had the support of Poletti, Badoglio, the Allied Control Commission, and the mafia. A World War I veteran and an ex-deputy, Musotto had remained aloof from politics for most of the Fascist regime. During that period, however, he had made important connections with landowners and the island's mafia, and defended many members against government persecution. Above all, Musotto's reputation was that of "a person who will look out for himself first."[79] His greatest asset was his service as the AMG-appointed prefect of Palermo. Although he had proven to be a capable administrator, he had also acquired a reputation as a separatist supporter.

Once discussions began in earnest, Badoglio vacillated, because he could not decide whether the appointee should be a political or a military figure. Nevertheless, he assured the Allies that any decision would be in total accord with their desires. At a meeting of the Council of Ministers on 17 February, it became evident that Badoglio did not fully approve of Musotto because of his reported sympathy for Sicilian independence. Badoglio attempted to nominate someone else for the position, but Poletti pressured him to withdraw the nomination. Badoglio then put forward several other names, all of whom were military figures, and the meeting ended without a decision. As the month wore on, the situation became more confused, and Musotto's position weakened with the withdrawal of Poletti from Palermo and the appointment of Colonel A. N. Hancock as his replacement.[80]

One of the primary reasons for the delay in the selection process was the support Finocchiaro Aprile and other separatists gave Musotto. The separatist leader hoped that Musotto would bolster the cause of independence and that his appointment would be regarded as an act of weakness on the part of the government and a concession to the separatist movement.

When official approval for Musotto came on 3 March 1944, it was not unanimous. Members of the Council of Ministers attacked him as a separatist, criticized him for having supported Lucio Tasca as mayor of Palermo, and accused him of having ties to the mafia. On the island, however, the local press greeted his appointment with satisfaction, as did the general populace.[81]

Musotto's attitudes about separatism did leave room for doubt. He understood the movement's roots and, in some ways viewed it favorably. He pointed out that separatists used the island's poor economic and social conditions to their advantage. Unless the situation im-

proved, the movement would gain followers from among the less educated and less powerful classes. Musotto credited separatists with
having brought to light the "Sicilian problem" which many opposition
leaders had wished to ignore. Like other reformers, he decried the
subservience of Sicilian industries to those of the north and wanted
the government to take measures to remedy the historically poor treatment of the island and institute a system of administrative autonomy.
Sounding like a separatist, Musotto pointed out that as an island, Sicily's problems differed from those of the rest of the south and urged
that any system of autonomy satisfy those particular needs.[82]

On 30 March 1944, Musotto was officially installed in the presence
of Badoglio, who made a historic trip to the island. Badoglio's visit
created little enthusiasm, despite his effort to conciliate local political groups.[83]

As high commissioner, Musotto sought to coordinate the activities
of the island's prefects and ensure that they followed uniform policies.
He had only limited decision-making powers, and the presence of an
advisory council that included many of his political opponents further
weakened his authority. Musotto summoned the committee as infrequently as possible.[84]

Musotto's appointment represented the first step toward the restoration of Italian control over Sicily. It also signified a minor victory for
the separatist movement and its mafia ally, which had reportedly influenced the selection.[85] During his tenure, Musotto placed few restrictions on the movement, which functioned unhindered by government
edicts and with little fear of retaliation. Musotto's tolerance, plus the
economic and political chaos of the period, allowed the separatist
movement to dominate the Sicilian political landscape for the next
eighteen months.

2

The Birth of the Separatist Movement

PRE-INVASION ORIGINS

ON the afternoon of 22 July 1943, advance units of the American army entered Palermo. Throughout the city, a proclamation signed by the "Committee for Sicilian Independence" appeared on many walls. It asked the Allies to permit the formation of a provisional government that would conduct a plebiscite to determine Sicily's future status. The Committee proclaimed the Savoy dynasty dead and asserted that Sicily deserved independence and sovereignty.[1]

This first appearance of the separatist movement was not a spontaneous or unexpected event. Regional or separatist movements had existed in the post-World War I period and the Fascist era. For the most part, these groups led an underground existence, but occasionally, regional sentiment bubbled to the surface. In 1919, the people of Riesi, in Caltanissetta province, proclaimed a republic. In mid-1920, authorities in Palermo, Messina, Catania, and Syracuse reported the existence of a separatist movement that had arisen as a result of the island's economic distress and from fears that the revolutionary activity in northern Italy might spread and lead to the formation of a leftist or anti-monarchical state. Like the 1943 separatists, the followers of the 1920 movement were divided among republicans, monarchists, and those desiring regional autonomy. One of the organization's major leaders was Ettore Pellegrino, a former parliamentary deputy who was also involved in the previously mentioned Soldino Movement. Lucio Tasca might also have played a role. Though Italian authorities believed that the movement presented no real threat, they closely monitored it.[2]

Despite Mussolini's desire to stamp out Sicilians' regional tendencies, such sentiments flourished under Fascism. Giovanni Rosa's autonomist movement, which existed between 1932 and 1938, again testified to the islanders' deep attachment to regionalism. Rosa, a young Ragusan student who was labeled an anarchist, socialist and anti-Fascist, established bases of operation in both Tunisia and Paris.[3]

His cadres had little concrete success except to fuel regional sentiment and prepare the groundwork for separatist centers in Tunisia.

In 1936, at the University of Palermo, a group of students demanded the separation of Sicily from Italy. The following year, during a visit to the island, Mussolini encountered demonstrations demanding the creation of a Sicilian republic.[4]

The presence of German troops, desperate economic conditions, and continuing Fascist repression all contributed to a rise in support for separatism. By 1941, a number of local political leaders had begun to debate seriously Sicily's relationship to the Italian state. They proposed to employ a radical solution to prevent the island's continued subjugation by Italy.

Between 1941 and 1943, many of these men coalesced around a separatist program. An American intelligence report of September 1941 indicated the existence of "a powerful movement" which sought to establish an independent Sicilian republic. Still, the writer of the memorandum prophesied that the movement would fail, "because it has no Italian national interest and . . . of its own weight."[5] By the end of 1942, separatist sentiments were so prevalent that both the United States and British governments took notice. Sources in Rome indicated that Sicilians were pro-Ally, and that an underground movement had been organized and was preparing to secede from Italy and join the Allied forces. A later report suggested that some separatist supporters had attempted a coup but had been crushed.[6]

In the two years prior to the invasion, the separatist movement began to take shape. Three distinct groups had begun to meet secretly and work in relative isolation from each other. In Palermo, Lucio Tasca Bordonaro, an ultra-conservative landowner pledged to preserve Sicily's feudal society, led the separatists. At one time, the Americans considered Tasca the leader of the separatist movement, but he recruited Andrea Finocchiaro Aprile, who ultimately filled that role. The Tasca cadre included Don Calogero Vizzini, the reputed head of the Sicilian mafia. A second cell operated out of Catania and was directed by a conservative group of nobles, including the di Carcaci family, Bruno di Belmonte, Santi Rindone and Attilio Castrogiovanni. These men became the most ardent and dedicated separatist leaders, disdaining cooperation with any of the island's anti-Fascist organizations, which they equated with those who wanted union with Italy. Canepa led the third faction which also operated out of Catania. He found most of his support from idealistic university students who supported the establishment of a republic.[7]

A number of smaller, less significant bodies also existed. Stefano La Motta commanded a group at Nicosia, while Luigi La Rosa, a dissident Catholic politician, led another faction in Caltagirone.[8]

SEPARATIST PROGRAMS

In the pre-invasion period, both Tasca and Canepa established themselves as leaders of the movement by publishing pamphlets promoting the idea of separation. Both agreed that Sicily should be independent, but disagreed on the nature of its society. Their differing attitudes foreshadowed the ideological divisions that crippled the movement from inception to dissolution.

Tasca's *L'elogio del latifondo,* published in 1942, represented the thought of one of the richest men in Sicily; he was a friend of the mafia and a political and social reactionary. Born in 1880 and residing in the Palermo area, Tasca had never held a major political position, although he had supported Sicilian autonomy and had authored a separatist declaration in 1920. American officials, however, knew few details about his pre-separatist background. According to American consul Alfred T. Nester, between 1933 and 1938 Tasca had not been a Fascist, but he "may have joined the party for reasons which are well known." Other American intelligence reports confirmed, however, that he had joined the party and claimed that he belonged to it up to the "last moment."[9]

Nester never elaborated on Tasca's reasons, but it can be surmised that the conservative landowner viewed the Fascist Party in the same light as he did the separatist movement—as a means to preserve his social and political power. Being an unknown quantity was to Tasca's advantage, and under the AMG administration he was appointed mayor of Palermo with the support of both Charles Poletti and Francesco Musotto, the AMG-appointed prefect.

Tasca was reportedly popular with the peasants and had a great deal of influence among them. In his own paternal fashion, he seemed interested in improving their standard of living. His demand for Sicilian independence derived from his desire to retain the aristocracy's traditional powers and privileges and reflected the fear of modernization and social reform that permeated his class. Rather than modernization, he advocated the retention of antiquated methods of agriculture and a feudal societal structure.[10]

While many politicians called for the dissolution of the island's large estates, Tasca staunchly defended them. He argued that the *latifondi* could be profitable and beneficial to all classes, but that state interference had crippled their productivity. The introduction of a system by which peasants rented land for a period of time had placed tracts in the care of ignorant and unproductive people. A Fascist law providing families twenty-five hectares of land had negatively impacted the rural classes, because it had isolated families, prevented women from attending church, and hampered the education of children. It also led farmers, Tasca claimed, into a primitive, subsistence-level existence. The replacement of animal labor by machinery was also an error, he felt, because modernization left agriculture prey to large capitalist enterprises and counterproductive technological changes. According to Tasca, those who were truly attached to the land and the old ways would fight modernization.[11] The *latifondi,* Tasca believed, were a local problem which only Sicilians could solve.

During the occupation period, two distinct factions emerged within the separatist movement. Lucio Tasca led the conservative group and it adhered to his ideas. During the separatist era, he never wavered from his basic ideology and often repeated these beliefs in speeches and pamphlets. He consistently claimed that the *latifondisti* were not the most conservative or reactionary class and that they did not dominate or control Sicilian agriculture.[12]

Antonio Canepa stood at the other end of the separatist spectrum and was representative of the movement's progressive faction. Canepa had Marxist leanings. Following his anti-Fascist efforts in Sicily, he fought in the Resistance in central and northern Italy. It is believed that he founded and belonged to the leftist-oriented Partito dei Lavoratori (Party of the Workers).[13]

Canepa had accepted the idea of *Sicilianità,* or the belief that Sicily represented a unique nation and people, early in his career. His work, *La Sicilia ai siciliani!* (Sicily to the Sicilians!), which appeared in late 1942, reflected this ideology. His call for independence was based on his perceptions of a free and rich Sicily as he thought it had once existed. Like other separatists, Canepa held to a romantic concept of the island's past. To this almost mythical image, he added both religion and geography. As an island, Canepa wrote, Sicily had been decreed by God to be a separate national entity and had been improperly joined to Italy.[14]

Canepa argued that history justified independence. He chronicled Sicily's fate from ancient times, and accused those who had conquered the island of reducing its people to misery, hunger, and slavery. On the other hand, he claimed: "Whenever Sicily has been independent, has governed itself, it has also been very rich and happy. Instead, whenever we have had to obey our rulers from the continent, we have been weak, poor, and exploited."[15]

In tracing the Italian state's persecution of the island, he attacked Mussolini for having treated Sicily as a "cancer at the foot of Italy." The Fascist regime had demolished peasant organizations, burdened the island with enormous taxes, and, under the guise of eradicating the mafia, had injured many innocent people and attempted to destroy the people's spirit of liberty. In fact, the Fascist state treated Ethiopia better than Sicily.

Canepa appealed to Sicilians of every social class and political perspective to ignore their differences and unite to regain independence. He urged them to form small conspiratorial groups with no more than ten members to plan for the moment of redemption. He anticipated that Sicily's liberation would be accomplished with ease, since the United States and Britain would favor it, but warned his followers to rely upon their own strength to achieve independence. The motto of the movement would be "Separate Us or Die," and he concluded by asserting, "If we are decisive, unified, and intransigent we will also be invincible."[16]

Canepa spent all of 1943 and most of 1944 in northern Italy fighting the Germans. This proved unfortunate for the progressive separatists, who needed his intransigence and leadership. By the time Canepa returned to Sicily in fall 1944, the conservative separatists were well entrenched, and several opportunities for revolution had passed. In Canepa's absence, Antonino Varvaro (the movement's second secretary—general) guided the progressives. He found his main base of support among the idealistic, middle-class youth in the Catania area who had republican leanings. Members of this group originally favored using violence as Canepa prescribed, but in his absence they followed a legalistic path.[17] Separatist progressives also found support from Concetto Battiato and his Partito Laburista Siciliano (Sicilian Labor Party) and the Partito del Lavoro (Party of Work) which was adhered to mainly by veterans.[18] They also found a measure of backing from Vincenzo Vacirca and his Sicilian Socialist Federation, which supported a broad plan of autonomy.

Canepa and Varvaro were the most conspicuous leaders of the reformist faction, but their group had less cohesiveness and less devotion to separatism than the Tasca contingent. Progressive separatists were among the movement's first defectors because they could find outlets in mainstream political parties. They realized early on that they had little in common with the conservatives who seemed unwilling to compromise their interests for the general welfare. Varvaro and others understood that in an independent Sicily, reform might be even more difficult given the continued dominance of the landowners and the mafia. By switching allegiances, progressives also avoided the possibility of arrest or persecution. As independence became a more improbable end, many of them joined the ranks of the Communist or Socialist parties.

While both the progressive and conservative factions believed in the need for independence and relied on the past to justify it, they differed greatly about the scale and type of political, social, and economic reforms that would be made in the new state. Supporters of Canepa and Varvaro wanted to modernize the island's infrastructure while Tasca and his followers wanted as little innovation as possible. The unwillingness of the two cliques to overcome their differences contributed heavily to the movement's failure to achieve independence for Sicily.

ANDREA FINOCCHIARO APRILE

Given the differences between the Tasca and Canepa camps, the separatist movement needed a leader skilled at compromise and politics. Andrea Finocchiaro Aprile was such a man. Between 1943 and 1948, he remained the most conspicuous separatist chieftain, and most of the rank and file looked to him for direction. Though he never enjoyed absolute authority, whatever success the movement had between 1943 and 1945 can be directly traced to him. Finocchiaro Aprile's past political status, skill as an orator, and adeptness at compromise enabled him to gain the allegiance of many who might otherwise have dismissed the separatist cause. As a skilled parliamentarian, his presence gave the movement an air of legitimacy, even though the British accused him of simply being a "vote getter."[19]

A self-proclaimed simple and modest man of the people with a great love for the poor, Finocchiaro Aprile had been involved either in politics or academia throughout his entire adult life. Born in Palermo on 26 June 1878, Finocchiaro Aprile studied law and taught at various Italian universities. In 1913, he was elected as a deputy from the Corleone district, a mafia stronghold. In the Nitti government of June 1919–May 1920, he served as undersecretary of state for war and undersecretary of state for the treasury.[20] During the Fascist period, Finocchiaro Aprile participated in the Aventine Secession and maintained contact with anti-Fascists. In one instance, he prevented the arrest of two of his future nemeses, Francesco Musotto and Franco Grasso. He also joined Giovanni Amendola's anti-Fascist National Union, and in the late thirties gained fame by providing legal assistance to Jews in Venezia Giulia and the Trentino from whom the government was attempting to take Italian citizenship.[21]

While the Fascist police kept him under surveillance, Finocchiaro Aprile maintained a sporadic correspondence with Mussolini.[22] Though anti-Fascist in sentiment, he sought to reap any possible benefits that he could under Mussolini's rule. Like many other exponents of traditional liberalism, Finocchiaro Aprile's ties to Fascism reached their peak during the Ethiopian conflict, but despite a telegram commending Mussolini for the Ethiopian triumph, his attempt to join the party was rebuffed. Still, Finocchiaro Aprile continued to express his admiration for the Duce. In 1938, he even asked Mussolini for an audience to personally proclaim his loyalty.[23]

Finocchiaro Aprile seems to have coveted the position of director of the Bank of Sicily, a post that he claimed to have turned down in 1920. In 1936, however, his "sense of duty" led to an unsuccessful request for the position. Two years later, when Guido D'Orso's impending dismissal as bank director became obvious, he again appealed to Mussolini.[24] There was some irony in that the bank director was losing the job because he was Jewish, a fact of which Finocchiaro Aprile was cognizant.

In April 1939, Finocchiaro Aprile complimented Mussolini for uniting Italy and Albania, expressing the satisfaction with which many Albanians in Sicily regarded the new situation. He claimed that transplanted Albanians residing in Sicily were among the first and most ardent supporters of the Duce. Although he had no basis for saying so, he asserted that many Sicilian-Albanians would be willing to work for the Fascist regime in their native land. Separatist opponents later used this letter to discredit him.[25]

Unlike the island's landowners, Finocchiaro Aprile supported Mussolini's plan to transform the *latifondi*. He believed this action would promote Sicily's economic rebirth, and congratulated Mussolini for having freed Sicily from "centuries of woeful abandon."[26] Given his future statements, this comment probably reflected Finocchiaro Aprile's true attitude.

In retrospect, Finocchiaro Aprile's contacts with the regime damaged his standing with the Americans. They knew of his attempts to join the Fascist Party. Furthermore, OSS reports labeled him "one of the first collaborators of Mussolini," and accused him of having befriended the English and Americans merely to "obtain information which could be useful to the present situation and the Fascist cause."[27]

Although he had never publicly expressed separatist sentiments, by 1941 Finocchiaro Aprile had begun to support the idea of an independent Sicily. Once "converted," it did not take him long to assume the mantle of leadership. In 1941, he nominally accepted the presidency of Sicilia e Libertà, an anti-Fascist faction to which many separatists adhered. This was especially true in Palermo, where the future leaders of the movement coalesced around this organization. In this role Finocchiaro Aprile demonstrated his political skills and gained popularity and prestige. In 1942, he assumed control of the existing separatist groups. The British noted that during his trip to the island there was a rise in pro-separatist and anti-Fascist sentiment.[28] Finocchiaro Aprile told his listeners to organize, and attempted to woo influential Sicilian politicians to the separatist cause. He argued for the inevitability of an Allied victory and predicted an invasion of Sicily. Like Canepa, he assured his listeners that America would support an independent Sicilian nation.[29]

The events of the ensuing months proved the truth of Finocchiaro Aprile's predictions of invasion, lending credence to his claims that the Allies supported Sicilian independence. This in turn reinforced support for the movement.

Finocchiaro Aprile assumed a centrist position and sought to unify the divergent social and ideological tendencies within the movement. He wanted to lift separatism above party politics and forge a Sicilian nationalist philosophy which would appeal to the entire political spectrum.[30] To maintain unity, and placate his conservative followers, Finocchiaro Aprile spoke little of concrete social and economic reforms. He understood the conflicting ambitions of the Allied powers and exploited the distrust that existed among the United States, Britain, and the Soviet Union. He talked of world leaders as if he knew them personally and was privy to their decisions. His personal charisma appealed to the Sicilian people. His familiar manner, his constant proposals of miraculous solutions for all of Sicily's ills, and his avoidance of substantive matters, contributed to his popularity.[31]

For all of his political skills, the nature of the separatist movement hampered Finocchiaro Aprile's leadership. His centrist position drew together individuals from all political persuasions. Unwilling to enforce ideological purity, Finocchiaro Aprile found himself in the unenviable position of trying to lead a mass movement that contained influential figures who held contrasting beliefs.[32] Moreover, many Sicilians supported separatism for personal motives and not because they believed in independence.

Finocchiaro Aprile rarely used statistical information or detailed facts, but relied instead on his power as an orator. He appealed to Sicilian traditions and emotions and consistently repeated the same themes. He asked Sicilians to lay aside their differences and restore their homeland's greatness. Through his work, separatism gained a mass following and both the Allies and the Italian government recognized his importance. The major emphasis of his speeches was that the Savoy dynasty was dead and that the state which had mistreated Sicily for eighty years had ceased to exist. The only solution, therefore, was the creation of a free and independent Sicilian republic.[33]

Ironically, Finocchiaro Aprile adhered to the long-standing idea that Sicilians were a separate race. This ethnic group, according to the separatist leader, also included Calabrians, Lucanians, and Sardinians. These peoples were not inferior to northerners, only different. By using race as an issue, Finocchiaro Aprile sought to attribute unique qualities to Sicilians and to establish an anthropological basis for independence. This also broadened his movement's appeal by grouping together all southern Italians whom the state had allegedly mistreated.

Opponents of separatism used these and other statements to accuse Finocchiaro Aprile of being anti-nationalist. He often argued, for example, that Sicilians were more than willing to participate in the war effort but only within battalions made up of Sicilian volunteers, commanded by Sicilian officers, and fighting under the flag of an independent Sicily. He did not object to the war, only to Sicilians fighting for the Italian state under Italian officials on the Italian front.[34]

Like Canepa, Finocchiaro Aprile used economics and history to buttress his arguments for independence. Since unification, Italy had treated Sicily like a colony, and the island had paid more in taxes than had been returned to it. Reforms had never been undertaken because landowners and northern capitalists who wished to exploit Sicily had stopped them. Unity had impeded the growth of industries and the formation of a working class. Northern bankers and industrialists in league with the government had purposely destroyed the island's economy, and its navigation, wine, and sulphur-mining industries to suit their own needs. New industries were suffocated before they ever appeared. Despite the exploitation, Sicily retained the capacity and resources for economic self-sufficiency and once free from Italian hegemony, it would again be the richest island in the Mediterranean.

Nothing had changed with the fall of Fascism. In Finocchiaro Aprile's view, the Badoglio government was simply an extension of the Fascist regime and was the primary enemy of the separatist movement. He shared the popular conviction that the king had aided the Fascist seizure of power and, like Mussolini, was responsible for the disastrous war Italy had fought.

Of course, the political atmosphere had much to do with Finocchiaro Aprile's anti-monarchical position. Many of his conservative followers had deep feeling for the royal family, but the king's identification with Fascism made anti-monarchism a safe and popular position in 1943.[35] Indeed, following the Sicilian invasion, Finocchiaro Aprile had asked the King to abdicate. He repeated this demand in February 1944, because he realized that Sicilian independence needed this legal justification. With the monarchy gone, all historical ties between the modern Italian state and Sicily would be severed.

Finocchiaro Aprile treated the Papacy differently. In an obvious appeal to Sicilian religious sentiment, the separatist leader invited Pope Pius XII to come to Sicily if he were expelled from Vatican City. Even if the Papacy remained in Rome, the new Sicilian state would negotiate a concordat aimed at having native personnel appointed to the leading church positions on the island. Finocchiaro Aprile's position toward the Church is best explained by two factors. First, the clergy's past behavior in inciting revolt led Finocchiaro Aprile to assume that many clerics would support the separatist movement. Second, he believed that the clergy had nothing in common with the leadership of the Christian Democrats, whom he accused of being more concerned with their own interests than with those of the Sicilian people. In fact, most island clergy remained aloof from the political struggles and failed to respond to separatist pleas. Finocchiaro Aprile's position on the Church surprised some observers, who believed that the separatists were anti-clerical. Others pointed out, however, that the movement and the Church made natural allies, because both feared revolutionary social changes on the mainland.[36]

Finocchiaro Aprile had ambivalent feelings toward the Communists. Originally, he labeled the island's Communists uncompromising enemies of separatism.[37] Yet, he described Lenin as one of the most important philosophers and political strategists of his time, and later suggested that many of his own economic and social ideas were similar to Communism. If separatism were defeated, he warned, separatists would support Communism. When he announced that the separatists' motto would be "Independence or Communism," Finocchiaro Aprile hoped to present Sicilians and the Allies with little choice. His statements about the ideological affinity between separatism and Communism were clearly designed to promote the movement as the one sure antidote to a Communist revolution. They were also designed to silence those who claimed that the movement aimed at preserving the privileges of the aristocracy at the expense of the peasants.

Faced with conservative opposition, Finocchiaro Aprile could never enunciate clear solutions for erasing the ills that afflicted the workers and the peasants. But he at least understood their problems and mentality. He described the peasants and workers as the bravest, most humble, and most dignified people and felt that continued unity between Italy and Sicily would only worsen their economic plight. To both groups, he promised not only jobs but dignity, as well as a prominent position in the political order of the new nation.

A detailed program for land reform would have helped convince critics that separatists were interested in aiding the peasants, but Finocchiaro Aprile never produced one. He spoke about using state funds to industrialize the *latifondi* and about creating peasant coop-eratives. Reclamation projects would make unusable land productive. Once these things had been accomplished, peasants would receive a landholding based on family size and their ability to work the fields.[38] Finocchiaro Aprile's thoughts on property went beyond the immediate needs of the Sicilian peasant. He believed the post-Fascist world would produce a new relationship between the individual and the right of property, and thus alter the structure of the world. Within the new order, Sicily would take its place among the great nations.[39]

The island's fate would be determined by a plebiscite held under international control. Prior to the vote, the island government would consist of a council including a tenth of all pre-Fascist deputies. The council would produce solutions for Sicily's most immediate problems, thereby preventing much of the confusion that would be expected after independence.

Once independence had been achieved, Sicily would consider join-ing other states in some form of federation. On this point, the separatist leader stated concisely, "for now the only necessity is the creation of a sovereign and independent Sicilian republic."[40] This grouping of states might be an Italian federation or a broader-based European alliance. Sicily would not, however, join an Italian federation if Italy became a Soviet or Bolshevik state or if it reconstituted itself into a Giobertian scheme with the Pope as president. Finocchiaro Aprile envisioned a European confederation in which each state retained its international character and armed forces. He rejected other models in which individ-ual states lost too much of their identity.[41]

LEADERSHIP AND SUPPORT

Finocchiaro Aprile's leadership abilities were greatly tested during the separatist era. Only his skills at compromise and political maneu-vering enabled the movement to maintain a semblance of unity. The movement's widespread following made cohesion difficult, and decisive revolutionary action nearly impossible. Separatists projected an image of strength because of their apparent numbers, but there existed only a small core of dedicated and fanatical followers. They were often poorly led or restrained by those who sought a legal solution to Sicily's status. Much of the support for separatism was superficial, and once the quest for independence appeared hopeless, or when government intervention seemed imminent, the less-strident followers deserted the cause.[42] To those on the scene, the movement always appeared to be in a state of internal crisis.

Separatists came from all political, economic, and social groups, and at one time or another the movement tied together, in a fluid and ever-changing mixture, landowners, mafia, anti-Fascists, students, intellectuals, and professionals.[43] Support for independence united people with contrasting ideologies and political philosophies. Finocchiaro Aprile, a Liberal Democrat, Giovanni Guarino Amella, a Social Democrat, Luigi La Rosa and Francesco Termini of the former Popular Party, Vincenzo Vacirca of the Sicilian Socialist Federation, and Fausto Montesanti and Mariano Costa, both of whom were socialists, all temporarily put aside party loyalties and banded together behind separatism. Finocchiaro Aprile once observed that "among the most zealous followers of the movement were conservatives, liberals, democrats, *popolari*, Socialists, and Communists."[44] Those who defected from other political parties often assumed ranking positions in the movement. They brought much in the way of political expertise, legitimacy, and prestige, but in some cases hurt the movement's progress with their infighting and lack of dedication.

Many of these political figures had been former deputies in the Italian parliament. They carried with them the baggage of the past and had been schooled in the art of "trasformismo," the quick-changing, heterogeneous, shifting coalitions necessitated by the great number of factions and lack of clear political consensus. These attitudes worked to limit and delay decisions when quick and radical action was required.

Those who led the movement came from three segments of society— the middle class, the large landowners, and mafia chieftains. Control was not shared equally, however, and for much of the separatist period, the middle-class leadership was manipulated and coerced by the land-owning clique and its mafia ally. The diversity of the leaders' professions, their life experiences, and their worldviews help to explain Finocchiaro Aprile's difficulty in holding his followers together, and in formulating concrete policy. It also accounts for the movement's failure to seize control of the island. Leaders could never overcome their ideological, economic, social, or personal views for the sake of independence. They hesitated out of fear of government reprisal, concerns about losing their powers and privileges, and apprehension about the aims and desires of the other leadership cliques.

Out of a list of approximately 200 prominent separatists comprised from Italian, American, or British documents, the profession or social standing of 131 is known. Fifty were lawyers. This group included some of the most important leaders, such as Finocchiaro Aprile, Luigi La Rosa, Sebastiano Lo Verde, Francesco Restuccia (a future leader of the separatist army), and Varvaro. Lawyers often occupied positions on national and regional separatist bodies. Another forty-nine leaders

came from nine different areas of professional life, including teachers
on both the university and lower levels, engineers, accountants, and
doctors. Others had their occupations listed as shipping agent, driver,
journalist, an industrialist, and a military figure. Fourteen were students, most of whom belonged to separatist committees at the island's
universities. Only seventeen were designated as proprietors, landowners, or aristocrats.

The presence of *latifondisti*, or owners of large estates, and aristocrats within leadership circles gave credence to anti-separatist claims
that they were manipulating the movement. The great landowners had
profited greatly from Italian unity and government policies. With the
cooperation of the state and northern capitalists, they had opposed
the modernization of Sicily's agricultural system and retained their
economic power at the peasants' expense. They had welcomed Fascism
and given the regime open support because they thought it would
preserve traditional institutions. In 1943, however, they feared a *Vento
del nord* ("wind from the north") or leftist revolution on the mainland,
which would destroy their powers by breaking their traditional alliances and redistributing their property.[45]

Not all landowners were aristocrats, the size of their holdings differed, and their numbers were small. According to surveys published
in 1927, the percentage of land covered by the *latifondi* had decreased
since the Fascist seizure of power in 1922. There were 1,055 landed
estates, which ranged in size from 200 to 5,000 hectares (a hectare is
approximately 2.5 acres). Most of the existing *latifondi*, however, were
in the 200- to 500-hectare range, and few 5,000-hectare estates existed.
Overall, the large rural concerns covered approximately twenty-two
percent of the island's agricultural-forest area. Caltanissetta had the
largest percentage of acreage covered by *latifondi*, Ragusa the least. On
the other hand, over seventy percent of Sicilian farms were three hectares or less in size, which meant there was a substantial number of
small landowners on the island.[46]

Larger landowners wished to retain, as Tasca had written in *L'elogio
del latifondo*, the island's archaic feudal structure and *latifondi*. They
also wanted the abolition of any controls over the agricultural economy, and objected to the introduction of any local industry since this
would destroy the notion that land represented the only real source
of wealth and status. This same feeling also extended into the ranks
of the smaller land proprietors.[47]

Finocchiaro Aprile tried to play down the role and influence of the
large landowners. He once branded them the movement's enemies,
and boasted that he had alienated them through his views on agrarian
reform. At one point, he stated that out of eighty-four *latifondisti*, only

three adhered to the separatist movement, while at least five or six belonged to the Communist Party. Later, however, he conceded that almost all large landowners were separatists.[48] Finocchiaro Aprile's true attitude toward the landowners is difficult to assess, but it appears that he viewed their support as a necessary evil during the struggle for independence.

Despite Finocchiaro Aprile's rhetoric, large landowners and nobles did exercise a powerful influence over the movement. The Tasca family, notably Lucio and Alessandro, played critical roles throughout the separatist period. Guglielmo di Carcaci, president of the separatist Lega Giovanile (Youth League), Gaspare Gattucio, head of the Propaganda Committee in August 1944, and Stefano La Motta, head of the separatists in Enna, were also influential.

The mafia supported separatism for its own purposes. Most mafiosi had an underlying dislike for the *latifondisti,* and the marriage between the two had always been one of convenience only. The landowners had not opposed the Fascist persecution of the criminal organization, but in 1943 mafia chiefs realigned with them because they and the separatist movement were the island's dominant political forces. In late 1943, Italian officials disclosed that the mafia had sanctioned the separatist movement, which identified itself with the landed proprietors and exploited the agricultural population. Fearful of this alliance, "agents of the Italian government" were working to lure the leaders of the mafia "away from the Separatist Movement" and reestablish ties to the House of Savoy.[49]

Links between the mafia and the separatist movement were thought to be so close that Finocchiaro Aprile was once erroneously listed as the head of the former.[50] He treated mafia allegiance the same way he did the *latifondisti*—he recognized mafiosi as a strong force capable of helping the island achieve independence. Afterwards, the new state would determine its relationship to the criminal organization.

The mafiosi who made common cause with separatism represented a traditional institution that used illegal methods that fell within the confines of Sicilian custom and culture. This "old" mafia operated out of Palermo and had played a significant role in island politics from time eternal. One complimentary Allied report characterized its chieftains as having a strong sense of "chivalry and justice" and distinguished them from the island's newly released criminal elements. Moreover, many of these individuals had the respect of their fellow islanders.[51]

Within the separatist hierarchy, Lucio Tasca had the strongest ties to the mafia. Tasca, the Allied-appointed mayor of Palermo, was regarded as the head of the "old Maffia who often call themselves the

Mutual Protective Association."[52] With Tasca acting as facilitator, the mafia easily infiltrated the movement's inner circles and forged a temporary alliance with Finocchiaro Aprile.

Formal ties between the mafia and the separatist movement were not established until December 1943, after the mafia had recouped its strength and regained a measure of political influence. The criminal body owed its renewal to Allied officials. At least two mafiosi played influential roles in AMG's administration. Don Calogero Vizzini had been appointed mayor of Villalba while Vito Genovese, Vizzini's old friend and a notorious Sicilian-American gangster, held a post with the Allied Command at Nola. The Americans seemed to have appreciated Vizzini, not only because of his political power, but also because he had opposed the Fascists. For his part, Vizzini liked to brag about his contacts with the Americans, and spoke of their support for the separatist movement. Vizzini was later to become an ally of Tasca and an important player during the separatist crisis. Genovese's appointment and continued employment seems to have been based on a case of confused identity, but it was not necessarily a unique situation. Several other mafiosi with "somewhat questionable political records" were appointed to AMG posts throughout the island.[53]

While many of these new officials sought only to further their own interests, these appointments gave the mafia an enormous amount of prestige, the power to control the local political situation, and an opportunity to resume its illicit and profitable criminal activities, and consolidate its hold over the black market. By late 1944, General Giuseppe Castellano, the island's military commander, judged the mafia the strongest force in Sicily.[54]

Though both the landowners and the mafia saw separatism as the best avenue through which to maintain the status quo, for the mass of Sicilians, separatism held the possibility of change. Sicilians at all levels were unified by their hatred of an Italian state that had exploited them. The middle class adhered to the movement in great numbers. Its members had suffered economically and socially under Italian rule, and, although they might have little in common with the island's elites, they were willing to align with them momentarily. Many of these same people had been hurt by Fascism, but like the conservative landowners, they also feared a leftist swing in the government. In a reconstructed unitary state, many who served in the local administration might lose their jobs to mainland Italians. In a free Sicily, their jobs, businesses and status seemed assured.[55]

Sicilian intellectuals saw independence as the only way to end the island's continual exploitation. Most of all, the intellectuals who were drawn to the separatist cause hoped that independence would help them achieve greatness as the cultural elite of a regenerated Sicilian nation.[56]

Separatism also had deep roots among the island's student population. As early as 1936, students had been attracted to the idea of independence, but did little except debate the subject in the pre-invasion period. Once the movement became public, students became some of separatism's most dedicated followers. For the young, separatism fulfilled both practical and idealistic needs. Sicilian independence meant the end of Italian military service. Any armed struggle would aim to free their homeland. A stronger magnet in pulling the young to the movement was the idealistic belief that separation would make Sicily a great nation.[57] Students often formed the bulk of separatist crowds, joined the movement's youth league in large numbers, and answered the leadership's calls to resist the draft.

The extent to which workers and peasants backed separatism is difficult to determine. They participated in rallies, attended meetings, and listened to separatist propaganda. But there is no evidence that they gave their full-fledged support to the movement. They had, as one source puts it, "a cautious mistrust" of the movement, mainly because the large landowners dominated it. For these groups, it made no sense to back an organization led by those cliques that had ruled them through intimidation and fear. On the other hand, separatism represented an attempt to stave off the winds of change through a revolutionary act, while preserving the island's traditions.[58] For this reason, they may have hoped for its success.

Landless peasants—comprising approximately forty percent of the island's agricultural population—had an obvious reason to resent the Italian government. The state had consistently failed to carry out meaningful land reforms to provide them productive parcels of land. Finocchiaro Aprile understood this attitude and exploited it to benefit the movement. He once wrote:

> the Sicilian peasants are individualistic and conservative, they long to have a piece of land all their own on which to build their own castle with a few animals. . . . Politics is estranged from them, and they are not interested. But they are independists, not only because they profoundly love their Sicilian homeland but because they are convinced that detaching Sicily from Italy would help them and end the ignoble exploitation that the agriculture of the island has undergone to the advantage of the North.[59]

Alienated from an insensitive bureaucracy, the peasants saw separatism as their best hope for the future. Finocchiaro Aprile promised land, and separatism meant that such reforms would be made without "alien" interference.[60] Thus, on a different level, and for somewhat

different reasons, the landowners and the peasants had the same objective: to prevent so-called "outsiders" from determining how they
would live.

Even if the peasantry did not join the separatist movement, many
of its numbers adhered to it simply through their traditional ties to
the landowning class. These attachments were maintained through
either a dominant personality whom the peasants followed, or the
southern intellectual who voiced the policies and needs of the dominant social class. In this case, the peasant, whether landed or not,
would follow the lead of the large landowners.[61]

To obtain peasant allegiance, separatists organized agricultural
leagues. In Catania they formed the Associazione Agraria, to which
both small and large landowners adhered. In Palermo, the Unione Siciliani Agricoltori Presidente Roosevelt had about 300 members.[62]

The Sicilian laboring classes—those involved in fishing, industry,
transportation, and communication—which made up about thirty percent of the population, also wanted to improve their wretched existence. The existence of virtually no local industry other than sulphur
mining makes assessing worker support for the movement problem-
atic. Since unification, the industry had sharply declined and, in the
post-invasion period, employment dropped dramatically from approximately 9,000 miners in 1943 to only 5,000 in 1944. What remained of
the industry centered on the most desolate and least-populated provinces, namely Agrigento, Caltanissetta, and Enna in the southern and
central parts of the island, and was crucial to the economy of these
areas. The miners suffered severe economic deprivation after the invasion, and sometimes went on strike to obtain equitable pay and working conditions. For the most part, however, the Allies and Italian
government sought to accommodate the workers, and separatism had
little success in recruiting them. Although Finocchiaro Aprile claimed
that they supported the movement in large numbers, there is no evidence to substantiate his opinion. Indeed, separatist organizations in
the sulphur mining provinces were among the weakest.[63]

By mid-1943, separatist leaders had laid the groundwork for their
movement. Their message appealed to all those Sicilians discontented
for one reason or another with Italian rule. Their demand for independence appealed to the island's historical traditions and seemed realistic
given Finocchiaro Aprile's assurances of Allied help. More importantly,
Finocchiaro Aprile had emerged as the movement's leader. He was a
man of standing and intelligence, and a man of politics. He and his
followers eagerly awaited the Allied invasion and Sicily's liberation.

3

The Struggle Begins

MISSED OPPORTUNITIES FOR POWER

Prior to the Allied assault, separatists tried to seize the political initiative. On 17 June 1943, Palermo separatists formed a provincial committee, and within a month Finocchiaro Aprile became its leader. Fausto Montesanti, the movement's first secretary general and Vincenzo La Manna, a former Socialist and editor of *Giornale di Sicilia,* were among those aligned with him. Once the occupation began, Sebastiano Lo Verde, director of *Sicilia Liberata,* also joined the movement. Through Lo Verde, Finocchiaro Aprile met Charles Poletti and influenced him to appoint numerous separatists to communal positions.[1]

In the days just before the Allied landing, Finocchiaro Aprile went to Palermo and planned anti-Fascist initiatives in league with the Party of Action and the Communists. One such scheme called for the occupation of municipal offices in Palermo prior to the English or American entrance into the city. On 22 July, leaders of Sicily's Action Party and Finocchiaro Aprile met to discuss final details, but they canceled their plans for fear of embarrassing the Allies, who were approaching Palermo. In all likelihood, Action Party leaders, who had cooperated with the OSS, were thankful that the plans had been shelved, for any move would have jeopardized their standing with the occupation forces. By failing to exploit the moment, separatists missed a crucial opportunity to gain control of the island's most important city and give themselves some standing as the legitimate spokesmen of the Sicilian people.[2]

Separatist leaders, including Finocchiaro Aprile, also apparently discussed a possible joint action with the Communists against the Germans and Fascists. Separatist chiefs rejected the proposal because they surmised that a move against the Fascist army was unnecessary, since it would not oppose the Allies. Finocchiaro Aprile also recognized that such an alliance might split the movement's leadership, because conservative separatists feared the Communists more than they did the central government.[3]

On the eve of the landings, separatists formed an island-wide Committee for Sicilian Independence and placed Finocchiaro Aprile at its head.[4] On 10 July, the committee issued its first public appeal, linking the debacle of the unitary state with the collapse of Fascism, and calling for a "national Sicilian rebirth." Unity between Sicily and Italy was declared to be irrevocably broken; Sicilians wanted to govern themselves. Separatists asked that the Allies assist in establishing an independent Sicilian republic, to be preceded by the formation of a provisional government and the admission of a Sicilian delegation to the future peace talks, where Sicily would act as a friend of the Allied powers.[5]

Although cautiously worded, the declaration strengthened separatist claims that they were the only group speaking for the Sicilian people. However, the Allied command, fearful of disorder in the early days of the occupation, forbade any political activity and warned separatists to halt their activities.[6]

Separatists ignored this caution. On 23 July, Finocchiaro Aprile addressed an appeal to General Alexander announcing that the Sicilian people desired independence, a sovereign state, and a republic. Autonomy, an old, worn-out concept, would not be enough. Separatists again called for a provisional government, elections, and a seat at the peace conference, and requested that all Sicilian prisoners of war be repatriated. The movement's slogan was simply: "Sicily to the Sicilians."[7]

Five days later, the Committee for Sicilian Independence repeated its demands for a provisional government and plebiscite and openly attacked the House of Savoy. Separatists accused the monarch of having ignored the needs of Sicilians, of having supported Fascism, and of having betrayed Italy's liberal institutions.[8]

THE ALLIES

This series of proclamations sounded the opening shot in the long and difficult struggle between the Italian government and the separatist movement. Over the next three years, this struggle threatened Italian stability, became a question of international importance, and helped to shape Italy's postwar institutional structure.

Many islanders believed that the movement owed its early success to either American or British influence. Neither power issued a formal statement disavowing the movement during the occupation, but from the beginning, the Americans tried to demonstrate that they never intended Sicilians to believe that liberation from Fascism meant separation from Italy. Indeed, if the Allies had really supported an independent island they could have easily done so "without even appearing to be responsible for such a development."[9] On the other hand, separatists hoped that either the British or Americans would make Sicily an independent Mediterranean state to serve as a bulwark against "the so-called Bolshevik peril."[10] Finocchiaro Aprile continuously exploited Allied fears about a Communist stronghold in the Mediterranean. As late as April 1944, he believed that the Allies would be "compelled to support separatism with a system of international guarantees in order to prevent the spreading of Communism in Sicily."[11]

Neither the British nor the Americans wanted an independent Sicily, and both were concerned with the island's fate only as long as the political direction of the Italian state and the outcome of the war remained muddled. In truth, the Allies tolerated the separatist movement following the invasion because its supporters aided the landing procedures and dominated the island's administration. They also exploited the movement's popularity in order to maintain calm on the island.[12]

Speculation has persisted that separatists made contact with Allied leaders prior to the invasion. One American source admitted that given their social position, as well as the "availability of money, and of private means of transportation, the vast network of personal relationships in the diplomatic and foreign field, and certain family relationships with Anglo-Saxon elements, the chiefs of the Separatist Movement succeeded in establishing contact with the Anglo-Saxon world before the occupation." Finocchiaro Aprile often spoke of letters that he sent to Allied officials, and it is believed that he communicated with friends in America and England through the Vatican.[13]

If there had been pre-invasion communications or agreements, they did little good after the offensive. Rennel denied having heard of a separatist movement prior to the landings, but admitted suspecting that such a movement would arise. During the occupation of the island, Rennel's suspicions were confirmed. In August, he reported that "from the first moment of our landing when my officers took charge, they have been assailed by Sicilian separatism and expressions of hope of people of all classes and all over the island that the liberating mission of the Allies involved the separation of Sicily from Italy." It was not surprising, Rennel explained, that the arrival of the Allied armies, having promised that people would have their own government, should have stimulated separatist sentiments. At the same time, he noted that separatist activity was more pronounced in the northern areas of the island than it was in the south and southeast. "We shall," concluded Rennel, "hear a great deal more about this Movement before we are through."[14] Rennel's associate, G.R. Gayre, who understood the roots of separatism, felt that the Allies were making a grave mistake by not realizing the movement's strength. American consul Nester noted widespread separatist sentiment and estimated that at least seventy-five percent of the population backed independence. Separatists also dominated the local administration and controlled ninety percent of Sicily's communal governments.[15]

Separatist estimates of their movement's strength paralleled those made by Allied officials. Finocchiaro Aprile once boasted that the movement had at least 400,000 adherents, an estimate he later increased to 630,000, including 130,000 men ready to fight under the command of Sicilian officers. His figures later climbed; he claimed at one point that his organization had "about 800,000 members and an army composed of 200,000 well-trained men," figures that Nester disputed. Alessandro Tasca, Lucio's brother, believed that at least ninety percent of the island's population supported Sicilian independence.[16]

While there was no way to substantiate these numbers or test the depth of separatist sentiment, it was obvious that the idea of Sicilian independence had at least attracted the attention of many islanders. Despite the movement's apparent popularity, AMG officials firmly stated their opposition to the creation of an independent Sicilian nation, and recommended that "the Sicilian Independence Movement, which was making itself felt throughout the island, should be discouraged and all meetings forbidden. We should discount all Sicilian statements that they would like to be governed by some other country."[17] The Allies accused separatists of using their offices for personal and economic gain, condemned them for their reactionary character, and charged them with having been Fascists. Local Allied personnel were instructed to discourage the movement and remove its supporters from public positions. They also published orders that anyone advocating separatism was subject to arrest.[18]

Notwithstanding such moves, the Allies bore partial responsibility for the persistent rumors that they were supporting the separatist movement. Although OSS officials called for public disavowal of the movement, they suggested using the threat of separatism to force Badoglio to accept terms for withdrawing from the war. OSS agents thought that "we may suggest that the future of Sicily depends on the present course of the Italian government." Italian unity could be guaranteed only if the Allies could militarily occupy the entire peninsula. OSS personnel also pointed out that control of Sicily and Italy's North Africa possessions provided the Allies leverage with which to pressure Italians into ceasing resistance by threatening the loss of both.[19]

Separatists exploited the lack of a formal proclamation disavowing their movement, and continually manufactured and spread rumors of

Allied support. Hopeful that the fabrications were true, some separatist leaders openly declared that they were partial to either an American or British protectorate.[20]

Opposition politicians complained with some justification that the separatists had found unexpected help from American authorities and that the movement's chiefs had access to AMG while they did not. The actions of Charles Poletti, the former lieutenant governor of New York and the chief civil affairs officer in Palermo lent weight to these accusations. In August 1943, he had publicly welcomed the movement's leaders, and later refused to see a group of unitarians. He also supported the creation of administrative bodies that appeared to lay the groundwork for the island's self-government. In his most important moves, Poletti pushed for Francesco Musotto's appointment as high commissioner and retained Lucio Tasca as mayor of Palermo in spite of his mafia and separatist connections. As mayor, Tasca seems to have done an adequate job, and was reportedly popular with a number of AMG officers. While in this position he made no attempt to hide his separatist sentiments. When unitarian politicians confronted Poletti and complained that separatists occupied all the administrative positions in Palermo province, Poletti responded that he had used "only the criterion of competence to be his guide."[21]

Finocchiaro Aprile and Poletti clashed over Allied policy. Poletti evidently angered him during an August meeting when he warned the separatist leader that AMG would not support any political activity. In February 1944, Poletti reiterated that the "aim of AMG has been to prepare Sicily to continue its historic mission as an important and integral part of a free Italy."[22] In response, Finocchiaro Aprile announced that Poletti was openly hostile to Sicilians, and cautioned him that his political future in New York would be ruined if he displeased Sicilian-Americans there. If, on the other hand, Poletti acted properly he would be welcomed back to the new Sicilian nation as the American ambassador. Despite his bickering with Poletti, Finocchiaro Aprile continually exploited the general appreciation that Sicilians had for their American rulers and often expressed his love for the United States.[23]

Poletti's allegedly pro-separatist activities reinforced British fears concerning American backing for the movement, and inflamed the mistrust that existed between the two occupying forces. "There seems to be little doubt," noted one British report, "that the Separatist Movement has received a measure of support from American officers." British personnel accused the island's base commander and other American officers of having permitted and attended separatist meetings. British officials were mystified by the attention paid by the American government to the movement since the United States had never

had much interest in the Mediterranean. Moreover, they believed that
the American government would derive no economic benefits from
an independent Sicily. The British surmised that "it therefore seems
probable that the innate snobbishness which so frequently leads the
average American to seek the companionship of the bearers of high
sounding titles may be a not diminutive factor in this situation . . . and
the Sicilian landowners are of course not infrequently the possessors
of ancient and impressive titles of nobility."[24]

Mutual suspicion concerning separatism was merely an outgrowth
of previous Anglo-American disputes over the formation and control
of AMG, the invasion of the island, and general Mediterranean strategy.
While the two powers had ultimately settled the first two issues, they
had done so only through tenuous compromises. Beyond invading and
occupying the island, the Allied powers had no long-range plans concerning the area. Strategically and historically, the British had good
reasons to back Sicilian independence. They had occupied the island
in 1812, and post-war control of Sicily would give them dominance in
the Mediterranean. They also sought revenge against Mussolini for his
invasion of France in 1940 and other anti-Anglo policies. Taking Sicily
would fulfill both desires. Many on the American side did not share
British attitudes. Roosevelt was hesitant about putting large numbers
of troops in Italy, and some American officials pushed for action in
the Pacific or, more importantly, a cross channel invasion in Western
Europe. They held that any further military action in the Mediterranean would detract from that effort.[25] Given Sicily's strategic location
and the differing American and British concerns, it was inevitable that
problems over separatism would arise.

Though British parliamentarians had spoken about respecting Italy's territorial integrity and had denied supporting separatism,
American fears persisted that the British wanted to reduce Italy to a
position of "complete dependence on their country" while making Sicily a British naval base.[26] Some American officials further suspected
that Finocchiaro Aprile had gained Churchill's approval for the movement before the invasion and that the Tasca brothers "would gamble
their heads on English domination of Sicily."[27] American authorities
at the highest level wanted to know the real intentions of the British,
and to this end, the Federal Bureau of Investigation (FBI) sought such
information. In October 1943, FBI Director, J. Edgar Hoover wrote Assistant Secretary of State Adolph A. Berle that the British were manipulating the movement in order to create a naval base in the
prospective republic, and their agents were working in all of the island's provinces to induce "anti-Fascists" to support secession. Hoover
was aware that any attempt to separate Sicily from Italy would cause

tremendous political problems in the United States, where Italians were strong enough politically to determine the outcome of an election. FBI agents also informed Hoover that Churchill supported the creation of an autonomous Sicilian republic, and that, although Roosevelt opposed the idea, he might acquiesce to Churchill's demands if the two argued over political matters. Churchill had reasoned that as long as Sicily remained tied to Italy, it would be impossible for the British to acquire naval bases on the island and gain control of the Mediterranean.[28]

In reality, most Sicilians would not have accepted either British or American rule, and, in general, Finocchiaro Aprile rejected both possibilities.[29] Yet these conflicts of interest and the suspicions they created made Sicily's fate an international question of some importance. The separatists profited from these differences.

SEIZING THE INITIATIVE

The absence of a well-organized political opposition, combined with Allied tolerance, social and political chaos, and the weakened condition of the Badoglio government, all played into separatist hands. The movement's supporters recognized, however, that as the Italian situation stabilized and the Allied role on the island diminished, their freedom of action would shrink while the danger of persecution would increase. Therefore, during the occupation period, separatist leaders worked frantically to make themselves the arbiters of Sicily's destiny.

To maintain their post-invasion momentum, separatists held meetings, issued declarations, clandestinely published newspapers, and disrupted opposition gatherings. They defied the Allied ban on political activity and confronted Italian security officials. These encounters often turned violent, as Italian police harassed separatists and ordered them to disperse. The separatists would usually refuse, provoking fights and gunshots. More often than not, the movement's adherents were blamed for the violence.[30]

Following its July propaganda blitz, the Committee for Sicilian Independence issued no major declarations for several months. This so-called national committee, was the most prominent separatist organ. It consisted of a president, secretary-general, the presidents and vice presidents of the provincial committees, and others designated by the committee itself.[31] In theory, the national committee controlled the numerous provincial and communal cells, as well as all other separatist organs. In reality, it served merely to demonstrate the leadership's diversity. At one time or another, its membership included some of the

most important separatist figures, but its actual numbers fluctuated
with the movement's fortunes. The majority of the time, only President
Finocchiaro Aprile and the secretary-general—(first Fausto Montesanti
and then Antonino Varvaro) signed the committee's declarations, and
the great majority of members had little if any input. Given the contrasting views of the committee's members, a select group usually
wrote and edited its manifestos.

On 4 October 1943 the national committee directed a statement at
the king and Badoglio. As president of the movement, Finocchiaro
Aprile signed what was essentially an anti-monarchical declaration
that was designed to take advantage of widespread anger over Victor
Emmanuel's role during the Fascist period. Although Alessandro Tasca
and others protested this position, the separatists temporarily joined
the anti-monarchical current in Italy.[32] The statement deplored the
king's compromise with Fascism and accused him of betraying the
ideals of the *Risorgimento*. "You and the monarchy," Finocchiaro
Aprile declared, "are the greatest obstacles to the durable union of
Sicily and Italy." If the dynasty disappeared, and if one or more Italian
states developed into republics similar to that planned for Sicily, then
an independent Sicily would join a federation of these Italian states.
This far-sighted but radical proposal bridged both the needs of autonomy and the desire for independence.

In reality, the national committee was little more than a propaganda
device. Instead, the central committee came closest to being the real
decision-making body for the movement. It contained anywhere from
eight to fourteen members, including Finocchiaro Aprile and the secretary-general. Other individuals who sat on the national committee
also participated in the central committee. Although the committee
theoretically contained delegates from all the provinces, this was not
always the case. Indeed, at one point in 1943, only Messina, Palermo,
Trapani, Agrigento, Syracuse and Catania had individual representation, while Finocchiaro Aprile spoke for the other provinces. The committee's membership changed constantly, and like the national
committee, the central committee concentrated much of the policy-
making process in the hands of a few leading personalities.[33]

On 9 December 1943, the central committee met in secret in Palermo. Twenty-eight people attended the crucial gathering, including
Don Calogero Vizzini. His presence signaled the old mafia's adherence
to the cause of independence, and aided the conservative separatists
in their attempt to control the movement.[34] Vizzini and Tasca held
common views, and despite protests by progressives, Vizzini remained
at the session as the representative from Caltanissetta. Vizzini's support of Tasca's platform gave conservative separatists an ally skilled in

the use of political coercion. It is not surprising, therefore, that the right wing pushed through a motion that called for the use of force, if necessary, to halt the meetings of all political parties having a "national character."[35]

Passage of this resolution encouraged the growth of separatist armed bands in the western part of the island. In early 1944, Allied sources reported that two separatists, Carlo Brandaleone and Paolo Virzi, were creating "action squads" to demonstrate against visiting government officials and create the impression that Communists and Socialists were to blame for the disturbances. Virzi had obtained a cache of arms that would be distributed to band members at the "opportune moment." Not surprisingly, these "action squads" would arise mainly from the Palermo area, a mafia stronghold.[36]

For public consumption, the committee circulated a more moderate "order of the day" that said nothing about mafia participation at the meeting or the possible use of violence. It lodged the usual accusations against the king and Badoglio for their role in establishing the Fascist state, and claimed that although islanders would not fight for the Italian monarchy, they were willing to contribute to the Allied war effort.[37]

The committee also expressed deep concern about the food situation and public security. Although it credited the Allies with having tried to treat the islanders fairly, it asserted that their failure to comprehend the situation fully had contributed to Sicily's horrible conditions. Despite the mistakes, separatists asked the Allies "to spare Sicily the misfortune of being consigned to the so-called Badoglio government" because it would bring more "sorrow" to the island.

The separatists called for the creation of a consultative committee, composed of men of proven technical and political ability from all parties, to suggest to the Allied command solutions to the island's crisis. The movement's leaders hoped that this body would include a large number of their supporters, simply because they dominated the island's political scene. The Allies' refusal to form this commission represented a significant setback, since it deprived separatists of a legitimate administrative body from which to influence Sicily's fate.

The meeting of 9 December 1943 was a critical event in the history of separatism. For the next two years, ties with the mafia allowed conservatives to control the movement, provided them an ally against any revolutionary upheaval on the island, and sheltered them against a government crackdown. In many ways, the separatist movement now depended upon mafia largesse for its survival. Those same connections brought to the forefront the dissension within the leadership. Progressives who had protested Vizzini's involvement would have a difficult time finding common ground with the conservatives, and would never control the movement.

The day after the 9 December meeting, thousands of separatist badges portraying Sicily as the forty-ninth state of the United States were distributed.[38] The badges were only part of an effort by the mafia to demonstrate its pro-American sympathies. Some mafia chieftains truly believed that they would fare better under American rule than they had or would under Italian rule. Moreover, they were thankful to the Americans for having restored them during the invasion and occupation. They also sought to take advantage of the island's pro-American attitude, which was rooted in the Sicilian vision of America and family ties. The idea that Sicily should become part of the United States became a fundamental point in the platform of the newly created Partito Democratico d'Ordine (Sicilian Democratic Party of Order). This group would play an important role in determining Sicily's fate. According to the OSS, "the party's leading exponents are rural agrarians, better known as the rural Maffia." Its platform demanded the creation of an independent Sicilian nation under an American sphere of influence. It also called for the establishment of a democratic republic with all the basic freedoms. All Fascist laws would be abolished and collaboration with all political parties "whose common objective is the supreme interest of the Sicilian Republic" would be welcomed. In addition, industries, banks, and commerce would be developed, property protected, and military service ended.[39]

The Partito Democratico d'Ordine's program ran counter to Finocchiaro Aprile's demand for true independence. Nonetheless, following the 9 December meeting, Finocchiaro Aprile sought to cement his ties to the mafia and take advantage of its protection. On 30 January, he spoke at a gathering in Misilmeri in Palermo province. Approximately 20 mafiosi attended to maintain order.[40] His connections were strengthened by public statements like those he made in February, when he declared, "if there was not a Mafia already, one would have to be invented. I am a friend of the Mafia even though personally I am against crime and violence."[41] Unlike opposition politicians, Finocchiaro Aprile spoke in mafia-controlled areas without incident, but only because mafia chiefs allowed him to do so.

The central committee's other important gathering took place on 8 January 1944. In addition to the committee's members, a number of other political leaders attended the meeting as observers.[42] In reality, these men had already given their support to either independence or autonomy, but by inviting them, separatist directors hoped to reinforce their organization's image as a broad-based coalition. The participants discussed a wide range of topics, including the Allied attitude toward independence, the international problem of separatism, and the continuing presence of Fascists in the island's administration. To coordinate the movement's activities, committee members decided to organize provincial sections for Catania, Agrigento, Trapani, Messina, and Palermo. Committee chairmen, some of whom were relative unknowns in separatism's highest circles, but important local personalities, were appointed to guide the work of these bodies.[43]

The formation of provincial and communal sections gave the movement a populist facade. Provincial sections had actually been formed in some locations prior to the 8 January meeting of the central committee, notably Palermo and Catania. Only later in 1944 did committees become firmly established in all the provinces except Caltanissetta, as per the recommendation of the central committee.[44] Ideally, these bodies adhered to the policies and orders of the central committee, but many provincial leaders took their own initiatives, followed their own programs, and published their own propaganda, all without regard to a coordinated plan. Indeed, the Catania committee, one of the most powerful, never really fell under Finocchiaro Aprile's control, and was often estranged from him.[45] Of all the provincial committees, the one in Palermo was the most notable because it acted as Finocchiaro Aprile's mouthpiece. On the other hand, some of the other committees never played influential roles in their provinces and disappeared early in the struggle for independence.[46]

The communal organizations appeared and dissolved almost daily, and it is impossible to estimate their number accurately. In areas where there was strong support for the movement, communal committees flourished, while in other places, they never appeared. While these communal sections did little to influence the national policies of the movement, they provided every supporter an opportunity to participate actively in the struggle. They often attempted to have an impact on the local scene, especially through small meetings, and the issuance of proclamations or other propaganda.

Although AMG prohibited the publication of political propaganda, Allied officials could do little to stop the dissemination of separatist literature. In its simplest forms, separatist propaganda relied on the traditional Italian method of spreading news by writing slogans on city walls, or distributing handbills and written notices detailing separatist activities or voicing the standard complaints. The messages continually expressed the movement's disdain for the Italian government and nation and the Savoy dynasty, and proclaimed that the island's economic and social renewal was contingent upon independence. Some adopted a menacing tone and urged the Sicilian people to "rise up and free Sicily."[47] Separatist authors relied on Sicily's glorious history to justify independence, and allusions to the past became an integral part of their writings. The revolt of the Vespers in 1282 became a common point of reference, and the symbol of the Vespers appeared on many placards and cards.[48] These simple slogans appealed to the emotions and were aimed at the unsophisticated.

For the more literate Sicilian, the separatist movement published several newspapers. *L'Indipendenza Siciliana* was the major press organ of the movement and served as the mouthpiece of the central committee, whose members were listed as its financial and political supporters.[49] First published in January 1944, the paper was distributed mainly in the Palermo area, and echoed many of Finocchiaro Aprile's policies and ideas. *L'Indipendenza Siciliana* avoided calls to violence and revolution, and simply repeated the usual separatist arguments. Its publication, however, upset Allied officials, who hunted down the printer and forced him to close his shop. Despite this action, *L'Indipendenza Siciliana* continued to be published periodically.[50]

Finocchiaro Aprile used the separatist press to spread his ideas. Under the pseudonym "Verax," he wrote articles for *La Repubblica Siciliana,* published by Concetto Battiato. *La Repubblica Siciliana* began publication in early 1944, but ceased in May after the prefect of Catania warned Battiato to stop his activities. Battiato was considered by some to be Finocchiaro Aprile's mouthpiece, and his paper publicized his program.[51]

Of all the separatist propagandists, the Allies considered Battiato to be the most important. His "Catechism of the Free Sicilian" was one of the most interesting works justifying independence. Dedicated to Finocchiaro Aprile, it echoed many of his positions. Battiato claimed that Sicily had once been a beautiful and rich country that its various conquerors had despoiled. The island had been the most anti-Fascist region, and Battiato argued that all true Sicilians agreed that it needed to become a "free land in a free sea." An independent Sicily would not be Italy's enemy but would cooperate with it and all the states in the area. Battiato, like other separatists, declared that Sicily must not belong to any other power, although he admitted that its geographic position made the island attractive to other nations; for this reason he labeled the island the "calamity of the Mediterranean."[52]

Like other separatist propagandists, Battiato used a religious-mystical approach to rationalize the need for Sicilian independence. He went so far as to rewrite the Ten Commandments and the prayers of the Roman Catholic church to fit separatist ideology. His Ten Commandments exhorted Sicilians never to take the island's name in vain, never to commit acts that would reflect badly on the dignity of a Sicilian, never to covet anyone else's land, and to use their abilities to improve their own property. Other prayers asked God to aid Sicilians in the quest for independence. One particular prayer went as follows: "I believe that [Sicily] represents geographically, ethnically, and politically, a national unit. . . . I believe in its right to withdraw forever from every tyranny and slavery; I believe in its resurrection and its liberty."[53]

Separatist propaganda had a profound effect. Independence became the dominant political question among the islanders.[54] Separatist events were usually well attended by all classes of people. It was not uncommon to see mafiosi, landowners, local officials, peasants, and workers at the same function. Audience reaction to speeches was usually favorable, especially those given by Finocchiaro Aprile, who crisscrossed the island to maintain enthusiasm for the movement.[55] To his listeners, Finocchiaro Aprile stressed his continuing contacts with Allied leaders, giving assurances that they supported the movement and would discuss it at the peace conference. Although most separatists appreciated and applauded his efforts, some opponents within the movement held meetings to propose their own solutions for Sicily's ills.[56]

The large crowds demonstrated the movement's appeal and made it painfully obvious to the Italian government that many Sicilians were dissatisfied with their treatment by the Italian state. The level of participation threatened officials because the possibility existed that many of these listeners would become active separatists if the island's conditions did not improve. In reality, however, channeling these supporters into the ranks of the movement became a major problem for the separatist leadership.[57]

Like other groups, separatists waited until the Allies lifted their ban on political activities to hold their first open meeting. On 16 January 1944, approximately 1,000 people from all social classes and political viewpoints attended a meeting sponsored by the Partito del Lavoro, a satellite separatist organization. Opponents heckled separatist speakers and demanded a statement concerning the future of the island's *latifondi*. The separatists rebuffed these demands, attacking instead the Italian government and confirming their support for the Allied policy of national self-determination.[58]

Finocchiaro Aprile used this forum for the first important public presentation of his ideas. His dependency on standard emotional arguments, his attack on the monarchy and the Italian state, and his halfhearted praise of the Allies became enduring characteristics of his presentations.

Separatists concentrated much of their activity on creating enthusiasm for a major meeting scheduled for 13 February 1944 in Palermo.

The date was decidedly crucial. The problem of the king's abdication and the transfer of Sicily to Italian control required a strong stance. More importantly, the meeting followed the Bari Congress, during which the parties of the Committee of National Liberation (CLN) had called for the king's immediate abdication, and supported the election of a Constituent Assembly following the war to write a new Italian constitution. Separatists were, therefore, under pressure to achieve independence before the post-war settlement. To gain their objective, separatist leaders needed to demonstrate the movement's popularity and maturity to the Allies, while avoiding becoming the cause of a military crisis on the island.[59] Between 6,000 and 8,000 people turned out to hear Finocchiaro Aprile and other separatists in Palermo. The crowd included people from the province's rural areas, members of the wealthy classes of Palermo, students, landowners, and Allied personnel. Opponents of separatism were also in evidence.[60]

As Finocchiaro Aprile began to speak, fighting and screaming erupted. The unitarians responsible for the disruption were, however, quickly ejected. A number of other violent altercations occurred during the gathering, and as many as fifty people were assaulted by the separatists, two of whom were "almost beaten to death." This episode led to Allied criticism of the movement and comparisons with Fascist violence.[61]

In his speech, Finocchiaro Aprile repeated his claim that the Sicilian people strongly supported independence, and that separatists came from all social classes and political parties. He explained that his federalist approach also included a possible European-wide system excluding Communist states.[62]

Such statements were merely pragmatic. By assuming a federalist stance, Finocchiaro Aprile hoped to make the movement more palatable to the struggling Badoglio government, the Allies, and many Sicilians. He sought to provide Badoglio with an opportunity to solve one of his more difficult problems. Perhaps Finocchiaro Aprile mistakenly assumed that the Italian leader might do anything to hold his government and the state together, including ridding the nation of its "ball and chain," a move that some anti-southern politicians might have supported. Additionally, federalism might appeal to the Allies and convince them to prod Badoglio into freeing the island if they had assurances it would remain anti-Communist and would not disturb the war effort.

In a reference to the Bari Congress, Finocchiaro Aprile agreed with Carlo Sforza regarding the need for a united front behind the Allies until final victory, and reminded the audience that the movement had sought to form volunteer battalions of Sicilians to fight with the Allied forces.[63]

Finocchiaro Aprile also addressed Sicily's return to Italian jurisdiction and the recent nomination of the Sicilian high commissioner. The separatist leader asserted that all Sicilians had welcomed the Allied government because it meant a release from the tyranny of the Savoy dynasty. But, in a major concession to the Allies, he agreed that if they thought it well to entrust the island to the Badoglio government, all Sicilians would welcome that decision. As a condition of acceptance, however, the Allies must nominate the high commissioner, whom the separatists hoped would be Musotto. If the Badoglio regime tried to impose a non-Sicilian on the island, Finocchiaro Aprile warned that Sicilians would wage a campaign of passive resistance and would neither pay taxes nor serve in the army. He promised a "struggle without quarter" in order to obtain Sicilian independence.[64]

Other separatists spoke, but their speeches were merely footnotes to Finocchiaro Aprile's oration. He had been interrupted by both cheers and jeers, and despite the violence, the general public considered the meeting a success.[65]

Musotto's appointment enhanced Finocchiaro Aprile's position, as it appeared that the government had surrendered to his threats. The selection also permitted separatists to take more aggressive actions and assume a more belligerent stance without much fear of retribution. On 29 February, in Palermo, the first cadre of the Lega Giovanile Separatista (Separatist Youth League) was established. A month later, Catanese separatists created a section and elected Guglielmo di Carcaci their leader. They declared their faith in separatism, and pledged their lives to it. Later, di Carcaci, who had been "absolutely estranged from political life," was elected national president of the league.[66] Like the other separatist organs, the Lega ultimately used the press to spread its platform. *Giallo Rosso* was a moderate newspaper in which the articles defended the movement and attacked the government.[67]

The formation of the Lega Giovanile frightened some officials, who saw it as the embryo of a separatist army, but it was more shadow than substance. Its activities were generally limited to public rallies and escorting separatist leaders at speaking engagements.[68] On the other hand, the Lega Giovanile served as a vehicle to draw Sicilian youth into the separatist movement. It provided young Sicilians who had been deprived a chance to fight the Germans an opportunity to struggle for Sicilian independence. Filled with a sense of idealism, many Sicilian youth joined the Lega Giovanile.

The first important meeting of the youth league took place on 23 April 1944 in Palermo, attended by approximately 1,000 people. Com-

munists tried to disrupt the assembly. As in most separatist engagements, Finocchiaro Aprile was the main attraction. He gave another of
his patented speeches and took credit for Musotto's appointment as
high commissioner. At the same time, he expressed disappointment
with Musotto and his advisory body.[69]

Two months after their Palermo meeting, the separatist organization
adopted its formal title: Movimento per l'Indipendenza della Sicilia
(The Movement for the Independence of Sicily).[70] By 1944, the separatists had laid the groundwork necessary to conduct their struggle for
independence. They and their movement had benefited from Allied
tolerance, the absence of a well-organized political opposition, and Musotto's appointment. Yet, every separatist chief understood that as Allied control over island affairs diminished, the risk of an attack by the
Italian government grew. From the beginning of the struggle, decisive
action was needed to achieve independence. The failure of the leadership to take that action cost it the ability to control Sicily's destiny and
gave its enemies time to regroup.

4

Separatism and Its Enemies

THE MUSOTTO PERIOD

Francesco Musotto's term as high commissioner of Sicily was marked by significant changes in the Italian political scene. On 24 April, Badoglio formed a second government that included Palmiro Togliatti from the Communist Party and Salvatore Aldisio from the Christian Democrats. Aldisio became minister of the interior. In the same month, Victor Emmanuel III declared that he would retire in favor of his son Umberto when the Allies took Rome. On 4 June, the Allies reached the capital and the king kept his promise. On 18 June Ivanoe Bonomi formed his first cabinet, signaling a decisive break from Fascism, a step toward national unity, and a new phase in the anti-separatist campaign.[1]

Musotto's selection as high commissioner in March 1944 demonstrated the Badoglio government's intention to assume firm control over Sicilian affairs. But at a time when the situation demanded cooperation among all political factions, unitarians attacked Musotto for having given public offices to separatist sympathizers, for not having joined any political party, for being too close to the Allies, and for not knowing enough about the island's problems. Observers continued to assume that he was a separatist supporter, although he was pledged to autonomy. Fearful of Musotto's true intentions, Badoglio filled his advisory council with anti-separatists, such as Salvatore Aldisio and Enrico La Loggia, and secretly ordered all island mayors to hinder separatist activities.[2]

Any separatist loyalty toward Musotto quickly disappeared after he alienated both Finocchiaro Aprile and Lucio Tasca. In April, Finocchiaro Aprile admitted that his original enthusiasm for the nomination had been a mistake, and wrote to Bonomi, the new Italian Prime Minister, that Musotto was "absolutely unequal to the situation." Soon after, the OSS reported that Musotto and Tasca were embroiled in a feud, the details of which were unknown.[3]

Finocchiaro Aprile's attitude was not totally unfounded, but blame could easily have been placed with Musotto's consultative committee, which was hostile to him, and whose operation and makeup he resented. The government had ignored the list of names submitted by Musotto, and the presence of Aldisio and La Loggia weakened his authority. Members of the council stifled and attacked Musotto's reform proposals out of concern that he was seeking to strengthen the separatists. On the other hand, Musotto should have been more forceful in forging consensus on popular issues such as defascistization.

The defascistization process begun by the Allies had been slow and ineffective. During Musotto's term, the trend continued. Defascistization committees continued to operate, but were slow to meet and take action. Even when former Fascists were dismissed, it was from insignificant posts.[4] When cases were presented to these committees for judgment, the large majority of accused were deemed innocent.[5]

Great resentment existed over the slow pace of defascistization. The continuing presence of Fascists in high-level positions contributed to a number of demonstrations.[6] Among islanders, there was a lack of confidence in the bureaucracy. None of the island's administrators inspired political loyalty, and complaints that racketeers held official positions also abounded.[7] Many administrators were simply unable or unwilling to deal with the bewildering economic and social problems confronting the populace. A number of prefects were attacked as disinterested or incapable. Others were criticized for being too closely tied to the local interests, which in many cases meant the separatists, and attacked for their partisan politics. Musotto had a measure of support from these prefects and when Aldisio, in his capacity as minister of the interior, tried to cleanse the local administration, Musotto opposed him.[8] In reality, the entire administrative infrastructure lay in shambles and the situation would not change dramatically until Aldisio replaced Musotto.

In the chaos following the invasion it would have been difficult for any government to administer Sicily efficiently, let alone one man without political consensus. Indeed, during Musotto's tenure, social and economic conditions actually worsened, and Sicilians suffered from numerous depredations. The inability of the administration to ease the situation reinforced traditional Sicilian disdain for outside authority. Rather than stand idly by, islanders expressed their discontent through a number of organized political parties.

THE REBIRTH OF SICILIAN POLITICS

Separatism did not develop in a political vacuum. Political groups had formed within days of the invasion, despite an Allied ban against all such activity. The order was neither rigidly applied nor obeyed. In general, the parties were anti-Fascist, and limited their activities to clandestine meetings and the distribution of political literature. In addition to the separatists, early reports listed the Socialists, Actionists, Christian Democrats, Communists, and Democratic Liberals as the island's major political forces.[9]

Political activity centered on the larger cities, such as Palermo, Agrigento, Trapani, and Catania. Caltanissetta, where the island's sulphur miners were concentrated, was the only rural area in which significant movement was noted.[10] As usual, Palermo became the center stage for Sicilian politics.

The Allies were suspicious of this political resurgence and assumed that a number of these organizations had been formed by "groups of irresponsible persons" who were "taking advantage of the food situation in Sicily to ferment trouble amongst the population." They also thought that some of the organizations were being used to cover up illegal activities by former criminals.[11] Sicilian political parties were considered so hostile toward one another that the Allies thought that it would be a serious error to give them control of the island.[12] Rather than create further tension by stopping all political development, however, the Allies gave tacit support to, and worked with, those parties that backed the war effort and were anti-Fascist. On the other hand, those groups that specifically violated Allied directives or disrupted the public order were actively prosecuted.[13]

AMG directors soon realized that they could do little to restrict the growth of local political bodies. Rather than fight the rising tide of activity, on 10 January 1944, the Allies instituted political liberty. Sicilians could now freely participate in any non-Fascist activity, as long as they did not disturb the public order. The Allies granted permission for peaceful assemblies and the publication and distribution of political literature. This proclamation guaranteed that the same freedoms would be permitted once the Italian government regained control of the island.[14] Since the regulations did not prohibit anti-national movements, the separatists could function without fear of suppression.

Almost all of the island's political groups focused on separatism and the structure of the future Italian state as the most serious issues. They advocated the continuation of Italian unity in some form, and placed all solutions for Sicily in this context. Most proposed some form of autonomy for Sicily, or the establishment of a federal system. All rejected independence as a solution to the island's ills. Despite sharing an anti-separatist orientation, ideological differences made inter-party cooperation difficult. To complicate matters, most parties were part of larger national organizations that did not regard liberated Sicily as their primary concern. It is not surprising, therefore, that separatism, which concentrated on island conditions while exploiting the traditional disdain for the mainland government, should enjoy a measure of popularity.[15]

The role of the local Committee of National Liberation (CLN) was one of the most striking features of early Sicilian political life. The central committee had been organized in Rome on 9 September 1943, the day after the armistice had been announced. In northern and central Italy, the CLN led the anti-Fascist resistance. In Sicily, the lack of any massive campaign of armed struggle, and the occupation of the island by friendly forces, rendered the island CLN's military function unnecessary. Opposition to separatism unified the committee, but the supporting parties (the Christian Democrats, Communists, Socialists, Liberals, and Actionists) often fought among themselves. A continuing schism between the Christian Democrats and the Communists proved especially divisive.[16] As a result, the local CLN served as nothing more than a loose coalition of anti-separatist groups. In spite of this difficulty, the opinions of CLN leaders carried a great deal of influence.

Enrico La Loggia informally headed the Palermo branch of the CLN. La Loggia had been a parliamentary deputy for Sicily in the pre-Fascist period and had been an avid supporter of autonomy. Soon after the invasion he arrived in Palermo, rebuilt his old power base, and formed the Fronte Unico Siciliano, a coalition of anti-separatist political figures from the various parties. La Loggia quickly became one of the most prominent anti-separatists.[17]

La Loggia's influence grew continually between 1943 and 1944. Although Poletti rebuffed his request for a meeting, the incident did not hurt La Loggia's standing within anti-separatist circles. La Loggia continuously pointed out the weaknesses of separatist ideology, accusing separatists of misrepresenting the complex causes of the island's dire economic circumstances. He firmly believed that these conditions contributed to the movement's popularity. La Loggia held that Sicily lacked the necessary resources to exist independently, and supported the establishment of a federal system.[18]

La Loggia personified the conventional character of the separatist opposition. He advocated programs that the Rome government and its political allies had proven unwilling to implement, and asked Sicilians to trust an Italian state that had mistreated them for nearly a century. Thus, he found himself at odds with those islanders who had tired of the historical relationship between the island and the mainland.

On the party level, the Christian Democrats had the most advanced political organization. Prior to the Fascist era, Luigi Sturzo's Popular Party had enjoyed strong roots in Sicily, and Sturzo's popularity remained enormous, although he had been in the United States since 1939. Following the invasion, Sturzo's disciples reorganized the remnants of the old Popular Party and renamed it Christian Democracy. By early 1944, the party had made its presence felt in all of the island's provinces and had found two capable leaders, Salvatore Aldisio and Bernardo Mattarella. Christian Democrat supporters came from all social classes, but the Americans felt that the group contained a number of reactionaries and Fascists.[19]

Sturzo's ideas on regionalism and autonomy formed the basis of the Christian Democrat platform for Sicily. The party called for a system of limited administrative and economic autonomy within the Italian state. Separatism was attacked as nothing more than a movement led by personally ambitious men seeking to take advantage of Sicily's plight. In a congress held in December 1943, the Christian Democrats reaffirmed their position on autonomy and independence.[20]

Despite official policy, a strong separatist current existed within Christian Democrat circles. At the December meeting, Silvio Milazzo from Caltagirone proposed that the party refrain from taking a stance on separatism, while allowing members to exercise freedom of thought. When the delegates refused to approve his idea, he led a number of supporters out of the gathering. Luigi La Rosa, an early follower of Sturzo, believed that Sicilians desired independence, and turned to separatism after Fascist rule. He attacked his former party for having adopted worn-out methods to solve Sicily's problems.[21]

Unlike the Christian Democrats, the Communist Party did not have strong roots in Sicily prior to the Fascist seizure of power. When the Fascist regime collapsed, the island's Communists had no leader and little organization, and were divided by ideological, strategic, and geographical differences. Some Communists wished to ally with the Committee of National Liberation, while others wanted to prepare for an eventual seizure of power. A schism also existed between those who wanted autonomy and those wishing for a highly centralized state. The former were based mainly in Messina and Catania while the latter operated out of Palermo.[22]

Although generally anti-separatist, as early as November 1943, reports suggested that Communists were aiding separatists with the intention of converting them to Communist objectives. Later, some Communist leaders reported having received instructions to support the cause of independence. To add to the confusion, others wished to permit separatists to join their ranks while many were anxious to crush them, through force if necessary.[23] This dissension resulted from a strong separatist current within the party. Led by Ignazio dell'Aria and Arturo Scardino from Catania, the Partito Comunista di

Sicilia (Communist Party of Sicily) had its headquarters in Palermo and justified Sicilian independence on the basis of the Italian government's past exploitation.[24] This group demanded that Sicilians alone solve the island's problems, and called the unitary Communists traitors. This separatist current gained in importance as agitation for independence persisted, and reached its zenith in late 1944.

Communist strength on the island continued to rise in spite of errors, Allied resistance, and government persecution. Demonstrations against private property, short-lived attempts to create soviets and seize control of town councils in Sicily, and the issuance of propaganda which advocated disrupting the advance of the British armies into Berlin so that the Soviets could occupy the city, only increased Allied fears about Communist intentions. Some Allied authorities believed that the Communists could not be successful on the island unless conditions deteriorated. Nevertheless, they permitted officials who had persecuted them during the Fascist regime to continue arresting them. These actions increased tension and prevented inter-party cooperation.[25]

Although the Allies would have liked the Communists to disappear, by late 1944 the Communists had become second only to the separatist movement in influence. In fact, in certain areas of the island, such as Catania, the Communists challenged separatist dominance as early as mid-1944.[26] Although the party had gained national prestige as a result of Palmiro Togliatti's cooperation with the Badoglio regime, in Sicily the leadership proved incapable of unifying the local factions.

Girolamo Li Causi's arrival in August 1944 marked a change in Communist fortunes. Li Causi worked to curb dissension, prevent violence, and block Sicilian separatism, while supporting autonomy.[27] Li Causi believed that Sicilians would benefit from autonomy. On the other hand, he believed that separatism, which represented a "vague sentimental attitude" that the island's reactionaries supported, would cause harm. These reactionaries included the large landowners, whom Li Causi accused of having supported Fascism. He labeled the *latifondo* Sicily's central problem.[28]

Li Causi's struggle was supported by the local publication of *Unità Proletaria* (Proletarian Unity) and by the national Communist press. Writers in *L'Unità* attacked separatism for impeding the anti-Fascist struggle and for hampering the reconstruction of Italian democracy. *L'Unità* smugly declared that Finocchiaro Aprile's movement would not accomplish much, since the peasants, workers, and intellectuals had already disowned it.[29]

Ultimately, Li Causi became Finocchiaro Aprile's main rival and the most consistent enemy of separatism. Wherever and whenever he spoke, he attracted large crowds. He consistently voiced his support for the political unity necessary to rebuild Italy and Sicily, and often criticized Sicilian politicians for their personal squabbling. He attained great popularity but developed numerous enemies among the island's conservatives.[30]

The Socialists were in a more precarious position. The Socialist Party had never been a force in local politics because many of the party's national leaders had ignored the needs of the south while focusing on those of workers in the north, and because Sicily lacked a large working class from which to draw support. The weakness of the island's branch led it into an alliance with communists in Palermo known as the Fronte del Lavoro (Labor Front). Socialist unity was destroyed in August 1943, following an announcement by the national organization that "the Italian Socialist Party is not in favor of Sicilian separatism, nor does it favor such movements elsewhere. The party supports the greatest possible autonomy within the structure of the future federal republic of Italy."[31]

Island unitarians supported this statement, and the national headquarters recognized them as the party's legitimate representatives. Many local Socialists, however, refused to adhere to this declaration, and supported the Sicilian Socialist Federation. Some leading separatists found a home in this political faction, including La Manna, Montesanti, Mariano Costa, and Domenico Cigna, all of whom sat on the Federation's executive committee in December 1943. Vincenzo Vacirca, an anti-Fascist who had lived in the United States, was the organization's main spokesman. Under the code name Pliny, Vacirca had worked for the OSS prior to and after the Sicilian landings. He left the United States for Sicily in September 1943, while still in the employ of the OSS.[32] Vacirca might have been one of the American consul's informants on the island, and his platform for Sicilian autonomy might have been a true reflection of American desires regarding Sicily's fate. As an OSS employee, Vacirca occupied a secure and protected position, while his platform offered the best alternative to total separation in calling for the broadest possible system of autonomy. His ideas so closely resembled those of the separatists, however, that some authorities believed that he had direct contact with Finocchiaro Aprile.

Vacirca's plan called for Sicily to have an independent judiciary, police force, and school system, as well as departments of commerce, communications, and finance and treasury. A legislative assembly elected through universal suffrage would have broad powers, including electing a first deputy, who would choose the cabinet. Vacirca's platform limited the Italian state's role to little more than an advisory one. The Rome government would be represented by a general commissar for

Sicily who would ensure that the Sicilian government followed the basic principles of the national constitution and of autonomy. He could veto laws of the Sicilian assembly, but the veto could be overridden. The central government could intervene in local affairs only if basic political rights were violated, and would control both foreign and military policy. Sicilian representatives would participate in the Italian parliament, and Sicily would pay taxes to Italy, based on its wealth and the services it received from the Italian state. Changes in the statute of autonomy could not be made without the consent of the Sicilian people.[33]

Unitary Socialists found Vacirca's ideas unacceptable. After a series of meetings in April 1944, Socialist Party chieftains realized that as long as the schism between the two factions existed, their influence on the island would be minimal.[34] By the time the conflict was resolved in 1945, local Socialists had lost much of their influence.

While the local party remained crippled by its internal conflict, leaders at the national level campaigned to discredit separatism. In one of the most famous anti-separatist articles, Pietro Nenni declared that just as Sicily could not survive alone (fara da sè), neither could Italy ever again treat the island as a colonial possession. To Nenni, separatism represented a narrowly based, illogical, reactionary movement, supported by the same forces that had backed Fascism. Autonomy, on the other hand, represented a healthy fear of government centralization and bureaucracy, but was the most logical plan for creating economic regions based on the development of local resources.[35]

The Action Party, the last of the major national parties on the island, had been created underground during the Fascist period as an outgrowth of the Giustizia e Libertà (Justice and Liberty) resistance organization. A conglomerate of many political personalities and philosophies, the Action Party had a great deal of influence and strength in Italy in the immediate post-war period. In Sicily, the party profited from its ties to the OSS and operated freely throughout the island. In 1943 and 1944, it enjoyed temporary popularity. Given its makeup, the party had an elastic if not well-defined program; its heterogeneous membership in fact prevented the adoption of a rigid ideological platform.[36]

The political careers of the party's main leaders, Vincenzo Purpura and Giuseppe Scialabba, reflected its elasticity. Both had undergone many changes in their political affiliations, and shared commitment to basic ideas, including opposition to the monarchy and the Badoglio government and support for regional autonomy.[37] Independence was considered illogical because all the regions shared a cultural heritage and markets. Autonomy, however, should be installed only in regions where popular sentiment demanded it. Action Party spokesmen denounced separatists as traitors, accusing them of having aided the Fascist seizure of power, and equated separatism with the despised Italian monarchy.[38] The Action Party progressively lost influence, especially after two of its leaders accepted positions in the Badoglio government, and it eventually proved to be no match for the other political forces on the island.

The presence of numerous small parties further confused the local political scene. Many of these groups were short-lived, but further splintered the population into non-cooperative factions.

The Liberal Party had great prestige on the mainland because the renowned philosopher Benedetto Croce supported it. In Sicily, however, its appeal was limited to the intellectual classes. Similarly, the Republican Party—despite its historical traditions—had almost no influence on the local political scene. Republicans strictly opposed the monarchy and supported giving each region broad autonomy. The Sicilian branch of the party, like the other political groups, contained a number of separatists. When the party's national leader, Randolfo Pacciardi, visited the island in 1945, rumors suggested that Republicans and separatists were working on a plan of mutual cooperation.[39]

The Party of Union had no national roots and developed on the island after the collapse of Fascism. Considered right-wing, it was intensely anti-Communist. Its supporters came from monarchist groups, including well-known members of the Catanese nobility, and professionals. The Party of Union was the only organized political group that openly supported the transfer of power from the Allies to the Badoglio government.[40]

At least four other parties that were proponents of separatism developed on the island. Concetto Battiato formed and led the Sicilian Labor Party. This group called for the creation of a Sicilian republic with a large degree of self-government. The platform called for extensive economic development and compulsory schooling, and held that "property is a material right that can be taken over for a social function." It demanded disarmament and the end of conscription. The new state would have its own currency and could form political and military alliances with the Allied powers.[41]

At first the Allies incorrectly considered this party independent of Finocchiaro Aprile, believing that it brought together Republicans, Socialists, and other supporters of Sicilian independence. In May 1944, however, the Allies recognized that this group represented nothing more than an outgrowth of the separatist movement.[42]

The Demoliberal Party had a small following and never played a major role in the separatist struggle, yet the faction represented a singular current within the movement. Its supporters reportedly came from the island's capitalist classes, and its leaders had close ties to the movement's inner circles.[43] In essence, this party was merely an offspring of the progressive wing of the separatist movement, and its inability to influence events attests to the dominance of the movement's conservatives.

Like the previously mentioned Sicilian Democratic Party of Order, the Sicilian Party of Reconstruction reflected the strong pro-American sentiment on the island. Led by Antonio Di Stefano, a former priest, the party used the Statue of Liberty as its symbol and claimed the support of 40,000 members from among the railroad unions, Catholics, and Masons. The leaders were university professors and high school teachers. The Party of Reconstruction's platform called for Sicily to become the 49th state of the United States. If this goal could not be accomplished, the party wanted the island to become part of the British Commonwealth, a United States of Italy, or a larger European confederation. In an interview, Di Stefano spoke about his party's plans for an independent Sicily, and mentioned the rebuilding of homes, ports, and the promotion of industry based on local products as a means to improve island conditions. Like Finocchiaro Aprile, however, he did not have a well-defined solution to the problem of the landed estates.[44]

THE FOOD CRISIS

Deliberately or not, the political parties helped the Italian state to combat separatism. They joined with the government in trying to persuade the Sicilian people that independence was not in their best interests. But neither the government nor any of the political parties could provide a solution to Sicily's most pressing problem: the critical shortage of food.

In June 1944, the Bonomi government attempted to solve the food crisis by creating the *granai del popolo,* or people's granaries. Largely the work of the Communist minister of agriculture, Fausto Gullo, the *granai* replaced the Fascist *amassi* and were designed to provide each province a measure of control over the supply of agricultural products, and supply necessities to consumers at a fixed price. *Granai* administrators supervised the purchase and collection of agricultural commodities from farmers and sold them to the population. The Allied Control Commission buttressed the system by supporting the regulated price.[45]

Although the *granai* arrangement provided some relief, the program failed in the long run. Farmers continued to hoard their crops because of the low prices paid to them. Sicilians, however, blamed the Allies and the Italian government for the continuing shortages. Problems associated with the *granai* not only fueled public distrust, but also increased suspicions about Allied motives. Some politicians accused the ACC administrator of "lacking the spirit of cooperation," while others concluded that the Allies sought to incite armed revolt for their own ends.[46] Rather than admit their mistake, the authorities tried to force the delivery of grain to the public markets. "If the measures to be enforced by the Italian government are stern ones for the collection of grain," Allied officials declared, "it is because the necessity of war and of feeding the people must override the selfishness of faction and of misguided individuals." Their campaign to make the *granai* a success, was "to be restricted to Sicily alone and will not be allowed publicity in the rest of liberated Italy. For liberated Italy we will play up to the full the facts of the successful harvest, recalling the beginnings of the *Granai del Popolo* campaign and giving details of how it has succeeded so far."[47]

Allied and Italian authorities blamed the crisis on local politicians, especially separatists and their mafia allies. The Americans claimed that separatists had induced farmers not to send their grain to the *granai* and were covertly working against the system, because they were for the most part large landowners who could make big profits from the black market. Moreover, mafia thugs were terrorizing peasants who had given their full quota to the *granai*. Allied officials recommended that the Italian government consider the "removal from Sicily (with the help, if necessary, of the Security Branch) of the heads of the Separatist Movement, especially Finocchiaro Aprile, Avvocato Di Martino, Baron Cesare Bruno di Belmonte, and other members of the so-called National Committee for the Independence of Sicily."[48]

This statement signaled a sharp change in Allied policy toward the movement. Tolerance had started to wear thin, but for the moment, the arrest and deportation of separatist leaders could only remain an empty threat, because economic and political conditions were so unstable. The fanaticism and militancy of the separatists was difficult to ascertain and, since the mafia still supported the movement, any action against it might have invited further chaos. Clearly, however, the Allies were more concerned with maintaining order and feeding the populace than with supporting the creation of an independent Sicilian state.

Separatists spoke against the *granai* and proposed a series of vague plans for improving Sicily's food situation. Finocchiaro Aprile charged that the pricing of grain represented a reckless action on the part of the Italian government that assured the starvation of the Sicilian people. He advocated instead a free-market system, infuriating the Allies with his inflammatory statements. "We solemnly declare," he proclaimed at Regalbuto, "that no one will deliver a single ear of grain. Particularly those who are near to us and those who have at heart the rebirth of this, our land of Sicily, will absolutely refrain from doing so. This constitutes a first and essential duty."[49]

Separatist propaganda relentlessly reinforced the notion of Italian responsibility for the island's food situation and claimed that Sicily could be self-sufficient if it were free from Italian theft. Catanese separatists instructed peasants that "the grain for which you have given your sweat through a whole year must not be stolen from you; the grain belongs to you and the Sicily which has produced it. What is required of you is a compact union, determined to break in every way the thefts of the Italian rulers."[50]

Despite the campaign against the *granai,* Finocchiaro Aprile denied that his supporters had undermined its success, and tried to rationalize the apparent shift in Allied sentiment. In June, he complained to a British official that an unfavorable attitude, originally adopted in order "not to arouse any suspicions in American circles," had now become British policy.[51]

In a ploy to regain Allied support and draw strength from the parties of the left, Finocchiaro Aprile claimed that as politics turned increasingly leftward, so would separatism.[52] This represented one part of a long-term effort to use the "red scare" tactic and make separatism more palatable to those who feared a Communist takeover more than an independent Sicily—including the Allied powers.

MOUNTING COMPETITION

With political pressure mounting, Finocchiaro Aprile took measures to coordinate the movement's activities and prepare for independence. He secretly proposed the creation of an administrative council to "govern" Sicily after a successful separatist revolt. This body was to be ready to assume responsibility by October 1944. This suggests that separatist chiefs planned for a seizure of power to coincide with their first national congress. This proposal, made during a series of private conferences that Finocchiaro Aprile held with separatist heads in Catania, sheds some light on the movement's decision-making process.[53] A clique had begun to develop policy without consulting other leaders or the rank and file. By the end of the year, the movement's public activities barely reflected the real decisions being made in secret.

During these same meetings in Catania the movement's leaders decided to create several new political parties with separatist aims designed to draw followers from the island's other major groups. A Sicilian Christian Democratic Party, a Sicilian Socialist Party that would oppose the autonomy platform of the Sicilian Socialist Federation, and a Sicilian Communist Party were all planned. Out of this decision arose the Partito Comunista di Sicilia in late 1944, led by Ignazio dell'Aria.[54] This tactic represented a skillful effort to undermine the political opposition while at the same time broadening the movement's appeal.

As the intensity of political competition increased, violent confrontation between separatists and their opponents became inevitable. Small-scale brawls and the throwing of objects became common occurrences at the movement's functions. The violence irritated the Allies, who felt that the incidents demonstrated "the political immaturity of many of separatism's followers."[55] The government responded by cracking down on separatists. Those who held administrative positions were pressured to resign, while prominent leaders, including Finocchiaro Aprile, were placed under surveillance. In response to rumors concerning the formation of action squads and the seizure of arms destined for separatist use, the government dispatched troops to the island.[56] Nevertheless, on 14 May, Finocchiaro Aprile, accompanied by other separatist leaders, presided over an unauthorized public meeting in Catania attended by approximately 500 provincial representatives. Although the chief of police employed an extra force of Carabinieri, a clash occurred in which three people were injured. Later, the police accused Finocchiaro Aprile and other separatist leaders of having incited the violence. But the trial held in December became a separatist victory when the accused were acquitted.[57]

The rivalry between separatists and Communists was especially dangerous. As each sought political dominance, violence increased. In late May at Randazzo, in the province of Catania, the separatists reportedly killed one Communist, while the Carabinieri apparently wounded two others.[58] Later that same month, another incident attracted world attention when separatists and Communists clashed at Regalbuto, on the slopes of Mount Etna. The town had endured countless bombings during the invasion, and the population suffered from hunger and unemployment. Although not a separatist stronghold, the area's large landowners supported the movement.[59]

On 27 May, Finocchiaro Aprile and other separatists arrived in Regalbuto, and hundreds of Communists demonstrated in front of the separatist meeting hall. Although police dispersed them, the Communists regrouped an hour later and struggled with the security forces and separatists at the building's entrance. Both sides fired shots, and at least one Communist was killed, and two men were injured.[60]

Separatists fully exploited the Regalbuto incident. They accused the prefect of Enna of having helped transport the Communists and their followers to the meeting. They also charged that the Communists had started the shooting and were behind a plan to assassinate Finocchiaro Aprile. Separatists warned that they would defend their freedom of speech at any cost.[61]

The minister of the interior, Salvatore Aldisio, reacted immediately by calling for the deployment of more troops to the island.[62] At the same time, the Allies used the violence to further distance themselves from the separatists. When Finocchiaro Aprile appealed to the Allied Commission for support, authorities retorted that policy did not allow them to interfere with the Italian administration and that the commission's sole concern was that Sicily make the "greatest possible contribution to the successful prosecution of the war and that it does not hinder the war effort." Colonel A. N. Hancock, the ACC's Deputy Regional Commissioner for Sicily, considered the situation an internal matter for the Italian government, but added that if asked, he would recommend "in the best interests of the war effort and public security in SICILY, Finocchiaro Aprile's removal to an internees camp, with other members of his group for company is to be advocated."[63]

Despite private misgivings, the British and Americans failed to renounce the separatist movement publicly, thereby fostering the impression that the separatists continued to enjoy their support. Rallies at which the American and British flags flew alongside that of independent Sicily and at which leaflets were distributed, further implied that Sicily was included in the list of oppressed nations to which Roosevelt and Churchill promised freedom.[64] Local officials hesitated to restrict the movement's activities in fear of offending the Allied powers. Thus, separatists enjoyed a larger amount of freedom than the Italian government found agreeable.

THE FOREIGN CAMPAIGN

Despite their public bravado, separatists realized that a full-scale crackdown was possible as Allied tolerance diminished and the government grew in strength. Moreover, although new separatist sections continued to form, overall the movement seemed to be losing strength, especially in the eastern and central areas. Challenged by opposition

parties and plagued by a failure to organize on a local level, the separatists had suffered significant attrition in Syracuse. In Catania the population was moving toward support for the Communists, Socialists, and
unity. Even in Messina the movement showed a loss of strength, while
in the sulphur-mining areas of Caltanissetta and Agrigento there were
no signs of separatist activity. Only in Palermo did the movement show
any growth, but this was understandable, since its main headquarters
was located there and its major advocates concentrated their activities
in that area. Some Allied officials responded to the apparent decline
by claiming that if separatists did not achieve some measure of success
soon, all hope for the cause would be lost.[65]

For the first time, it also appeared that Finocchiaro Aprile might
be losing some of his authority. In June, the Committee for Sicilian
Independence criticized the separatist leader as "incapable of giving
the Separatist Movement an ideal program which could attract intellectuals." It also pointed out organizational problems and accused him of
planning an armed march on Palermo. Rumors concerning Finocchiaro Aprile's possible assassination spread, although there is evidence
to suggest that he had begun the rumors himself in order to appear
"cloaked in the halo of a martyr."[66]

In the face of these problems, separatists sought to increase tension
in the hope that the government would use severely repressive measures. They calculated that this would arouse foreign protection for
the movement. Separatists became increasingly strident. After a small
disturbance between members of the Lega Giovanile and the Italian
military, Finocchiaro Aprile rejected the government's accusation of
separatist provocation and instead charged that soldiers had obeyed
orders from their superiors to rough up his young followers. He threatened repercussions, the responsibility for which would fall on the
"provocateurs."[67]

Rather than instigate an armed challenge, Finocchiaro Aprile and
his followers sought another avenue to undercut the government while
gaining sympathy for their movement. In the midst of the political
chaos of mid-1944, they began a massive campaign to enlist foreign
assistance.

Popular belief continued to assume that either the British or Americans backed the separatist movement. The foreign campaign aimed at
garnering further support by publicizing the situation on the island.
Separatists portrayed themselves as freedom fighters to those countries
that had fought the Axis and suffered under Nazi oppression.

Reports in mid-1944 suggested that the separatists were already re-
ceiving aid and sympathy from foreign nationals. Evidence indicates
that Finocchiaro Aprile had made contact with two Yugoslavs, and

authorities assumed that Finocchiaro Aprile was conspiring to dismember Italy. At almost the same time, separatist sympathizers among Sicilian settlers in Tangiers held meetings to form a political party known as "Trinacria" (the three-legged symbol for Sicily) which called for separation from Italy.[68] Little is known about the group's strength or whether it received its instructions from Sicily.

Finocchiaro Aprile actually announced the foreign campaign in a letter written to Bonomi in late June. In it, the separatist leader surveyed the Sicilian political situation, attacked Musotto, and labeled the prefect of Palermo, Paolo D'Antoni, "a drunkard and a political chameleon." He accused D'Antoni of prohibiting separatist meetings and threatening publishing houses that disseminated the movement's literature. Finocchiaro Aprile warned that he would not assume responsibility for the reaction of his followers and demanded that his movement be protected since it operated within legal limits. In the time-honored tradition of Sicilian nationalism, he argued that the government would make Sicilians slaves of the industrialized North. "Only if you will consider the eventuality of a federation," he warned, "will Sicily and Italy be able to understand each other. Otherwise each one must proceed on its own way. I have already placed the problem on an international basis."[69]

Separatists directed their first international appeal to Sicilians in the United States. It asked Sicilian-Americans to use their wealth and influence at the voting booth to sway Washington's policies. It reminded these emigrants of the constant exploitation of Sicily, and urged those who had contributed so much to their new homeland to exhort the United States to aid the separatist cause. The manifesto emphasized the bonds and benefits that would be created between an independent Sicily and an actively interested United States. Sicilians in America were urged to persuade the government to support a plebiscite to determine Sicily's fate. In a last appeal to sentiment, the separatists declared, "Above all, in the name of God do not remain inert, and remember that all that you do is for your holy mother: Sicily."[70]

This message demonstrated the often unrealistic presumptions of the movement's directors. Clearly, they understood the potential political power of the approximately six million Italian-Americans, many of whom were of Sicilian origin. A show of solid support from this group might force an alteration in American policy, yet it is doubtful that many in the Italian-American community supported the separatist movement. While many Italian-American leaders expressed concern about Sicily's fate, they did so because they believed that the separatists had British support and feared that the island might fall under British control. In fact, most of those who voiced their opinion wanted Sicily reunited with the mainland.[71]

On the same day, another separatist proclamation, aimed simultaneously at Sicilians and Anglo-Americans, called upon the Allies to reassume control over Sicily to prevent a Communist takeover. Sicilians had anticipated that the Anglo-American invasion would bring liberty to their island, but now they felt betrayed: "Now, oh Anglo-Americans, you remind us of Dante, Manzoni, and Berchet. You teach us at our own expense that it is sinful to hope that foreigners will work to obtain liberty for us." The Allies had built up Sicilian hopes for an independent state through their pre-invasion propaganda, but had failed to understand the islanders' character. Through their errors, the Allies might have hastened a Communist takeover: "Italian Communists together with Russia are preparing a war against England and America." The Allies' biggest mistake, accused the proclamation, had been to return control of the island to Italy. This had permitted the government, the Committee of Liberation, and Italian military units to abuse separatists. The Allies were warned that "you will become aware of this only when several thousands will be taken to prison or sent to the concentration camps like common criminals. Perhaps here again the new government will exceed the Fascist regime. . . . Keep the promises which you have repeated for four years. . . . Return to govern us till the day of the plebiscite. Do not suffocate us. Prevent a civil war. Prevent Communism from triumphing over us. Do not allow liberty to be spoiled by abandon. Only thus shall we be eternally grateful."[72]

Some separatist leaders tried other avenues to reach the outside world. On 5 July, Lucio Tasca attempted to send a telegram to President Franklin Roosevelt through the Allied Control Commission. The telegram, which read "glory to those nations which have the joy and the faith of celebrating their independence," was rejected for transmittal by ACC officials.[73]

Finocchiaro Aprile, on the other hand, had a bit more success. On 10 July, he sent a letter to Roosevelt explaining that the Italian government was abusing and oppressing the separatist movement. He accused the ACC of doing nothing to halt the government's activities, and begged the president to intervene. Although the letter evidently reached Washington, Roosevelt, who knew of the movement's existence, never responded.[74]

While the movement looked for outside assistance, Finocchiaro Aprile sought again to mollify Allied authorities by making a conciliatory address on Radio Palermo. He planned to thank the Allies for liberating Sicily and express Sicilian willingness to march on the side of the United States and Britain. More importantly, he intended to retract his earlier attacks on the *granai* and declare that all Sicilians were duty-bound to send their grain to the *granai,* even though the government had made a mistake in its pricing policies.[75] Allied and Italian officials denied Finocchiaro Aprile permission to speak, but it is clear from the episode that the separatist leader had come to realize that the movement had to stop irritating the Allies.

To the dismay of their enemies, the separatists seemed to achieve some success in Britain. In mid-July, an article in the London *Times* strengthened the perception that the movement enjoyed broad support among the British. The article pointed out the racial differences between Sicilians and northern Italians, stressed Sicilian resentment over the "rigged" results of the 1860 plebiscite, and explained why Sicilians felt exploited. It also pointed out that the movement's leaders were large landowners, whose major motivation was their desire to preserve their property in the face of a predicted leftist revolution.[76] Although the article was non-committal, its publication boosted separatist hopes that the British might aid their cause.

The appeal for outside help also caught the attention of Soviet officials. One of their representatives asked the Italian foreign ministry "in a personal and friendly way" to prepare a review of separatism. The report contained the usual anti-separatist rhetoric, but admitted that fear of a communist triumph in Italy, and historical resentment, had contributed to the movement's growth. Most Sicilians, the report continued, supported autonomy and federalism, and separatists were extremists who desired to retain their positions. It was impossible to evaluate the movement's strength fully, but its following would increase if extremists gained control on the mainland or if past wrongs were not addressed. The best means to fight separatism was to treat the island as equal to the rest of the nation. Moreover, the application of autonomy would end the separatist threat.[77] Although the Soviets expressed interest in the Sicilian situation, there was no sign that their policy of preserving Italian territorial integrity had changed.

Buoyed by some apparent success, the separatists renewed their foreign campaign on 20 July by issuing a manifesto pointing out similarities between conditions on the island and those that had existed in Nazi-occupied Europe: "We live here under a regime of the most abominable oppression. Not only are all liberties denied to us, but we are exposed to violence of all kinds. . . . It is to be borne in mind that the Italian government is taking everything out of Sicily as if to punish her for her hostile attitude. Railway rolling stock, autobuses . . . materials and goods of every kind are being taken away to Italy, rendering our life impossible. The Italian government cares not that Sicily is deprived of everything." Separatists asked that the United States and

Britain reoccupy the island to end this situation. If this did not occur, the national committee promised to continue the fight for the separation of the two nations.[78]

Reaction to the 20 July manifesto was almost universally negative.[79] Some Sicilians were indignant that the separatists had requested foreign intervention; many realized the illogical nature of the appeal—separatists wanted independence, but were willing to look for foreign powers to aid them without any guarantee that these same nations would not try to assume control over the island.

If the declaration offended Sicilians, it infuriated the Allies, who considered the note "full of mis-statement and perversion of the truth, and . . . composed with evident intent to mislead." They observed that the removal of material to the mainland was the result of urgent military necessity.[80] British officials reported that Rome might come to regard the latest manifesto as "something near treason" and that officials "were wondering whether they could let this go by without reacting." But the Italian government stopped short of taking harsh action against the separatists on the advice of Colonel Hancock. In August, he counseled that "it would be a great mistake for the Italian government to attempt to take any steps against Aprile at any rate at the present time."[81]

Although the Allies saved Finocchiaro Aprile and others from arrest, they were clearly disenchanted with him:

He may have been sufficiently far-sighted enough to return to Palermo from Rome to capitalize on the Allied landings. His protestations that he has no personal ambitions, are so frequent as to give reasons for doubt, and he is unscrupulous in his attempts to gain popular sympathy. [We are] not yet in a position to judge whether he is capable of militant action, but his verbal onslaughts on authority are capable of producing a tension among his younger followers which may get beyond his control. It is also known that FINOCCHIARO has attempted to curry favour with the British at the expense of the Americans, and vice-versa, and would not hesitate to misquote and twist any statement made by an Allied spokesman to suit his own political ends.[82]

THE ALDISIO PERIOD

While a full-scale suppression of the movement was for the moment impossible, the Bonomi government did remove Francesco Musotto as high commissioner. Musotto had never lived down the suspicion that he had separatist tendencies, nor had he dealt successfully with his opposition. In some cases, he proved to be his own worst enemy by creating antagonism between himself and other officials. One of his biggest problems lay in Palermo, where he had tried to extend his influence into the provincial administration. Paolo D'Antoni, the prefect, refused to assume responsibility for many of Musotto's policies, and Musotto's attempt to encroach on his authority angered him. On the other hand, D'Antoni's desire to communicate directly with the Rome government threatened Musotto.[83]

Musotto had retained his position under Badoglio because of Allied influence and political uncertainty, but his removal became inevitable once Bonomi assumed power in June 1944. Bonomi's government marked a clear break from Fascism and a step toward national unity. Musotto's removal gave Bonomi an early opportunity to demonstrate that he was independent of Allied pressure.

The support of La Loggia, the Palermo section of the Committee of National Liberation, and many of the island's anti-separatist politicians, virtually guaranteed that Salvatore Aldisio would replace Musotto. While ACC officials thought the change inopportune, they did not actively interfere.[84]

Aldisio's appointment became official in late July and signaled the start of a deliberate campaign against separatism and its supporters. Aldisio viewed his selection as an opportunity to wage war against the separatist movement. He recognized that the movement had benefited from the conditions on the island, but believed that it lacked popular roots. In his view, isolated elements who feared losing their rights and privileges, especially the large landowners, had started and supported the movement.[85] He thought that Sicily's recovery could be best achieved through a system of decentralized administrative autonomy. In a series of secret meetings with separatist-oriented Christian Democrats, he revealed that his program "did not include the non-payment of taxes by Sicilians to the Italian state."[86] This was an essential question, since separatists claimed that the island had always paid more to the state than it had received in program benefits.

Finocchiaro Aprile opposed Aldisio's appointment for personal as well as political reasons. The separatist leader correctly surmised that Aldisio had two aims as high commissioner: to crush the separatist movement and aid the Christian Democratic Party, of which he was a leading member. He also claimed that he and Aldisio had met soon after the invasion, and that Aldisio had supported the idea of a provisional Sicilian government. Aldisio, however, denied that he had made any such agreement.[87] The hostility between the two men set the tone for the next three years.

Once in office, Aldisio attacked separatism on several fronts. First, he contacted the island's mafia leaders. The OSS reported that Aldisio and Vizzini, both Christian Democrats, were friends. Vizzini even offered to meet with Aldisio to solve the island's grain problem, thus implying that he had the power to do so. While there is no evidence that Aldisio and Vizzini ever met to discuss the food issue, the new high commissioner did, however, invite Calogero Volpe, a leading mafia official and friend of Vizzini, to the secret gatherings with Christian Democrats.[88] Volpe's attendance represented the first step in the formation of the government's alliance with the mafia. Mafia chieftains perceived Aldisio's appointment as a first sign of the government's determination to crush the separatist movement, and forced them to reconsider their loyalty to it.

While he slowly moved to co-opt the mafia and other conservative elements, Aldisio also worked to intimidate separatism's supporters. He ended Musotto's benign policies, endorsed police measures against separatist leaders, and permitted the local Committee of National Liberation to carry out a vociferous anti-separatist campaign.[89] Aldisio also targeted separatists who held public office, removing mayors and municipal committee members from their posts. From prefects, he obtained lists of separatist agitators, and placed them under surveillance. Those who resisted Aldisio's orders were purged. Separatist leaders protested to no avail that many of those removed had done an efficient job, and that many of the new appointees lacked the necessary training.[90]

Lucio Tasca became the most significant casualty in Aldisio's crusade. Because the Allies had appointed Tasca mayor of Palermo, his removal, like that of Musotto, was a test of the Bonomi government's independence. Tasca had sealed his fate in May when he presided over a meeting of provincial officials that called for administrative elections, the abolition of the high commissioner's consultative committee, and the creation of a body made up of representatives from all the provinces.[91] Tasca's elimination highlighted the inability of the movement to mobilize its followers for decisive action, and showed the growing isolation in which the movement found itself. Only separatists protested Tasca's dismissal.

Tasca blamed his banishment on the Committee of National Liberation and asserted that his administration had always had both popular and Allied support. "The future of the country," he told the people of Palermo, "is in your hands, you will forge your destiny with love, faith, and the courage necessary in the decisive moment in the history of a people. With this faith in you and with the hope of a glorious future for our island, at the moment of leaving the first mayoralty of free Palermo, I address to you my fraternal and solitary thought."[92]

Tasca also wrote to his former benefactor, Charles Poletti, claiming that his eleven months in office had been torture, and that he returned home "happy, contented, and burdened by praise from all the authorities, from the high commissioner to the prefect." He added that "I am returning first to my dear latifondo and I hope always, with your help, to Sicilian Independence! Thanks, dearest friend, for the assistance and aid which you have always given to our country, which I hope you will continue to assist for the conquest of its supreme good and that is . . . independence."[93]

Aldisio's actions forced separatists to work harder to maintain their viability. Local committees now arose in areas where they had never existed previously. Elsewhere, separatist support increased, appearing for the first time in an organized fashion. Some groups began to dominate the local political situation and overwhelm the anti-separatist bloc.[94] This was in marked contrast to the condition that had existed less than two months before.

THE MAFIA AND THE 49TH STATE

Despite Aldisio's campaign of intimidation, large audiences continued to show up at separatist gatherings. The police chief of Bagheria (near Palermo) prohibited a meeting planned for 25 June because he feared violence, but it took place on 6 August after the Allies and mafia applied pressure. Perhaps 3,000 people attended, many waving the banner of the Lega Giovanile. Finocchiaro Aprile, whose appearance was greeted with wild cheering, and Antonino Varvaro made major addresses. Varvaro accused the opposition of trying to suffocate separatism, and claimed that it was a popular movement, free from foreign influence. He echoed Finocchiaro Aprile's latest call for Sicilians to deliver their grain to the *granai*.[95]

Finocchiaro Aprile saluted the Allies, Roosevelt, and the Sicilians of America, arguing that separatists preferred Allied military occupation to Italian control, but indicating a willingness to negotiate a plan of federation with Italy on the basis of equality. Sicily, he said, was entitled to self-government and "many leading international personalities . . . including La Guardia" had affirmed that right.[96]

At the end of his speech, Finocchiaro Aprile spoke directly to the large number of people who were wearing badges bearing a picture of the American flag with the green silhouette of Sicily in the center. These were members, or supporters, of the mafia-organized Partito Democratico d'Ordine, which in late April or early May had changed its name to the Fronte Democratico d'Ordine Siciliano (Sicilian Democratic Front of Order). "Mafia," he again proclaimed, "is an institution which should be created if it did not already exist. We have to distinguish between mafia and criminality. Mafia is an organization of order, discipline, and political justice."[97]

This statement was an effort by Finocchiaro Aprile to appease those of his mafia followers who were already distancing themselves from him. In Misilmeri, a town in Palermo province, one mafia group was already collaborating with Finocchiaro Aprile's opponents. Given that this was the area from which Finocchiaro Aprile had first been elected as a deputy, the OSS concluded that he was losing favor with the criminal organization.[98]

The program of the Fronte Democratico d'Ordine Siciliano proposed an alternative to Finocchiaro Aprile's aims and copied those of the earlier Partito Democratico d'Ordine, whose leaders, the OSS concluded, "were all members and lieutenants of the high Mafia." Nester believed the Fronte's purpose was to draw other mafiosi, as well as pro-American Sicilians, into the movement but away from Finocchiaro Aprile.[99]

The Fronte called for the independence of Sicily under an American sphere of influence and the establishment of a democratic republic with official representation in the government at Washington. The twenty-point program included such concepts as respect for private property, compulsory elementary education, introduction of the dollar as the official currency, and abolition of military service. Declaring that they had "headquarters in every commune of the Island and branches in each community of Sicilians existing in the world," the party's platform exhorted Sicilians to "prepare ourselves for the rebirth, which depends exclusively on the remodeling of our life in the sphere of a powerful America, which will allow us, among other things to resume intimate ties with our 4,000,000 brothers living across the Atlantic."[100]

At first, Finocchiaro Aprile seems to have welcomed the appearance of the Fronte. In a letter to Girolamo Valenti, the editor of La Parola in New York, the separatist leader claimed that the Fronte, "which was of purely American origin," supported his movement's objectives. He claimed that he wanted the future Sicilian republic to move toward "unison" with the United States in order to help its economic rebirth while protecting its own interests.[101]

Despite Finocchiaro Aprile's optimism, the mafia and his movement were on a collision course. By changing the name of their organization, mafia leaders hoped to broaden their appeal and place themselves above the local political struggle, presenting themselves as representative of Sicilian needs rather than a narrowly based interest group. Most importantly, their call for American control represented a genuine, if unrealistic, desire, for mafiosi saw the reimposition of Italian rule as a threat. The presence of a powerful mafia in the United States and the seeming willingness of American officials to work with them encouraged Sicilian chieftains. At the least, mafia leaders hoped to use the Fronte as leverage to force the Italian government to bargain with them over Sicily's destiny and their own.

In response to Aldisio's actions and the growth of political opposition, separatist rhetoric became increasingly radical. At a congress held in August 1944, separatists announced that they were prepared to fight.[102] Guglielmo di Carcaci, the leader of the Lega Giovanile, proclaimed that the slogan of the organization should not be "Plebiscito e Indipendenza" (Plebiscite and Independence), but "Indipendenza o Morto" (Independence or Death). Di Carcaci demanded "a machine of steel capable of scattering and destroying the obstacles" that prevented Sicilian independence and prosperity. The young had to provide an example in what had become a life-and-death struggle. Furthermore, he threatened that his organization represented a "potent reality, quick to smash each plan, quick to defend tightly around the red and yellow flag, with life if necessary, its ideals and that of the people, of the true Sicilian people."[103]

The slogan "independence or death," which became widely used, had important psychological consequences. Although there was no overt move toward widespread violence in the summer of 1944, Italian officials feared the specter of a full scale separatist revolt. Certainly, the slogan suggested that a peaceful resolution of the separatist problem seemed less likely with every passing day. Although outwardly committed to achieving independence through legal means, Finocchiaro Aprile and others were slowly modifying their views.

5

On the Rise

POLITICAL VIOLENCE

In the second half of 1944 the level of political hostility in Sicily escalated as both separatists and their opponents assumed more strident positions.[1] Finocchiaro Aprile's followers rejected compromise, and threatened to prevent public meetings by their adversaries. In response, these parties called upon the government to take action.[2]

With the situation degenerating, Aldisio called for quick action against the separatists and administrative autonomy for the island.[3] On 31 August and 1 September, the Council of Ministers voted in favor of "regional autonomy and decentralization" for Sicily, and approved measures to combat separatist propaganda and improve economic and social conditions. The Constituent Assembly, which would meet following the war, would have final approval over the plan.[4]

In response to the government's move, Finocchiaro Aprile dispatched a short note to Bonomi: "The National Committee of Sicilian Independence disregards the new threats and new deceit. The Italian government's promises are futile. We will intensify open propaganda until the last sacrifice for the realization of independence, the only salvation of the Sicilian people."[5]

Meeting in Palermo, the national committee asserted that the government lacked popular support and the constitutional power to legislate for the Sicilian people, who alone had the right to determine their future. In defiance, the leaders pledged to maintain their anti-government stance, intensify their propaganda efforts for independence, and continue their appeals to the United Nations. They insisted on a Sicilian plebiscite and warned that the government would have to assume responsibility for the consequences of its actions.[6]

In an unusual display of unity, some of the movement's most prominent bodies adopted similar positions. The provincial committee of Messina attacked the right of the Constituent Assembly to provide final approval for autonomy. That body, and any other government organ, they claimed, would be dominated by unitarians who would deny Sicily independence. Committee members asserted that unitarians feared a plebiscite because they knew that they would lose. Messinese separatists promised to continue the struggle for independence and warned that they would not be deceived by "useless promises."[7]

The Lega Giovanile of Messina took a more militant stance, calling upon Sicilian youth to help write "the first page of our true history." Sicily would enjoy well-deserved prosperity if independent. "Each one of us," the declaration asserted, "has the categorical duty of participating in the struggle for our redemption." All young men were therefore ordered to report to separatist headquarters.[8]

This call to action contributed to rumors that separatists planned to seize Palermo and take control of the island as soon as peace terms were announced. Some Allied officials dismissed these threats, but others believed that serious armed disorders might arise.[9]

While they verbally protested the government's policy, separatists carried out their promise to restrict opposition gatherings. On 13 September 1944, minister without portfolio Meuccio Ruini was scheduled to speak at a meeting sponsored by the Democratic Party of Labor. Several hundred separatists infiltrated the gathering and, as Ruini began to talk, they interrupted him, shouting, whistling, and flooding the hall with pamphlets and leaflets. Police intervened and ejected those responsible for the disturbance, but Ruini could not resume, and he was forced to leave the hall.[10]

As the mob moved out of the theater, it headed toward separatist headquarters. There, Finocchiaro Aprile congratulated his followers, gloating that after Ruini's defeat "no Italian politician will dare to speak at Palermo or in any other Sicilian town. Our people will prevent it. He who is against independence," Finocchiaro Aprile proclaimed, "is against Sicily, and he is a very mean traitor who will have to pay for his crime." In a veiled threat of violence, he mentioned a "new Sicilian Vespers" as an avenue to independence and asked the crowd to salute the United States and Great Britain, "who are going to give the world peace which everybody wants and with whom we want to face our new and brilliant fate."[11]

Separatists considered the episode a victory, for they had demonstrated their audacity and a willingness to confront the state by preventing an important official from speaking, and then holding an unauthorized meeting.[12] All this had occurred without government retribution. The entire incident gave Sicilians pause to contemplate separatist influence among those sworn to uphold order.

The Ruini visit had immediate consequences. The prefect of Palermo, D'Antoni, faced the possibility of losing his position and took a forced leave, while the police chief, Garbo, was transferred to Pisa. Moreover, opposition leader Alberto Cianca of the Action Party felt pressured enough by events to ask Finocchiaro Aprile for written assurance that he would be permitted to speak unmolested during a scheduled meeting in Palermo.[13]

What Finocchiaro Aprile might not have known, however, was that Ruini and D'Antoni met privately with the Tasca brothers the day after the incident. The prefect castigated Lucio and Alessandro for the separatists' conduct the previous day, but the two men denied any involvement in the incident. They, in turn, attacked the Committee of Liberation as dictatorial. The most important part of the discussion centered on the question of whether the Tascas would support a plan for Sicilian autonomy within a national framework. The Tascas responded by stating their willingness to formulate "such a project with the help of their friends."[14]

The agreement represented a potentially stunning blow to the separatist cause. Lucio's ties to the mafia made him the obvious choice to act as intermediary between the government and mafia chieftains. If he could convince the mafia to accept autonomy as an alternative to independence or the establishment of an American protectorate, and persuade them to renounce Finocchiaro Aprile, the movement would lose its strongest arm. While the process would take some time, the stage was set for the mafia and the government to become anti-separatist allies.

INCIDENT AT VILLALBA

The Ruini incident soon faded into obscurity in light of a more significant confrontation. Had it not been for the personalities involved, the Villalba incident of 16 September might have passed as nothing more than another encounter in the growing struggle between the Communists and separatists for domination of Sicilian affairs. But this clash represented much more. Girolamo Li Causi had galvanized widespread support for the Communist Party. Opposing him in Villalba was Calogero Vizzini, the reputed chief of the Sicilian mafia, leader of the Fronte Democratico, and supporter of the Christian Democrats. Vizzini was one of the most important symbols of the old order, and the episode in Villalba—which he ruled like a fiefdom—represented in microcosm the struggle between the forces of tradition and those of change.

The atmosphere in Villalba made it ripe for a showdown. The Vizzini and Farina families had been on poor terms with the Pantaleone family for some time, and a decision favoring the Vizzini family in a property dispute had inflamed the bitterness between them. As one report noted, the land decision "called for a reprisal from Pantaleone."[15] Political competition further raised the level of antagonism. Vizzini and Farina supported the Christian Democrats, and Pantaleone the "Socialist-Communists."

On the morning of 16 September, tensions rose as Beniamino Farina, the Christian Democratic mayor, and Vizzini's relative, angered local Communists by ordering all hammer-and-sickle signs erased from buildings along the road on which Li Causi would travel into town. When Li Causi's supporters protested, they were intimidated by separatists and thugs.[16]

Li Causi's meeting began in late afternoon. Vizzini had agreed to permit the gathering as long as the speakers did not deal with land problems, the large estates, or the mafia. Both speakers who preceded Li Causi, Luigi Michele Pantaleone of the Villalba Socialists and Luigi Cardamone, secretary of the Caltanissetta Communist section, followed Vizzini's commands. Li Causi did not. Addressing the question of agricultural socialization, he argued for the elimination of the *gabelloti*, or middlemen, between the farm owners and laborers. When Li Causi labeled them extortionists, Vizzini immediately interrupted and denied the charge. This served as the signal for violence. Communists were beaten when they protested Vizzini's remarks, and Vizzini's followers began to shoot. Separatist followers threw three bombs at Li Causi's group, and pistol shots targeted the Communist leader. Li Causi abandoned the piazza while Vizzini and his followers gloated. Fourteen people were injured in the hail of bullets and bombs, including Li Causi, who was shot in the right leg.[17]

The Carabinieri quickly restored order and arrested eight people, including the mayor. Several others, including Vizzini, evaded the police dragnet. Sixty persons were interrogated, but the investigation was doomed from the start.[18]

Vizzini's own written account, "La Verità sui Fatti di Villalba" (The Truth About the Events in Villalba) appeared in separatist newspapers, and differed from the official report. The American consul, Nester, considered Vizzini's version "a fair and just summary of what occurred."[19] According to Vizzini, notice of Li Causi's meeting did not cause any great alarm among the populace, and the appearance of the Communist slogans in the town had surprised everyone, since no such inscriptions had been seen previously. He recalled that it had caused a quarrel between the chief of the Carabinieri and one of the town's citizens that had to be ended by Mayor Farina's intervention. During this altercation, a large crowd gathered and was soon joined by the Communists.

The Communist presence, Vizzini continued, alarmed many of the villagers, but Vizzini calmed them while he offered the Communists cigarettes and coffee. Sometime around five o'clock, Pantaleone and Li Causi arrived and asked Vizzini if they were in hostile territory and whether their meeting might be disturbed. He "assured them that they were free to hold their meeting without any fear of disturbance if they were careful enough not to speak on local matters." Once the speeches began, Christian Democrats and Communists lined up on different parts of the square. According to Vizzini's statement, peace reigned until Li Causi warned the peasants, "Do not let yourselves be fooled by a landowner (whom was he referring to?) who promises a *salma* (land measure) of earth in order to keep you with him."

Vizzini admitted that he interrupted Li Causi to tell him that he was wrong and that he had planned to accuse the Communists of having been Fascists and of having exploited the town's peasants and workers. Before he could finish his statement, however, the Communists began shooting. Vizzini claimed responsibility for contacting the Carabinieri, who were reluctant to intervene. Vizzini then left the square. "It was easy to see," he said, "on which side the battle had begun and from where the bombs were hurled."[20]

Reaction to the incident reflected political attitudes. The Communist and Socialist presses declared that Li Causi had been assaulted by the separatist mafia. *L'Unità* claimed that the meeting had been attended by women and children and that mafia members, assisted by separatist barons, had broken up the gathering by throwing hand grenades.[21]

Separatists accused left-wing newspapers of perverting the truth, and supported Vizzini's version. Separatist reports charged Li Causi with having been accompanied and aided by Fascists, who hated the populace of Villalba for having turned anti-Fascist after the invasion. They even claimed that Li Causi had been injured by Communist shooting. When Finocchiaro Aprile had been welcomed by the people of Villalba, they pointed out, there had been no violence. According to *L'Indipendente,* the Communists had provoked the entire incident, and Vizzini was merely an innocent bystander who tried to calm the crowd. The separatists concluded that the episode was the result "of an almost diabolical and internal action minutely planned and organized by a group of hotheads and criminals."[22]

The Villalba incident signaled an escalation of violence, to which the government contributed. The state grew more belligerent in its treatment of Sicilians, and regarded every protest or rally as a separatist ploy to subvert the political order. The government's attitude only served to heighten tension. A violent confrontation between islanders and the state seemed inevitable.

VICTORIES IN THE COURTS

Had Rome acted decisively against Finocchiaro Aprile, it would have seriously weakened the separatist cause, but the government squandered many opportunities to do so. In September 1944, during an unauthorized meeting in Valdese, a scuffle broke out between security forces and separatists, and Finocchiaro Aprile seems to have been an instigator of the mild disturbance.[23] On 19 September, the police charged him with trespassing, violence, resistance against public security forces, and holding a public meeting without authorization. Although the indictments were forwarded for investigation, no immediate action resulted. The failure to act lay directly with Bonomi, who felt that it was not the appropriate time to arrest the separatist leader. He did, however, order tight surveillance on Finocchiaro Aprile, and instructed Aldisio to prosecute the separatist movement vigorously, especially when its leaders violated the law. Bonomi authorized Aldisio to use all legal means to crush the movement.[24]

Aldisio's legal campaign against the movement was, however, constantly thwarted by the judicial system. When brought to court, separatist leaders were judged innocent and released. These defeats brought tremendous pressure to bear on government officials and raised fears about the influence of separatists upon the judiciary. The government was hesitant to try other separatists following its defeat in both the Cangemi and Di Natale cases.

On 19 September, Edoardo Milio Cangemi, a propagandist for the movement, was brought to trial for having distributed a separatist manifesto without police permission. Giovanni Millemaggi (a Communist supporter of the movement) and Finocchiaro Aprile defended Cangemi. Given the nature of the trial, interest was extremely high, and elements from all political parties attended. Separatist attorneys used the hearing as a forum to denounce the government and call for Sicily's independence. Millemaggi declared that "we are not in truth the accused, but the accusers, we accuse the Italian government, its premier, Bonomi, and the Committee of National Liberation of being arbitrarily constituted organs which are a new Fascist Grand Council designed to oppress the liberty of the Sicilian people." Finocchiaro Aprile announced defiantly: "We shall republish that manifesto and without asking the permission of any authority, because we do not recognize in Sicily the power of any constituted Italian authority." Despite the judge's admonitions to stop, he continued: "I want it publicly known that when Bonomi wanted to have me arrested, the Allied authorities laughed. And if I am here today, it is because the Allies want me to be."[25]

Cangemi was acquitted on a technicality. The court decided that he could not be convicted of having personally distributed the manifesto that had been found on the ground. The verdict was considered a farce and the Allies, who probably wanted Cangemi convicted and imprisoned to prove that they were not protecting the movement, accused the *questura* of Messina of mishandling the case. *La Voce Communista* demanded that action be taken to halt separatist activities and urged judicial authorities to overturn the verdict.[26]

At the same time, the Di Natale case was working its way through the system. Enrico Di Natale and six separatists had been accused of criminal activities under the Italian penal code. The case had originated in February 1944, when Di Natale, a professor of history and philosophy at the University of Syracuse, was accused of having posted copies of a separatist newspaper on public walls. In March, the attorney general brought the case before a military tribunal.[27]

The case caught the attention of Finocchiaro Aprile and, more importantly, Allied officials. For Finocchiaro Aprile, it represented simply another instance of unjust persecution, since Di Natale had done nothing except to voice his political beliefs. He implored Allied officials to intercede and called for the immediate release of Di Natale and his followers. Finocchiaro Aprile's appeal proved unnecessary, since the Allies were already pressuring Italian authorities to lessen or drop charges. The Allies feared that under a military tribunal, Di Natale might be condemned to death. Carrying out such a sentence would drive the separatist movement underground and anger thousands of Sicilians. In March, therefore, the ACC decided as policy that "no prosecution or proceedings against the party is to be tolerated."[28]

Allied pressure on the Italian government continued through 1944. In late October, the government rescinded the most serious charges, but decided to prosecute Di Natale for a lesser offense. Aldisio assured the Allies that Di Natale would be absolved. Indeed, the military tribunal in Palermo eventually decided that Di Natale and his fellow accused would not be prosecuted.[29]

The decisions struck a serious blow to the government's campaign to destroy the movement through legal means. Courts and judges could not be relied upon to rule against separatists as a result of political pressure. If Rome wanted to use the law to end the separatist threat, it would have to wait for the movement to take illegal action. On the

other hand, the verdicts gave hope to the separatists that their movement could survive if it acted lawfully.

AMERICAN-BRITISH DENUNCIATIONS

While the verdicts caused joy within separatist ranks, they coincided
with a decisive downturn in the movement's fortunes. American and
British denunciations of the movement led Finocchiaro Aprile and
other separatists to consider a more radical position regarding the use
of violence, and contributed to the mafia's decision to reconsider its
support for the movement.

Separatists had continually exploited the Allied failure to renounce
the movement, and in mid-1944, opposition politicians and newspaper
editors asked the Americans and British for a clear policy statement
concerning the movement. Some journalists complained that they
wanted to print anti-separatist materials, but feared to do so without
an official Allied disavowal of the movement. They believed that a decisive repudiation could emasculate separatism and destroy it. Even the
New York paper, *Il Progresso Italo-Americano* recognized the need for
an official Allied rejection.[30] These pressures came at an opportune
time for the western democracies. They wanted to restore the national
integrity of the Italian state and give the new government legitimacy. Thus, Finocchiaro Aprile's brand of separatism had to be denounced. Federalism could remain a possibility but without Sicilian
independence.

American and British statements are important not only for what
they contained, but for what they omitted. As one American official
explained, such a statement "need not necessarily denounce Separatism, but simply make clear that Separatist claims of Allied support are
wholly unfounded."[31] Basically, as long as Finocchiaro Aprile headed
the movement, neither the British nor the Americans could support
it, because they believed him an untrustworthy leader who flirted with
Communism and Russian support, as well as a man who would use
any deception or accept any assistance to achieve his goals. While they
might despise Finocchiaro Aprile, the unsettled Italian political scene
forced the Allies to hedge their statements so as to avoid alienating
Sicilians who adhered to separatism, especially those who belonged to
the Fronte Democratico or had pro-British sympathies. If a Communist
tide engulfed Italy, the Allies might want an independent Sicily in the
Mediterranean.

Even before the issuance of an official statement, Nester and Alexander Kirk, the American ambassador in Rome, tried to discourage

any belief that the United States was promoting the movement. Nester voiced his opinion that separatism was entirely "an internal problem." Kirk concurred, urging American officials to make their denunciations prior to the separatist congress scheduled for 15 October in Catania.[32]

American authorities followed this advice. In October, a statement was broadcast by the Office of War Information: "The Voice of America is authorized to declare that the Government of the United States neither recognizes nor supports any group that seeks to obtain the separation of a part of Italy from the rest of the nation. Our government gives its support to the present Italian government of national unity. The Voice of America is therefore authorized to declare that the government of the United States desires that its position be made known to all Italians and particularly to the Sicilians."[33]

The British response to separatism was more important in light of Britain's intense interest in the region. In September, Churchill met with Prince Umberto in Rome. During their conversation, the prince reportedly suggested that England supported separatism. Churchill responded by claiming "that was definitely not true."[34] In early October, Sir Noel Charles, the British ambassador, made the same point to Bonomi, saying that his government had authorized him to publish a statement that allegations concerning British support for the movement were groundless.[35] Some days later the British foreign secretary was asked in Parliament whether he was aware of the existence of a movement to separate Sicily from the rest of Italy and whether he would indicate the views of His Majesty's Government. George Hall, under secretary for foreign affairs, replied: "I am aware that such a movement exists and is active at the present time. It has also come to my knowledge that this movement is alleged to have the support of the Allies. I am glad, therefore, to take this opportunity of stating that as far as His Majesty's Government are concerned all rumors to this effect are entirely without foundation."[36]

News of the disavowals spread quickly. *Giornale di Sicilia* proclaimed that the announcements had eliminated all confusion over the Allied stance on separatism. Another paper credited the American declaration with having proven that Italy was not merely a "geographical expression." Government officials and a portion of the island's population welcomed the statements, which immediately led some of the movement's more timid supporters to abandon it.[37]

The Allied announcements caused dismay and confusion among those who remained committed to the cause. Finocchiaro Aprile explained the rejections in the context of the world political situation. He argued that Britain and the United States were attempting to appease Russia, not the Bonomi government. He emphasized that the

British said only that they did not "sponsor" separatism, but certainly the movement had the sympathies of some of the British people. In fact, in October, he claimed to have received a letter from Churchill expressing sympathy for the movement. The OSS thought this pronouncement meant that "Finocchiaro is either 'crazy' or actually has British backing in a maneuver typical of England's politics."[38]

Lucio Tasca also placed the denunciations in a positive context. He wrote to Roosevelt, Churchill, and other world leaders, alleging that although the Allied governments no longer supported the movement, they did not obstruct it. Their rejections, he said, had freed the movement from the misconception that it operated for the benefit of the English. Separatists would continue to claim England's friendship based on the historical bonds between the two islands. He drew parallels between the events of 1811–1812 and 1943–1944, and claimed that in the past, Sicily and England were the closest of collaborators. But, he warned, "Sicily will never be a help to the Allies," until separatist supporters controlled the government. The Allies, he said, were at fault for not having freed Sicily from "nearly a century of servitude to Piedmont," for the invasion had been taken as a sign that this domination would end. The time had come to restructure the state, and independence for Sicily was the "only possible salvation for Italy." Tasca concluded by appealing for outside help so that the "Sicilian people could have their sacred and secular rights restored to them."[39]

THE PALERMO RIOTS

The separatist movement had come to another important crossroads. When the Allies distanced themselves from the movement, a potential buffer against government repression disappeared. Separatists could still threaten a popular uprising with mafia aid, but a good part of their leverage against the state was now gone. This led them to adopt several new policies. For the first time the movement's leaders seriously considered a violent seizure of power, laying specific plans in the fall of 1944.

Island conditions in the fall of 1944 differed little from those of the occupation period. Prices remained high, salaries low, unemployment steep, and food and medical supplies insufficient. Large number of "beggars and vagabonds" who gathered in the large cities reflected the gravity of the situation. Demonstrations became common, and crowds of men and women often responded with small arms or stones after being fired upon by Italian security forces. A number of Sicilians believed that the Italian government had no interest in improving the island's predicament, and blamed the prefect of Palermo and the high commissioner for failing to keep Rome informed.[40]

As the disturbances multiplied, public-security officials excused the use of strong-arm tactics against the crowds. In spite of often contradictory testimony, when violent confrontation occurred the government's version was almost always the same: the crowd had fired first or had thrown bombs, and the military had reacted in self-defense. On the other hand, Sicilians were generally convinced that soldiers had initiated the fighting.

In October, Palermo became the focal point of violence. Between 16 and 19 October, provincial and communal workers in the city demanded and received promises of pay raises and concessions identical to those given state employees. On the 19th, staff in private firms went on strike to obtain the same adjustments. These demonstrators were joined by others protesting economic conditions, and a crowd began to loot stores and steal food. Some 3,000 gathered at the prefect's office, demanding bread and pasta. Fearing violence, the vice prefect called in the military.[41]

The men who answered the alarm were inexperienced soldiers without a high-ranking officer to lead them. They had formerly belonged to the elite Sabauda division, which had previously dealt with separatists and Sicilians. About forty soldiers reached the scene on a truck, and according to an early official version, someone from the crowd threw a hand grenade at them. The soldiers responded with gunfire and hand grenades. When the firing ended, the toll was 26 dead and 156 wounded.[42]

Sicilians reacted sharply to what they saw as a deliberate act of aggression by the Italian state. Some accused the military of having fired upon unarmed civilians, and several public authorities disputed the early reports. One of them, Antonio Ramirez, an undersecretary in the naval ministry, went so far as to declare the official account of events false, noting that women and children demanding bread and pasta formed a large part of the crowd. He also claimed that the gathering had been easily controlled by a small group of Carabinieri and that the soldiers had fired without provocation.[43]

The government had no choice but to launch an investigation. It became evident, however, that it would be impossible to place specific blame. Reconstructing the exact sequence of events proved difficult, especially with all the contradictory testimony. The report concluded that the violence had not been premeditated, but was the result of panic and disorganization among the young soldiers who had been intimidated by the mob. The report made no mention of separatist involvement.[44]

Carr, the ACC's Regional Commissioner for Sicily, agreed with this view, doubting that the situation had warranted arming the troops and issuing hand grenades. Moreover, if they had approached the crowd in a more circumspect manner rather than driving right into the middle of it, Carr believed that confrontation could have been avoided.[45] Despite his own anti-separatist feelings, he too made no mention of separatist involvement.

The Palermo massacre had far-reaching political ramifications. At a meeting of the Council of Ministers, Finocchiaro Aprile's arrest was considered. Aldisio, Giuseppe Saragat, and Carlo Sforza supported such an action, but nothing was done. Later, Aldisio held a press conference in Rome where, despite the lack of evidence of separatist involvement in the disturbances, and the Allied denunciations, he blamed the Sicilian situation on Allied support for the separatist movement. Some days later, he accused the parties of the left and the separatists of having exploited the events of the 19th, and claimed that only the army could insure unity and order in Sicily.[46]

American officials also assessed the political damage done by the Palermo incident. A month after the shootings, a meeting was held at the American consulate in Palermo. Those in attendance included Nester, Brigadier General Carr, the commander of Public Security in Sicily for the ACC, Colonel Snook, and other Allied personnel. They discussed the economic and political situation on the island and decided that the positions of both the prefect of Palermo and Aldisio were no longer tenable. They expressed concern that the parties of the left would try to take advantage of the situation.[47]

In truth, a Communist or separatist seizure seemed imminent, and for one brief moment, the two parties united on a single issue. The Communist Party accused the soldiers of having fired on the crowd without warning, and claimed that they had monarchical sympathies. It surmised that the incident would increase pro-separatist sentiment.[48] To Aldisio, the criticisms placed the leftists alongside the separatists as enemies of the Italian state.

Separatists also strongly condemned the government's actions. In a telegram to Bonomi, Finocchiaro Aprile voiced his "profound indignation" at the events in Palermo and warned that a government assault against the movement would have grave consequences.[49]

Finocchiaro Aprile and Varvaro tried to send a telegram to Roosevelt attacking the Italian government for a "cruel massacre at Palermo." They asked that American authorities on the island conduct an investigation and prevent any "dangerous repercussions against (the) reactionary government detested by the Sicilian people."[50] In a similar letter addressed to Secretary of State Cordell Hull, Finocchiaro Aprile again blamed Bonomi's government for the bloodshed and denied separatist responsibility for the riot. He made still another appeal for foreign assistance to end the oppression of the Sicilian people.[51]

Giallo Rosso, the press organ of the Lega Giovanile, declared that the shooting of innocent, hungry civilians was incomprehensible, and warned, "You must be the first to pay for your treachery, and . . . upon you will fall the hatred of our people and the inexorable law of divine justice." Other separatist propagandists declared that the military had been sent to the island to strip Sicilians of their liberty through terror, but they stressed their will to strive for independence, and swore never to recognize in Sicily any form of government except a republic.[52]

The Palermo riot presented a perfect opportunity for a separatist seizure of power. But while Sicilians shed their blood in the streets of Palermo, the separatists were holding their first national congress at the resort town of Taormina on the eastern side of the island. They were caught off guard even as they began to prepare the groundwork for their own revolution. The riot and the aftershocks came much too quickly for the separatists, and they lost an important opportunity to seize power.

6

At the Height

THE FIRST NATIONAL CONGRESS

THE Taormina Congress of 20–22 October 1944 took place at a critical moment in the history of the separatist movement. The island was in chaos, the Italian government was consolidating its power, the Allies had renounced separatism, and the movement's internal problems had worsened. Many of the newly formed local bodies refused to cooperate with the national committee, which retaliated by refusing to grant official recognition. Moreover, provincial sections had little or no contact with separatist leaders, who were compelled to travel throughout the island to halt a continuing trend toward decentralization.[1]

In contrast, the Taormina congress presented the movement as well organized and cohesive. The meeting actually took place on two levels: in a public session, open to all members of the movement, and a more secretive assembly open only to a select group. From these hidden sessions emerged a plan for the seizure of power and a provisional government.

The number of delegates was estimated to be between 150 and 350, including some twenty women and a large number of landowners. Most delegates came from Catania, Messina, and Palermo, and about half were Sicilians in their twenties. The hall was decorated with red and yellow drapes and emblems of the Trinacria, the three-legged symbol of Sicily.[2]

All the leading separatists attended, including Finocchiaro Aprile, Varvaro, Lucio Tasca, La Rosa, the di Carcacis, and Battiato. Representatives from the movement's satellite political organizations were given official recognition. These included Varvaro's Unione Siciliana dell'Ordine Democratico, Scardino's Partito Sociale-Communista, Giuseppe Caltabiano's Partito Democratico Siciliano, and Millemaggi's and dell'Aria's Sicilian Communist Party. Don Calogero Vizzini represented the Fronte Democratico.[3]

The selection of committees reinforced the facade of unity. Representatives from all geographical areas and political viewpoints were

106

appointed. Professor Santi Rindone of Catania was selected as president of the congress, while Luigi La Rosa (Caltagirone), Edoardo Cangemi (Messina), Lucio Tasca (Palermo), Francesco Poma (Trapani), and Bruno di Belmonte (Catania) served as vice-presidents. Secretaries and members of a clandestine press office were also chosen. Those in the press bureau included Concetto Gallo of Catania and Francesco Restuccia of Messina.[4]

Finocchiaro Aprile dominated the meeting. An assassination threat delayed his opening speech for two hours, but once Finocchiaro Aprile began, he covered a number of relevant subjects and was often interrupted by thunderous applause. He predicted that a change in the island's status was inevitable. Furthermore, he said, Sicily merited the right to participate in debate concerning colonies since "Sicily has a right to those colonies where her countrymen are in a majority or to those closest to Sicily with which she has racial affinities . . . there is no reason why an equitable distribution of colonies should not be made to the new Sicilian state. Libya as well as Tunisia would become ours because they are inhabited by a majority of Sicilians."[5]

In what some Allied officials believed to be a reference to a possible separatist coup, Finocchiaro Aprile expressed his belief "that a solution to the Sicilian problem will be found shortly; it will perhaps be found before the peace conference, which will then only have to ratify a de facto situation." He lashed out at the Bonomi government and portrayed leaders of the Italian Communists and Socialists as Russian agents who were simply awaiting the moment to install a "red" dictatorship in Italy.

To encourage his followers, Finocchiaro Aprile claimed that new members were joining every day and that the movement was steadily proceeding toward its goals. The unitarian parties were declining in strength, and to prove the point, he called off a list of those groups that adhered to the movement.

Finocchiaro Aprile expressed his indignation over the Palermo riots as the audience cheered. Despite the apparent support, when he proposed to postpone the conference to return to Palermo, the delegates decided that they should remain in Taormina.[6]

Speakers who followed Finocchiaro Aprile repeated many of his points. Loud applause greeted each reference to Sicilian independence, and one speaker, Millemaggi, proposed that a republican form of government be installed in an independent Sicily with Finocchiaro Aprile as president. Although the delegates disapproved of the plan, this scheme of government was developed more fully in the weeks following the congress. None of the orators however, attempted to deal with the difficult problems of social reform, the *latifondi*, or the use of violence.[7] The avoidance of such sensitive issues insured that the conference would be free of ideological dissent.

The second day of the congress opened with a dramatic announcement. Santi Rindone informed the audience that separatists in Palermo were pleading for Finocchiaro Aprile and others to come to the city in the aftermath of the riots. Calls for action and a series of angry speeches followed, including one by Finocchiaro Aprile that whipped his audience into a frenzy. In a highly emotional statement, he offered to resign if his followers did not think him capable of leading the movement because of his age. Predictably, the audience burst into wild applause and declared their willingness to go immediately to Palermo.[8]

Varvaro then reported that heads of action squads should be nominated and sent to Palermo. After approving this proposal, the congress suspended itself for an hour. After building up the crowd's anticipation, however, the separatist leadership made a critical error. The central committee, meeting in secret, decided that it was impractical to go to Palermo, since there was no way of getting there until the twenty-third.[9] The decision by separatist leaders to remain safe in Taormina rather than exploiting the chaos in Palermo damaged their chances for success. By remaining inert, they lost their best opportunity to seize power since the opening days of the invasion. Had separatists been willing to act decisively, they might have successfully utilized popular discontent to stage their revolution.

When the congress resumed, the audience learned that Finocchiaro Aprile would not go to Palermo until he had all the facts. The rest of the day was taken up by repetitive speeches. Finocchiaro Aprile again spoke, and warned that the movement had left the preparatory stage and that future action was possible.[10]

Little more of importance happened at Taormina in the public sessions. The congress's motion concerned itself with separatist organization rather than current politics. It reaffirmed Finocchiaro Aprile's preeminent position and established a council to assist him. This body included five members in Palermo, and was headed by Santi Rindone. In addition, the statement called for the formation of committees in each provincial capital, with sections and subsections, and either a local president or vice-president. The congress ended by establishing Finocchiaro Aprile's program as representative of the movement.[11]

During the closed sessions, however, there was much activity. In one of these meetings the Statute of Sicilian Independence was written. It omitted any reference to the major social issues or plans for reform. Instead, it confirmed the pro-Allied feeling of the Sicilian people and attacked the current government as more "hideous than the Fascist one." The statement reaffirmed the movement's basic premises, including Finocchiaro Aprile's original federalist plan. It also repeated the request for Allied intervention to conduct a plebiscite and protect separatist freedoms, but affirmed separatist intentions to act legally.[12]

The Taormina congress had been an important personal success for Finocchiaro Aprile. He remained the undisputed leader of the separatist movement, and all policy reflected his beliefs. More importantly, the gathering had not been marred by any incidents, a fact which the Allies recognized. "Although the delegates have different political views," one Allied report reflected, "there is complete unanimity over the fundamental aims of the movement—Sicilian independence from Italy and a republican form of government under the Presidency of Finocchiaro Aprile."[13]

REVOLUTIONARY AMBITIONS

Although the movement publicly proclaimed its intention to follow legal avenues to obtain independence, behind the scenes, plans for a violent seizure of power were being conceived. Three secret committees were organized to operate in Catania, Messina, and Taormina. One was to plot an armed revolt that would begin in the island's most depressed rural centers and then spread to pre-chosen cities such as Palermo and Catania. Separatist forces would occupy town halls, military barracks, munitions dumps, and radio stations. The committee would also gather arms and munitions and transport the materials to the designated points of revolt. To maintain secrecy, the armed bands would gather only after a designated signal and at predetermined points. The other two committees would plan and finance the revolution and continue to propagandize.[14]

Preparations for the uprising continued after the congress. On 23 October, a secret meeting of the separatist leadership took place at a Taormina hotel. The members proposed the constitution of an executive committee, otherwise known as the "Sicilian government." The composition of this committee is uncertain, because it operated in such a secretive manner, but it probably included Varvaro, Lucio Tasca, Salvatore Arrigo, and Pasquale Ameduri, all of whom came from Palermo. This body had overall responsibility for preparing, organizing, and directing the revolt. Once separatists controlled the island, the committee would temporarily assume power and officially declare itself the new government. Separatists not on the committee would also become government officials—most importantly Finocchiaro Aprile as president, Antonio Canepa as minister of the armed forces, Guglielmo di Carcaci as minister of the interior and Luigi La Rosa as minister of agriculture. All opposition political parties would be excluded from the new administration.[15]

American consul Nester had little fear of an uprising. The formation of the executive committee, in his opinion, was nothing more than a self-serving move by Finocchiaro Aprile so that he could not be "blamed personally for any infraction of Italian law" that might give Aldisio a reason to arrest the separatist leaders.[16]

Nester incorrectly assessed the situation. During the last week of October, the committee met in Catania and made additional plans. With the assistance of a wealthy Tunisian businessman of Sicilian heritage, the committee organized a ministry of colonies, press and propaganda in Tunis. It also set up a special office somewhere in North Africa where the "most important files of the movement" would be kept. Fearing the loss of this material, they planned to deceive the Allies about the bureau's existence. The committee also decided to organize action squads, the leaders of which would be appointed before the next meeting. Each troop would maintain contact with the executive committee through a specified provincial chief. Bands would operate in each commune and would contain between fifteen and one hundred men. Ten thousand men were available immediately, but it was thought that 100,000 could be organized within one month. Action squads organized in Algiers and Tunisia would act as reinforcements if the Allies blocked the revolution, and a munitions dump had already been organized in the Syracuse area.[17]

Antonio Canepa's task was to hire automobiles to transport weapons and maintain close contact with Finocchiaro Aprile. To try to garner support from Christian Democrats and high-ranking church officials on the island, the committee planned to establish an embassy of the "Sicilian Republic to the Holy See" in Catania. To achieve Communist backing, separatists planned an embassy to the Soviet Union near Messina. This office would maintain contact with the Soviet Union and Togliatti. Leaders also requested the "Pastoral Blessing" of eighteen of the island's leading clergymen.[18]

Although he had previously espoused legal avenues to achieve independence, Finocchiaro Aprile threw his support to the planned revolt. After hearing of government intentions to prosecute the movement's leaders, he argued that the time had come for immediate action. The threat of imminent arrest and the declining Allied influence in Sicily contributed to his decision. He assumed that separatists could act before the unitarian parties could retaliate, but was unsure about the Allied reaction. With Finocchiaro Aprile's support, Lucio Tasca was ordered to transmit the mobilization order to all the provinces while Finocchiaro Aprile and Varvaro remained inconspicuous in Palermo.[19]

Although most of the planning never went beyond the preparatory stage, separatist leaders had obviously concluded that revolution was their only hope for success, a feeling that many of their followers shared. Though all preparations were supposed to be made secretly, rumors of the revolt quickly spread. Aldisio received notices that separatist forces were gathering around many cities and that an attack on government offices was possible. In light of these reports, many of which were unverified, Aldisio asked that appropriate security measures be taken.[20]

Belief in an imminent uprising caused some civil servants to resist enforcing anti-separatist measures, because they feared retribution. It appeared that separatist sympathizers in the postal and telegraph services were leaking information in messages between Palermo and Rome, and Aldisio believed that some Carabinieri officials and magistrates worked for the movement.[21]

Though several American officials knew of the separatist plans and believed that the movement could be paralyzed by arresting the leadership, they advised caution. In a meeting with Aldisio, American officers urged him to practice restraint until definite grounds existed for an anti-separatist action. Others on the scene discounted any imminent uprising. Nester did not anticipate any immediate revolt unless something happened to trigger it. In his view, separatist leaders were simply taking advantage of the government's weakness following the Palermo riots.[22]

The Italian government was cognizant of the separatist plot, and ordered the movement's leaders prosecuted on charges of endangering state security. Lucio Tasca and others knew of these directives and discussed them openly during a 26 October meeting, showing no fear of the Rome government. Instead, they emphasized a possible Communist shift toward the movement.[23]

Aldisio continued to prepare security measures. He planned to arrest separatists and intern them in former Fascist prison camps on various islands. He ordered prefects to prepare lists of separatist supporters so that those with prison records and without funds to support themselves could be arrested or warned about their activities. He believed that "with such measures, we can achieve two objectives: to strike at delinquency and separatism at one time."[24]

Officials also tried again to use legal avenues to attack the separatist leadership. Following the Palermo riots, separatists published an anti-military article, posting copies on city walls and throwing them from the windows of separatist headquarters in Palermo. In response, Anselmo Sessa, the new police chief and an ally of Aldisio, authorized a search of the headquarters. During their investigation, public security officials confiscated much material detailing the movement's activities. This included a membership roster containing over 23,000 names, donation lists, and correspondence concerning past meetings. Also found were 1,000 identification cards, a list of the 33 members of the municipal council of Palermo, rosters of those who belonged to the separatist women's committee, and future appointees to various island sections. Aldisio labeled the material subversive and closed the building. Ten separatists were arrested and taken to jail but were later released.[25]

This incident alarmed even some of the opposition forces. *La Voce Communista* denounced the raid as a violation of the people's freedom to meet and declared that it had raised a "new alarm in the Sicilian population." Some correctly perceived this condemnation as a sign of a Communist shift toward the separatists.[26] In reality, Communists feared that they would be the government's next target.

Separatists threatened reprisals if their office was not reopened and Tasca told Carr, the regional commissioner, that he could not be held responsible for future events. Carr apparently refused to aid the separatists, who then tried to enlist the help of the police chief. He informed them that he was under orders to close the office and report their followers to judicial authorities.[27]

To stave off another strike by the authorities, Varvaro and Tasca canceled planned public meetings. Moreover, separatists failed to protest Aldisio's actions. In fact, they seemed to lack any coordination, and it was apparent that certain leaders, like Tasca, had adopted a wait-and-see attitude in response to government policies.

In the meantime, police chief Sessa acted to place separatists on trial for what he considered their anti-national activities. Based on papers confiscated in the raid, he decided that the actions of the separatist leaders constituted an offense against the penal code. Sessa accused Finocchiaro Aprile of planning a revolution to achieve Sicilian independence, and criticized him for urging Sicilians to disobey the government's orders, refuse to pay taxes, and avoid the draft. Sessa labeled these "the whole ends of the separatist movement, which aims at dissolving the unity of the Italian state by detaching Sicily from the Fatherland."[28]

Sessa's indictment denounced other important separatist officers for treasonous activities, including Fausto Montesanti, Lucio and Alessandro Tasca, and Antonino Varvaro. But, at the same time, he wanted to prove that the separatist conspiracy extended beyond the movement's provincial groups. Sessa's plan was obvious—indict and imprison the movement's major leaders and frighten those in the countryside into inaction. All this would be done legally, a fact that would, it was hoped, quell any Allied protest.

While he supported Sessa's work, Aldisio lamented the police chief's decision to forward his indictment to judicial authorities without having consulted him, and felt that the procedure had been "too rushed." Nonetheless, during a talk with D'Antoni, the prefect of Palermo, Aldisio and Sessa went one step further by proposing that D'Antoni issue a decree dissolving the movement's Palermo section. D'Antoni, who attacked Sessa's indictment for being too broad, disliked both Aldisio and Sessa. While the police chief and high commissioner wanted a hard line policy to crush the separatists, D'Antoni preferred that the government take a more tolerant approach. Confronted by the two men, D'Antoni refused to sign the order to close the headquarters.[29]

All of Sessa's work came to naught. Much to his surprise, on 8 November, Aldisio ordered authorities to return to separatists the keys to their headquarters.[30]

Aldisio's decision was probably based on his knowledge of Judge Vito Barone's forthcoming decision on Sessa's accusations. Barone, whom Sessa implied had separatist sympathies, argued that the mere expression of an opinion did not constitute a treasonous crime, and interpreted the article of law to apply only to actual criminal activities, not preparatory acts. According to Barone, "It is clear that the propaganda undertaken by ex-deputy Finocchiaro Aprile does not constitute executed activity directed at breaking the unity of the state as long as it is contained in the field of propaganda." Barone decided that dissolving the separatist movement was not within his jurisdiction and that it was the responsibility of the minister of the interior and the Council of Ministers.[31]

Separatists openly celebrated their victory. Finocchiaro Aprile gave a defiant address in which he told his approximately 800 listeners that the movement's strength had increased and that the Taormina congress had attracted international attention. Speaking of Sessa's accusations, Finocchiaro Aprile claimed that separatists were being persecuted for an idea, and "the propaganda of ideas has never been a crime. We have done nothing which could authorize the high commissioner to proceed against us." Even if the facts did exist, the Italian state had no authority since it was not a legitimate government. Moreover, he considered the closure of separatist headquarters an illegal act, and sneered at the authorities who had been forced to reopen the building. If the government accused him and a few others, then it would have to charge another 520,000 Sicilians with the same crimes. He ended with a clear threat: "We will continue our propaganda. If they want a struggle, they will have one, and if they want war, they will have war."[32]

Frustrated by the continuous string of separatist victories, Aldisio asked the government to enunciate a more precise policy regarding the nature of the movement. He noted a general lack of certainty among state officials about which policies to follow in dealing with separatism. If an anti-separatist declaration was not forthcoming, he complained, his campaign would be limited to surveillance of the leaders and members.[33]

SEPARATIST-COMMUNIST DISCUSSIONS

Uncertainty regarding separatism also permeated the island's major political factions. Separatists helped to foster this mood by creating independence-oriented offshoots of the major opposition parties. This political shift was in conjunction with planning for the revolution and was an attempt to create a more populist image for the movement. In late October, a separatist-oriented Sicilian Christian Democratic Party appeared, headed by Luigi La Rosa. A number of unitarian Christian Democrats immediately joined the organization, the formation of which had been delayed until separatist leaders were certain of having their support.[34] The party's emergence lent further credence to Finocchiaro Aprile's claim that separatism was above party politics, and strengthened the movement's appeal to indecisive conservatives.

A more important pro-separatist shift occurred among a number of Communists.[35] The events of 19 October in Palermo had robbed the Communists of any credibility that they had influence with the national or regional government. Their press had been censored, and Aldisio had listed them alongside the separatists as a destructive and anti-national element. Their political isolation increased their vulnerability, and it seemed logical to approach the separatists, since they represented the strongest anti-government sentiment on the island. Ideologically, Communists could justify aligning with the progressive wing of the movement, since some of its members had leftist sympathies.[36]

Despite his previous anti-Communist rhetoric, Finocchiaro Aprile gave impetus to a separatist-Communist alliance during a number of speeches in November and December. He commented that separatism was leftist-oriented because it was a movement of the workers and peasants. He had been among the first in Italy to study Lenin, whom he praised as one of the great European philosophers. He also noted that Russia had never expressed hostility to the movement, and thanked Stalin and Molotov for their lack of animosity. He flirted with creating a Soviet Republic in Sicily and stated, "Should the Sicilian people request a soviet republic, we will give them a Soviet Republic. What more do they want? An open declaration of friendship? I am happy to declare that we are friends of Russia."[37]

The formation in Palermo of the Communist Party of Sicily represented another sign of political realignment. Its leaders seemed to have had little prior connection to the movement. Its platform called for the establishment of a Sicilian republic "with complete economic and administrative autonomy in the framework of the confederation of Communist republics." Sicily had been systematically exploited by the Italian government for 84 years, and independence was necessary to avoid paying for the reconstruction of northern Italy's industries. Reunification meant that Sicily would again be deprived of roads, hospitals, and schools. The party supported the struggles of the proletariat and warned that the war effort was senseless unless directed against the monarchy, past and present Fascists, and oppressors of every country. In particular, the party declared, "the problems of Sicily must be treated and resolved by Sicilians and only Sicilians."[38]

In the last two months of 1944, separatists and Communists actually discussed an alliance. American officials knew of the meetings but none of the details. Communist leader Giuseppe Montalbano openly declared that he had instructions to follow the separatist movement, but he would not reveal from whom those directions had come. "Neither England nor America, Montalbano claimed, would have the last word regarding the future destiny of Sicily because Russia is also among the United Nations."[39]

The Communists evidently wanted to reach an agreement with separatists in case of revolution on the island. By participating in the creation of an independent Sicily, Communists might be able to lay the groundwork for a future peninsula-wide uprising. In Catania, members of the separatist Sicilian Communist Party and representatives of the Italian Communist Party discussed some sort of an agreement. The talks were extremely secretive, and even some Communists in Catania did not know of their progress. No formal plans were made, but further deliberations were scheduled for a late December meeting of the executive committee.[40]

If further conversations ever took place they obviously failed. Communist negotiators probably rejected the notion of acting as a separatist tool without guarantees. Moreover, the number of Communists who switched their allegiance to the separatists remained small, and the Communist Party of Sicily had little impact even as an organ of propaganda. Even while negotiations were being held, animosities surfaced.

Montalbano labeled Finocchiaro Aprile's attempt to gain Soviet support "treacherous separatist propaganda," and there was confirmation of a separatist-backed assassination plot against Togliatti.[41]

By early 1945, almost all hope of a separatist-Communist rapprochement disappeared. Only the possibility of a monarchist revolt seemed to frighten Communist leaders enough for them to reconsider a coalition with separatists. When such a threat appeared in February 1945, Montalbano claimed that the creation of any government favoring the monarchy would result in an alliance with separatists to bring about the "separation of Sicily from Italy."[42] When the scheme failed to materialize, all hopes for separatist-Communist cooperation disappeared.

THE MAFIA-SEPARATIST ALLIANCE DISSOLVES

Finocchiaro Aprile's political vacillations prompted mafia chieftains to distance themselves from separatism. In reality, their support of the separatist movement had always been tenuous. They had joined with the movement to avoid political isolation and, just as they had done with other movements in the past, they had used separatism's popularity to consolidate their own strength.

The Fronte Democratico d'Ordine Siciliano had already demonstrated the mafia's hesitation to fully commit to the movement. Its original platform had rejected many of Finocchiaro Aprile's ideas but placed the organization on the political fringe. Despite its radical nature, the Fronte was popular. Though the Americans "strongly emphasized that the United States did not want Sicily as the 49th state," in late 1944, at least one source claimed that the Fronte's ideas were the result of American propaganda that had "encouraged separatism" prior to the invasion.[43] Indeed, Fronte leaders spread rumors that they had the backing and protection of the United States. Nester expressed concern that the Fronte's influence had spread so rapidly and that it had gained many supporters from the uneducated classes and the peasantry. Reportedly, 2000 "port laborers" in Catania had given it their unanimous support, and it apparently had a large following in the city. Moreover, many of the large landowners had deserted Finocchiaro Aprile and were cooperating with the Fronte.[44]

The Fronte claimed with exaggeration that it had branches in every Sicilian community in the world and that its aim was to introduce American principles and systems. Many of its members were "lieutenants in the high Maffia" and Calogero Vizzini was considered its leader.[45]

Fronte members also operated within non-separatist circles. Pro-American separatist factions, led by mafia members, operated independently of Finocchiaro Aprile and existed in every political party. At least one of the Fronte's supporters, Michele Buongiorno, was so effective within the ranks of the Christian Democrats in Agrigento that Aldisio asked him to represent the party in that province.[46]

No American official ever acted to discourage the Fronte, for fear that the British had designs on the island. If the Fronte grew influential enough, its presence would deter the British from pursuing their plans.

Anti-British sentiments helped convince Fronte leaders to transform their organization into a regular political party in September 1944. According to OSS informants, the mafia had decided to act because its leaders concluded that Finocchiaro Aprile's organization had become a tool of the British and the Communists. When speaking of a possible victory by the "pro-British separatists" one Fronte member said, "We will come down with machine guns and cannon, which we still have buried here, and will declare a state of siege. It is all right to speak of the United States of America, but otherwise our weapons will always be ready."[47]

In September, Fronte organizers prepared to establish sections throughout the island, hold public meetings, and publish a newspaper in Catania. Concetto Battiato, the "former henchman of Finocchiaro," would direct the publication. Leaders of the Fronte believed that they could expand their movement without much difficulty except for some possible British opposition.[48]

Finocchiaro Aprile clearly understood the repercussions of the Fronte's impending split from his movement. The mafia's withdrawal would cripple his organization, leave it virtually defenseless, limit his ability to propagandize, and possibly endanger his life. He had, therefore, tried to penetrate and then co-opt the Fronte by inviting its members to attend the separatist congress in Taormina.

Finocchiaro Aprile tried to use a former Fascist from Palermo known only as Ferrara to infiltrate the Fronte and act as his personal informant. Before he could gain any useful information, however, a Fronte leader advised Ferrara to disappear or "run the risk of being beaten up."[49]

Prior to the Taormina Congress, Fronte leaders met in secret and formed a provisional national committee and an executive committee. Antonio Lupo, a major in the Bersaglieri, became president, while Concetto Battiato sat on the national committee. Since "many requests for adhesion" to the Fronte came from the "intellectual and commercial classes," they deemed it necessary to distance themselves from Finocchiaro Aprile's clique. Fronte leaders decided to continue their clandestine propaganda campaign against Finocchiaro Aprile ("it is about time that Finocchiaro Aprile is disgraced"). Because of his pro-British and pro-Communist sympathies, the participants decided that Finocchiaro Aprile had to be stopped, by force if necessary.[50]

Fronte directors also decided to change their platform by deleting almost all references to the United States, especially anything that referred to placing Sicily under an American sphere of influence. Fronte leaders made these modifications because they feared being arrested under Article 241 of the Italian Penal Code, which threatened anyone responsible for turning a portion of Italy over to a foreign power, or weakening Italian unity, with arrest and punishment by death.[51]

Fronte executives—including Volpe, Francesco Di Pietra, Giovanni La Cara, and Giuseppe Pirrone—met in October 1944 to discuss the alterations, and proposed a "federal form of government which will permit Sicily to have political and economic autonomy." Di Pietra proposed a constitution based on the following principles:

(1) a united political bloc of all Sicilians (*Fronte*); (2) the organization of Sicilian social and economic life on the principles which inspire the United States of America (*Democratico*); (3) affirmation of "the principles of ORDER" in the sphere of "a wholesome democratic life" based on work, prosperity, social and political peace, and progress (*Ordine*).[52]

At the same time, delegates to the Taormina Congress, including Di Pietra and La Cara, were selected. These individuals would announce the Fronte's new positions and formalize the break with Finocchiaro Aprile.

Through his network of OSS contacts, Consul Nester obtained a copy of the Fronte's final program. The leaders planned to present it to the government along with a request for status as a political party.[53] The Fronte made it clear that it operated independently of Finocchiaro Aprile. It "was not subservient to any political program of the past and had no hidden interests to defend, nor privileges to safeguard. . . ."[54]

The platform repeated Di Pietra's points and dealt with the rejuvenation of Sicilian economic, social, and political life. Sounding like separatists, the Fronte claimed that Sicily's rebirth could be accomplished by using its own resources. The island's economic structure had to be radically altered to prevent unemployment and to promote a system of public works. The bureaucracy had to be reformed and the people educated according to the basic principles of the "United States of America which imply the guaranty of the citizen's liberty within the limits of respect for the law and exclusion of violence." Education was especially important for the lower classes, which had to be assured that their work would benefit everyone, not just a "privileged minority."[55]

The program ended with an overt threat: "if the warning of order and discipline is disregarded, if anyone makes an attempt to sabotage the work of reconstruction and rebirth which has already begun, he need fool himself no longer, because FDOS will undertake the necessary process of eliminating undesirable elements in its efforts to lead the people towards the wholesome principles of democracy and moral cooperation of all citizens for the supreme welfare of the island."[56]

Much to Finocchiaro Aprile's chagrin, Fronte representatives publicized the schism at the Taormina congress. Di Pietra implied that the differences between his organization and Finocchiaro Aprile were so deep that he did not even belong at a separatist gathering. Fronte representatives were present only because "this [separatist] movement has solemnly declared the supreme welfare of Sicily as its goal. And since we are Sicilians, we are for the conciliation and tolerance which should animate each party towards other parties, which leads us not to despise a Federalist hypothesis not only of Italian states but also of the United States of Europe." He claimed that most liberated Italians hated the separatist movement even though they might have the same justifications for supporting such an effort in their regions. Ultimately, the people would have to decide their form of government and society, but he hoped that the principles of American democracy would guide Sicily's economic and social life.[57]

At a later meeting with separatist leaders (the date is unknown), Giovanni La Cara further clarified the Fronte's position. The new platform, according to La Cara, represented the "exact expression" of the Sicilian people and directed them toward a "more serene and objective end than in the past." The movement was conscious of the "international situation" and therefore had decided to adopt a federalist position. La Cara also reaffirmed the Fronte's advocacy of the principles of American democracy, in which every Sicilian should be indoctrinated.[58]

There was no attempt to cover up the schism and it rapidly became public knowledge. In fact, the prefect in Palermo announced that with its new program, the Fronte had distanced itself from Finocchiaro Aprile.[59] Indeed, by making these pronouncements, mafia chieftains essentially entered the mainstream of Sicilian political life. They could no longer be accused of treason, since all the other "legitimate" political factions backed some form of Sicilian autonomy or federalism.

THE CASTELLANO INITIATIVE

As the separatist position seemed to weaken, Lucio Tasca sought to ensure his political survival. The conservative leader had been frightened by Finocchiaro Aprile's leftist rhetoric and vacillations on Communism. He began to seek a solution to the Sicilian crisis which would better suit his true desires. He got his opportunity when Prince Castel Cicala, a member of the Savoyard court, approached him with a plan designed to satisfy federalists and monarchists. The Prince thought that Tasca could influence a large number of separatists to support an autonomous Sicily ruled by the House of Savoy.[60] These initial discussions eventually led to further talks between monarchists and separatists in 1945.

Tasca also got involved in discussions between the Italian government, mafiosi, and political leaders. Italian authorities had first approached Tasca and his brother Alessandro in September 1944 following the Ruini incident. During their talks with Minister Ruini, the two had agreed to support Sicilian autonomy, thereby becoming potential weapons to be used against Finocchiaro Aprile. The following month, General Giuseppe Castellano arrived in Sicily as the commander of the Aosta Division. Castellano had clearly been empowered to hold political talks in an effort to resolve the separatist threat. At first he tried to appease separatists by obtaining permission for them to publish a newspaper, believing that "such an action is imperative to maintain law and order." He tried to obtain Aldisio's consent for such a move, but the high commissioner refused.[61]

Castellano soon concluded that peace on the island did not require appeasing Finocchiaro Aprile. Instead, he became "convinced that the strongest political and social force to be reckoned with is the Maffia." Castellano became "extremely anxious to establish cordial relations with high Maffia leaders."[62] The general also believed that law and order could be restored if "the system formerly employed by the old and respected Maffia should return to the Sicilian scene."[63]

Over the next few weeks Castellano made contacts with mafia leaders and met with them several times. He gained the cooperation of Vizzini, who was prepared for a change in the island's political situation. Vizzini had not only led the move to reorient the Fronte's platform, but he had also become disenchanted with Aldisio. Reportedly, the two had clashed when Aldisio "requested" Vizzini's "unconditional adherence to the Christian Democratic Party." Vizzini had responded that he would support the party if it based its platform on separatist ideas. When it became obvious that such an agreement was impossible, Vizzini told Aldisio, "if we are on two roads, we will meet, if on the same road in opposite directions, we will clash." Later, Vizzini declined Aldisio's invitation to "solicit the support of the old Maffia of the provinces of Caltanissetta, Agrigento, Enna and Catania" for the Christian Democrats, no doubt because he wanted to put all his efforts into enlarging the Fronte. By October 1944, Vizzini had broken off all friendly relations with the high commissioner and was calling for his removal.[64]

Within a few weeks, Castellano submitted a plan to Rome that contained five major points: (1) immediate emergency relief measures to reduce popular unrest in Sicily; (2) temporary but limited freedom of speech and assembly for the separatists in order to temper extremist opinion; (3) support for regional autonomy, "which will deflate the program of the separatists"; (4) the imposition of "extraordinary measures in the administrative-judicial department" to eliminate "banditry and criminal elements"; and (5) a propaganda campaign to counteract separatist ideas. Castellano stressed that "to suppress delinquency, of which the Separatists, themselves make such use, would result in depriving them of the means of fighting." Although his plan suggested arbitrary police action, it reflected his belief that the mafia was the key to ending the island's crisis. "The Maffia in Sicily," Castellano stated, "is not a negligible force. It will be necessary to select the most influential leaders (who are also capable) and confer responsible posts upon them."[65]

Castellano called together mafia and separatist leaders and other Sicilian politicians. The first series of meetings took place in the middle of November in Palermo. Approximately twenty mafia leaders, some of whom were leaders of the Fronte Democratico, and several prominent separatists attended, including Vizzini, Calogero Volpe, Vincenzo Palermo, Guglielmo di Carcaci, Nino Leanza, Mauro Seminara, Giuseppe Russo, and Pietro Vinciguerra. The general purpose of the gathering was to organize a movement for Sicilian autonomy sponsored by the Fronte and the mafia-dominated Agricultural League. The mafia presented a list of demands that required changes in the central government, the elimination of the anti-Fascist Committee of National Liberation from Sicilian politics, and the replacement of Aldisio. Virgilio Nasi, whom Nester labeled the "boss of Trapani province," was nominated to lead the new autonomy movement. Vizzini and the other maflosi approved of Nasi, and it was hoped that ultimately, he would replace Aldisio. The participants also agreed to try to lure Finocchiaro Aprile away from a position of absolute separatism. A secret meeting had been reportedly arranged with the separatist leader for this purpose. All of the discussions were posed in the context of the mafia's concern that the Sicilian masses were being wooed by mainland Communists and that the Americans and British would break with the Soviets over the "Polish and Balkan problems." More importantly, they felt that what happened in Sicily would determine Italy's role in the post-war struggle for power between the West and the Soviet Union.[66]

Castellano, Vizzini, and other mafiosi approached Nasi on 18 November in Castellammare del Golfo. They asked him to assume the leadership of the embryonic mafia-supported movement for autonomy, replace Aldisio, and ultimately "go to Rome and issue an ultimatum to the Italian government in the name of the Sicilian masses." Evidently, Nasi accepted all three proposals, thereby creating a powerful triumvirate along with Castellano and Vizzini. Castellano also secured a pledge from Vizzini that the vastly powerful leagues of landowners dominated by the mafia would throw their weight behind autonomy and "line up the Tasca brothers, Alessandro and Lucio, separatist and Maffia leaders in the Palermo province." The ability to re-create the traditional alliance between the landowners and the mafia gave the mafia its real strength and struck a decisive blow against separatism. Supporters of the new mafia-backed movement announced that "any idea of an independent Sicilian republic such as demanded by Finocchiaro Aprile is definitely discarded." They planned to call for immediate recognition of Sicilian problems by the government and institution of a relief program to aid Sicilian industry and other sectors of the economy. In addition, they assured all the concerned parties that this new organization would not be pro-Communist, and called on the government to prevent any repetition of the Palermo massacre.[67]

The OSS took a favorable view of the new alliance of Vizzini, Nasi, and Castellano. This faction and its program, it advised, "is not to be mistaken as another form of separatism in view of the plan of large autonomy, probably Federalist, to be developed in the interests of Sicily, in spite of the separatist ideals of the Maffia from top to bottom."[68]

As soon as the newly backed autonomist movement gained momentum, Castellano, a member of the Liberal Party, pledged to remove himself from active participation. He would be kept informed of events by two of Nasi's "lieutenants" and leading members of the Agricultural League. The League, which contained landowners and agricultural workers, would play an active role in the new mafia autonomy movement.[69]

Nester appreciated the danger that this new group presented for Finocchiaro Aprile. He surmised that "quite likely many of the followers of Finocchiaro Aprile, who is losing popularity and the confidence of the people, will join the Nasi followers." He concluded that "Finocchiaro Aprile is considered by this movement a menace and doing

Sicily more harm than good with his dramatic speeches, demand for an independent republic and his move toward Communism."[70]

To broaden the appeal of this initiative, Castellano and some of his supporters met individually with representatives of the mafia and leaders of the island's Committee of National Liberation in late December 1944 and January 1945. Castellano hoped to obtain approval for a round-table discussion to solve the island's problems and select a spokesman for the Sicilian people. Calogero Volpe, a mafia mouthpiece, conducted talks between "Maffia chieftains and members of the CLN (Committee of National Liberation), such as Dr. Girolamo Li Causi, Communist Party Inspector, High Commissioner Aldisio for the Democratic Christians and others."[71]

Castellano held a separate meeting with all three Tasca brothers, Lucio, Paolo, and Alessandro, in early December, pointing out that disorder on the island "could not be tolerated." He indicated to the three separatists that it was important "to set an example at that time." The Tascas promised cooperation but warned that if the islanders failed to receive "bread and pasta" they could not bear responsibility for future events.[72]

Prime Minister Bonomi indicated that he would meet with someone "representative of Sicilian thought."[73] This ruled out Finocchiaro Aprile or any other hard-line separatist. Castellano's idea for a conference found support from much of the island's political leadership including the Vizzini-led mafia. Hoping to bring his idea to fruition, Castellano sought to have elder statesman Vittorio Emanuele Orlando, himself a former premier, chair the meeting. Orlando had been kept informed of the Sicilian situation and had some previous contact with Lucio Tasca.[74] Orlando favored a federalist approach to the Sicilian problem and, like many others, thought that the British were manipulating the separatist movement because they wanted an autonomous Sicilian state through which to control the Mediterranean. If the separatist movement were successful, Orlando claimed, "it will not owe its success to the support of the Sicilian people, but rather to a group of landowners fostered by elements of the old Maffia and encouraged by the British."[75]

In January, Orlando visited Palermo and talked with Castellano. He agreed to chair the session, but only on the "condition that Finocchiaro Aprile and Lucio Tasca can be induced to join the conference."[76]

By setting this condition, Orlando acknowledged the power and influence of the separatist leaders. Indeed, Castellano also understood the strength of both men when he admitted that most Sicilians were "predominantly separatist and not followers of the Committee of Liberation parties."[77] When Finocchiaro Aprile stubbornly refused to attend any such gathering because of his hatred for the Committee of Liberation and the government, the plan fell through. To make matters worse, while Alessandro Tasca agreed to participate, Lucio Tasca, rejected such a conference as "impossible."[78]

The collapse of the round-table discussion plan did not end Castellano's efforts. He continued to seek a spokesman who would be "really representative of the thought and ideals of the Sicilians—not necessarily a separatist, who would be received by Bonomi and who would press for the needs and desires of the Sicilian masses in the form of an ultimatum." Castellano wanted to use Orlando in this role, but first Orlando would have to renounce definitively his support of the Italian monarchy.[79]

Orlando's major hurdle was convincing Finocchiaro Aprile to accept autonomy or some other sort of bargain. After meeting with Orlando in January 1945, he rejected the creation of an Italian federal republic with Orlando as President. This plan already had Tasca's and Vizzini's support, but despite their pleas, Finocchiaro Aprile stood firm. He could accept federation only if Sicily became a sovereign republic "be it only for a day."[80] Negotiations between the parties broke down.

Although Orlando continued to believe that he and Finocchiaro Aprile might come to an agreement, in reality no such bargain was possible.[81] Finocchiaro Aprile did not trust Orlando and continued to find support from a large number of followers. He believed that the struggle for independence was not yet over and sought to create a fighting force to replace the mafia. For him, the fight for independence had simply moved to another plane.

Despite Finocchiaro Aprile's refusal to compromise, Orlando's representatives maintained contact with mafia chiefs and government officials as late as April 1945. Mafiosi wanted Orlando to lead their "Italian Republican Movement in Sicily," but they demanded that he denounce the monarchy. While they awaited his decision, hopes were raised that if "a coalition of Maffia and extreme separatists, under the leadership of Orlando could be worked out, it might result in the salvation of the island and avoid future disorders and bloodshed."[82] Obviously, if Orlando and the mafia could have formed this coalition, Finocchiaro Aprile would have become expendable. But the bloc never materialized.

Even threats of liquidation by the mafia could not force Finocchiaro Aprile to compromise. While others spoke of moderation, Finocchiaro Aprile became more extreme, a development that struck fear into officials close to the situation. "In all the confused political picture of Sicily," Nester warned, "Finocchiaro Aprile is probably the most unstable and unreliable element. He is quick to turn the situation of the moment to his advantage and is unscrupulous.... When dealing with Finocchiaro Aprile the future cannot be predicted with any certainty."[83]

Although Castellano failed to topple Finocchiaro Aprile, his mission had been a success. Reportedly, the movement's following declined "noticeably" in early 1945. Some of the defectors established groups calling for various degrees of autonomy.[84] Castellano's work had also broken the separatist-mafia alliance. His reliance on the mafia provided the organization another boost in its recovery from the depredations of Mori and Mussolini. Following the Castellano initiative, the mafia became a force of order and stability on the island. When anti-government draft riots swept Sicily in December 1944 and January 1945, mafiosi limited the damage by using "a restraining hand in the areas where their influence" was the strongest.[85] By acting to support the state in 1944 and 1945, the mafia planted the seeds of a partnership from which it would reap tremendous benefit. In the meantime, mafiosi worked to prevent a separatist revolution by muzzling extremist elements within the movement.

Although Castellano's work had weakened Finocchiaro Aprile, the struggle between his movement and the state was far from over. Even as the separatists seemed to be losing control of their ability to determine Sicily's destiny, they received a temporary boost from the government. The state's decision to draft Sicilians into the Italian army created further bitterness, led to a series of destructive disorders, and provided separatists one last opportunity to complete their revolution.

7

In the Balance

LOSING GROUND

In spite of Aldisio's measures and the breakdown of its alliance with the mafia, separatism remained a potent political force. The government's reluctance to act against the movement and its failure to formulate a wide-ranging policy to alleviate the island's social and economic crisis helped to nourish pro-separatist sentiment. Even the most rabid anti-separatist officials had come to realize the movement's appeal. When Aldisio conceded in late 1944 that the movement had more than 400,000 official members and sympathizers, the commanding general of the Carabinieri acknowledged the accuracy of the estimate. These adherents were rumored to be well armed with guns and even artillery.[1]

To the further dismay of officials, the separatist movement appeared to have become the dominant party on the island. According to a count made by the Ministry of the Interior, Finocchiaro Aprile's followers numbered 480,000 while those of the Christian Democrats and the Communists amounted to 35,000 and 25,000 respectively.[2]

This report supported separatist claims about the breadth of their popularity, and was exploited heavily by the movement's press once it became common knowledge. Moreover, separatists claimed that even these figures were too low, because many members of the opposition parties supported their cause, a fact the Americans did not dispute.[3]

Despite these statistics, other government reports presented a quite different picture. But, although these numbers cannot be relied upon for accuracy in themselves, they denote overall trends which were ominous for the movement.[4] These estimates indicated that support for the movement had ceased to grow and in fact was in a state of decline. They also suggest that separatist membership lagged behind that of the Christian Democrats and Communists, and that the majority of Sicilians had remained aloof from the political process. Indeed, membership in any single party never reached the hundred thousands, and total membership for all parties rarely went above 200,000.[5]

The reports confirmed that in the opening months of 1945, the separatist movement had entered a period of stagnation, registering a net gain of only one provincial section. Even this figure is deceptive. The increase appeared only because four new sections opened in Messina province in January 1945, two of which were closed by March. In fact, in only three of the island's nine provinces, Enna, Messina, and Catania, was there any movement by separatist forces.[6]

Although the movement had a sizable following, it had failed to overcome its own form of sectionalism. As Rennel had noted in 1943, separatism originally found its strength in the northern part of the island, including Palermo and Messina as well as Catania. After two years of struggle, little had changed. Only Syracuse was mentioned as an additional stronghold. In spite of all the rhetoric, separatism had remained an urban phenomenon of the wealthier, eastern portion of the island, which derived its leadership and a large part of its direction from Palermo. The movement had made little headway in attracting a following in the poorer areas such as Agrigento in the south, Trapani in the west, and Caltanissetta in the interior.

While it was true that separatism was weakest in the poorest provinces, its appeal varied from region to region. The movement's largest following was in Palermo, where its followers were considered most fervent. Within the province, the landowners formed the bulk of separatist support, while most of the middle class, with few exceptions, rejected the cause.[7] In Messina, the movement appeared weaker in the city than in the remainder of the province. Nonetheless, the Messinese separatists were as fanatical as those in Palermo and were noted for their ability to make trouble and gain attention.[8]

The Catanese separatists were among the most radical. They were a relatively unified group, as compared to the movement as a whole, and they often acted independently of the national organization. In spite of their large numbers and extremism, however, they failed to dominate the political life of the city; local leaders could threaten and cajole, but would not act. By late 1944, slogan writing seemed to have become their major activity, and they were perceived as a minor threat to the established order.[9] Syracuse underwent more change and was the weakest of any separatist stronghold. By August 1944, the Communists had gained a dominance in the area that they would maintain into 1945. Syracusan separatists were also hurt by ineffectual leadership.[10]

In the island's other five provinces, the separatists were weak and disorganized. In Enna and Ragusa they faced heavy opposition from the other political parties and had few members. By late 1944, separatists in Ragusa lacked any leadership and had sections only in the provincial capital and Modica.[11]

The separatist movement had never attracted much of a following in the provinces of Caltanissetta, Agrigento, and Trapani. In July 1944, there was little if any sign of separatist activity or organization in Caltanissetta, and the only important section was located in Villalba, the home of Don Calogero Vizzini.[12] In Agrigento and Trapani, separatist fortunes reached their nadir. In Agrigento there was a highly organized and well-established Communist organization, while in Trapani most reports confirmed that no separatist committee structure existed.[13]

It had become painfully obvious that while separatism may have had a great deal of popularity among certain classes in specific provinces, it had never gained the deep-rooted allegiance of the masses. The movement was essentially the elitist clique that its opponents had claimed it to be. Moreover, separatist leaders had failed to exploit their popularity because they lacked the necessary dedication and fanaticism. Men like Finocchiaro Aprile, Lucio Tasca, and Antonino Varvaro may have been brilliant politicians, administrators, propagandists and speech makers, but they were never really willing to risk their own lives or those of their followers for the sake of independence. More importantly, by failing to weld all of the movement's factions into a tightly knit organization, they doomed their own cause.

The movement's continuing inability to attract a following from the poorer areas can be explained by changes in the general political and economic situation. Despite the collapse of the first Bonomi cabinet in late November, the state quickly recovered, and the second Bonomi government was formed on 12 December 1944.[14] The relatively easy transition in a crisis demonstrated that the Italian government was becoming a functional entity. Separatist opponents could only hope that as the state gained more strength it would act against the movement.

The landless peasantry was helped by Communist participation in the government. Fausto Gullo's decrees, approved in October 1944, permitted peasants to take control of uncultivated lands as long as they formed cooperatives, attempted to regulate agricultural contracts, and gave peasants a more reasonable share of agricultural produce. These edicts, which met great resistance from the landed classes and their supporters, drove the peasants into the Communist ranks. The Communists became defenders of the landless peasants against the landowners, many of whom were separatists or Christian Democrats. The measures also increased support for the Italian government, which for the first time appeared to be concerned with peasant needs and problems.[15] Though the laws ultimately met with varying degrees of success, they were a historic move and led to a series of land seizures starting in the fall of 1944.

THE DECEMBER RIOTS

The unrest in the countryside only added to the chaos on the island. In late 1944, Sicily continued to suffer from the effects of a grain shortage. Less than half the grain quota was being delivered to the open markets, and the Allies had actually discussed lowering the bread ration in Sicily to supply food to northern Italy. This exacerbated the situation and added a degree of truth to separatist propaganda that the needs of the north had priority over those of the island. To many locals it also seemed unfair that Sicilian men were about to be drafted and removed from the agricultural sphere where they were desperately needed.[16]

In mid-December, Brigadier General Carr paid an emergency visit to the American commander of the Palermo naval base. They were joined by a member of the OSS, who agreed with Carr that serious trouble on the island was a real possibility. All admitted that Sicily was not self-sufficient as the Allies had believed prior to the July invasion. All grain supplies would be gone by the end of December. They agreed that these conditions "would irrevocably lead to rioting, and bloodshed and such troubles will be aggravated by the political parties in Sicily who will undoubtedly try to restore Allied control of Sicily in place of Italian control which is cordially hated by a very large number of thinking and intelligent Sicilians." To make matters worse, Italian troops on the island would be unable to control the situation, and their intervention would only cause further disorder. Any major disturbances in Palermo might "create a loss of efficiency at the naval base."[17]

Given popular anger over the poor conditions, the government's plan to draft Sicilians could not have been more ill-timed. Poor organization and planning made the actual call-up a complete disaster. Conscripts were supposed to report in late December and during two periods in January 1945, but at no time did the government convince Sicilians to accept a place in the Italian army. Common belief held that the war was all but over, and Sicilians did not want to participate in a struggle that promised nothing for them or their families. And, there was uncertainty about Italy's status as an ally, the conditions of the armistice, and the possibility of territorial changes once the war was completed.[18]

Separatist propaganda encouraged resistance to the draft. As early as February 1944, Finocchiaro Aprile had made conscription an issue when he declared that Sicilians would not accept being drafted into the Italian army. He and other separatists continually stressed the disadvantages of serving in the Italian military, but Finocchiaro Aprile had counseled his followers not to oppose the call-up openly, because the movement wanted to work with the Allies. But he did argue that Sicilians were unwilling to fight under a Savoyard flag. Once the draft began, however, separatists encouraged conscripts not to present themselves, and instead invited them to fight for the "freedom and liberty" of their island, not that of Italy.[19]

Demonstrations against the draft and the crippling social problems on the island began in late November and continued through January 1945. In general, there were few casualties but extensive property damage. Intense separatist activity exploiting the anger of the general populace preceded the outbreak of the riots. Separatist leaders held meetings throughout the island, especially in their eastern strongholds, where some of the worst demonstrations took place. In the days before the major riot in Catania, both Finocchiaro Aprile and Varvaro shifted their attention there. [20]

As the actual call-up date approached, rioting became more intense. The high point of the cycle was reached on 14–15 December, when violence broke out in Catania. The death of Antonio Stampinato, a student, stimulated the riots and as they progressed, gunfire erupted, government buildings were burned, and Carabinieri vehicles destroyed. Only the appearance of military units prevented further destruction.[21] These disturbances bore little resemblance to those of October in Palermo, because there were few demands for more food in December. Moreover, in the Catania riots, the crowd initiated the violence and the police failed to take decisive action. In fact, Aldisio believed that an effective display of strength by the security forces would have stopped the turmoil before it really began.[22]

There was widespread disagreement over the extent of separatist participation in the Catania disturbances and those in other parts of the island. Although most Italian and Allied authorities agreed that separatists bore at least indirect responsibility for the protests, they also believed that other political factions as well as criminal elements had much to do with the two-day rampage. When the riot began, only about fifty of the five hundred demonstrators were recognized as separatists, the only notable figure being Guglielmo di Carcaci.[23] General Branca, commander of the island's Carabinieri, reported that although the separatists might have planned the riots, members of the other political parties had quickly joined in. He warned that further violence was imminent.[24] Allied reports reveal no evidence to prove separatist complicity in organizing the disturbances, although they admitted that separatist propaganda had certainly influenced the situation. Some analyses claimed that the initial riot in Catania had been sparked by the Lega Giovanile, but as it gained in intensity, criminal elements who represented no political idea or party replaced the separatists as the dominant force.[25]

Separatists themselves denied any involvement in the tumult. The national committee deplored the Catania incident and claimed that supporters had tried to calm the populace. Varvaro accused the government of spreading lies, and reiterated the movement's willingness to pursue legal avenues to accomplish its ends. Months later, Finocchiaro Aprile denied separatist responsibility, but admitted that his movement had encouraged Sicilian youth to desert from the Italian army. He also debunked Aldisio's claim that separatists and Communists shared responsibility for the destruction, placing total blame on the Communists and appealing to British and American fears by warning that there was a grave danger that Sicily would become "Bolshevist."[26]

Though it is possible the Catania riot and other disturbances were part of a separatist blueprint for revolution, in fact the disorders may have frustrated their plans by making the situation too difficult to control. Although separatists had started to plan an uprising in October, they lacked the organization to take advantage of the turmoil.[27]

Aldisio used the chaos to attack the separatists vocally. He criticized them for their involvement and called for stern anti-separatist measures. He also accused the parties of the left of complicity. He contended that the demonstrations were in part caused by the "excitement to riot constantly made by the directors of the separatist movement and by other parties of the left, those who have made and continue to compete in exploiting all the negative elements of each situation in order to excite the population and throw them unconsciously toward anarchy." Aldisio also faulted the separatists, Communists, Socialists, and the Party of Action for having carried on a press campaign that had demoralized the police and weakened their response to public disorders.[28]

In a speech following the Catania riots, Aldisio appealed to Sicilians to stop. The disorders had resulted from a "sudden gush of insanity" that arose from the multitude of problems on the island. He understood that the people lacked everything, but reasoned that the destruction would only make recovery more difficult. He asked those in Sicily to "stop with the criminal speculation, stop with the work of breaking up the morale of the people, stop with the daily attempts against order and discipline," and instead to see autonomy as a fresh start. The recent declaration by the government proved that autonomy would soon be a reality.[29]

Rather than blame the separatists, Orlando and Castellano attacked Aldisio. During a conversation with an OSS informer, Orlando criticized Aldisio and the government for having failed to understand conditions on the island. He intended to inform Bonomi of the situation and present a solution to the crisis. He believed that an increase in the number of security personnel and the transfer of those with questionable loyalties might alleviate the situation. He suggested, too, that Aldisio's work be investigated and that a "substitution be made if Aldisio is found responsible for the aggravation of general conditions on the island."[30]

Of course, Orlando was deeply involved in the Castellano-mafia initiative that supported Aldisio's removal. It is not surprising, therefore, that Castellano buttressed Orlando's sentiments. Castellano lambasted the Italian government for its handling of the draft. In his opinion, much of the difficulty could have been avoided had the government informed Sicilians of the impending call-up. Although he did not directly criticize Aldisio as incompetent, he pointed out that his removal was being considered. For the present, however, he was going to recommend that Aldisio be retained.[31]

During a meeting with Francesco Battiati, the new prefect of Palermo, and Montalbano, the Communist leader, Nester had listened to Montalbano blame the separatists for having influenced the students to riot while at the same time admitting that the movement had no strong following at the universities. Nester rejected the Communist leader's argument, responding that he had no indication that separatists were involved in the demonstrations. In reality, he felt that Fascism was the strongest political force at the universities.[32]

Clearly, a large number of young Sicilians did not want to serve in the Italian army. This protest lent strength to Finocchiaro Aprile's demands for Sicilian battalions. Although Aldisio claimed that ninety-five percent of the men called up had responded, Allied officials estimated that of the 32,000 men expected to report, only 3,200 had come forward, and out of those only 1,300 were accepted for service. Nester reported in late December that only 500 men out of 7,000 had reported for service, while other unconfirmed reports, probably separatist-authored, claimed that only one percent of eligible men were responding.[33]

THE PROMISE OF AUTONOMY

The government acted swiftly to prevent further disturbances. A mobile force of Carabinieri was distributed throughout the island to support local police officials who often waited to confront a situation until they had received orders from superiors removed from the problem. Aldisio also prohibited assemblies in public places, and assigned a new prefect to Catania.[34]

Aldisio again asked the government to define the legal position of separatism, and sanction action against the movement, including the arrest of separatist leaders and the closing of their regional offices.[35] Alone he could do nothing, since these measures required action from the central government, which up to now had refused to act.

Bonomi complied with Aldisio's requests. On 20 December, the government announced its intention to fight any movement seeking to dismember Italy. Although worded generally, the declaration was aimed specifically at the Sicilian situation. Any movement that sought to make an Italian region a "distinct state" was "intolerable." Factions whose leaders spoke of joining their independent states to a future Italian federation were branded "enemies of Italian unity and contrary to the interests, the sentiments, and the ideal of the nation." The same declaration broadened the powers of the high commissioner and promised Sicily regional autonomy; Sicilians would have the right to express their views through a regional council.[36]

Bonomi assured Aldisio that the government would immediately respond to illegal separatist acts. All measures, however, would be carried out within the limits of the existing penal code, the public security laws, and the laws of war. More repressive procedures would have to wait until military reinforcements had been distributed throughout the island.[37] A week later, Aldisio's powers were more clearly defined. He was given authority to oversee state administrative employees, civil and military, as well as those organizations responsible for security. In addition, he was empowered to coordinate the island's prefects and civil authorities to ensure uniform policies. He also assumed direction over ministries that controlled the island's natural resources.[38]

The government's new policy sent many separatists underground. In their public responses, separatists combined restraint and militancy. An article written by Canepa under his pseudonym of Mario Turri, claimed that government restrictions on voting, speech, and the press hampered the ability of Sicilians to express their true desires. The members of the regional council would not be popularly elected, but would be picked by Aldisio. In truth, Canepa warned, Rome, not the Sicilian people, would determine the extent of autonomy.[39]

Declarations issued by separatist committees emphasized Finocchiaro Aprile's policies. In Palermo, a statement accused the government of unjustly attacking the separatist movement and the legitimate goals of the Sicilian people. It appealed to the separatist national committee for direction in case the government tried to further circumvent the people's desires. The proclamation, signed by Giuseppe Tasca, pledged that committee members were "ready to confront any event."[40]

On 22 December, the national committee declared that the decisions of the Bonomi government were unconstitutional, since the government was a fraud and not an expression of the people's will. The Sicilian people wanted to decide their own fate and could never accept autonomy, which would place Sicily at the mercy of the northern Italian capitalists and the government. A more preferable solution was the formation of a federation between an independent Sicily and Italy. This system would "maintain the ties of language, culture and history existing between the two countries." Separatists hoped that such a plan might be worked out with a different Italian government, one that would be "less incomprehensible than the Bonomi cabinet." Throwing down the gauntlet, the national committee vowed not to retreat and not to change its policies.[41]

THE REVOLUTION THAT NEVER HAPPENED

A growing sense of desperation permeated separatist ranks. Decisive action was needed, for even if a revolution failed, it might create a situation in which Allied intervention would become necessary to insure the island's "military efficiency." Such a maneuver would forestall the government's anti-separatist campaign and allow time to devise new strategies.

Separatist militants considered the government's announcement a victory because it had been forced into an uncompromising stance against the movement.[42] Spokesmen for the Lega Giovanile took this attitude a step further. The moment for revolution had arrived, they proclaimed, and the current situation justified the use of violence. The uprising had a good chance of success, they claimed, because there were arms and munitions in the island's interior ready for use.[43]

Finocchiaro Aprile sensed the shift among his followers and reaffirmed his support for revolutionary action by declaring that he would support violence "if it were the will of the majority." At a 24 December meeting in Palermo, he told his audience that it had entered the "heroic phase of our movement." Separatists, he said, would never recognize the Italian government. Italy was headed toward bankruptcy and its plan for autonomy was nothing more than a "shady deal." Only respect for the Allies had stopped separatists from seizing power, but the movement now intended to proceed toward its goals. Varvaro added his support for revolutionary action when he urged the young men in the audience to begin a more intensive propaganda campaign to prepare the soldiers of the separatist army, which would redeem Sicily, but cautioned that the moment was not yet opportune.[44]

Italian authorities were disturbed at talk of a revolt. The police chief of Palermo, Sessa, surmised that "after January 12, the separatist movement will pass from the preparatory stage to that of action." Rumors also spread that separatists were continuing to instigate disturbances in eastern Sicily.[45] In Messina, an Italian admiral learned that an uprising was imminent. According to reports, the preceding riots had merely been the first manifestation of the separatist revolt. A reputed "sealed letter," which had been distributed to all provincial committees, laid out the plans for the oncoming full-scale revolution. The instructions called for concentrating the separatist army in the island's interior. This force would be composed mainly of men who had refused to report for military service. To supply this army, each separatist was to collect his own arms. Instructions were also issued for the occupation of public buildings. The revolution would start after receipt of orders from separatist headquarters in Palermo.[46]

In both Palermo and Messina, it appeared that separatist soldiers were gathering. In the Palermo area, an armed force of some 2,000 men had established headquarters at Monte Pellegrino above the city. One group of young men had left Messina and would be followed by large numbers of other youths, all of whom would meet in the island's center. It was believed that an "action squad" had been formed and had taken a "death oath of allegiance" to initiate the revolution and maintain its positions until reinforcements arrived.[47]

While United States naval personnel in Palermo feared a revolt in early 1945, most American officials believed that the panic over the "sealed letter" was needless. Nester and others had been "repeatedly assured" that separatists had no intention of starting a revolt as long as the war continued, but the consul pointed out that the younger, more impulsive followers might cause trouble that the leaders could not control. In this case, "there probably would be nothing for Tasca, Finocchiaro Aprile, Varvaro and others to do except to go along with the majority. Of these three, Finocchiaro Aprile is the least trustworthy and might not keep his word."[48]

In fact, the movement's leadership was badly divided over the use of force. Those who wanted action believed that a strike had to be made before the government could act against the movement and that conditions on the island were favorable for an uprising. Those who opposed an armed struggle thought that the movement should continue to stress its desire for a plebiscite. This faction also feared that any insurrection would meet Allied and Italian resistance. For a brief moment it appeared that the more militant elements might initiate the uprising. Yet, a short time after Christmas, the movement's major leaders, including Lucio Tasca, decided against a violent takeover.[49] In reality, without a military force to replace the mafia, an unplanned separatist revolt was doomed to failure. The demise of an uprising at Comiso in Ragusa province provided ample proof that further preparation was needed. There, in the first week of January, a republic had been declared and a provisional government established. After heavy fighting the rebellion was crushed.[50]

The beginning of 1945 marked a crucial juncture in the separatist struggle. In the face of further government pressure, the movement's leadership became more fractured over ideological differences and the use of violence. Nevertheless, in the first months of 1945, separatists announced that they had created an army capable of carrying out their revolution. Furthermore, they conducted another campaign to attract world sympathy in an effort to pressure the Italian government. The movement had entered its most radical phase.

8

The Radical Phase

MODERATES VERSUS EXTREMISTS

THE mafia's exit from the separatist coalition had radically altered the movement's internal make-up. While on the surface it appeared that most separatist leaders continued to support independence, the Castellano initiative had led to the emergence of a faction that favored the establishment of an autonomous Sicilian republic within an Italian federation. The split openly manifested itself in Catania where the "federalists" sought to open their own headquarters.[1]

By 1945, the Italian state had grudgingly accepted autonomy as the basis for its future relationship with Sicily. It had been pushed to this position under pressure from the separatist movement. Adherence to this moderate group was, therefore, safe, prestigious, and politically profitable, since those supporting autonomy might influence the final result and gain positions in the new regional government. Moreover, autonomy had gained the support of many major political figures, some of whom, Li Causi included, were in contact with this group.[2]

The moderate faction contained some of the more important island figures, besides those involved in the mafia-government talks and the Castellano initiative. Both Vizzini and the Tasca brothers were aligned with this group even though Lucio still portrayed himself as a supporter of independence, and sought to manipulate the political situation in his favor. His failure to champion the December revolution demonstrated that he intended to protect himself by not supporting any radical action.

The Bonomi government's decision to fight separatism had frightened the movement's more timid or uncertain supporters, thus strengthening the position of the moderates. More and more separatists, leaders and followers, realized the futility of struggling for independence, and came to accept autonomy as their goal. After having promised autonomy, the government strengthened its position by taking decisive measures to prove that the plan was not simply a "shady deal." Aldisio moved quickly to dispel doubts by holding the first meeting of the regional council on 25 February 1945. He instructed its members that they had the task of tightening the bonds between the island and the mainland, as well as responsibility for improving economic and political conditions.[3]

Extremist separatists rejected autonomy and continued to demand absolute independence.[4] Led by Finocchiaro Aprile, they disdained any compromise with the Italian government and refused to support the initiatives of either Castellano or Aldisio. Although this group continued to shrink throughout 1945, Finocchiaro Aprile gave it residual strength and prestige.

While he continued to speak of achieving independence through legal avenues, Finocchiaro Aprile's public pronouncements testified to his growing radicalism. In one message to the Allies, he warned that if the Bonomi government continued to abridge separatist rights, the separatists would seize Sicily by force. As long as Allied officials remained in Sicily, he promised he would do all he could to prevent a revolution, but after their departure there would be nothing to stop the revolutionaries, especially since there was no shortage of arms on the island. The revolution, he warned, would be a "very bloody and bitter struggle," and unless Sicilian desires were satisfied, there would be no peace in the Mediterranean.[5]

Once again, Finocchiaro Aprile and his followers planned a revolt. On 15 and 16 January, some 40 members of the national committee met in Palermo. The meeting had been called because of "strong pressure being brought on local leaders to institute immediate and violent action." After a series of "stormy sessions," the committee issued an ultimatum demanding that either the Allies reoccupy the island or the movement act to assume power. It is unclear to whom the statement was directed, but the national committee decided that if it was not accepted, "the movement would seize power by using force" and proclaim Sicilian independence. The executive committee was again given power to direct the revolution while the Lega Giovanile was ordered to begin a widespread propaganda campaign.[6]

Out of this same meeting came a "provocative" declaration asking the United Nations to give control of the island to the national committee. It was also one of the most detailed policy statements ever made by the movement. If the national committee was given control of Sicily, it would administer the island and enforce the law with the help of the Allied powers. Sicily would "give its maximum contribution to the war effort of the Allies." The committee promised to begin immediately the process of electing members to a Sicilian Constituent Assembly, which would write a constitution "based on the historical traditions of the State of Sicily, assuring the largest autonomy to the towns and villages of the Island." The declaration provided details as to how the island would be divided into electoral districts and who would be eligible to vote. It also assured the Allied powers that the new Sicilian nation would assume a position of neutrality in world affairs, but that it would be willing to federate with Italy "if it would be so required by post-war political circumstance."[7]

The timing for the planned seizure of power is uncertain, but one report warned that it would begin on the "following *Sabato Santo* precisely at the moment during which the church bells announced Christ's resurrection during Easter." The revolution's leaders would be recognized by an olive leaf in their button holes.[8]

Indecisive as always, separatist chiefs tried to back away from their plans once they realized the possible repercussions. On 10–11 February, members of the executive committee met and decided that any violence had to be delayed until the end of the war. A revolt, they believed, would be opposed by the Allies and would be too disorganized to succeed. Rather than fight, they counseled the movement's followers to concentrate on regaining all public offices from which separatists had been removed.[9]

Once again, separatist discipline proved to be illusory, as many followers ignored these recommendations. These revolutionaries had no intention of giving up their dream of independence and had no wish to listen to the pronouncements of their more timid leaders. They did understand that they needed time to prepare the groundwork for a seizure of power. Unplanned disturbances in the cities or countryside were doomed to fail. Popular support, an armed force, and outside assistance were all necessary for a successful revolution. Extremist propaganda sought to appeal to the nationalist sentiments of Sicilians, and reminded them that they had often fought to throw off the chains of oppression. Propaganda continually compared the present government to that of the Fascists, and noted that the time had passed for supplication, protest, and peaceful demonstration. Separatist followers were ordered to "fight against the flag," to remove Italian flags "whenever flown," or to deface them "with paint or other means."[10]

Separatists also tried to discredit government officials through an increasingly vociferous and personalized campaign. Aldisio became the focal point of the attack. In February, Finocchiaro Aprile rebuffed an effort by Aldisio to make peace, telling him that it was "too late" for any discussion, and that he would never collaborate with him or the Christian Democrats. Separatists assailed the high commissioner as nothing more than the instrument of foreign oppression, because he had been appointed by the Italian government. One piece of separatist propaganda attempted to link Aldisio to Mussolini:

Dear Aldisio,

I have received news of the strong actions which you undertake in the geographical center of our lost empire. In recognition of your good works, I am disposed to concede you the honor of a membership badge (of the Fascist Party) with seniority from 1922. Stand straight. Stand fast. You will earn the highest Fascist decoration. At my return you will have a portfolio, perhaps that of the Colonies, because Sicily is the only colony which remains. Thanks for the hospitality that you have given to my faithful in the Christian-Democratic Party. To whom does Sicily belong? To us!

Mussolini[11]

In late February, Pietro Nenni, the secretary-general of the Italian Socialist Party, visited the island. Separatists tried to interfere with one of his meetings, but were stopped by security officials. During his trip, Nenni expressed little sympathy for Sicily's past treatment, declaring at one point that if the island sought to find a solution for its problems through separatism, it would become the colony of a foreign power. In his view, the Sicilian problem was no different from that of Lombardy, Calabria, or Emilia, and the solution to it could best be found within the framework of the nation.[12]

A more compromising attitude was taken by Randolfo Pacciardi, the leader of the Italian Republican Party, who toured the island soon after Nenni. Reports claimed that his visit was prompted by invitations extended by the Party of Action and the separatists. Perhaps this explains why, as Pacciardi spoke in Palermo, Messina, and Syracuse, he avoided any open attack on the separatist movement. Instead, he stressed his party's anti-monarchist stance, and pointed out that it wished to unite with others in that particular struggle. This political line gave credence to rumors that Pacciardi intended to form a republican coalition with the separatists and the Party of Action in Sicily.[13] Pacciardi's position won the conditional support of some anti-monarchical separatists, but they disagreed with his concept that Italy should become a federation of regions rather than independent states.[14]

THE ARMY FOR SICILIAN INDEPENDENCE

While separatist efforts to undermine faith in the government and autonomy continued, the extremists also worked to develop a military force. Since the defection of the mafia, an entirely new body was needed to initiate the seizure of power.

The basis for a military organization already existed in the form of the Lega Giovanile, from which the Corpo della Guardia alla Bandiera (Guard for the Flag) had evolved. Concetto Gallo and Guglielmo di Carcaci commanded the Corpo and during the ceremony marking its formation, Gallo had reinforced the group's militant image by making a menacing speech. The Corpo was organized as a military force, and for a short time it appeared to be the embryo of the separatist army, but it never evolved to that level. Members of this group were recruited for an "Army for the Liberation of Sicily" and were incorporated into the ranks of EVIS (Esercito Volontario per l'Indipendenza Siciliana)— The Volunteer Army for Sicilian Independence. Gallo later became a commander in this separatist army, which had minimal ties to the Lega Giovanile and the Corpo.[15]

In the fall of 1944, Antonio Canepa returned to Sicily from the mainland. During his interval away from the island, Canepa had continued to work for the British secret service by organizing groups to disrupt the German retreat and help American and British prisoners escape. He had fought in the Italian resistance, first in the Abruzzi area and later in and around Tuscany, where he led a partisan group known as the Matteotti Brigade. He adopted the pseudonym Tolù, and founded the socialist-oriented Partito dei Lavoratori.[16]

Supported by Attilio Castrogiovanni, Varvaro, and members of the Catanese separatist organization, Canepa pushed for the formation of an armed force. On 23 October he met with Finocchiaro Aprile in Catania, and a week later with Guglielmo di Carcaci, the head of the Lega Giovanile. They gave Canepa the task of forming a clandestine organization that would be prepared to take revolutionary action.[17] Canepa became the organizer and the first commander of EVIS. He was the only possible choice, since he stood alone in terms of military and organizational experience.

Conservative separatists and those supporting autonomy feared Canepa's leftist beliefs, and from the beginning inhibited his activities. Canepa was fully committed to Sicilian independence, and like Finocchiaro Aprile, never wavered in his desire. In truth, Canepa's return to Sicily, his ties to the left, and his successful recruitment efforts for EVIS might have helped stimulate the Castellano initiative and the mafia secession from the separatist movement. From the start, Canepa represented a threat to the established order.

Although many of Canepa's organizational activities are obscure, it is clear that during the formative period of EVIS, he remained in contact with separatist leaders, who lent him support and money, including Finocchiaro Aprile, Lucio and Giuseppe Tasca, and Francesco Restuccia.[18] In Catania, Canepa recruited his former anti-Fascist comrades, most of whom were young, and managed to obtain weapons. But potential soldiers for EVIS existed throughout the island. Some youths had organized clandestine groups in 1942 or had tried to form action squads in 1944.[19] Those youths who enlisted in EVIS did so for a number of reasons. Some were idealists or Sicilian nationalists, while others simply hated the Italian government or joined for personal reasons. Students who had demonstrated against the draft and had participated in the violence also joined. Other potential soldiers included members of bandit groups, the unemployed, and the disenchanted, as well as "Italian and Allied deserters, foreign partisans, and Jews and Yugoslav royalists from the internment camp at Eboli."[20] If Canepa could unite them, he would have a sizable force.

Ultimately, students and bandits formed the majority of EVIS soldiers. The students lacked military training, and separatist leaders did not expect to have time to train them. Instead, they sought to enlist those who already had weapons and a proclivity toward violence, and turned to the bandits. These brigands operated independently of the mafia and resorted to kidnaping and extortion to maintain themselves. Some twenty bands operated on the island, most in the western portion. Palermo, Trapani, Caltanissetta, Messina, Syracuse, Agrigento, and Catania all had their share.[21] The members of these groups hated the Italian state and joined the separatists because they hoped that in an independent Sicily they would be free from persecution.

Incorporating these bands into a cohesive fighting force was difficult. It is unclear who convinced these men to join the separatist army or when the alliance was consummated. Although some authorities believed that Vizzini was responsible, this is incorrect. Given the past conversations between the government and the mafia, it would not have made sense for Vizzini to encourage more disorder. In fact, in early 1945, Vizzini and his followers were trying to bring order to the island by stifling the activities of the armed bands. In March 1945, mafia leaders met in Palermo to formulate a policy concerning the bandits and the island's crime problem. Vizzini, at the forefront of these efforts, noted that "Sicily must have tranquillity in the country and on the roads. A few hundred have been eliminated. But about one hundred more must fall." Fascism was responsible for the island's condition but "today," Vizzini continued, "Sicily must be considered a jewel in the Mediterranean by the Americans."[22] Mafia leaders found support from police officials in this campaign. Several times, Carabinieri and police officials had requested the mafia's assistance in crushing the lawbreakers. At other times, they simply neglected to investigate the killing of bandits or delinquents by the mafia.[23]

By January 1945, an EVIS nucleus had been organized. The initials "EVIS" or the entire name of the army appeared on wall posters protesting the draft in Catania and attacking Aldisio. In this same month, Finocchiaro Aprile admitted that his movement had an army, but that they were holding off any action until the Allies had left Sicily.[24]

The structure of EVIS reflected Canepa's experience as a resistance leader and his egalitarian beliefs. For the most part, however, his organizational work was only theoretical.[25] Canepa devised a detailed chain of command. The commander of EVIS was the head of the general staff. A colonel in charge of official plans, and a number of majors who controlled different logistical areas, assisted the commander. The regimental leaders formed the last link in the general staff. Subsidiary organizations of the general staff included the revolutionary tribunal, the secretary of the commanding general, information office, prisoner office, and a map office.

In theory, each EVIS soldier was to receive a daily ration of 200 grams of pasta, 400 grams of bread, possibly as much as 200 grams of wine, three cigarettes, and additional foodstuffs. Separatist soldiers also would be paid a monthly wage depending on their rank. Gradations were only 500 lire between ranks, thus keeping the gap between soldier and leader to a minimum. As a final incentive, each EVIS soldier would retain his rank in the army of an independent Sicilian nation.

EVIS soldiers were provided a Decalogue, or ten commandments, that precisely outlined what Canepa expected of them. EVIS followers were to fight for the island's independence and obey orders given them by the Committee for Sicilian Independence. To maintain security, members had to obey the organization's supreme law: secrecy. "Those who tell what they know or what they have done are despicable. Those who betray EVIS will die." Members had to be punctual at any cost and maintain "disciplines of steel." No one would receive payment until the establishment of the new state and at mealtime, soldiers ate before officers. Moreover, "Everything that goes badly is the fault of the officials, everything that goes well was due to the soldier's good work." Knowing that EVIS forces would usually be outnumbered or outgunned, Canepa advised that "rather than using force, be shrewd whenever possible, but if it is necessary to use force, then fight until the end." No action was considered too repugnant if used in the separatist cause.[26]

Since EVIS operated as a guerrilla force, each member was to be prepared to carry much of his equipment and all necessary arms and munitions. EVIS had to be capable of moving quickly and fighting at a moment's notice. In theory, EVIS was perfectly designed for the guerrilla-style campaign that Canepa realized would have to be fought. An all-out attack against the Italian military would be senseless, but with hit-and-run tactics and the support of the people, a guerrilla force might achieve success.

Despite Canepa's best efforts, EVIS was unable to play a decisive role in the first six months of 1945. Indeed, it is nearly impossible to distinguish its activities from those of the island's armed bands, which roamed the countryside and plundered at will. EVIS was often credited with these actions and was thought to have created more disorder and presented more of a threat than it actually did.[27]

If separatist leaders intended to use the specter of EVIS to frighten Italian authorities, they succeeded. Italian officials considered EVIS the "first embryonic plan for the practical formation of a military organism."[28] Any activity credited to EVIS heightened their fears of revolution and increased the pressure on them to end the separatist threat. Other observers, however, painted a more realistic picture of EVIS strength and recognized that it was merely another tool with which separatists could manipulate the government. One American official bluntly wrote, "The EVIS is evidently an army that does not exist despite the fact that all over the island the following inscriptions are seen on the walls: Viva l'EVIS, Viva Truman or Viva l'EVIS—Viva l'America. Furthermore, the EVIS seems to be something built up by shrewd propagandists to lend weight to their demands."[29] For the time being, EVIS was too disorganized to influence events, thus forcing the movement to rely on other means to pressure the government.

THE SAN FRANCISCO DECLARATION

Despite Allied antagonism, separatists continued to spread rumors that AMG was returning to Sicily and that American and British officials on the island still supported their cause. Leaders like Santi Rindone of Catania openly voiced his belief that the United States would assist Sicily in attaining independence. At the same time, he attacked Great Britain as an "imperialistic power and the enemy of democracy."[30] Italian officials often panicked at such statements, and acted as if they were true. Bonomi, who should have known better, antagonized American officials when he intimated that certain Americans on the island backed separatism.[31]

If the Americans had championed separatism and wished to exploit it, Bonomi would have had good reason to worry. Pro-American sentiment was still widespread among islanders. One separatist spokesman claimed, with some legitimacy, that "seventy percent of the Sicilian population was pro-American separatists and one hundred percent of the industrialists and businessmen, ninety percent of all Sports Club members, most of the laborers at the American Naval Base, 700 out of every 800 port workers, a great percentage of Public Safety functionaries, all the Bank of Sicily personnel of Cassa di Risparmio, Banca del Sud and Banca Nazionale del Lavoro are pro-American separatists . . . let no one be deceived. The people's decision will reveal their solidarity for America. We intend to fight two enemies: Great Britain and Communism. These two must disappear from Sicily."[32]

Media coverage made it apparent that separatism still had the potential to become a question of international importance. When Drew Pearson wrote in 1945 that secret terms in the Italian armistice gave Britain control of Lampedusa and Pantellaria in return for allowing the United States to annex Sicily, he fueled the rumors. Both the British and Americans said that the story was too ridiculous to merit denial, while one official commented that "Mr. Pearson would appear to be hard up for news. His story is a year out of date. The only suggestion that I have ever heard seriously put forward that Sicily or parts of southern Italy should join the United States was made in the first three months after our landing among certain local Sicilians and Italians who had been in America and had connections. The story long ago faded away for lack of any basis in fact or encouragement from the Allies."[33]

Articles in the *New York Times* implied that under certain conditions, the United States might support an independent Sicily. Vanni Montana, the director of the Italian American Labor Committee and a trade union leader born in Sicily, gave the impression that Sicilian-Americans would support separatism if the movement could prove that it was not merely a tool of the British. Furthermore, when Montana toured the island, he discovered that separatism was a "real, popular movement."[34] The question for Italian authorities was whether the United States or Britain might come to the aid of a "popular movement" for their own purposes.

The British continued to mistrust American intentions and tried to exploit what little pro-British feeling existed. In doing so they gave Finocchiaro Aprile additional leverage against the government and contributed to the lingering belief that they backed the separatist movement. Even though Sicily had faded from the war front, it continued to cause friction between the United States and Britain. The latter was not about to permit the establishment of an American sphere of influence in the Mediterranean while under pressure to surrender its own imperial holdings.

Finocchiaro Aprile capitalized on the clouded situation. He left a three-and-a-half hour meeting with British officer George R. Gayre (the former public education officer for AMG), satisfied but reluctant to divulge any information about the discussion. According to an informant, however, a British officer had confirmed that his nation supported separatism, and Finocchiaro Aprile had stated that "we can finally believe in Sicilian independence under a British sphere of influence. This cannot displease the Americans, who incidentally are not interested in the Mediterranean." The British, according to the informant, had already approved the "administrative and political lists to be published when Sicilian independence was proclaimed."[35]

Finocchiaro Aprile inflamed the situation further by alleging that he had reached important agreements with the British. Apparently, he had sacrificed control of the movement for British aid when he declared that "I shall not take a step unless precise orders are issued, for a blunder might compromise the entire situation. Therefore, I shall not act without orders."[36] To increase tension, separatist leaders decided to broaden their call for assistance to the entire world in an attempt to make separatism a question of international importance.

In early March, Finocchiaro Aprile announced to separatists gathered in Syracuse that Roosevelt and Churchill had discussed Sicily at the Yalta conference and had decided that the issue would be solved at the upcoming San Francisco Conference. On 30 March, Lucio Tasca went to the American consulate on behalf of Finocchiaro Aprile. In his possession was a declaration addressed to the delegates at the San Francisco Conference, the meeting to write the charter of the United Nations. Officials denied him permission to transmit the manifesto through the diplomatic pouch and he was told that the American government would in no way assist or encourage the separatist movement. Tasca made the same request at the British consulate and the British field security section, but met with the same answer. In desperation he sought a military officer who would deliver the documents.[37]

It is unclear whether any copies of the statement ever reached the San Francisco Conference, and there is no reference to Sicilian separatism in the official records. Copies of the declaration were distributed in Palermo and other parts of the island. Dated 31 March 1945, the 663rd anniversary of the Sicilian Vespers, it presented a detailed explanation of the separatist position and justification for the movement. The document's purpose, according to the national committee, was to focus the attention of the conference on the "grave situation existing in Sicily so that a decision might be made on the island's future." The statement outlined Sicily's past and argued that the island had historically existed more or less as a sovereign state, prosperous and at the center of the world's cultural activities.[38]

The declaration pointed out that in 1860, contrary to the wishes of Sicilian patriots, the island was annexed to the Italian state. Thus began a period of systematic oppression, robbery, and slavery that had lasted for the past eighty-five years. During this time, Sicily had been treated like a colony and had been deprived of all the benefits of modern civilization and those enjoyed by other Italian states. The island was continually exploited through higher rates of taxation, the absorption of all of her economic resources, and by the retardation of industrial initiatives in favor of the north. Continued unity with Italy would only cause further deterioration.

In light of this situation, the manifesto continued, Sicilians had decided to form their own independent state. They had repeatedly expressed this desire to the governments of the United States, Britain, and the Soviet Union. This latest declaration represented an attempt to make the islanders' plight and their desires known to all the other Allied powers and to invoke their aid "for the solution of the intolerable and miserable conditions of the oppressed Sicilian nation." These conditions had deteriorated since Mussolini's fall because of policies followed by the new Italian government. Calling those in power "addicted to the most disgusting political opportunism," the declaration accused the government and its allies of caring only for themselves and their fortunes. "Sicily will achieve her destiny at whatever cost; nothing can stop the people of the Vespers. If it takes up arms, then it will be with the certainty of success. . . . If the bloody conflict can be avoided, if it is possible to avoid upsetting the peace of the Mediterranean, the people of Sicily will be glad and happy, they who sincerely love order and civil progress and who want to be elements of tranquillity and stabilization."[39]

Separatists asked for the intervention of those at San Francisco to prevent bloodshed. Only the United Nations could stop the flow of events. "The noble task of the guardianship of the supreme interests of the Sicilian people devolves on them, and they who will declare the independence of Austria and of other countries will see that the independence of Sicily is an act of grace and justice."[40]

Although the Sicilian issue was not debated in San Francisco, Finocchiaro Aprile claimed that the memorandum had been discussed and that thirty-one nations had voted in favor of examining the question of Sicilian independence at the peace conference following the war. The eight votes against the separatist declaration had come from states tied to the Soviet Union, but the opposition had been based on procedural questions. Three nations had abstained. The vote marked the first instance in which the United States clashed openly with Great Britain, for the Americans had forced the issue before the conference despite British opposition. The results were a great victory and, almost guaranteed Sicily's independence.[41]

On 11 June 1945, Finocchiaro Aprile wrote to Churchill, repeating his claim about the San Francisco vote. He expressed the movement's "deepest gratitude for the very noble work that we supposed you accomplished on our behalf. Sicily is today enthusiastically eulogizing Great Britain and yourself who direct her destiny with a sure hand and who are the greatest architect of the new world order." Finocchiaro Aprile asked that an observer delegation from Sicily be admitted to the peace conference since it might be useful to "know our views at first hand."[42]

Allied officials knew nothing of a discussion on the Sicilian question. "I have never heard any mention of Sicily at San Francisco," one British official commented. "It seems most improbable." Some days later a letter directed to Finocchiaro Aprile repeated the British government's statement of October 1944 in which it had denied any support for the separatist movement.[43] The Americans also disavowed any knowledge of a San Francisco vote. Nester sent Aldisio a letter in which he denied that the separatist memorandum had been approved at the conference or that a discussion of the movement had taken place. American officials also decided that a statement of American sentiments and a denial of Finocchiaro Aprile's claims would be issued over the radio.[44]

In reality, separatists knew that no discussion of their declaration had ever taken place, but they tried to take advantage of the islanders' lack of information to increase tension within government circles. The separatist strategy backfired, however, because the proclamation contributed to a storm of anti-separatist feeling. Pietro Nenni, the Socialist leader, accused separatists of treason and wrote that they had clearly demonstrated that they planned to use foreign accomplices to gain independence. There was no longer any doubt, he declared, about the movement's reactionary nature, and it was obvious that it stood against Italian democracy.[45] The island's Committee of National Liberation also attacked the separatists, because they had requested foreign intervention for their cause. The movement was seditious, outside the law, and an obstacle to the island's reconstruction. Representatives of the committee asked the high commissioner and the government to take legal action to destroy the movement.[46]

Aldisio reported that the public responded to the declaration with indignation and disgust.[47] Indeed, the statement could not have been more ill-timed or done more harm to the separatist cause. Its appearance coincided with rumors concerning the loss of Italian territory. Separatists became accomplices of those foreign powers seeking to dismember the nation. The San Francisco memorandum did more to stir the anti-separatist forces than all the previous measures taken by the government. Sicilians who had waited for Rome to take action made their feelings apparent, thereby strengthening the anti-separatist coalition. The separatist leadership, surprised by the popular response against them, was forced to take even more extreme measures. From this point, the history of the movement was a litany of self-destructive actions that ultimately led to the demise of the independence wing and gave the autonomists their victory.

9

Decline

OPPOSITION INTENSIFIES

THE San Francisco Declaration aroused the anti-separatist opposition. Organizations and groups that had remained submerged now surfaced to speak out in support of unity and against independence. Political factions that had previously taken an anti-separatist profile stepped up their attacks amid a growing perception that public opinion was turning in their favor. These organizations exploited nationalist sentiment on the island and escalated and focused popular resistance to separatism. In doing so, they aided the government's effort to destroy the movement.

The end of the war was one of the key events in turning the tide against separatism. At the beginning of April, the Allied powers began their final attack against the Germans and Fascists. On 28 April, Italian partisans shot Mussolini and then hung his body on display in Milan. Within days, the Allied powers took control of all of Italy and the war effectively ended for the Italian people. For Sicilians, these events meant little in material terms. Instead, with the conflict's end, all attention focused on the problem of Sicily's future status. Islanders faced the reality of having to decide whether they wanted the uncertainty of independence, or autonomy within the Italian state.

Anti-separatist factions worked quickly to make their case. The leading press organ of the Christian Democrats, *Il Popolo,* intensified the criticism that it had begun earlier in the year. *Il Popolo* contended that Sicilians were estranged from separatism and that political gangs had prearranged the disturbances of the previous year. The paper compared separatists to Fascists and claimed that they followed similar methods and ends. It accused Finocchiaro Aprile of rewriting history to demonstrate that Garibaldi had made a mistake by liberating Sicily in 1860.[1] He profoundly humiliated the traditions of "island patriotism" that had always supported Italian political renewal. According to *Il Popolo,* separatism was founded on bad faith during a tragic period of history and was essentially a myth that needed to be eradicated.[2]

150

While it lambasted separatists, *Il Popolo* praised Aldisio as a temperate and democratic man who worked for the best interests of the island and the nation. Accusations that he was working in common with the island's large landowners were unjustified.[3]

A number of political organizations designed to combat separatism also made their presence known. These groups did not have large followings, suffered internal dissension, and their leaders were more concerned with personal ambition than with separatism. They also lacked funds, which prevented them from carrying out a very active propaganda campaign. Their members were mainly Sicilians who had emigrated to the mainland and received financial and material support from the Italian government. The most important of these included the Comitato Nazionale Movimento Antiseparatista ed Unitaria (National Committee for the Antiseparatist and Unitary Movement) headed by Luigi Gasparotto; the Unione Siciliana Lavoro Giustizia e Libertà (the Sicilian Union of Work, Justice and Liberty) headed by Baldassone Gambino; the Sicilian Association of Rome dominated by Giovanni Cascino; and the Movimento Antiseparatista della Sicilia per l'Unità (the Sicilian Antiseparatist Movement for Unity) led by Giuseppe Amilcare Oddo.[4]

Continuing Intransigence

Separatists did little to change public perceptions during their second national congress, held in Palermo 14–16 April. The congress was not a time for moderation, and threats of violence and fiery speeches dominated the meeting.[5]

Some 1,500 separatists attended the congress, 500 from the Palermo area and 250 from Catania. There were 150 representatives from Messina, 25 from Enna, 10 from Ragusa, 2 from Alcamo, 1 from Marsala, and 20 from Lercara Friddi. The foremost separatist leaders, many of whom still supported independence, presided over the gathering. These included Finocchiaro Aprile, Giuseppe Tasca, Luigi La Rosa, Attilio Castrogiovanni, Concetto Gallo, Bruno di Belmonte, Francesco di Carcaci, Guglielmo di Carcaci, Edoardo Milio Cangemi, Francesco Restuccia, and Francesco Montalbano.[6]

For most, this meeting was the last large separatist gathering, and for Finocchiaro Aprile, it represented the climax of his undisputed leadership. His position, weakened by the factionalism of late 1944, would be further undermined after the conference. During the Palermo session, Finocchiaro Aprile spoke of his plans for Sicily, but many now realized that the achievement of independence was improbable.

In his opening address, Finocchiaro Aprile simply bemoaned the death of Roosevelt. The president's passing was crucial, he said, since Roosevelt would have attended the San Francisco Conference.

A litany of speeches threatening revolution followed Finocchiaro Aprile's short statement. Bruno di Belmonte criticized the government and threatened that if the Sicilian problem was not resolved in the international field, it would be dealt with by Sicilians. Filippo Sanfilippo of Palermo suggested that Sicily acquire her independence at any cost, including that of blood. Pietro Giganti, president of the Lega Giovanile in Palermo, predicted the immediate realization of independence through the use of force. Francesco Restuccia, a future EVIS leader, also mentioned the forthcoming revolution and asked Finocchiaro Aprile how long the movement's followers would need to wait before acting.[7]

The calls for revolution appealed to separatists who had waited two years for the leadership to take decisive action. They understood that the movement had entered a final, critical phase. Many believed that the success of their program was imminent, a feeling reinforced by the government's apparent inability to crush the movement.[8]

Finocchiaro Aprile's one major speech, the highlight of the congress, emphasized his populist positions. Speaking of the "rising maturity" of the working class, he extolled the separatist-oriented Partito Social-Communista and claimed that many cultivated and intelligent Communists, who at first had assumed an anti-separatist position, were now joining the movement. Numerous workers in Catania followed the cause, while in Messina, separatist-Communists were constantly increasing their activity. Communists supported the movement wholeheartedly, he declared, because they had discovered the similarities between Bolshevist doctrine and the concepts that guided the separatist movement. Also, they recognized independence as a first step toward the gradual triumph of Communism.[9]

Claiming to have been among the first to encourage the formation of the Sicilian Socialist Federation, Finocchiaro Aprile argued that most serious members of the organization had remained separatists and some, like Varvaro, had attained high positions in the movement. "This flow on the part of the workers and the almost total consent of the peasants for the movement, defines the character of the movement, which contrary to the statements of Communists and Socialists, was a movement of the left, rather of the extreme left, because the world, after the infamous experiment of Nazi-Fascism, was moving decisively to the left, toward the people, toward the workers of intellect and strength."[10]

The separatist leader concluded by thanking the leadership of the separatist-oriented Sicilian Communist Party of Catania for the honorary membership given to him. Finocchiaro Aprile characterized it as an act of sympathy, solidarity, and recognition of the democratic character of the movement.

Once again, Finocchiaro Aprile had tried to portray himself as the leader of all Sicilians rather than the head of a narrow clique. Of course, his remarks must be understood in the context of current events, including the mafia's desertion of his movement. He had reminded conservatives and the mafia that there existed unpleasant alternatives to an independent Sicily. By holding the threat of Communism over his errant followers, Finocchiaro Aprile was trying to bring them back into the separatist fold.

Finocchiaro Aprile had indeed touched a raw nerve among his fellow separatists. The day after the congress ended, the national committee secretly met in the movement's Palermo headquarters. Those present surmised that Togliatti had signed some sort of agreement with Tito to carry out a Communist coup d'etat in Italy. On the other hand, members of the separatist intelligence service informed the committee that separatists had infiltrated the American intelligence services in Rome which "faithfully transmitted all reports provided by the Separatist Intelligence Service." Moreover, an American major had reportedly advised separatists to revolt to prove that they represented majority opinion. Only then, he had informed the separatists, "could the Allies help them."[11]

POPULAR BACKLASH

By reaffirming their support for an independent Sicily, separatists further antagonized pro-Italian nationalists on the island. The demand for detachment coincided with a growing fear on the part of many Italians that their nation might lose territory as punishment for its alliance with Hitler. Of particular concern was the possible loss of Italian territory to Yugoslavia. Some months before, the Yugoslav foreign minister had announced that peace between Italy and Yugoslavia could come about only after the cession of certain districts that had been formerly annexed to Italy. This statement had set off a rash of anti-Tito and anti-Yugoslav comment in the press.[12]

In April, Yugoslav forces occupied Venezia-Giulia, thereby inflaming nationalist passions on the island. On 21 April between 3,000 and 5,000 people, most of whom were students, protested in Palermo to support Italy's continued dominance over Trieste. As it moved along the city streets, the crowd grew in size and began to sing the national anthem and wave the Italian tricolor. At one point, the crowd followed Via Ruggero Settimo, on which the separatist headquarters was located. Separatists began to throw stones and pieces of wood from the building's windows, and spit and scream insults at the crowd. Evidently, some separatists went outside and challenged the demonstrators. A brawl followed and despite efforts at restraint by the police, the crowd invaded the separatist offices and damaged the interior. Security forces evicted the mob, occupied the structure, and forbade entry. At least eight people suffered injuries, and to the dismay of separatists, the public did not seem to mind that government forces had been slow to halt the disturbance or that they had occupied the building.[13] The shuttered office stood as a grim reminder of governmental determination to end the separatist crisis.

Following the incident, rumors of a separatist reprisal spread, and Aldisio prepared to arrest the movement's leaders at the first signs of such an action, though he believed that the rumors were exaggerated.[14]

In fact, no retaliation followed. Canepa was not ready to use EVIS, and while Nester feared that young separatists might start trouble, he was confident that "more level headed groups such as Vizzini and the Maffia may keep matters in check."[15] Within days, Nester credited Vizzini with "having seen to it that the youths remain quiet" and predicted that it was "unlikely that any disturbance will occur in the immediate future. The extremist elements, the Finocchiaro Aprile and Tasca group seem to be confused and disorganized."[16] This failure to strike back at the authorities was the first sign of the damage done to the movement by the mafia's withdrawal.

The protest in Palermo was followed by a series of incidents in which separatists were attacked and arrested, and their offices closed. In Messina, during the last week of April, nationalist students clashed with separatists during demonstrations supporting Italian claims to Trieste and celebrating northern Italy's liberation. Quick police action prevented a major confrontation, but subsequent demonstrations led to the arrest of twenty-seven people, including Francesco Restuccia, a vice president of the movement and an EVIS supporter.[17]

In Catania, separatists fared no better. On 2–4 May, nationalist demonstrations led to attacks on separatist strongholds. Students invaded and occupied the separatist offices despite an effort to blockade the building's entrance with electrically charged wire. Although the maneuver kept the students out, separatists soon found themselves dispossessed by police, who occupied the structure.[18]

In Ionia, Acireale, Aci Sant Antonio, Randazzo, and Vizzini, separatist offices were closed, sometimes by separatists themselves, who wished to avoid popular prodding to do so. Although meetings continued in provisional locations, clearly the movement had suffered a massive blow. The government seized on the moment to close several presses in Palermo where separatist propaganda was printed and to seize separatist literature.[19]

These incidents aided Aldisio's campaign to quash the movement. In March, he had urged the government to take stronger actions against the separatists, and voiced doubts that the policy of forbidding their gatherings could be enforced. He had complained that the separatist office in Palermo was used for daily gatherings during which speakers would give lectures without the prior notification required by law. Aldisio again questioned the movement's compatibility with the national interests, and insisted that it be declared illegal, its offices immediately closed down, and its leaders warned that they might be hauled before a military tribunal. If, however, the government decided to tolerate the movement, then the only alternative was to contain it.[20] Thanks to the demonstrators, Aldisio's goals were being accomplished. Separatist offices had been closed, meetings had been obstructed, and the more timid followers had been silenced, out of fear of retribution.

Paolo Berardi, the military commander of the island, held similar views. He believed that the government's continuing unwillingness to confront the separatists had actually provided the movement a degree of strength. It was now time to act. The nationalist demonstrations had stirred the Sicilian people. By acting forcibly, the government would regain the people's trust and restore its prestige. He suggested that the separatist movement be declared illegal, its offices occupied, and its leaders arrested.[21]

Still, the government chose to do nothing. Given the movement's recent missteps, its inability to protect its offices or retaliate, and the rising tide of public opposition, Rome had in fact chosen the most sensible policy. From the government's point of view, separatism was in a state of decline, and might disappear as a viable force over the course of time. There was no need for a rash attack which might reverse the trend of events.

Separatists responded to events in the only way available to them, and launched a propaganda barrage. They accused the government of resorting to violence and of having destroyed the Palermo offices in a vain attempt to show the San Francisco delegates that the island's populace hated the movement. The national committee expressed its hatred of the Italian government and urged the population to remain calm. The "hour of revolt will sound," it warned. "We shall have our vendetta."[22]

Separatists also disputed the government's version of events in Palermo, charging that Christian Democrats and members of the Action Party had been part of the mob that attacked separatist headquarters, and accusing the Carabinieri and police of having led the assault against the fifty defenseless persons in the building, many of whom were beaten and hospitalized. There had been no retaliation, they claimed, because the government would have reacted by taking further measures.[23]

Finocchiaro Aprile again appealed to the Americans for help. He wrote two letters to Admiral Ellery Stone, the executive head of the Allied Commission, and two letters to the American ambassador, Alexander Kirk, blaming the Italian government for the destruction of the Palermo headquarters, and claiming that the incidents were an attempt to influence events at the San Francisco Conference. He warned that although separatists had tried to avoid disorders, after the incident, "serious reactions could be expected. The responsibility for any such reactions will lie exclusively with the Government."[24] To prevent this, Finocchiaro Aprile called for Allied intervention, appealed directly for American assistance, and praised the United States as "a great country of liberty which we love" and "to which we would like to unite our destinies."[25]

Attilio Castrogiovanni, secretary of the Catania provincial committee, and Giuseppe Tasca protested the destruction of their headquarters to Nester, handing him a letter informing him that they could not be held responsible for any retaliation caused by "hot headed members of their organization." Tasca also warned that separatists would revolt when the war ended in Europe and implied that they would be successful because "Italian troops in Sicily would have to be withdrawn to fight the Communist menace which would develop in North Italy." Nester merely accepted the statement as an admission "that the separatists were not strong enough to combat the troops which are now stationed on the island."[26] On the other hand, he disputed Aldisio's assumption that the movement was on the verge of disintegration, and wrote that "any movement or party in Sicily which has the backing of the Maffia will not disintegrate."[27]

On 6 May, the national committee met at Alcamo to discuss this newest crisis. Its members reaffirmed the decision to use legal methods even in the face of government illegality, referring to the Barone decision of November 1944 to show that the distribution of separatist propaganda did not constitute an unlawful act. The committee also used the opinions in the Di Natale case to show that the occupation of separatist headquarters could not be justified on the basis of protecting public security. Because closing the offices had created a climate in which reprisals were possible, the committee urged the high commissioner to reopen all of them, except the one in Palermo where there was an ongoing lawsuit concerning compensation for damages.[28]

These events led Aldisio to send Bonomi a surprisingly hopeful report in May. He was encouraged by the separatists' inability to recover their offices and their failure to act. Separatists seemed to lack direction, and the government had shown strength by denying them permission to reopen their offices.[29] Yet Aldisio still feared the movement. He characterized its supporters as seditious and violent radicals who sought to benefit from the disorder on the island, and dismissed the notion that they would accept federalism. He believed this was merely a maneuver to save themselves from public indignation and further security measures. Aldisio claimed that though the movement was all but dead, government inaction or indecision could resuscitate it. Stringent measures, including the permanent closure of all separatist offices, were needed. He had wished to issue such an order, but the government's failure to declare the movement illegal prevented him from doing so.[30]

In many ways, Aldisio's confidence was not misplaced. After the 21 April incident in Palermo and those that followed elsewhere, the separatist movement seems to have lost popular support as the Sicilian people became increasingly irritated with Finocchiaro Aprile and his followers. Despite separatist claims of non-cooperation, more youths began to register for the draft. In Messina, posters labeled Finocchiaro Aprile a Fascist and called for his downfall. More importantly, there were notable defections to other political parties. In places where the movement had been moribund, it all but disappeared. In locales like Palermo, membership decreased, while in other areas, members moved over to opposition parties. Even though an increase in membership was recorded in Catania and Messina, the general picture was extremely bleak.[31]

THE BREAKDOWN OF UNITY

At this critical juncture, the movement's followers desperately needed direction from their leaders. But Finocchiaro Aprile, the one man who could hold all the factions together, set in motion a chain of events that weakened his position and opened a fissure among separatist followers that would ultimately lead to the movement's collapse.

In spite of the anti-monarchical spirit of many of his supporters, Finocchiaro Aprile made favorable gestures toward the monarchy, hoping to regain the support of conservatives, many of whom now leaned toward autonomy while harboring monarchical sentiments. He hoped that perhaps they would accept a new platform—an independent Sicily with some form of monarchical relationship. It is difficult to evaluate whether this was a true reversal or simply another pragmatic shift in Finocchiaro Aprile's politics. Whatever the case, his actions proved extremely destructive to the movement.

In the first week of May, Finocchiaro Aprile sent a seemingly innocuous message to Prince Umberto: "Prohibited by local authorities any public manifestation, in the name of the Sicilian Independence Movement, I manifest to your Highness the sentiments of our jubilation over the complete Italian liberation." This simple message was, as an Allied source correctly estimated, "his [Finocchiaro Aprile's] outstanding political mistake."[32]

The telegram immediately caused a sharp drop in Finocchiaro Aprile's popularity and alienated his younger followers. In a 10 May meeting of the Palermo committee held at the home of Filippo Sanfilippo, a resolution was introduced criticizing Finocchiaro Aprile for his telegram to Umberto. Others wanted to expel Finocchiaro Aprile from the movement. Some leaders resigned in protest, while a group of militant Catanese separatists resolved not to deal with the crown at all.[33]

The strength of the reaction forced Finocchiaro Aprile to discuss publicly the reasoning behind his message. He explained that "the Separatist Movement has always sent its congratulations to the heads of governments and armies of the Allied nations for every victory achieved against Nazi-Fascism." The movement, therefore, could not fail to express its joy at the liberation of northern Italy "since many of our countrymen are scattered throughout that area." He did not, however, send a message to the prime minister, who had repeatedly insulted the movement.[34]

Separatist leaders denied that the message signaled a change in policy, and repeated that they would continue to pursue republican ends. But as reaction against the message continued to mount, separatists claimed that the pro-monarchist stance represented another avenue to Sicilian independence, for monarchists would help them gain control over high administrative positions on the island. Once free, the new Sicilian state would become a republic.[35]

Although one separatist writer characterized Finocchiaro Aprile's telegram as a spontaneous act, this is unlikely.[36] Negotiations between supporters of the movement and monarchists had been progressing for several months, and for a moment it appeared that the two sides might come to some sort of agreement. Lucio Tasca had been the primary catalyst behind these discussions. Tasca was a long-term supporter of the monarchy, and had backed the republican platform of the movement simply as a political diversion. He had, according to reports, used the movement to gain time to build support for an independent Sicily with a monarchist government, and to insure that the institutional question remained unsolved until the right moment. By mid-1945, Tasca no longer believed that a "republican" inspired separatist revolt would succeed. Moreover, with men like Canepa in command, the revolution might bring unwanted change to the island. Thus even as he bargained with the government and the mafia, Tasca sought a monarchist solution to the separatist crisis. He therefore allied himself to members of the nobility who supported the monarchy and hoped to obtain a broad range of autonomy for Sicily.[37]

As early as March, Tasca had been made aware of a secret plan to unite the monarchist and separatist movements. Supporters of this initiative believed that the best way to solve the crisis was by forming an independent Sicily that would have a "personal union" with the Italian sovereign. Tasca informed Finocchiaro Aprile of this scheme, and told him that the "movement would be destroyed by the hostile attitudes of the Allied and Italian governments." Upset by the lack of a positive response from the Allied powers to his past protests, Finocchiaro Aprile relented and gave Tasca permission to go on with the contacts. Some secret talks did occur in March with a representative of the monarchy, and it appeared that Umberto approved the plans.[38]

The telegram to Umberto paved the way for better relations and in May, two representatives of the monarchy came to Palermo to meet with Finocchiaro Aprile, Bruno di Belmonte, and Vizzini. The monarchists appealed to the men to support the monarchy "in exchange for a wide autonomy in Sicily and a limited recognition of the movement." They told Vizzini, however, that Umberto could not recognize Finocchiaro Aprile and that the movement had to select another leader before an agreement could be made. Vizzini objected, claiming that his supporters had committed themselves to a "Republican-Democracy." Undaunted by Vizzini's hesitation, the monarchists suggested that separatists send a "secret mission" to talk with Umberto in Rome and that they arrange transportation with General Berardi, who was considered a prime link to the crown.[39]

In late May, a Tasca contact spoke with Umberto, who seemed interested in the Sicilian situation but objected to the San Francisco Declaration. Though talks continued into June, Umberto proved too timid to act, and there were too many differences to overcome. Moreover, mafia chiefs had refused to depose Finocchiaro Aprile and replace him with Orlando, about whom they had doubts. After Orlando had visited Palermo in March, mafia leaders and separatists had held a series of meetings. They discussed which man to support, but could not come to a clear-cut decision. The mafia leaders could afford to delay, however, because they had been gaining in prestige ever since announcing their support for their modified form of separatism.[40] Thus, they were in the strongest possible position to decide the island's future.

In spite of misgivings, in June, Vizzini and the mafia decided to retain Finocchiaro Aprile as head of the movement.[41] To regain the mafia's support, Finocchiaro Aprile might have promised to support autonomy or assured mafia chieftains about their position in the new Sicilian state. He might have also promised to restrain Canepa and EVIS or, more ominously, agreed to allow the criminal organization to plan Canepa's death. Whatever the bargain, Finocchiaro Aprile had lost his independence, and the movement had finally become what its detractors had always claimed—a movement supported by and established for the preservation of the conservative order in Sicily.

For mafia chieftains, supporting Finocchiaro Aprile was the price of rejecting Orlando. Evidently, the decision was final and some individuals who had supported the Castellano initiative hinted to Italian officials that Umberto should meet with Finocchiaro Aprile to discuss the Sicilian question.[42]

Although Finocchiaro Aprile had weathered another storm, his flirtation with the monarchy further splintered the movement. Young supporters who had called for revolution in late 1944 and early 1945 were especially disillusioned. They had been repeatedly disappointed by the failure of separatist leaders to act. They now accused Finocchiaro Aprile and others of treason. Many left the movement, especially from the ranks of the Lega Giovanile. Some of the more extreme leaders to whom the youth had allegiance, such as Concetto Gallo, took matters into their own hands. Gallo went into the mountains to organize a fighting force to carry out the separatist revolution while Francesco Restuccia, reportedly also split from Finocchiaro Aprile.[43]

Some separatist leaders chose another option. Frightened by growing anti-separatist sentiment, the pro-monarchical drift, and the government's strength, some of the most important local leaders now retired from active participation in the movement, leaving a void at a crucial moment.[44]

Other leaders sought to save themselves by negotiating with the government. Varvaro tried to strike a bargain with Aldisio that would reopen the movement's offices and allow publication of a newspaper. He spoke to Aldisio about turning the movement toward federalism and eliminating any foreign influence. Varvaro was willing to rule out foreign intervention or internal violence as a means to accomplish independence. Instead, he promised, the movement's activities would concentrate on structural and legal discussions with the government.

Aldisio replied that he needed a binding statement in order to change government policy. Varvaro presented him with such a letter, but Aldisio decided that it was not explicit enough, and asked Varvaro to accompany him to Rome to discuss the matter.[45] Varvaro accepted the offer, but did nothing until the summer of 1945.

Aldisio's hopes that separatism could be channeled into a unitarian or lawful movement were soon dashed. Although the national committee still existed, it had declined in importance. Technically, Finocchiaro Aprile remained its head and it still included the representatives of the movement's provincial sections. But, as evidence of separatism's regional appeal and declining fortunes, Trapani, Agrigento, Caltanissetta, and Enna had no representation. Committee members included separatist luminaries such as Varvaro, Attilio Castrogiovanni, Cesare Bruno di Belmonte, Santi Rindone, Luigi La Rosa, Concetto Gallo, and Raffaele Di Martino. The committee had not met for some time and following Finocchiaro Aprile's pro-monarchist actions, its prestige had dipped.[46]

To prevent further deterioration, restrict Finocchiaro Aprile, and centralize the movement's direction in the hands of the strongest separatist cadre, the "Pentarchy" was created in mid-1945. The Pentarchy included five of the most important remaining separatist leaders from Palermo: Varvaro, Attilio Castrogiovanni, Salvo Di Matteo, Lucio Tasca, and Pasquale Ameduri. This move was a compromise designed to halt an effort by other separatists to replace Finocchiaro Aprile with a triumvirate of Varvaro, Bruno di Belmonte, and Edoardo Millemaggi. Such a coalition would have reinforced the movement's anti-monarchical and leftist character and would have offended the conservatives who had just confirmed Finocchiaro Aprile's position.[47]

This reorganization actually created further friction. Catanese separatists objected to the Pentarchy because it did not include one of their own. Since they also disagreed with the pro-monarchist stance, the Catanese found themselves isolated from the Palermo branch. To accentuate their autonomy, Catanese separatists organized an intelligence service headed by Concetto Gallo. The office operated without regard to the national committee and Pentarchy. Gallo explained that the bureau was needed because "we must be in a position to report on even Finocchiaro Aprile and for that reason we need complete independence."[48]

Although Varvaro remained on the Pentarchy, all signs suggested that the movement was headed in a more conservative direction. Thus, in mid-1945, many so called "left" separatist factions vanished from the scene, including Vacirca's Sicilian Socialist Federation. Furthermore, by this time, Varvaro's efforts to create a separatist-leaning Sicilian Socialist Party had also failed.[49]

By mid-1945, the Sicilian crisis was moving rapidly toward its climax. In June 1945, Ferruccio Parri, leader of the Action Party, formed a new government. Despite a multitude of economic and political difficulties, the institutional question and scheduled elections for the Constituent Assembly took precedence. Discussion of these matters forced separatist leaders to be more specific in their pronouncements, and, as a result, they exhibited their differences and the lack of cohesion among their followers. Increasingly, Antonio Canepa and his EVIS units emerged as the last hope of those who wanted an independent Sicilian republic.

10

The State Acts

By April 1945, officials in Rome had concluded that EVIS represented a real threat to island stability. Once authorities were alerted to EVIS activity, they acted to prevent what they thought were preparations for a revolt by Canepa and his followers.[1]

On 13 April, Canepa and four EVIS soldiers left Catania and headed toward the commune of Cesarò near Messina. They apparently set up a camp there and circulated in the general vicinity. On 17 May, the prefect of Messina received a report that a band of approximately fifty armed separatists had been sighted in Biviera, a town in the commune of Cesarò. After a few days, the band was sighted in the Sambuchello area, where they occupied an unused forestry guard barracks.[2]

In this locale, the EVIS soldiers established an arms cache for later use. Government officials soon learned about the depository in conjunction with rumors that some 200 separatists planned to meet in Cesarò and, with the aid and collaboration of other bands, march on Palermo. On 31 May, about 400 Italian soldiers raided the munitions dump. No EVIS soldiers were there, but authorities did seize ammunition, arms, food, and equipment. More importantly, they confiscated many documents, some of which described the organization of the armed bands and EVIS. The information confirmed that separatists had informants in state offices on the island and in the army. It even appeared that a member of the Italian General Staff on leave in Catania had expressed an interest in helping to organize the separatist armed forces.[3]

From their intelligence, officials concluded that EVIS activities centered in the provinces of Palermo, Messina, Catania, and Enna. Police faced great difficulties, however, locating or capturing EVIS soldiers. Aid given by separatist sympathizers in the countryside and cities rendered ordinary search techniques useless. Military units, acting without professional or technical advice, were consistently frustrated in their efforts.[4] But the authorities now had a clear picture of EVIS and developed a plan to render it impotent by arresting Canepa, his closest aide Carmelo Rosano, and Attilio Castrogiovanni, an EVIS supporter.[5]

THE DEATH OF CANEPA

The authorities organized roadblocks in the four provinces. Canepa, ever wary of capture, shifted his location often. At first, he tried to work his way to Bronte where he believed he could find shelter. The presence of a Carabinieri group forced him to return to Catania. On 10 June, he went to Cesarò to hide some arms and a few days later met with some of his followers who wished to make a punitive raid against the mayor of Cesarò, who was holding the family of Salvatore Schifani, an EVIS sponsor. An attack planned for 16 June was aborted, because the van to be used developed mechanical difficulties. Canepa decided that the next day, he and his cohorts would go to Francovilla to retrieve some arms.[6]

According to official reports, at 8:00 A.M. on 17 June the van, filled with six people, including Canepa and Rosano, approached the Carabinieri roadblock at Randazzo. Despite a signal to stop, the vehicle accelerated and crashed through the blockade. Security forces reportedly shot into the air as a warning, but the vehicle continued. Those in the van returned fire and slightly wounded two of the security personnel. A grenade that was about to be tossed by one of the men inside exploded, wounding two of the passengers. Once the van stopped, two EVIS followers exited and prepared to throw hand grenades, but before they could do so, they were shot by the Italian forces. Despite their serious wounds, they managed to flee the scene and disappear. Canepa and Rosano were found with the vehicle. Both were wounded, and Canepa could not respond to any questions. In the van the military found weapons, equipment, and money.[7]

By the time Canepa arrived at the hospital in Randazzo, he was dead. Rosano and Giuseppe Giudice, another EVIS soldier, also died from their wounds. Immediately after the incident, the military launched a giant manhunt, but the other participants had fled into hiding.

There are varying accounts of the episode. The driver of the van admitted accelerating the vehicle when asked to stop, and claimed that although Canepa had not given any orders to fire, he did have some words with the Carabinieri marshal while passing the blockade. Shots then rang out and the vehicle stopped only after it had rounded a curve in the road. He saw that Canepa and Rosano had been badly wounded, while two other youths had managed to flee. The driver claimed that he had dropped the injured men with some people and asked that they be taken to the hospital, but the men were thought to be common bandits and help was slow in arriving.[8]

Separatists claimed that Canepa and his people had fired only in response to an attack by government officials, who had continued shooting even after they had seen that Rosano was wounded. Moreover, the vehicle's driver had maintained his composure during the hail of gunfire and had taken Rosano to get medical assistance.[9]

Separatists made Canepa a martyr. In religious ceremonies, they extolled his courage and treated him and the other dead men as heroes. Separatist propaganda claimed that the government had set up its blockades to hunt down the men and kill them. Canepa and the others had been ambushed and had sacrificed their lives for the freedom of the fatherland. Separatist statements urged Sicilians to take revenge against the authorities.[10]

There are a number of theories as to who was responsible for Canepa's death. The most outlandish claims involve the British secret service, for which Canepa had worked. It was rumored that the British wanted separatist leaders to hand over Canepa as a compromise with the government. British intelligence feared Canepa's leftist views and his knowledge about their organization. Reportedly, separatist leaders accepted the deal and gave the mafia responsibility for the murder.

A more believable theory is that Canepa's assassination was either the end result of Finocchiaro Aprile's deal with the mafia or a decision by mafiosi and conservative separatists to end what they recognized as a threat to the status quo. The mafia eliminated Canepa because it served their interests and those of the established order. It made sense that the death of a Marxist-separatist would provoke little outcry from government officials. It is reasonable to assume, therefore, that mafia figures and conservative separatists aided the Carabinieri in locating and killing Canepa. In fact, it appears that the Carabinieri knew of Canepa's travel plans and set up a well-organized ambush. At least one account of the incident claimed that Canepa and his companions were cut down in a hail of gunfire as they left the van after it had stopped.[11] Canepa should have been able to protect himself through the system of informants that separatists had within the army and the bureaucracy. He might have delayed his mission or changed his route had he been made aware of the roadblocks. Certainly, other separatists, such as Giuseppe Tasca, Concetto Gallo, and Guglielmo di Carcaci, evaded these checkpoints and eluded capture as they tried to rebuild EVIS. All the evidence indicates that someone or some group betrayed Antonio Canepa and that his murder was a well-planned trap constructed by Italian officials, conservative separatists, and the mafia.

Nester clearly understood the significance of Canepa's death. Within days of the incident he wrote, "EVIS is not an organized army nor can it be considered the cadre of a future army to be organized by the separatists." He urged that "in order to estimate the efficiency of EVIS, one should distinguish between the armed bands and the weapons cache."[12] Some Italian authorities agreed that Canepa's death crippled EVIS, while others correctly predicted a merger between the island's bandits and the remnants of the separatist force. The bandits would profit from such an alliance, because they would be able to conduct their operations under the guise of separatism. Such an occurrence would have serious consequences for the military, since the bandits fought differently than EVIS. Military authorities, therefore, called for decisive action against the brigands.[13]

Following Canepa's death, authorities initiated a full-blown campaign against what were believed to be EVIS formations and supporters. Messina and Catania became the main theaters of operation. Several minor separatists were quickly arrested, including Vincenzo and Antonio Oddo, who were accused of kidnaping and extortion. Police also confiscated weapons and munitions from their homes. In other searches, authorities located information detailing the formation of the armed bands, including a list of fourteen names and particulars on EVIS members. In another investigation, police found a letter directed to a group of criminals in which separatists asked for their assistance. The letter promised the bandits that they would receive the rank of officer in the army of the future Sicilian republic. The letter also claimed that Salvatore Giuliano's band had already reached an agreement with the separatists. Still other papers documented the roles of Gallo, La Rosa, and di Carcaci as promoters and organizers of the armed bands.[14]

The raids and arrests destroyed EVIS formations in and around Cesarò. EVIS soldiers were either dispersed or captured, and the arms that the military seized were reported to be all that the separatists in the area possessed. Searches to apprehend any remnants of EVIS in Messina continued as the government tried to completely cripple the separatist army's ability to reform and retaliate.[15]

In Catania province the government was less successful. In Randazzo, 300 separatists had reportedly gathered with the intention of avenging Canepa's death. Panicked by this report, authorities sent out a force of soldiers and a group of armed carriers. These units conducted a fruitless search without finding any trace of such a unit.[16]

Canepa's death frightened many separatist leaders into renouncing EVIS and the use of violence. The executive committee declared that EVIS had always been estranged from it, while in Messina, Finocchiaro

Aprile now cautioned that the movement could not achieve success through force. Instead, he urged his followers to limit their activity to propaganda.[17] He also made it clear that he adamantly opposed the formation of armed bands composed of young men controlled by other leaders.

Some separatist leaders continued to be defiant. Guglielmo di Carcaci received a proposal by the prefect of Catania that EVIS followers lay down their arms. But because it carried no guarantee of immunity for the former soldiers, di Carcaci refused to accept it. Less strident separatists, however, like Santi Rindone, wanted to accept the offer.[18]

On 30 July, Varvaro and Lucio Tasca arrived in Trapani and held lengthy discussions with several individuals, including the former prefect of Palermo, Paolo D'Antoni. Varvaro, who had supported the use of EVIS as long as it was controlled by Canepa, now changed his position. He feared that the separatist army might now be used as tool by conservative separatists against progressive forces on the island. The prefect of Trapani believed that separatist leaders were discussing the reorganization of EVIS in their meeting with D'Antoni, but Varvaro and Tasca actually wanted to dismantle EVIS or convince its followers to renounce violence.[19]

SALVATORE GIULIANO, SEPARATIST

Those seeking to rebuild EVIS made a concerted effort to conclude an agreement with the island's bandits. Guglielmo di Carcaci and Gallo were at the forefront of this undertaking. They conducted their efforts under extreme pressure, since they were the subjects of a massive manhunt. They eluded capture by constantly moving from place to place and hiding in the homes of supporters. They also understood that they did not have time to recruit and train an army. Therefore, they turned to the bandits who already possessed arms and a willingness to use them.

Their efforts brought the most famous Sicilian bandit, Salvatore Giuliano, into the separatist camp. Giuliano had begun his career of crime in September 1943 when he killed a Carabiniere who had caught him illegally transporting grain. Until the beginning of 1945, he had simply been another in a long line of brigands who controlled the Sicilian countryside. He was something of a hero to the peasants, who protected him while he extorted money and produce from the aristocratic landlords in the area.[20] By 1945, Giuliano had grown powerful, and his band virtually controlled the area around Palermo. Canepa had tried unsuccessfully to make contact with Giuliano to convince him to channel his efforts into the separatist struggle.

In May, prior to Canepa's death, Attilio Castrogiovanni, a separatist, met with Giuliano. Giuliano assured Castrogiovanni that he was a separatist by "instinct" and had always fought the state. Castrogiovanni, however, reminded the bandit leader that separatism was a political movement and that his actions would have to be governed accordingly. After this conversation, Giuliano agreed to work with EVIS, but no explicit partnership was established.[21]

The delay in creating a formal alliance might have contributed to Canepa's death because he grew impatient, and probably began to travel in order to make further contacts and conclude the agreement. Following Canepa's death, Gallo and di Carcaci approached Giuliano again. With Giuseppe Tasca's aid and the inadvertent help of an American official, the two managed to evade roadblocks and, after some delay, arrived in Palermo. There they organized a makeshift headquarters that separatists such as Giuseppe Tasca and Stefano La Motta frequented.[22]

Before their encounter with Giuliano, the two participated in a gathering at Lucio Tasca's villa. Besides di Carcaci and Gallo, Finocchiaro Aprile, Lucio Tasca, Varvaro, Sirio Rossi, and Vizzini attended. Two questions dominated the meeting: the movement's financial difficulties and EVIS. Although they had many ideological differences, these leaders agreed to try to hold the movement together. Since no final agreement on autonomy, or their safety, had been made with the government, the movement and EVIS had to be maintained. Despite the critical nature of the situation, the leaders failed to reach a unanimous agreement. When Gallo requested that he be given leadership of the military organization, he received Tasca's support, but Varvaro attacked the idea so vehemently that the session ended without resolution.[23]

Varvaro's opposition to armed resistance was not only based on his distrust of Gallo and Tasca, but was also the end result of negotiations that he was conducting with the government. This effort was an extension of Varvaro's previous discussions with Aldisio. At Varvaro's insistence, certain separatists planned to offer the Parri government a deal to bring peace to the island. The offer included a separatist promise to stop attacking the Italian government if Parri would enact Sicilian autonomy.[24] Negotiations between Varvaro and the government continued through July, and by August a firm pact had been made. Varvaro and Finocchiaro Aprile were prepared to go to Rome to finalize the negotiations. According to the agreement, the government would recognize the separatist movement and grant it equality with those parties not belonging to the Committee of National Liberation. In addition, it could participate in administrative elections scheduled for later in the summer and would have freedom of assembly and press. Separatists agreed to curtail their meetings, dissolve EVIS, and not disturb the public order. All separatists would be urged to turn in their weapons, but followers could maintain a policy of "mild government opposition." To consummate the agreement, Parri's government pledged to enforce autonomy while permitting the movement's leaders to take partial credit for the arrangement.[25]

Actions by some separatists dashed any hope for the bargain's completion and reinforced the perception that Finocchiaro Aprile and his followers were not trustworthy. Those who wanted armed confrontation had refused to halt their activities, thereby forcing the government to take radical countermeasures. Gallo played a leading role in demolishing the settlement. His desire to lead EVIS and emulate Canepa led him to assume the pseudonym of "Secondo Turri." He issued manifestos in that name claiming that there were still things to be done before EVIS could accomplish its purpose. He offered his life for Sicily's independence.[26]

Gallo also took the lead in completing the alliance with Giuliano. The historic meeting between the two took place some time between the end of August and the first ten days of September 1945. Stefano La Motta, Guglielmo di Carcaci, and Castrogiovanni (who was trying to reorganize EVIS in the Etna region) accompanied Gallo. They had a short discussion during which Giuliano's political sentiments were questioned, and the separatists explained their platform. The separatists made no explicit promises to the bandit leader, who remained cautious, wanting to discuss the situation further. Gallo stayed with him for two days, gaining the confidence of the bandit, who finally decided to embrace the struggle for independence.[27]

Giuliano's decision had little immediate effect on the political situation. His presence did not necessarily strengthen the separatist military because there was no coordination between Giuliano in the west and Gallo, who was building an EVIS formation in the eastern part of the island.

THE APPEAL TO THE LONDON CONFERENCE

Sicily's post-war fate, the movement's apparent willingness to use outside assistance, and fear of an impending revolution afforded the government a rationale for action. Finocchiaro Aprile aggravated the situation by telling his followers that 15,000 Americans were coming to take control of the island and supervise the plebiscite.[28] At other times he confided that after the war, Sicily would either be given a trusteeship administration, which would involve separation from Italy, or would be unified with Italy but militarily and politically occupied by an Allied power to protect the island's military installations.[29] He regarded any of these alternatives as acceptable as long as Italian control ended.

These statements forced the government to go on the defensive. Aldisio went so far as to call the commander of the American naval base in Palermo, who once again assured him that all the activities on the post were normal and that the "American people and government have not had and do not have any territorial designs, and have no intention of interfering with the internal affairs of the Italian state."[30] Aldisio published an account of his interview with the American commander, but most Sicilians had already adopted a wait-and-see attitude.

In September 1945, out of desperation, the movement's national committee issued a declaration to the London Conference of Ministers. The foreign ministers of the Allied powers had assembled to deal with a number of unresolved wartime issues. The manifesto explained that the separatist movement had arisen out of long tradition and as a reaction against Fascism. Separatism embraced men from all social classes and represented the wishes of the majority of the Sicilian people. The committee requested that a plebiscite be held under international supervision. The Sicilian people would use this vote to regain their independence. Using history as a rationale for independence, the document claimed that Sicilians had once had their own parliament, and because the parliamentary statutes had never been abrogated, Sicilians retained the right to recall the legislature. The vote in 1860 that united Italy and Sicily had been a fraud and since then, the Italian government had employed violence to subjugate the island. Sicily had been treated as a colony and had been the target of ever-increasing exploitation. Under the Americans and British, Sicilians had enjoyed new-found liberties, but this condition ended when the Italian government regained jurisdiction. Since then, separatists had lost their civil rights, and their offices had been closed or destroyed. They had been arrested and imprisoned without cause. All of these events had rendered the island's situation intolerable and made unity between the island and Italy impossible.[31]

The London Declaration was a senseless political maneuver. It had absolutely no chance of success, and strengthened fears that an independent Sicily might fall under the control of a foreign power. Furthermore, since doubts still existed about Allied intentions concerning

Italy, the government saw the London Declaration as a threat to the nation's territorial integrity.

It is not known whether any copies of the declaration ever reached the outside world. Although dated 1 September, the proclamation was still being finalized in mid-September. During a raid by security forces, many copies were seized, and Salvatore La Manna, a leading separatist organizer, was arrested.[32]

The London Declaration was not as well publicized as the San Francisco Declaration, nor did it elicit the same sort of reaction among Sicilians. It did, however, serve as another reason for the government to act against the separatist movement. The timing for such an action was perfect, because EVIS was in no condition to mount an armed struggle and the mafia chieftains would not risk their position to save Finocchiaro Aprile and Varvaro. Without Finocchiaro Aprile, there would be no leader capable of holding all the separatist factions together. The movement would come totally under the domain of the conservatives, none of whom were capable or popular enough to replace Finocchiaro Aprile.

Roundup

The government was confident that separatists would not react to the arrest of the leaders, for there had been almost no response to the arrests on 13 September of Attilio Castrogiovanni, an EVIS organizer, and Salvatore La Manna, the provincial president of the Lega Giovanile in Palermo.[33] La Manna was seized while carrying copies of the London Declaration and other documents, including membership lists from Palermo, the names of Lega Giovanile members, correspondence, and propaganda material. After La Manna's arrest, police searched the house of two other separatists, where they found Castrogiovanni, whom they had sought ever since the previous summer. Castrogiovanni charged that he was lucky to have been apprehended by the police and not by the Carabinieri, since the latter had orders to assassinate him. He was immediately transferred to Catania to await trial, but La Manna was quickly released.[34] Castrogiovanni was able to smuggle work for the movement from prison via his relatives and sympathizers, but none of his fellow separatists raised more than their voices to protest his imprisonment. In fact, other separatist leaders who feared imminent arrest fled into hiding.[35]

Encouraged by these successes, the government moved against the major leaders amid rumors that a separatist uprising was planned for late September. These suggestions gained strength with reports about the establishment of EVIS camps and the intimidation of people in the countryside by separatist bands. The appearance of a new armed separatist group, Comitato Siciliano Anti-Fascista Brigate Volontari della Libertà, (Sicilian Anti-Fascist Committee of Volunteer Brigades for Liberty) gave the government further reason to worry, although no one seemed to know to whom or to which separatist faction this group was loyal. Finally, the existence of a separatist radio station that broadcast a signal every evening further increased tension.[36]

Aldisio asked for assistance to destroy the station, and other authorities hoped that 2,000 men could be sent to the island to aid the beleaguered police forces, though some believed that this number was inadequate.[37]

A final plan of revolt did exist. Separatist military leaders had decided to leave EVIS members to their own devices until they received a prearranged signal for an attack. In such a case, they would carry out their actions in localities that were not heavily patrolled by military or police forces. They would provoke disorders in various centers and impede any massing by the military. Separatist activists would provide their own weapons, and it was pointed out that "there was not a family which did not have arms at home."[38] By fighting a guerrilla-style campaign, separatists would make it difficult for the government to destroy them.

To create further chaos, separatists planned to carry out lightning strikes against government installations, assassinate government figures and leading opposition politicians, and infiltrate the public security forces. They also intended to create civilian bands to patrol areas at night in the name of public safety. It was hoped that these bands would gain official sanction by protecting private property and would actually serve as auxiliary organizations for incorporation into EVIS.[39] The plan called for the occupation of police barracks and public buildings on 26 September. All actions would be taken in concert with the island's bandit groups to which promises of immunity and pardons had been made.[40]

Pressure on the government increased as dissatisfaction surfaced about the amount of freedom that Finocchiaro Aprile enjoyed. Public officials echoed these complaints and awaited specific policy decisions, while opposition politicians demanded firm action.[41]

On 25 and 26 September, Aldisio received two telegrams. One, from Prime Minister Parri, declared that the separatist movement had been tolerated for a long period in the hope that it would move to an autonomist position within a system of federalism. Instead, the movement had continued to propagandize against national unity and had demonstrated its intention to use violence. To protect public order, Parri authorized Aldisio to close all separatist offices, stop the movement's propaganda, and arrest and intern Finocchiaro Aprile, Francesco Restuccia, and Varvaro. Moreover, all signers of the London Declaration would be warned that they faced charges and arrest.[42]

A second note from the prime minister's office confirmed Parri's orders and insisted on the quick arrest of the separatist leaders and an immediate decision regarding the place of internment. The message also instructed Aldisio to concentrate his forces in the island's most important centers in case of a violent reaction, because in such an event, Aldisio could not expect immediate reinforcements.[43]

On 26 September, Aldisio met with the police chief of Palermo, the prefect of Palermo, a brigade commander of the Carabinieri, and the commander of the armed forces in Palermo. When Aldisio informed them of the pending arrest of the separatist leaders, all the participants balked, arguing that from both a political and psychological viewpoint it was the worst moment for such an act. The working class was discontented because of their miserable living conditions. The landed classes and the middle classes had gravitated towards separatism. This trend was especially alarming, because it was happening in places that had previously been immune to separatism. Aldisio was warned that the arrest of separatist leaders would lead to many small revolts and disturbances, making it impossible for the island's public security forces to maintain order. The presence of armed bands in the countryside further complicated the situation. An outbreak of separatist-backed violence would defeat the government's campaign to dissolve these bands.

Though many of the observations concerning the movement's condition contradicted the reports of the last few months, Aldisio agreed with them. He feared that arresting the leaders would create martyrs. If the government wanted the separatist chiefs taken into custody, all agreed that they had to be moved to a more distant locale. Since forces to combat a separatist retaliation were limited, Aldisio wanted specific instructions regarding his powers in the face of the expected reaction. Under these circumstances, Aldisio believed that warning the leadership and closing their offices would be harsh enough. If the government accepted his suggestion, then he wanted the option of arrest kept open so that it could be used later.[44]

Aldisio held another meeting on the morning of 30 September. The next evening, 1 October, public security forces seized Finocchiaro Aprile and Varvaro. Neither man resisted forcefully. Both were placed on the vessel *Pomona*, which quickly departed for the island of Ponza, which had been long used as a penal colony. Sixteen public-security agents kept the two under guard until they reached the island the following morning. Following their arrival they were informed that

Francesco Restuccia, who had been arrested in Messina, was also on his way.[45]

On 4 October 1945, Parri signed the order for the internment of the separatist leaders. The three were indicted for their leadership in the movement, and accused of working to subvert violently the political and social order of the Italian state. The government had deemed it necessary to act because the leaders' presence threatened Sicily's peace and tranquillity.[46]

The quiet that greeted the arrests reduced fears regarding an outbreak of separatist violence. Encouraged by the calm, Aldisio issued orders to the island's prefects echoing those sent him by Parri and calling for the energetic repression of all separatist demonstrations. He also told local officials to warn all provincial leaders that their continued activities would lead to indictment under the penal code.[47] In Messina, Palermo, Syracuse, Trapani, Ragusa, and Agrigento, separatist offices were closed and the leaders warned to refrain from their activities. A number of those whose names had appeared on the London Declaration denied having signed the appeal, and others promised to refrain from further activity. Only a small group remained defiant, and reaffirmed their faith in Sicilian independence.[48]

Three days after the arrests, Aldisio discussed the government's actions. The seizures had been delayed because officials believed the movement to be in transition toward acceptance of autonomy or federation. The creation of EVIS, however, clearly violated the Italian penal code. Rather than independence, most Sicilians favored autonomy, Aldisio declared, and an attempt to form such a movement in Messina was already in progress. As for possible retaliation from EVIS, Aldisio stated, "If I were to say EVIS does not exist I would be guilty of exaggeration, but I should not be far from the truth. There is certainly a central headquarters and a general staff of EVIS, but it is a general staff whose army is more on paper than in the field." The movement, he concluded, had only "six or seven thousand deluded followers."[49]

With Finocchiaro Aprile's arrest, survival became the priority of the remaining separatist leaders. Without his leadership, all cohesion among the factions disappeared. The end of the movement as a viable political force was at hand.

11

The End

REACTION TO THE ARRESTS

REACTION to Finocchiaro Aprile's arrest exposed the movement's weakness and isolation. The immediate separatist response was limited to a propaganda campaign that glorified the imprisoned leaders. Propagandists assured their followers that a revolution remained possible.[1] Opposition comment almost universally supported the seizures. Socialists felt that the government's action had freed the Sicilian people from the threat of bloodshed and revolution, while the Communists considered the arrests a victory for their side, though they lamented the government's delay in acting.[2] Despite the movement's apparent impotence, Italian authorities worried that radical separatists might take matters into their own hands and react with violence. As a precaution, several asked the government to take further anti-separatist measures.[3]

The British and Americans had been willing to use separatism as an ally during the invasion and occupation. By October 1945, their fear of Germany had been replaced by anxiety about Soviet expansion in the Mediterranean. Under these circumstances it was clearly advantageous to have Sicily attached to a non-Communist Italy. Finocchiaro Aprile and his movement were now expendable.

Nester accurately reflected the American and British view that Finocchiaro Aprile's arrest was the only way to end the separatist crisis. "It is hoped," Nester wrote, "that he [Finocchiaro Aprile] will remain in confinement indefinitely for he has done the Sicilian people much harm in the eyes of the world and if he should be released, he is not the type of person who can keep out of politics and the public eye. More than likely he would resort to his former methods and policies."[4]

Only George R. Gayre, the pro-separatist AMG official, protested the arrests, arguing that the movement represented the will of the Sicilian people. He attacked the government's characterization of separatists as Fascists and labeled the deportations as being in "good totalitarian

tradition." Gayre feared that British interests would suffer if independence was not supported, and warned the foreign office that "separatism is a genuine aspiration and it will be achieved ultimately at
whatever cost. If we support a Roman government we may find ourselves one day in a very difficult position. To make enemies of the
Separatists as we are in danger of doing might mean a very difficult
position should we have our hands full with an Arab League, and Russia and the Straits." Gayre was certain that "separation will come by
force of armed rebellion. The Separatists have the whole Mafia organization behind them and I can see no Italian government sufficiently
strong to stamp out the Mafia: they have unlimited arms and while the
archbishops are not on their side, the parish clergy are and that is
what counts with the people."[5]

Schism in the Mafia

Gayre correctly surmised that no Italian government would be
strong enough to destroy the mafia, but he miscalculated mafia support
for independence and Finocchiaro Aprile. Gayre was probably unaware
that although they had recently reaffirmed their support for Finocchiaro Aprile, for mafia leaders he was the only acceptable choice. Actually, the arrest of the separatist leader caused a schism in the mafia
and completed the shift of a major part of the organization toward
autonomy and the government.

On 21 November 1945, mafia leaders from Palermo, Trapani, and
Agrigento met in Palermo. Those in attendance included Paolo Virzi
of Palermo, Mazzaro del Vallo Bruno of Trapani, Sciacca Russo of Agrigento, and Giuseppe Cottone Sr. and Jr. of Trapani. Conspicuously ab-
sent was Calogero Vizzini, who was being "completely ignored" by this
mafia faction as a result of his "close association with separatism and
the fantastic ideas of Finocchiaro Aprile."[6] This small meeting was a
prelude to a larger gathering during which mafia chieftains would "discuss the future policy and program of the organization and work out
some coordination within their ranks which is not existent up to the
present time." Nester believed that if a meeting took place with any
degree of success, then "it may mean the foundation of the strongest
political movement which has yet existed in Sicily."[7]

This small gathering, decided that their faction would try to influence or control all political parties and candidates no matter what
their "political affiliation." They also reaffirmed their support of a federal system "which would embrace limited autonomy for Sicily and
other parts of Italy and result in a form of government similar to that

existing in the United States." They favored a republican form, but pledged to support the monarchy as long as Italy became a democracy. Most importantly, the group fully rejected Sicilian independence and pledged to work toward maintaining law and order.[8]

Within days, forty-seven mafia chieftains from throughout Sicily came together to reaffirm their rejection of Finocchiaro Aprile and emphasize their support of "administrative and political autonomy for Sicily."[9] They repeated their "intention to work and cooperate with the authorities in maintaining tranquillity throughout the island" and added that they did not "intend to back any one political party." Mafia leaders did admit, however, that they were completely opposed to Communism. Again, Vizzini was excluded from the discussions. He was tainted by his association with Finocchiaro Aprile and Lucio Tasca. Also, this new faction wanted nothing to do with either the island's bandits or EVIS, to which Vizzini and Lucio Tasca were thought to be connected.[10]

At this meeting a "steering committee" was chosen. Through a conversation with one of its leaders, Giuseppe Cottone from Trapani, Nester learned about the mafia's new strategy. Cottone claimed that the mafia would not cooperate with the Communist Party, but would seek to defeat it through "peaceful means." If necessary, he warned, the mafia was prepared for an armed struggle with the Communists, whom Cottone believed were the best-organized party on the island.

Cottone also claimed that Orlando had declared his support for political and administrative autonomy. If this was the case, Nester believed that Orlando would have the support of the mafia. More importantly, Nester correctly assumed that if the mafia continued "its present peaceful and cooperative policy," its prestige would increase and, "that organization may be expected to go forward with leaps and bounds."[11]

As for Finocchiaro Aprile, the new mafia faction proposed that the separatist leader be freed not to return to Sicily, but to live in the "northern part of the country." Ultimately the mafia faction discarded this plan and instead decided not to use its influence for his release.[12]

The mafia schism was an indication of the change that the organization would later undergo. New leaders would eventually emerge to challenge mafia traditions and alter the way in which the organization functioned. For the moment, however, the rift signaled the final dissolution of the separatist-mafia alliance. Instead, the mafia had shifted its attention to the future political order. Mafia support for autonomy made it a near certainty that the new administrative system could be instituted without much open opposition or much change. In this "new" Sicily, the criminal organization would have the opportunity to re-establish its power base by asserting control over local politicians and the economic infrastructure. The mafia's opposition to Communism provided a further measure of protection. No Italian government would challenge an organization that was its most reliable ally against the "red threat." The mafia cycle of recovery that had begun with the Allied invasion in July 1943, was now complete.

Alessandro Tasca also deserted the separatist cause. In November, he gave his "blessing and support" to the Movimento per l'Autonomia Siciliana (Movement for Sicilian Autonomy), which first appeared in Messina in September and in Palermo in late October. The founding of the movement was recognized as a major political event. It immediately gained a good deal of popular backing, and several former separatists, besides Tasca, joined and led it. Nester predicted that certain mafia factions with which Tasca "is in close contact," particularly those elements loyal to Vizzini, would cooperate with the movement.[13] But Vizzini was more absorbed in trying to maintain control of the mafia, and there is no evidence to suggest that he aided the Movimento per l'Autonomia. Moreover, the Movimento per l'Autonomia lost some following when it began to appeal too strongly to monarchists for assistance.

THE DESTRUCTION OF THE SEPARATIST ARMY

Radical separatists suggested that the arrests of their leaders clearly demonstrated that anti-separatism had no valid argument except the use of force.[14] Since the mafia had moved toward a closer association with the state, the separatists were left with violence as their only possible response. With Giuliano operating in the western portion of the island and Gallo in the east, the stage was set for the climactic confrontation between EVIS and the government.

The union between Giuliano and separatist leaders came to fruition in the latter part of 1945. Giuliano entered EVIS as a colonel and was promised that in the event of a separatist victory, he would be pardoned for his crimes and appointed to some position in the newly independent state. Defenders of the Giuliano-separatist alliance justified the agreement by claiming that Giuliano had been forced to become a bandit by the cruelty and injustice of the Italian state.[15]

Although an EVIS commander, Giuliano remained cautious about subordinating himself to the movement's leadership. He confined his activities to the western part of the island, while Gallo fought in the east. This decision crippled EVIS' fighting ability and forced Gallo to change completely his plans for a revolt and seek alliances with other island bandits.[16]

To complement EVIS, a military body was formed as an arm of the Lega Giovanile. It is unclear whether the two organizations operated jointly or separately. Even the organization's name was a mystery. The initials GRIS stood for either the Gruppi Rivoluzionari Indipendenza Siciliana (Revolutionary Groups for Sicilian Independence) or Gioventù Rivoluzionaria per l'Indipendenza della Sicilia (Young Revolutionaries for Sicilian Independence). Most sources agree that this auxiliary army existed by late 1945 when the last separatist offensive began. It appears that GRIS was meant to serve as the vehicle through which the island's bandits would be incorporated into EVIS. Lucio Tasca seems to have been one of the prime instigators in forming this organization; the leadership included Giuseppe Tasca, Guglielmo di Carcaci, Stefano La Motta, and Sirio Rossi, most of whom also had ties to EVIS.[17]

In October 1945, separatist military leaders decided to follow through on their plans for a guerrilla-style war. They hoped that the government would respond by ordering the arrest of all of their followers, thereby provoking a massive retaliation. In that event, more troops would have to be dispatched to the island, thereby demonstrating the government's inability to control the situation. Then, perhaps outside forces would intervene in the movement's favor.[18]

The campaign began when separatist elements attacked, occupied, and removed food and munitions from the Carabinieri station at Falcone in the province of Messina. Authorities struck back and recovered the arms and munitions, forced the separatist militants to evacuate their base, and arrested several people connected with the raid, some of whom had no clear separatist connections.[19] In other incidents, however, the government had a more difficult time quelling the separatist forces. On 16 October, a heavily armed band, possibly led by Gallo, attacked a group of Carabinieri at Niscemi. During the raid, three men were killed and two were wounded.[20]

On 26 December, Giuliano launched an assault on a Carabinieri barracks at Bellolampo. Heavily armed, Giuliano and about forty followers met at prearranged locations and then attacked the building. Little blood was shed, since there were only four officials in the quarters, and they hid once the firing began. After four hours of shooting, and painting separatist slogans, Giuliano and his followers returned to Palermo.[21] Giuliano hoped to distract the government's attention from Gallo in the east. But, rather than diverting its forces, the government planned an assault on Gallo's camp at San Mauro di Caltagirone, in Catania province, which reportedly contained the main separatist force. Government leaders were determined to crush Gallo's army before it could take the initiative.

Gallo had begun preparation of this encampment in late October. Elements from separatist factions in Catania, Messina, and Caltagirone came to the location. Many of the soldiers were armed with American- and German-made machine guns and automatic rifles. Rumors abounded about the imminent arrival of cannons or artillery pieces. Within the camp, the men were informally divided between those enrolled in EVIS or GRIS and those considered bandits. The camp contained an emergency clinic, and bandits allied to EVIS supplied provisions. The men were drilled and rigid discipline enforced, but desertions were commonplace. Although they arrived at the encampment full of enthusiasm, recruits quickly became aware of the dangers they faced. Furthermore, they were not paid, and many left the camp at night to return to their families.[22]

Appearances by separatist leaders helped to maintain morale. In mid-November, Lucio Tasca and Guglielmo di Carcaci visited Gallo. Tasca urged him to be patient because he was involved in important discussions with General Berardi, the island's military commander. Evidently, Berardi was serving as a mediator between EVIS forces and the police in an effort to avoid bloodshed. He and Tasca had decided to approach the government with a proposal under which EVIS members would be given an amnesty. In return, all remaining separatists would be "channeled toward monarchist activities."[23] Gallo told Tasca that in light of these negotiations, he would not take up arms. Gallo decided to take precautions, however, so that he and his men would not be sacrificed to insure Tasca's safety. Thus Gallo continued to plan an attack and met with Giuliano. Meanwhile, both Giuliano and Gallo's informers in the Italian command provided information about the military's plans.[24]

Gallo never had the opportunity to launch an offensive. The Italian government struck first. According to the official report on the battle at San Mauro, at 10 o'clock on 29 December, 250 Carabinieri and 350 men from the Sabauda Division made contact with approximately 150 EVIS soldiers. The separatists were reported to have fired first and killed some of the Italian soldiers. The battle continued for hours, but in the afternoon, Italian forces launched a mortar barrage and destroyed the separatist positions. Soon after, officials took Gallo and two of his soldiers into custody. The following morning, government forces renewed their attack, but discovered that the remaining separatist fighters had abandoned their positions. EVIS suffered two dead and several wounded.[25]

Gallo claimed that government forces had fired first and that he and a small squad had held off the enemy so that the bulk of his men could retreat rather than be sacrificed. Gallo took command of the volunteers and placed his flag in full view so that "God and the world would know that in Sicily they fought for the people's liberty." Gallo's troops continued to fight, but late in the afternoon, following the government's mortar barrage, the situation became critical. Gallo ordered his men to retreat, but his most loyal followers refused, and were captured with him. After the battle, he was taken to Catania.[26]

Those in retreat went to a farm near Caltagirone, and some of the wounded were later transported to the Villa Carcaci in Catania. At the estate, Santi Rindone examined the injured while Stefano La Motta helped move them to a more secure place because the estate was under surveillance. Later, La Motta was arrested for his actions, a move that left a deep impression on area separatists, especially those in Nicosia, La Motta's home territory.[27]

Italian agents continued their assault on separatists in eastern Sicily. On 9 February 1946, officials raided the Villa Carcaci, but failed to seize any separatist leaders. Other searches took place throughout the countryside. By maintaining the pressure, the government kept the remaining separatist leaders off balance and in constant flight, thereby crippling their ability to retaliate. Within weeks, authorities had completely stifled the remaining EVIS factions and "pacified" eastern Sicily.[28]

Giuliano, on the other hand, remained a long-term problem for authorities. He continued to fight the Italian government in the name of the separatist movement. His attacks gained worldwide attention and made him a legend. In January 1946, at Montedoro, Giuliano and his band fought a brutal battle with authorities in which perhaps a thousand separatists took part. His actions kept alive the vision of Sicilian independence accomplished through force of arms.[29]

Police and military forces were unable to destroy Giuliano's EVIS formations. In fact, with the aid of the peasants—many of whom saw Giuliano as sort of a Robin Hood—and the landowners—who feared him—Giuliano continued to operate almost untouched. But as more separatist leaders were arrested, his funds became limited and he was forced to find new sources of supply. He eventually alienated himself from the peasants and became a tool of the landowners and conservatives. In this role he was manipulated to slaughter innocent peasants in the name of halting Communism in May 1947.[30]

For the time being, however, Giuliano refused to disavow the separatist cause. He continued to believe that the United States supported the separatist movement and would aid him at the necessary time. Giuliano showed his feelings by forming the Movement for the Annexation of Sicily to the American Confederation. The organization existed solely on the basis of Giuliano's charisma, and had no American backing. In May 1947, he wrote to President Truman offering his services to the United States and requesting the President's support. He claimed that "his only aim is the annihilation of Communism in Sicily and the admission of that island as the forty-ninth state of the American Union." In April 1948, he again wrote to Truman proclaiming that although Russian agents had tried to enlist him in their cause, he remained committed to democracy.[31]

Except for Giuliano's continuing presence, the government's campaign to destroy the remnants of EVIS and GRIS was eventually successful. Leaders of the two bodies were arrested, as were many soldiers, often while moving to reinforce other bands. Those seized were imprisoned, isolating remaining cadres in the countryside. It soon became apparent that what remained in the countryside were not elements of EVIS but groups of common criminals seeking to take advantage of the continuing problems on the island. By March 1946, *Avanti!* could legitimately claim that EVIS had been broken.[32]

As the number of imprisoned separatist leaders grew and as EVIS forces repeatedly met defeat, conservative separatists and mafia chieftains who had collaborated with the government consolidated their control of the movement. They remained free by virtue of that cooperation and now moved to disown EVIS and purge the movement of its republican or moderate followers. In January 1946, when the national committee met, both Vizzini and Lucio Tasca were present.[33] Despite their leadership roles and suspect activities, both had remained untouched.

Following Finocchiaro Aprile's arrest, Lucio Tasca had become the recognized leader of the movement. In October 1945, he had warned that he had the power "to order an armed uprising" but wanted to avoid "bloodshed." On the other hand, he confirmed that he "would not instigate a serious revolt unless it had a reasonable chance of success."[34] Authorities considered Lucio and his son Giuseppe primary supporters of EVIS and the bandits, and held them responsible for much of the disorder. At one point Lucio's arrest was considered "a final solution" to the island's problems.[35] Following Gallo's defeat and the campaign against EVIS, Tasca had a change of heart. As early as January and again in March and April 1946, he claimed that he had no intention of supporting EVIS and that it never had any connection with the separatist movement. To further protect himself from criminal charges, he announced that the movement would never adopt illegal methods while awaiting the release of the separatist leaders. Other leaders followed Tasca, assuring authorities that they were trying to dissolve the army. Indeed, General Berardi was asked to ease the situation by extending a general amnesty to all those involved in EVIS activities, except for those considered common criminals like Giuliano.[36]

IMPRISONMENT AND RELEASE

At Ponza, Finocchiaro Aprile, Varvaro, and Restuccia lived under strict, but not harsh, conditions imposed by Italian security officials. A guard always accompanied them, and their mail and visitors were carefully screened. The three separatists protested to Italian authorities that the arrests were illegal, that their detention imposed harsh conditions on their persons and that their imprisonment violated their civil rights.[37]

In the eyes of government officials, "confessions" elicited from the three leaders legitimized their incarceration. All justified the separatist movement's existence and defended their actions. Finocchiaro Aprile claimed that the San Francisco and London Declarations had been issued because all other legal avenues for appeal had been exhausted. The separatist manifestos (on which his arrest had been based), were perfectly legitimate instruments of protest. Therefore, he had been imprisoned unjustly.[38] Varvaro complained that he had been wrongfully deprived of his personal liberty and the ability to pursue his occupation. He also protested that his health was adversely affected by his imprisonment. He admitted his collaboration on, and approval of, the London Declaration but stated that all the members of the national committee shared responsibility.[39] His actions, however, were perfectly legal.

In a meaningless gesture, the detainees drew up a memorandum addressed to the Allies defending the separatist movement and the formation of EVIS, attacking the Italian government as dictatorial and totalitarian, and protesting that the arrests had been carried out under an old Fascist law used to stifle political opposition. The seizures were timed, the statement claimed, to help the unitary parties in the upcoming campaign for the Constituent Assembly. The government had planned to arrest, intimidate, and suppress supporters of the movement, thereby assuring the victory of the unitary parties. Separatists pleaded that the Allies act in the "profoundly democratic spirit of English Laborism, the traditional and unmistakable liberal and democratic spirit of the heirs of Abraham Lincoln and Roosevelt."[40]

Procedures to free the separatist leaders began immediately after the arrests. In October 1945, Orlando went to Palermo and "promised" Lucio Tasca that the government would release the three leaders if he would come to Rome to discuss the Sicilian situation.[41] Tasca refused, perhaps because he was trying to cement his own leadership position. In a demonstration of loyalty, Tasca sent a protest concerning the arrests to Allied headquarters at Caserta. He asserted that the arrests of the separatist leaders were illegal and that they violated the authority of the Allies whom he considered the supreme power in Italy "in the absence of a legal Italian government." American officials took the appeal as a sign that the separatists were still not convinced that neither they nor the British supported the movement.[42]

Appeals were also made directly to government officials, including Giuseppe Romita, the minister of the interior. Separatist leaders assured him that the movement would follow a peaceful course once the leaders were released. In March 1946, they were freed.[43]

The erroneous belief that Finocchiaro Aprile had changed his position on Sicilian independence might have hastened his release. Rumors abounded that he had renounced his stance in a letter to the Italian statesman, Nitti, and some papers carried a statement that he intended to carry out peaceful propaganda during the electoral campaign, as well as a denial of any separatist allegations.[44] The rumors were all incorrect. Finocchiaro Aprile had not rejected the idea of independence and his liberation guaranteed that he would have time to campaign for a seat in the Constituent Assembly. At a 22 March meeting of the separatist national committee in Rome, with Minister Romita present, he affirmed that the movement's position had not changed.[45]

Finocchiaro Aprile confirmed his stance during a tumultuous welcome given him at the Palermo airport upon his return to the island. He chided the government for having believed that the movement could be destroyed by simply arresting its leaders. The state had failed to understand that separatism had popular roots. He assured his listeners that his policies had never changed, and repeated his demands that Sicily must have its independence before joining an Italian or European confederation of states.[46]

Restuccia also received an enthusiastic welcome in Messina. His arrival stimulated local separatists to propagandize actively and hold meetings. Their statements echoed Finocchiaro Aprile's platform. The return of both men, especially Finocchiaro Aprile, gave the movement a temporary boost and encouraged activity by EVIS remnants and separatist believers.[47]

Finocchiaro Aprile now realized that independence was an impossibility, but he hoped that by serving in the Constituent Assembly, he and his followers could fight for a system of autonomy that would provide Sicily the maximum freedom within the Italian state. If separatists could win enough seats in the forthcoming elections, they might have enough influence to dictate the form of autonomy.

Epilogue

The Constituent Campaign

Separatists had little impact on the first elections held on the island in over twenty years. Between 10 March and 7 April 1946, a series of elections was held to determine control of the island's local administrations. The results gave the Christian Democrats control of eighty-five communes and the parties of the left sixty-three. The remainder of the administrations fell into the hands of rightist groups.[1]

This defeat did not alter separatist plans to battle for seats in the Constituent Assembly that would ultimately decide Sicily's fate. But separatist chiefs were divided on the methods to be used and the policies to be followed. Factions had first surfaced during a "closed door" meeting held in Rome soon after Finocchiaro Aprile's release. Approximately thirty separatist leaders, including Finocchiaro Aprile and Varvaro, debated the movement's positions and policies for the upcoming elections. No decisions were reached, but the session was reportedly "quite animated."[2] Later, however, some separatists decided to pursue a campaign of intimidation that might sway voters to them and the mafia.[3] Mafiosi who still supported the movement contacted American officials for assistance and a number of separatists sought advice from Luciano, who had been deported from the United States to Italy in February 1946. Luciano was reported to be very interested in the movement.[4] Lucio Tasca and Finocchiaro Aprile discussed the formation of a single electoral list with Orlando. Such an agreement would have provided an alternative for those unwilling to support the Socialists, Communists, or Christian Democrats.[5] In Messina, however, a number of young separatists broke ranks and decided not to participate in the campaign until amnesty had been given to those accused of EVIS activities. They were angry with Finocchiaro Aprile for not having settled the issue upon his release.[6] To preserve a facade of unity, separatists temporarily abandoned their factionalism and on 30 March 1946 announced their intention to participate in the campaign with their own lists of candidates and a platform proposing the creation of an Italian state of independent republics.[7]

As the Constituent campaign progressed, cohesion could not be maintained. Some separatists continued to emphasize an anti-monarchical platform, while a large faction favored the king and an autonomy solution to the Sicilian question. A number of separatists sought to form a coalition with other monarchists to reconstruct the Kingdom of the Two Sicilies. Rumors developed that a separatist group would offer the crown to a member of the Savoy family. There were reports that the separatists, mafia, and Giuliano had pledged to support the monarchy and that a monarchist coup was possible if the republicans were victorious.[8]

The pro-monarchist faction was actually attuned to the desires of the Sicilian people. In late May, when Umberto visited the island, Sicilians made it obvious that they supported the monarchy. Umberto received an enthusiastic welcome and was carried through the streets of Palermo.[9]

In May, Tasca and Finocchiaro Aprile discussed the Sicilian situation with Romita. The interior minister pledged to try to bring peace to the island, while the separatist leaders refuted charges that the movement had caused local disturbances. They accused the police, the Communists, and the government of having committed violent acts against the movement. They also assured Romita that the separatist movement had no connection with EVIS. Following the meeting, Tasca received permission to reopen separatist headquarters in Palermo. This event seemed to symbolize a rapprochement between the movement and the government. Many leftists now feared that workers would desert their unions if the separatists resumed their propaganda campaign.[10]

During the Constituent campaign, separatists complained that local authorities or opposition parties, in particular the Christian Democrats, hampered their activities.[11] But despite this interference, separatists drew large crowds. The possibility of a separatist electoral victory frightened the Italian government and forced it to take radical action to undercut separatist appeal. On 15 May 1946, less than a month before the election, the Italian government granted Sicily a wide-ranging system of autonomy. Sicily would have its own assembly, president, and regional council. The assembly would be elected by universal suffrage and called into session by the regional president. Deputies would work for the benefit of both Italy and Sicily, and if members defied Italian law, the national government could dissolve the body. The assembly had exclusive jurisdiction over areas of Sicilian life such as agriculture, industry, commerce, public works, tourism, education, and the region's budget. The island would have its own police force, but would have no control over foreign affairs.

The plan of autonomy was designed to pacify and keep the island closely tied to the Italian state, and to put the issue of independence to rest. All acts passed by the assembly had to be in fundamental agreement with the needs and interests of the Italian state. Sicily's economic survival remained tied to that of the mainland. Many Sicilians doubted that the statute would ever be applied or respected by the government, while others feared that the law's application would not improve Sicily's condition.[12]

Despite doubts about autonomy, islanders refused to vote for the separatist movement in any great numbers on 2 June. The elections for the Constituent Assembly proved a resounding defeat for the movement. Its candidates received only 8.71 percent or 166,609 votes, and out of the 49 deputies from Sicily to the Constituent, only four—Attilio Castrogiovanni and Concetto Gallo from Catania, and Finocchiaro Aprile and Varvaro from Palermo—were separatists.[13]

Although separatists failed to dominate the elections for deputies, the pro-monarchist segment of the movement achieved a moral victory. While mainland Italians opted for the establishment of a republic, in Sicily over 64 percent of the voters favored the monarchy. The defeat of the House of Savoy left many Sicilians angry. These sentiments gave rise to fears that southern Italy and Sicily might secede from the Italian state, or that Finocchiaro Aprile and the separatists would stage a revolt and restore the monarchy in Sicily in some form. Actually, elements of the Monarchist Party did contact the Lega Giovanile, but with few concrete results.[14]

THE COLLAPSE

The electoral defeat accelerated the movement's final dissolution. Separatist supporters of the monarchy, who had restrained themselves for years, now made their feelings known openly. On 9 and 10 June, forty-five separatist leaders, including Finocchiaro Aprile, Varvaro, Restuccia, and Di Martino, met in Enna to discuss the movement's position in light of the election results. After several discussions, most of the meeting's participants came out in favor of the Savoy dynasty. Delegates argued that the referendum of 2 June had abolished the monarchy against the desires of the Sicilian people. Reversing their earlier stance, separatists now claimed that in 1860, the Sicilian people had decided that they wanted a unified Italian state under the rule of Victor Emmanuel II and his descendants. With the end of the monarchy and the establishment of a republic, Sicily had regained its sovereignty and right of self-determination.[15]

Other separatists openly rejected this position. A group of Messinese agreed that the union between Italy and Sicily had been broken, but argued that Umberto would never consent to be the king of Sicily after having served as king of Italy. Since a monarchy was impossible, the best solution was an independent Sicilian republic federated to Italy. In this situation Sicily would have some measure of self rule, its own parliament and constitution, and "free exchange with foreign nations." A heated debate between monarchists and republicans made clear the depth of the split.[16]

In Palermo, the regional committee planned to meet to discuss the dissolution of the movement, while Lucio Tasca attacked separatists who supported a republic. He accused Varvaro and others of having had their campaign for the Constituent financed by EVIS bands and the Giuliano family. He was so disgusted by their conduct that he threatened to withdraw from the movement.[17]

True to form, Finocchiaro Aprile remained relatively silent on the monarchical-republican split once it became controversial. Instead, he focused his energies on the Constituent Assembly, which held its first meeting on 25 June 1946. As a deputy, Finocchiaro Aprile waged a vociferous struggle for Sicilian independence. His behavior led the British to label him as "slightly crazy" and to note that he "seems to be treated by the rest as a bad joke."[18] While Gallo and Castrogiovanni lent support to his efforts, Varvaro did not. The secretary-general did not favor the pro-monarchist direction of the movement and disagreed with Finocchiaro Aprile's methods and ideas.

In the assembly, Finocchiaro Aprile repeated the themes he had spoken on for the past three years. He argued that Sicily and the rest of the Italian south needed a broad form of autonomy different from that proposed by the government. The proposed system would aggravate current conditions and leave the southern regions under Italian domination. Because he viewed autonomy not as an end, but as a first step to independence, he asked the Constituent not to disregard his plan, in which an independent Sicilian state would be joined to the Italian state in a loose confederation.[19] If nothing else, Finocchiaro Aprile disabused his critics of the belief that he was simply an opportunist. At this point, with nothing left to lose except the final struggle, Finocchiaro Aprile proved that he was the true separatist that he had always claimed to be.

While Finocchiaro Aprile fought in the Constituent, the monarchist-republican split tore the movement apart. Varvaro and others declared their adherence to republicanism, while Tasca and Finocchiaro Aprile supported the monarchy. These differences led some long-standing participants to quit the movement. In August, prominent separatists surrendered their local offices. Santi Rindone and Bruno di Belmonte resigned their provincial positions, and the Catania committee fell under the control of Gallo and Castrogiovanni.[20] In Messina, two groups appeared, one supporting Finocchiaro Aprile, and one backing Anselmo Crisafulli, a pro-Varvaro separatist. In both Messina and Ragusa, leftist separatists were cooperating with Communists against the movement.[21]

In September 1946, as a direct result of the republican-monarchical split, Varvaro formally resigned as secretary-general. He had attacked Finocchiaro Aprile for his work in the Constituent and claimed that the break between the two could not be repaired. He admitted that he and the separatist president had been "on different paths" for some time, but that he had remained in his position to help the movement. With Varvaro's departure, the Finocchiaro Aprile faction became a monarchist-conservative coalition. Varvaro, however, did not desert the cause. In early 1947, he formed a republican-oriented separatist group, the Movimento per l'Indipendenza Siciliana Democratico Repubblicano (Republican Democratic Movement for Sicilian Independence), or MISDR.[22]

Varvaro's resignation forced an internal reorganization. The remaining leaders wrote new statutes governing the movement's officers and followers. Simultaneously, new officials were elected. Finocchiaro Aprile was the only leader to retain his position, while Castrogiovanni, one of Finocchiaro Aprile's most fervent supporters, became the movement's new secretary-general.[23]

At the third national congress of the movement, held in Taormina from 31 January to 3 February 1947, Finocchiaro Aprile and Castrogiovanni used their powers to expel Varvaro and his followers. Approximately 400 people attended the meeting during which a controversy arose over Varvaro's admittance to the gathering. In his opening speech, Finocchiaro Aprile repeated the movement's desire to establish an independent Sicilian state and then made mention of a newspaper article in which Varvaro had accused Finocchiaro Aprile, Castrogiovanni, Restuccia and other separatist leaders of having monarchist tendencies and of being reactionaries. This comment brought shouts of disapproval from Varvaro's followers and led to fighting between his supporters and enemies. Once the brawl ended, Finocchiaro Aprile resumed his speech and asked those in attendance if they wanted him to continue to preside over the conference. As usual, the delegates gave him a vote of confidence. He later ended the meeting by proposing that a vote on Varvaro's admission to the congress be taken the following day.[24]

As the next day's session opened, Castrogiovanni announced that Varvaro had been expelled from the movement. Varvaro had been asked to appear before a disciplinary committee but had refused to do so because he did not recognize its authority. Castrogiovanni claimed that Varvaro lacked the proper spirit and attacked him for having withdrawn from active participation in the movement out of fear of being returned to Ponza. When Castrogiovanni finished his tirade, Gallo asked that Varvaro resign his position as a deputy in the Constituent.[25] The rest of the day's session was spent debating the institutional question. Separatists reiterated that once the island gained its independence, the people would be free to choose their own form of government. One speaker warned that continued discussion on the institutional question would divert the movement from its principal interest.[26]

During the meeting's last two days, Castrogiovanni and others outlined the main parts of the separatist program. The movement repeated its demand for the establishment of an independent Sicilian state. Separatists supported a democratic form of government for the island, wished to improve the economic status and cultural life of all classes and wanted to revive and improve local industries. Michele Crisafulli declared that any Sicilian, no matter what their political ideology, could join the movement. Members could be expelled, censured, or suspended for disloyalty or if they adhered to an opposition political party. He also discussed the internal structure of the movement, describing the functions of the communal, provincial and national organs. From now on, the movement's president could hold office for only one year and then face reelection.[27]

While the Finocchiaro Aprile faction met, the MISDR held its own well-attended congress in Taormina. Varvaro became the movement's president, while Enrico Mondini was selected secretary-general. Followers claimed that they were the legitimate representatives of the separatist movement, since they followed its original goals and platform. MISDR cells appeared in parts of the island and gained a fair number of adherents, with one section in Palermo province claiming 1700 members.[28] The formation of Varvaro's group marked the first time that progressive separatists could freely function to influence the island's political future. But it was too late to make a difference.

FINOCCHIARO APRILE RESIGNS

The existence of two separatist organizations split sympathizers during the campaign for the first Sicilian Regional Assembly and guaran-

teed the movement's final electoral defeat. Personal attacks against
Varvaro claimed that he was Giuliano's tool and intimate friend. One
note even claimed that Giuliano was protecting Varvaro's
organization.[29]

In the elections for the Regional Assembly, held on 20 April 1947,
Sicilians again disowned separatist candidates. Finocchiaro Aprile's
faction managed to garner only 8.77 percent of the votes or approximately 171,000 out of two-and-a-half million. Varvaro's branch won a
mere one percent. Out of the 90 deputies elected to the assembly, only
eight were separatists, all of whom came from the more-recognized
Finocchiaro Aprile group. They included Finocchiaro Aprile, Concetto
Gallo, Attilio Castrogiovanni, Rosario Cacopardo, Gaetano Drago, Gioacchino Germanà, Pietro Landolina, and Giuseppe Caltabiano.[30]

In February 1948, the Sicilian statute of autonomy became law and
ended the struggle for independence. Nevertheless, one last rebuff
awaited Finocchiaro Aprile. In April 1948, national elections were held
for the Senate and Chamber of Deputies under the new constitution.
Despite some internal opposition, a faction led by Finocchiaro Aprile
decided to participate, but not one separatist claimed a seat.[31]

Rejected by the Sicilian people, in April 1948, Finocchiaro Aprile
resigned as president of the movement. In a letter to Castrogiovanni,
he expressed bitterness and sadness over his electoral defeat and the
failure of the movement. He complained that Sicilians had demonstrated "on several occasions that they did not understand at all the
greatness or beauty of the cause which we fought for them."[32] In a
public notice of his resignation, Finocchiaro Aprile thanked his friends
and supporters for their assistance, and claimed that he was resigning
so that they could pursue their own political goals.[33]

THE LEGACY

Finocchiaro Aprile's retirement ended his role in the struggle for
Sicilian independence. Incredibly, some leaders still tried to keep the
movement alive. Lucio Tasca, Giuseppe Bruno, and Gioacchino Salamone formed a triumvirate and pronounced the movement a political
force of the center-right, and pledged to continue the struggle. Supporters agreed to participate in future elections for the Regional Assembly
but not in those of national scope.[34]

In July 1950, approximately 350 people attended the fourth national
congress of the separatist movement at Taormina. While many personalities had long since abandoned the movement, Castrogiovanni, Cacopardo, Bruno, Caltabiano, and Drago were still active. One speaker

admitted that in the past four years, the movement had accomplished little because of its weakness and factionalism. Participants agreed that separatist deputies in the Sicilian Regional Assembly should work to insure that the central government respected the principles of autonomy in its dealings with the island and resolved that the movement "would struggle exclusively for Sicilian independence."[35] For those separatists who remembered the tumultuous and hopeful days of 1943, 1944 and 1945 it must have been a sad moment.

Despite its failure to achieve independence, the separatist movement had a measure of success. Separatist pressure had forced the Italian government to initiate a new relationship between the island and the mainland. Autonomy represented the first sign of Sicily's new status as an integral and equal part of the Italian state. The new system was supposed to promote economic and social rejuvenation, but instead, Sicily remains one of Italy's poorest regions.

The primary reason for autonomy's failure is the continuing dominance of the mafia. Under autonomy, the mafia has flourished as never before. Mafiosi adjusted to changing economic and political conditions in post-war Italy and, just as they had done earlier with the separatists, they aligned with the dominant party, the Christian Democrats, and other national leaders. Christian Democrat politicians rationalized mafia support by claiming that it was a bulwark against Communist influence in the south. In return for electoral support, mafiosi received protection from and positions in the new regional government. They profited by steering government contracts to their own businesses and by using their monetary gain to expand their control of Sicilian political and economic life. In the 1970s, the mafia enriched itself through the drug trade. With their new-found profits, mafiosi extended their connections to the highest levels of national government, finance, and politics. Christian Democrats stood by as mafia leaders continued to extend electoral support while giving Sicily nothing but death and turmoil. Money bred greed, and mafiosi began to slaughter each other as they sought to control their newly found profits and power. What is more important, they turned on the Italian state in a drive for further influence. The revelations of government-mafia cooperation and a series of brutal murders in the 1980s and early 1990s finally convinced the Italian people and their leaders that the mafia was a threat to and not a pillar of national stability. As Judith Chubb has pointed out so clearly, the latest struggle between the mafia and the government was not an attempt by the mafia to "destroy the state," but was aimed at insuring "control of the state for the mafia and its political allies," thereby insuring "the continuation or restoration of a political status quo which guarantees the unfettered pursuit of mafia interests."[36] This struggle led to the collapse of the partnership between the mafia and the Italian state. But, it will take years of concerted judicial action combined with social, economic, and political reform to break the mafia's influence in Sicily and throughout Italy.

The corruption and chaos foisted by the mafia on the Italian people has contributed to criticism of the government, the repudiation of the old political structure, and a resurgence in anti-southern attitudes. The meteoric rise of Umberto Bossi is a clear indication of the discontent that many Italians feel toward their government and fellow citizens. Bossi, who became involved in the Lombard League in the 1980s, now stands at the height of national power. He and the Northern League, which is an umbrella organization for several regional leagues, are twisted reflections of the Sicilian separatists. Like Finocchiaro Aprile, Bossi relies on historical symbolism to justify federalism or separatism. He makes reference to Carlo Cattaneo and evokes memories of the twelfth-century Lombard League that gained independence for several northern Italian states after defeating the German emperor Frederick Barbarossa. Like Finocchiaro Aprile, Bossi's program is purposefully vague and flexible in order to maintain his broad-based but superficial support. At one moment he speaks of dividing Italy into autonomous "macro-regions" while at another he talks of separating the nation into three distinct states—Padania in the north, Etruria in the center, and a Republic of the South. Much like Finocchiaro Aprile, Bossi makes bombastic statements for political gain but is often forced to retreat from his most extreme positions. Finally, like Finocchiaro Aprile, Bossi is opportunistic and makes alliances with other political factions with which his league has little in common except a desire to govern.

The appearance of the regional leagues is the direct result of popular dissatisfaction with government policies. Bossi's middle-class followers resent the state's inability to deal with crime and corruption, and its failure to deliver the most basic services. But, unlike Finocchiaro Aprile, who argued that Sicily was impoverished because of exploitative national policies, Bossi and his supporters claim that as Italy's most prosperous region, the north has been mistreated because government resources are diverted to the south in return for electoral support. Northern League followers complain that the south is an economic drag on the nation and that it is dominated by corrupt politicians and the mafia.[37]

In essence, the popularity of the Northern League shows the fragile nature of Italian unity. And, while Bossi grabs the headlines and comes dangerously close to power, Sicilians remain restless as well. In the 1980s, as regional leagues flourished in the north, there existed in

Sicily a number of separatist factions of varying political orientation.[38] Their grievances were essentially the same as those of 1943.

Although the separatist movement of 1943 is formally dead and its leaders gone, the spirit and aims of Finocchiaro Aprile and his followers still exist. Until the grim realities of Sicilian life are improved, the thirst for independence will remain alive among the Sicilian people, at least in popular memory.

Notes

ABBREVIATIONS

ACS: Archivio Centrale dello Stato
  AG: Atti del Gabinetto
  CAA: Comando Anglo Americano
  CPC: Casellario Politico Centrale
  Gov. del Sud.: *Governo del Sud, Min. Int.*, DGPS, AA.GG.RR., 1943–44
  MI: Ministero dell'Interno
  DGPS: Direzione Generale Pubblica Sicurezza
  AA.GG.RR.: Affari Generali e Riservati
  PCM: Presidenza del Consiglio dei Ministri
  SPD/CO: Segreteria Particolare del Duce, Carteggio Ordinario
  b.: busta
  f.: fascicolo
  sf.: sottofascicolo
CIA: Central Intelligence Agency
FBI: Department of Justice, Federal Bureau of Investigation
MAE: Ministero Affari Esteri
NA: National Archives and Record Service
  RG: Record Group
OSS: Office of Strategic Services
Poletti Papers: Herbert H. Lehman Papers, Columbia University, Charles Poletti Papers
PRO: Public Records Office
  FO: Foreign Office
  WO: War Office

INTRODUCTION

1. A useful survey of Sicilian history is M. I. Finley, Denis Mack Smith, and Christopher Duggan, *A History of Sicily* (London: Chatto & Windus, 1986); see also M. I. Finley, *A History of Sicily: Ancient Sicily To the Arab Conquest* (New York: Viking Press, 1968); Denis Mack Smith, *Medieval Sicily, 800–1713* and *Modern Sicily: After 1713* (New York: Viking Press, 1968).

2. The classic work on the revolt is Steven Runciman, *The Sicilian Vespers: A History of the Mediterranean World in the Later Thirteenth Century* (Cambridge: Cambridge University Press, 1958); see John Rosselli, *Lord William Bentinck and the British Occupation of Sicily, 1811–1814* (Cambridge: Cambridge University Press, 1956).

3. Nino Cortese, *La prima rivoluzione separatista siciliana, 1820–1821* (Naples: Libreria Scientifica, 1951); Rosario Romeo, *Il risorgimento in Sicilia* (Bari: Laterza, 1959).

4. At least one author feels that unification was destined to fail because of differences between the Bourbons of the south and the Piedmontese of the north. Massimo Simili, *I siciliani vogliono il re* (Milan: Riunite, 1946), 10–11. On the "southern question" see Rosario Villari, ed., *Il sud nella storia d'Italia* (Bari: Laterza, 1963); Salvatore F. Romano, *Storia della questione meridionale* (Palermo: Pantea, 1945); Giuseppe Vella, *Gli orizzonti scientifici della cosidetta "questione meridionale"* (Catania: Moderno, 1934). For a brief treatment of Sicily's history and economic conditions see Giuseppe Gennuso, *La questione siciliana* (O.E.T.—Edizioni del Secolo: Rome, 1945).

5. On the post-unification period and the *Fasci siciliani* see Paolo Alatri, *Lotte politiche in Sicilia sotto il governo della destra* (Turin: Einaudi, 1954); Salvatore F. Romano, *Storia dei fasci siciliani* (Bari: Laterza, 1959); Massimo F. Ganci, *I fasci dei lavoratori* (Caltanissetta: Sciascia, 1977).

6. The literature on the mafia is extensive but uneven. See especially Duggan, *Fascism and the Mafia*, 1–91; Pino Arlacchi, *Mafia Business: The Mafia Ethic and the Spirit of Capitalism*, trans. Martin Pyle (London: Verso, 1986); by the same author, *Mafia, Peasants, and Great Estates: Society in Traditional Calabria*, trans. Jonathan Steinberg (Cambridge: Cambridge University Press, 1983); Anton Blok, *The Mafia of a Sicilian Village, 1860–1960: A Study of Violent Peasant Entrepreneurs* (New York: Harper and Row, 1974); Judith Chubb, *The Mafia and Politics: The Italian State Under Siege* (Center for International Studies: Cornell University, 1989); by the same author *Patronage, Power, and Poverty in Southern Italy: A Tale of Two Cities* (Cambridge: Cambridge University Press, 1982); Diego Gambetta, *The Sicilian Mafia: The Business of Private Protection* (Cambridge, Massachusetts: Harvard University Press, 1993); Henner Hess, *Mafia and Mafiosi: The Structure of Power*, trans. Ewald Osers (Westread, England: Saxon House, 1973); Jane Schneider and Peter Schneider. *Culture and Political Economy in Western Sicily* (New York: Academic Press, 1976); Salvatore Lupo, *Storia della mafia dalle origini ai giorni nostri* (Rome: Donzelli, 1993).

7. The more recent and scholarly literature accepts this interpretation. See Hess, *Mafia and Mafiosi,* 75–125; see also Chubb, *Mafia and Politics,* 3–9; Jane and Peter Schneider, *Culture and Political Economy,* 186–194; Blok, *The Mafia of a Sicilian Village,* 141–145; Raimondo Catanzaro, *Men of Respect: A Social History of the Sicilian Mafia* (New York: The Free Press, 1988), 42–43. For the "godfather" or "grand council" idea see Norman Lewis, *The Honored Society: A Searching Look at the Mafia* (New York: G. P. Putnam's Sons, 1964), 88–90. Pantaleone seems to imply that there was one chief leader in Sicily even while discussing regional mafias: Michele Pantaleone, *The Mafia and Politics* (New York: Coward McCann, 1966).

8. Chubb, *Mafia and Politics,* 3. For a discussion of these concepts see Jane and Peter Schneider, *Culture and Political Economy,* 186–192; Hess, *Mafia and Mafiosi,* 60.

9. For a discussion of these ideas see Chubb, *The Mafia and Politics;* Arlacchi, *Mafia Business;* Blok, *The Mafia of a Sicilian Village;* Catanzaro, *Men of Respect;* Gambetta, *The Sicilian Mafia: The Business of Private Protection;* Hess, *Mafia and Mafiosi;* Lewis, *The Honored Society;* Pantaleone, *The Mafia and Politics;* Jane and Peter Schneider, *Culture and Political Economy.*

Chapter 1. Sicily from Mussolini and Badoglio

1. Works on Sicily during the Fascist period include the following: Giacomo de Antonellis, *Il sud durante il fascismo* (Manduria: Lacaita Editore,

1977); Giuseppe Miccichè, *Dopoguerra e fascismo in Sicilia* (Rome: Riuniti, 1976); Pippo Ragusa, *Storia dello squadrismo fascista palermitano* (Palermo: Tip. Italia-G. di Bella, 1934); Pietro Nicolosi, *Gli "antemarci"a di Sicilia, 23 Marzo 1919–28 Ottobre 1922* (Catania: Niccolò Giannotta, 1922); Antonino Trizzino, *Che vuole la Sicilia?* (Rome: G. STEI, 1944), 9–38; Giuseppe Carlo Marino, *Partiti e lotta di classe in Sicilia* (Bari: De Donato, 1976); Jack E. Reece, "Fascism, the Mafia and the Emergence of Sicilian Separatism: 1919–1943," *Journal of Modern History* 45 (June 1973), 261–276; for Mussolini's comments see his speech in Palermo, 19 August 1937 in Edoardo and Duilio Susmel, eds., *Opera omnia di Benito Mussolini*, 36 vols. (Florence: La Fenice, 1951–1963), 28:240.

2. Massimo S. Ganci, *L'Italia antimoderata: Radicali, repubblicani, socialisti, autonomisti dall'unità a oggi* (Parma: Edizioni Guanda, 1968), 262–263; Renzo De Felice, *Mussolini il fascista*, vol. I (Turin: Einaudi, 1966), 409–410; de Antonellis, *Il sud*, 207; Reece, "Fascism, the Mafia," 261–262; Giuseppe Gennuso, *La questione siciliana* (Rome: O. E. T., 1945), 25; Marcello Cimino, Ettore Serio, Giuseppe Cardaci, eds., *La Sicilia nella resistenza* (Palermo: Quaderno di Cronache Parlamentari Siciliane, 1975), 79. As of July 1923, of the 500,000 members of the Fascist Party only 25,031 were residents of Sicily. Only in Calabria, Basilicata, and Sardinia were there fewer members of the party. See de Antonellis, *Il sud*, 207, 213. In the Fascist youth organizations Sicilians made up less than ten percent of the total membership. See OSS, *Intelligence and Research Reports, Part IV, Germany and Its Occupied Territories During World War II, "Italy,"* OSS/State Department, Washington, D.C. (A Microfilm Project of University Publications of America, 1977).

3. Michele Pantaleone, *Mafia and Politics*, 45–46; de Antonellis, *Il sud*, 205.

4. De Felice, *Mussolini il fascista*, vol. I, 409; Pantaleone, *Mafia and Politics*, 45–46; de Antonellis, *Il sud*, 198.

5. De Felice, *Mussolini il fascista*, vol. I, 457; de Antonellis, *Il sud*, 212–213, 219; Francesco Paterno, Duca di Carcaci, *Il movimento per l'indipendenza della Sicilia: Memorie del Duca di Carcaci* (Palermo: S.F. Flaccovio, 1977), 36; Reece, "Fascism, the Mafia," 262; Trizzino, *Che vuole la Sicilia?*, 10-12; Marcello Saija, *Un "Soldino" contro il fascismo: Istituzioni ed elites politiche nella Sicilia del 1923* (Catania: Cooperativa Universitaria Libraria Catanese, 1981). On the anti-fascist resistance in Sicily, see Ganci, *L'Italia antimoderata*, 260–262.

6. Cimino, et. al., *La Sicilia nella resistenza*, 79, 83; de Antonellis, *Il sud*, 213–214; Mack Smith, *Modern Sicily*, 509; Reece, "Fascism, the Mafia," 267.

7. Francesco Renda, *Il movimento contadino in Sicilia e la fine del blocco agrario nel mezzogiorno* (Bari: De Donato, 1976), 212; Pantaleone, *Mafia and Politics*, 46.

8. Cesare Mori, *The Last Struggle with the Mafia*, trans. Orlo Williams (London and New York: Putnam, 1933); Raimondo Catanzaro, *Men of Respect: A Social History of the Sicilian Mafia*, trans. Raymond Rosenthal (New York: The Free Press, 1988), 108–112; de Antonellis, *Il sud*, 214, 216; Pantaleone, *Mafia and Politics*, 49–50. See also Domenico Novacco, *Inchiesta sulla mafia* (Milan: Feltrinelli, 1963), 280–288; Lewis, *Honored Society*, 67–76.

9. American officials knew of Mussolini's anti-mafia campaign. See Edward Nathan to Secretary of State, "Italian Authorities Attempt to Repress Criminality and Mafia Organization," 24 March 1926, NA, RG 59, 865.108/

3; Nathan to Secretary of State, "Measures of Italian Authorities to Repress Criminality and Mafia Organization," 15 June 1926, 865.108/6; Nathan to Secretary of State, "References in Prime Minister's Speech to Eradication of Criminality in Sicily," 31 May 1927, 865.108/10. From the same record group see Nathan's dispatches to the Secretary of State dated 13 April 1926 and 15 May 1926 numbered 865.108/4 and 865.108/5; Henry P. Fletcher to Secretary of State, 26 October 1927, 865.108/11; and Warren D. Robbins to Secretary of State, 27 January 1928, 865.108/12. Lord Rennel believed that the anti-mafia campaign had brought it under control and into a period of decline but also warned that the mafia was one of the most important forces in post-invasion Sicily. Report by Rennel, August 1943, NA, RG 165, Entry 77, Box 1906, File 6960. Gayre, the educational advisor to AMG, believed that the mafia had been cleaned up by Mussolini's regime. George R. Gayre, *Italy in Transition: Extracts from the Private Journal of G. R. Gayre* (London: Faber and Faber Limited, 1946), 41. See also Lamberto Mercuri, "La Sicilia e gli alleati," *Storia Contemporanea*, 3 (December 1972), 949; de Antonellis, *Il sud*, 200. Chubb, *Mafia and Politics*, 23. For the entire story of this period see Christopher Duggan, *Fascism and the Mafia* (New Haven: Yale University Press, 1989).

10. Mack Smith, *Modern Sicily*, 518.

11. De Antonellis, *Il sud*, 200–201; Mack Smith, *Modern Sicily*, 520–521; Carlo Ruini, *Le vicende del latifondo siciliano* (Florence: G.C. Sansoni, 1946), 177–193.

12. His stay in 1937 lasted from 12 August to 20 August. Mussolini was reportedly welcomed by cheering crowds. De Antonellis, *Il sud*, 224. According to Ganci, separatist tendencies were already present and probably contributed to Mussolini's decision to visit. See Ganci, *L'Italia antimoderata*, 260. See also Cimino, et. al., *La Sicilia nella resistenza*, 14.

13. Ganci, *L'Italia antimoderata*, 268; Cimino, et. al., *La Sicilia nella resistenza*, 38–39.

14. De Antonellis, *Il sud*, 222, 225–226.

15. Canepa has gone relatively unnoticed by historians. The best studies of his life are Ettore Canalis, *Alcuni aspetti del movimento per l'indipendenza siciliana ed una breve ricerca sulla figura di Antonio Canepa*, thesis, University of Rome, 1974, 87–95; Salvo Barbagallo, *Una rivoluzione mancata* (Catania: Bonanno, 1974), 34–37; Giuseppe Carlo Marino, *Storia del separatismo siciliano* (Rome: Riuniti, 1979), 163; Filippo Gaja, *L'esercito della lupara* (Milan: Area Editore, 1962), 125; Ganci, *L'Italia antimoderata*, 262. Also see the article on Canepa in Cimino, et. al., *La Sicilia nella resistenza*, 35–39; Salvatore Nicolosi, *Sicilia contro Italia* (Catania: Carmelo Tringale, 1981), 50–65; Lewis, *Honored Society*, 140–143.

16. Antonio Canepa, *Sistema di dottrina del fascismo*, 2 vols. (Rome: Formiggini, 1937); Canalis, *Alcuni aspetti*, 96–97.

17. Cimino, et. al., *La Sicilia nella resistenza*, 37–38; Canalis, *Alcuni aspetti*, 98.

18. Cimino, et. al., *La Sicilia nella resistenza*, 36–37.

19. De Antonellis, *Il sud*, 225; on the invasion see Sandro Attanasio, *Sicilia senza Italia, Luglio-Agosto 1943* (Milan: Mursia, 1976); Carlo D'Este, *Bitter Victory: The Battle for Sicily, July-August 1943* (New York: Harper Collins, 1991); Emilio Faldella, *Lo sbarco e la difesa della Sicilia* (Rome: L'Aniene, 1956); Albert Garland and Howard McGaw Smyth, *Sicily and the Surrender of Italy*, The United States Army in World War II, Mediterranean Theatre of

Operations, (Washington, D.C.: Office of Chief of Military History, 1965); Michael Howard, *Grand Strategy, August 1942-September 1943,* History of the Second World War, United Kingdom Military Series. Sir James Butler, ed., (London: Her Majesty's Stationery Office, 1972), IV, 359–370, 466–475; Samuel Mitcham Jr. and Friedrich von Stauffenberg, *The Battle of Sicily: How the Allies Lost Their Chance for Total Victory* (New York: Orion, 1991); C. J. C. Molony, et. al., *The Mediterranean and Middle East,* History of the Second World War, United Kingdom Military Series, Sir James Butler, ed. (London: Her Majesty's Stationery Office, 1973); V, 1–169; Nino Savarese, *Cronachetta siciliana* (Rome: Sandron, 1944); Mary H. Williams, comp., *Chronology 1941–1945,* The United States Army in World War II, Special Studies, (Washington, D.C.: Department of the Army, 1960), 117–128; Gerald W.L. Nicholson, *The Canadians in Italy: 1943–1945, Official* History of the Canadian Army in the Second World War, (Ottawa: Queen's Printer and Controller of Stationery, 1966), 3–179; Gaetano Zingali, *L'invasione della Sicilia, 1943: Avvenimenti militari e responsabilità politiche* (Catania: Università di Catania, 1962); Mercuri, "Sicilia e alleati," 897–968; Elena Aga Rossi, "La politica degli alleati verso l'Italia nel 1943," *Storia Contemporanea,* IV (December 1972), 847–896.

20. Mercuri, "Sicilia e alleati," 914; Ganci, *L'Italia antimoderata,* 259; Howard, *Grand Strategy,* IV, 466–469. The loyalty of these troops had been doubted even before the invasion. See also Rodney Campbell, *The Luciano Project: The Secret Wartime Collaboration of the Mafia and the United States Navy* (New York: McGraw Hill, 1977), 134.

21. D'Este, *Bitter Victory,* 552, 597, 606–609; Howard, *Grand Strategy,* 475.

22. The FBI documents cited here and elsewhere in the text were obtained as a result of Freedom of Information Act requests made in the 1980s and 1990s. Mr. Tamm to Mr. Tolson, 17 May 1946, FBI, File: "Charles Lucky Luciano," 39-2141-40; A. Rosen to Mr. E. A. Tamm, "Subject: Charles 'Lucky' Luciano, Parole, Miscellaneous; Information Concerning," 17 May 1946, FBI, 39-2141-39. On the subject of mafia-U.S. cooperation see Campbell, *The Luciano Project;* Mercuri, "Sicilia e alleati," 955–957; Ganci, *L'Italia antimoderata,* 282; D'Este, *Bitter Victory,* 622–625; Attanasio, *Sicilia senza Italia,* 187–205; Martin A. Gosch and Richard Hammer, *The Last Testament of Lucky Luciano* (Boston: Little, Brown and Company, 1974), 262–268; 269–270. The Kefauver Committee investigated the matter in the 1950s but came up with inconclusive answers. See Estes Kefauver, *Crime in America,* ed. Sidney Shallet (Garden City, New York: Doubleday and Company, Inc., 1951), 31–32.

23. FBI, "Salvatore Lucania, with Aliases Charles Luciano, Charles Lucania, Lucky Luciano, Charles Lane," 13 March 1946, FBI, 39-2141-10. From the same source see E. E. Conroy to J. Edgar Hoover, 1 March 1946, FBI, 39-2141-8. See also Campbell, *The Luciano Project,* 23–53.

24. FBI, "Salvatore Lucania, with Aliases Charles Luciano, Charles Lucania, Lucky Luciano, Charles Lane," 13 March 1946, FBI, 39-2141-10. From the same source see E. E. Conroy to J. Edgar Hoover, 1 March 1946, FBI, 39-2141-8; See also Director FBI, "Charles Lucky Luciano, Miscellaneous Information Concerning Parole and Deportation," 9 May 1946, FBI, 39-2141-44. From the same source "Salvatore Lucania with Aliases, Charles Lucanio, Charles Lucania, Lucky Luciano, Charles Lane," 2 July 1946, FBI, 39-2141-46. See also A. Rosen to E. A. Tamm, "Charles 'Lucky' Luciano, Parole, Miscellaneous; Infor-

mation Concerning," 17 May 1946, FBI, 39-2141-39; Campbell, *The Luciano Project,* 83–110.

25. Memorandum to Mr. Rosen, "Charles 'Lucky' Luciano, Parole, Miscellaneous; Information Concerning," 17 May 1946, FBI, 39-2141-39; Campbell, *The Luciano Project,* 111–127.

26. Rosen to Tamm, "Charles 'Lucky' Luciano, Parole, Miscellaneous; Information Concerning," 17 May 1946, FBI, 39-2141-39; Campbell, *Luciano Project,* 143–147. Information was also sought in libraries and from veterans. See also Max Corvo, *The OSS in Italy, 1942–1945: A Personal Memoir* (New York: Praeger, 1990), 27–28.

27. Campbell, *The Luciano Project,* 133.

28. To Mr. Rosen, "Charles 'Lucky' Luciano, Parole," 22 March 1946, FBI, 39-2141-45. On the recruitment of Sicilian-Americans see Earl Brennan to H. Gregory Thomas, "Statement Relative to Recruiting of Sicilians in New York Area," 1 October 1942, NA, RG 226, Entry 142, Box 2, Folder 14. From the same location see the memo from Thomas to Brennan dated 28 September 1943. On the impact that Sicilians might play in overthrowing Fascism see Richard Rohman to Mr. Dewitt C. Poole, "Sicilians in the United States," 15 July 1942, NA, RG 226, Entry 142, Box 2, Folder 14.

29. FBI, "Salvatore Lucania with Aliases: Charles Lucanio, Charles Lucania, Lucky Luciano, Charles Lane," 13 March 1946, FBI, 39-2141-10; Campbell, *The Luciano Project,* 199.

30. Navy Department, Office of Chief of Naval Operations, Memorandum for J. Edgar Hoover, "Subject Luciano, Charles," 10 May 1946, FBI, 39-2141-43; Luciano denied having helped the American government or army in the invasion. See Gosch and Hammer, *Last Testament,* 268.

31. Campbell, *Luciano Project,* 176–177. The FBI's investigation of this matter occurred after speculation arose that naval officials who had dealt with Luciano during the war had helped him get parole in 1946. See A. Rosen to E. A. Tamm, "Charles 'Lucky' Luciano, Parole, Miscellaneous; Information Concerning," 17 May 1946, FBI, 39-2141-39; in the same location see A. Rosen to E. A. Tamm, "Charles 'Lucky' Luciano, Parole," 6 May 1946.

32. Richard Rohman to Mr. Dewitt C. Poole, "Sicilians in the United States," 15 July 1942, NA, RG 226, Entry 142, Box 2, Folder 14.

33. Exp. Det. G-3 Sicily To: Exp. Det. G-3, Algiers, 13 August 1943, NA, RG 226, Entry 99, Box 39, Folder 195A. For a discussion on the relationship between the Allies and the mafia as well as the mafia's rebirth see Salvatore Lupo, "The Allies and the mafia." *Journal of Modern Italian Studies* 2 (Spring 1997), 21–33. On the Action Party see Giuseppe Mammarella, *Italy After Fascism: A Political History, 1943–1965* (Notre Dame, University of Notre Dame Press, 1966), 48–50.

34. Exp. Det. G-3 Sicily To: Exp. Det. G-3, Algiers, 13 August 1943, NA, RG 226, Entry 99, Box 39, Folder 195A.

35. Ibid.

36. Ibid. According to Corvo, prior to the invasion the OSS had decided not to have contact with anyone connected with the syndicate because such a connection might prove embarrassing. See Corvo, *OSS in Italy,* 22–23; see also Emanuele Macaluso, *La Mafia e lo stato* (Rome: Riuniti, 1972), 65.

37. Exp. Det G-3 Sicily To: Exp. Det. G-3, Algiers, 13 August 1943, NA, RG 226, Entry 99, Box 39, Folder 195A. In the same location see "Report on the Activities of the OSS Group on Temporary Duty with the CIC from July 21st

to August 2, 1943"; Headquarters, 2677th Regiment OSS, U.S. Army, Italian Division, "Closing Out Report," 26 July 1945, NA, RG 226, Entry 99, Box 25, Folder 123. In December 1943 it was reported that American and British officials were cooperating with criminal elements on Sicily that were not considered part of the mafia. See Office of Chief of Naval Operations, Intelligence Report, "Italy, Government, Political Parties in Sicily, Maffia and Separatist Movement," 10 December 1943, NA, RG 38, Register No. 9632-H, File C-10-f.

38. For a complete list of the men who served in the Badoglio government, see Mario Missori, *Governi, alte cariche dello stato e prefetti del regno d'Italia* (Rome: Ministero dell'Interno, 1973), 152–155.

39. On the Forty-Five Days and British attitudes toward the Badoglio government, see Agostino degli Espinosa, *Il regno del sud* (Rome: Riuniti, 1973), 3–39; 53–89; H. Stuart Hughes, *The United States and Italy* (Cambridge: Harvard University Press, 1953), 127–132; Mammarella, *Italy After Fascism,* 19–59.

40. On this period of Italian history see Roberto Battaglia, *Storia della resistenza italiana* (Turin: Einaudi, 1952); Ivanoe Bonomi, *Diario di un anno: 2 Giugno 1943–10 Giugno 1944* (Milan: Garzanti, 1947); Benedetto Croce, *Quando l'Italia era tagliata in due, Luglio 1943-Giugno 1944* (Bari: Laterza, 1948); degli Espinosa, *Il regno del sud;* Norman Kogan, *Italy and the Allies* (Cambridge, Mass.: Harvard University Press, 1956). On the CLN in Italy see Charles Delzell, *Mussolini's Enemies: The Italian Anti-Fascist Resistance* (Princeton: Princeton University Press, 1961); Guido Quazza, Leo Valiani, and Edoardo Volterra, *Il governo dei CLN* (Turin: G. Giappichelli, 1966).

41. On the formation of AMG see Harry L. Coles and Albert K. Weinberg, *Civil Affairs: Soldiers Become Governors,* The United States Army in World War II, Special Studies, (Washington, D.C.: Department of the Army, 1964), 3–187; Charles R. S. Harris, *Allied Military Administration of Italy, 1943–1945.* History of the Second World War. United Kingdom Military Series. Sir James Butler, ed. (London: Her Majesty's Stationery Office, 1957), 1–29. As of October 1943, AMGOT became known as Allied Military Government (AMG). For this book, therefore, AMG will used as the designation for Allied Military Government.

42. Coles and Weinberg, *Soldiers Become Governors,* 153.

43. Harris, *Allied Military Administration,* 27.

44. Aga Rossi, "La politica degli alleati," 874; "Proposed Directive From Combined Chiefs of Staff to General Eisenhower As Commander in Chief Relating to Organization and Operation of Military Government in the Territory Involved in Operation Husky," undated, Poletti Papers, AMG General Files, S-3.

45. Mercuri, "Sicilia e alleati," 904–905; Coles and Weinberg, *Soldiers Become Governors,* 182; "Secret—Bigot, Headquarters Force 343," 9 June 1943, Poletti Papers, AMG General Files, S-3. For a critical examination of AMG see George C. S. Benson and Maurice Neufeld, "Allied Military Government in Italy," in Carl J. Friedrich, et. al., *American Experiences in Military Government in World War II* (New York: Rinehart & Company, Inc., 1948), 111–147.

46. Algiers to ETOUSA, "Incoming Message," 17 August 1943, PRO, FO 371, 37325; di Carcaci, *Memorie,* 21.

47. On defascistization, see Giarrizzo, *Sicilia politica,* 9–10; Coles and Weinberg, *Soldiers Become Governors,* 386–399. Sicilians had never fully accepted the Fascist regime. For Sicilian politics see Marino, *Partiti e lotta di classe;* Rosario Villari, *Il sud nella storia d'Italia* (Bari: Laterza, 1963).

48. Mercuri, "Sicilia e alleati," 900–901.

49. Coles and Weinberg, *Soldiers Become Governors,* 165–166; Aga Rossi, "La politica degli alleati," 849–851. In the fall of 1943, Carlo Sforza urged Italian-Americans to use their influence for the good of Italy and warned that "five million Italian-American voters would not permit Italy to be defrauded of her rights." OSS, "Present State of Italian Politics in the United States," 1 December 1943, NA, RG 165, Entry 77, Box 1951, File 3800–3810.

50. "Preliminary Report on Conditions in Sicily," 15 February 1943, NA, RG 226, 30052.

51. Poletti to John McCloy, 27 September 1943, Poletti Papers, AMG General File, S-3; Coles and Weinberg, *Soldiers Become Governors,* 166–167.

52. Iantaffi to MI, "La delinquenza in Sicilia—Sua recrudescenza e causa," 15 September 1944, ACS, *MI,* AG, 1944–1946, b. 2, f. 149.

53. Elena Aga Rossi, "La situazione politica ed economica nell'Italia nel periodo 1944–45: I governi Bonomi," *Quaderni dell'Istituto Romano per la Storia d'Italia dal Fascismo alla Resistenza,* 2 (1971), 21.

54. Headquarters Seventh Army, Civil Affairs Section, "Memorandum to Fifteenth Army Group—AMG—Siracusa," Enclosure, 31 July 1943, Poletti Papers, AMG General File, S-3. From the same location see Poletti to Chief Civil Affairs Officer, AMG, "Civil Affairs Report," 15 July 1943. See also Coles and Weinberg, *Soldiers Become Governors,* 187; *The New York Times,* 14 August 1943. For all of AMG's proclamations, see Allied Military Government of Occupied Territory, *Sicily Gazette,* No. 1, July 1943; No. 2, 17 September 1943; No. 3, 20 October 1943; NA, RG 165, Entry 77, Box 1906, File 6960. At least one source characterizes AMG officials as totally indifferent to the population's problems: V. Sansone and G. Ingrasci, *Sei anni di banditismo in Sicilia* (Milan: Edizioni Sociali, 1950), 50.

55. "To Palermo," undated, unsigned, Poletti Papers, AMG General File, S-3.

56. Report by Rennel, August 1943, PRO, FO 371, 37326

57. Ibid.

58. Coles and Weinberg, *Soldiers Become Governors,* 189; Harris, *Allied Military Administration,* 36–37; OSS Report, "Weekly Political Bulletin from Sicily," 17 March 1944, NA, RG 165, Entry 77, Box 1949, File 3200–3300. For an Italian assessment of the situation, see Legione Territoriale dei Carabinieri Reali di Catanzaro, to Il Generale Comandante la 7 Armata, "Situazione politica ed economica della Sicilia in regime di occupazione," 29 October 1943, ACS, *MI,* AG, 1944–1946, b. 24, f. 1878.

59. Legione Territoriale dei Carabinieri Reali di Bari, "Notiziario," 11 November 1943, ACS, *PCM,* Governo di Salerno, 1943–1944, Cat. 4, f. 4/10, sf. 6.

60. Coles and Weinberg, *Soldiers Become Governors,* 204. At least one report disagreed with this view and pointed out that Sicily "seems on the whole a bit worse off than the mainland." OSS, "Preliminary Report on Conditions in Sicily," 15 February 1943, NA, RG 226, 30052.

61. Harris, *Allied Military Administration,* 21.

62. Coles and Weinberg, *Soldiers Become Governors,* 197, 312-314; Harris, *Allied Military Administration,* 38–40, 45–47; Headquarters, Seventh Army, Civil Affairs Section, "Memorandum to Fifteenth Army Group—AMG—Siracusa", Enclosure, 31 July 1943, Poletti Papers, AMG General File S-3.

63. OSS, "Weekly Political Bulletin from Sicily," 17 March 1944, NA, RG 165, Entry 77, Box 1949, File 3200–3300; Coles and Weinberg, *Soldiers Become Governors,* 306. For a comparison of black market and amassi prices,

see Legione Territoriale dei Carabinieri Reali di Bari, "Notiziario," 11 November 1943, ACS, *PCM,* Governo di Salerno, 1943–1944, Cat. 4, f. 4/10, sf. 6; Surveys of Public Opinion Held in Sicily, November 1943–January 1944, Report 4, "A Survey on Food Supply and Distribution," December 1943, Sheets 1, 2, and 3, NA, RG 165, Entry 77, Box 1909, Folder 6960.

64. Coles and Weinberg, *Soldiers Become Governors,* 347; Harris, *Allied Military Administration,* 46; "Security Intelligence Report," 4 March and 11 March 1944, ACS, *CAA,* Appendice, b. 1, f. 5; Allied Military Government, Province of Enna to Allied Control Commission, Sicilia Region, HQ, "Disturbances at Villarosa," 3 March 1944, NA, RG 331, 10100/143/276; Office of Chief of Naval Operations, Intelligence Report, "Italy, Sicily, Civilian Unrest In," 27 December 1943, NA, RG 38, Register No. 11033-6, File C-10-h.

65. Salvo Di Matteo, *Anni roventi: La Sicilia dal 1943 al 1947, cronache di un quinquennio* (Palermo: G. Denaro, 1968), 135, 149; Surveys of Public Opinion Held in Sicily, November 1943–January 1944, Report 4, "A Survey on Shelter and Clothing," December 1943, Sheets 1 and 2, NA, RG 165, Entry 77, Box 1909, Folder 6960. From the same source see "A Survey on Food Supply and Distribution," Sheet 4. See also Maurice Neufield, "The Failure of Allied Military Government in Italy," *Public Administration Review,* VI (April 1946), 142.

66. Di Matteo, *Anni roventi,* 137.

67. Pantaleone, *Mafia and Politics,* 70; Surveys of Public Opinion Held in Sicily, November 1943–January 1944, Report 7, "A Survey on Public Security," December 1943, Sheet 7, NA, RG 165, Entry 77, Box 1909, Folder 6960; Office of Chief of Naval Operations, Intelligence Report, "Italy, Sicily, Civilian Unrest In," 27 December 1943, NA, RG 38, Register No. 11033-6, File C-10-h.

68. In February 1944, police in Sicily were engaged in operations to crush the brigands, but they had little success. "Security Intelligence Report," 19 February 1944, ACS, *CAA,* Appendice, b. 1, f. 5.

69. Michele Iantaffi to MI, "La delinquenza in Sicilia—Sua recrudescenza e causa," 15 September 1944, ACS, *MI,* AG, 1944–1946, b. 2, f. 149; Surveys of Public Opinion Held in Sicily, November 1943–January 1944, Report 7, "A Survey on Public Security," December 1943, Sheets 1 and 14, NA, RG 165, Entry 77, Box 1909, Folder 6960.

70. Coles and Weinberg, *Soldiers Become Governors,* 238.

71. Harris, *Allied Military Administration,* 122; Coles and Weinberg, *Soldiers Become Governors,* 237–240, 245–247, 275–305; degli Espinosa, *Il regno del sud,* 332–336.

72. "Copy of the Declaration of the Meeting of the Prefects Held in Palermo," 14 December 1943, NA, RG 331, 10000/132/152; Poletti to ?, 10 December 1943, Poletti Papers, AMG General File, S-4.

73. Coles and Weinberg, *Soldiers Become Governors,* 298–305; Harris, *Allied Military Administration,* 105–128; Hughes, *The United States and Italy,* 134. According to Rennel, the installation of ACC personnel to help control Sicily was a mistake. He believed that they would destroy much that AMG had accomplished. Gayre, *Italy in Transition,* 14–15.

74. Poletti to General McSherry, "Memorandum," 23 September 1943, Poletti Papers, AMG General File, S-3; Poletti to Robert Murphy and John J. McCloy, 10 December 1943, Poletti Papers, AMG General File, S-4; OSS, "McFarlane and Free Sicily," 15 January 1944, NA, RG 165, Entry 77, Box 1909, Folder 6960.

75. Combined Civil Affairs Committee, "Operation of AMG in Sicily and Italy," 27 December 1943, NA, RG 165, Entry 77, Box 2013, Folder 6960. Rennel believed that Poletti enjoyed administrative power because it made him feel important and considered his possible appointment to Allied Commission Headquarters a poor choice. Rennel to ?, January 1944, PRO, FO 371, 43918.

76. "Security Intelligence Report," 19 February 1944, ACS, *CAA*, Appendice b. 1, f. 5; "Psychological Warfare Weekly Roundup, No.24," 29 August–4 September 1943, NA, RG 226, Entry 106, Box, 1, Folder 10; Poletti to Robert Murphy and John J. McCloy, 10 December 1943, Poletti Papers, AMG General File, S-4; M. E. Brod to Regional Public Safety Commissioner, "Public Reaction on a Military Governor," 10 February 1944, Poletti Papers, AMG General File, S-5; Legione Territoriale dei Carabinieri Reali di Messina alla Commissione Alleata di Controllo, "Passaggio della Sicilia al Governo Badoglio," 17 February 1944, NA, RG 331, 10103/143/28; Headquarters, Seventh Army, to Major Raffa, "Correction of Previous Report on Number of Communists in Palermo," 10 December 1943, NA, RG 331, 10100/142/414. For the "death blow" idea see Aldisio to Sturzo, 31 March 1944, in Luigi Sturzo, *Scritti ineditti*, vol. 3, edited by Francesco Malgeri (Rome: Edizioni Cinque Lune, 1976), 245. See also Coles and Weinberg, *Soldiers Become Governors*, 303.

77. Comando Arma dei Carabinieri Reali dell'Italia Liberata to MI, "Restituzione della Sicilia al Governo Nazionale," 2 March 1944, ACS, *MI*, AG, 1944-1946, b. 6, f. 426.

78. OSS, "Badoglio and Government of Sicily; Amella Versus Musotto for Governor of Sicily," 10 January 1944, NA, RG 226, 55277. Poletti believed that the appointment of a high commissioner would make it possible to withdraw the great majority of civil affairs officers from Sicily and provide Italian officials a great deal of latitude in governing the island. Combined Civil Affairs Committee, "Operation of AMG in Sicily and Italy," 27 December 1943, NA, RG 165, Entry 77, Box 1909, File 6960.

79. As early as 7 February the Allies supported Musotto for the post. Poletti to Lush, 7 February 1944, NA, RG 331, 10000/132/152. OSS, "Badoglio and the Government of Sicily; Amella Versus Musotto for Governor of Sicily," 10 January 1944, NA, RG 226, 55277; To Colonel (illegible) from OSS, X-2, "Political Situation in Sicily," 2 March 1944, CIA. From the same source see OSS, "Development of Political Parties in Sicily; Political Personalities," 19 November 1943. M. E. Brod to Regional Public Safety Commissioner, "Public Reaction on a Military Governor," 10 February 1944, Poletti Papers, AMG General File, S-5. The OSS characterized Castellano as a man of "slight intellectual background and dubious moral standards." The same report also lambasted his actions during the armistice negotiations. OSS, "Italian Generals," 5 September 1945, NA, RG 226, Entry 153A, Roll 1. One Italian report labeled Castellano too young and inexperienced while claiming that Musotto's appointment would be viewed as a sign of weakness on the part of the government. Comando Arma dei Carabinieri Reali dell'Italia Liberata to MI, "Restituzione della Sicilia al Governo Nazionale," 2 March 1944, ACS, *MI*, AG, 1944–1946, b. 6, f. 426. Ganci claims that Musotto was an enemy of the mafia. Ganci, *L'Italia antimoderata*, 285.

80. Badoglio to MacFarlane, 14 February 1944, NA, RG 331, 10000/132/152; Questura di Catania to Lt. Colonel French, "Nomination of a Civil Commissioner for Sicily," 28 February 1944, NA, RG 331, 10103/142/28; M. E. Brod to Regional Public Safety Commissioner, "Public Reaction on a Military Gover-

nor," 10 February 1944, Poletti Papers, AMG General File, S-5. Badoglio believed that the movement planned to place the island under foreign control. Pietro Badoglio, *L'Italia nella seconda guerra mondiale* (Verona: Mondadori, 1946), 182.

81. See the report on this meeting in ACS, *PCM,* Governo di Salerno, 1943–1944, Cat. 4, f. "Musotto: Nomina di Alto Commissario"; *Sicilia Liberata,* 8 March 1944; Allied Force HQ, Information and Censorship Section, Psychological Warfare Branch, "Political Intelligence Report on Italy, Number 53," 12 March 1944, NA, RG 165, Entry 77, Box 1949, File 3200–3300; R. Prefettura di Palermo, 8 March 1944, Poletti Papers, AMG General File, S-5.

82. Alto Commissariato per la Sicilia to MI, "Rapporto sulla situazione della Sicilia," 26 July 1944, ACS, *MI,* AG, 1944–1946, b.24, f. 1878.

83. "Security Intelligence Report," 1 April 1944, ACS, *CAA,* Appendice, b. 1, f. 5; from the same source see "Security Intelligence Report," 8 April 1944.

84. Giarrizzo, *Sicilia politica,* 35–37; OSS, "Weekly Political Bulletin from Sicily," 17 March 1944, NA, RG 165, Entry 77, Box 1949, File 3200–3300. On Aldisio see A. E. Heath to ?, 21 January 1946, PRO, FO 371, 60655. On the high commission and its powers see Jacoviello, *La Sicilia,* 41–43.

85. OSS, "Badoglio and Government of Sicily; Amella Versus Musotto for Governor of Sicily," 10 January 1944, NA, RG 226, 55277.

Chapter 2. The Birth of the Separatist Movement

1. Ganci, *L'Italia antimoderata,* 275; Barbagallo, *Rivoluzione mancata,* 73–74.

2. De Antonellis, *Il sud,* 199; Reece, "Fascism, the Mafia," 262. For Tasca's involvement see di Carcaci, *Memorie,* 33–36. For information on the 1920 movement see ACS, *MI,* DGPS, AA.GG.RR., 1920, b. 45, "Voci di un movimento separatista." In 1919, another separatist group was founded. The Circolo per l'Indipendenza Siciliana was suppressed by the Fascists but resumed activity in April 1944. OSS, "Inauguration of the Circolo per l'Indipendenza Siciliana," 20 April 1944, CIA.

3. For information on this movement see ACS, *MI,* DGPS, Divisione Polizia Politica, 1927–1944, Cat. K-161, b. 148, "Movimento autonomista siciliana, 1932–1938"; on Rosa see ACS, *CPC,* f. 4410, "Rosa, Giovanni." See also ACS, *MI,* DGPS, AA.GG.RR., 1943, Cat. K-4, b. 88, "Sicilia—Movimento Autonomista."

4. Gaja, *L'esercito,* 123; *Newsweek,* 30 October 1944. For information on other autonomist movements see Reece, "Fascism, the Mafia," 271–274.

5. Office of Chief of Naval Operations, Intelligence Report, "Italy—Social Forces, Oppressed Minorities, Revolutionary Forces," 30 September 1941, NA, RG 165, Entry 77, Box 1948, File 3020.

6. It is possible that the British source of information was either Canepa or Finocchiaro Aprile. "Memo on Sicily Under Italian Rule," 1 December 1942, PRO, FO 371, 33251.

7. Ganci, *L'Italia antimoderata,* 268; Finocchiaro Aprile, *Il movimento indipendentista,* 91; Gaja, *L'esercito,* 125; Barbagallo, *Rivoluzione mancata,* 69.

8. Gaja, *L'esercito,* 125; Chilanti, *Chi è Milazzo?,* 70–72.

9. Alfred T. Nester to Secretary of State, "Separatist Movement: Letter Addressed to the President of the United States and the Prime Minister of

England as Well as to All Responsible for the Allied Nations, Written by Lucio Tasca," 9 December 1944, NA, RG 59, 865.01/12-944; OSS, "Development of Political Parties in Sicily; Political Personalities," 19 November 1943, CIA; di Carcaci, *Memorie,* 33–36. Tasca had served as the Bank of Sicily's representative to the Central Committee for Agrarian Credit. Duggan, *Fascism and the Mafia,* 206; Lewis, *Honored Society,* 144–146.

10. Nester to Secretary of State, "Separatist Movement: Letter Addressed to the President of the United States and the Prime Minister of England as Well as to All Responsible for the Allied Nations, Written by Lucio Tasca," 9 December 1944, NA, RG 59, 865.01/12-944. In 1928, Tasca was honored as one of the most successful wheat growers in Palermo province. Duggan, *Fascism and the Mafia,* 252.

11. Canalis, *Alcuni aspetti,* 25–27; Ganci, *L'Italia antimoderata,* 264; Gaja, *L'esercito,* 123–124.

12. Tasca maintained his beliefs for the remainder of his life and wrote two tracts discussing the island's agriculture. Lucio Tasca Bordonaro, *Elogio del latifondo siciliano: La riforma della fame* (Palermo: S. F. Flaccovio, 1950) and *Le gioie della riforma: Hanno trasformato il latifondo? o rovinato l'agricoltura?* (Palermo: S. F. Flaccovio, 1951); "Verità sul latifondo siciliano," undated, ACS, *MI,* AG, 1944–1946, b. 8, f. 559, sf. 1; Lucio Tasca, "Il Pensiero Siciliano nel secolo XIX," ACS, *PCM,* 1944–1946, 8-2-10912.

13. Ganci, *L'Italia antimoderata,* 262; Cimino, et. al., *La Sicilia nella resistenza,* 38; Canalis, *Alcuni aspetti,* 112–122; Barbagallo, *Rivoluzione mancata,* 51–65.

14. Canepa's teacher was Antonio de Stefano, an ardent anti-Fascist. Ganci, *L'Italia antimoderata,* 262; Mario Turri [Antonio Canepa], *La Sicilia ai siciliani!,* (Catania: 1942), 5; Ganci, *L'Italia antimoderata,* 264–268.

15. Turri, *La Sicilia,* 6.

16. Ibid., 39–40. For a work that supports the separatist position by tracing Sicilian history and politics, see Antonino Trizzino, *Vento del sud* (Rome: Editrice Faro, 1945); for one that rebuts separatist arguments see Carmelo Caristia, *La Sicilia d'oggi e di ieri: Breve saggio-documentario su alcune grandi verità rivelate dall'istoriografia separatista* (Turin: Societa Editrice Internazionale, 1944).

17. Varvaro later joined the Communist Party and became a deputy in the Sicilian Regional Assembly. Pantaleone, *Mafia and Politics,* 74; Giarrizzo, *Sicilia politica,* 29.

18. The Americans labeled Battiato "the separatists' principal mouthpiece." "Appendix 'A' to Fortnightly Security Report for Period Ending 28 July 1944," 28 July 1944, NA, RG 331, 10100/143/275; Giarrizzo, *Sicilia politica,* 29.

19. Pantaleone, *Mafia and Politics,* 74; Ganci, *L'Italia antimoderata,* 271; Lord Rennel described him as "somewhat garrulous and not very outstanding in ability." Report by Rennel, August 1943, NA, RG 165, Entry 77, Box 1906, File 6960; *Gaja, L'esercito,* 126. The parallels between Finocchiaro Aprile's ideas and those of Umberto Bossi are numerous and are discussed in the epilogue.

20. Finocchiaro Aprile, *Il movimento indipendentista,* 15, 101; Ganci, *L'Italia antimoderata,* 267–270; Missori, *Governi,* 116; *Il Messaggero,* 16 January 1964. For his activities as minister of state see ACS, *PCM,* 1921, b. 611, f. 1/1.

21. "Appendix 'A' to Fortnightly Security Report for Period Ending 28 July 1944," 28 July 1944, NA, RG 331, 10100/143/275; Ganci, *L'Italia antimoderata,* 270; Cimino, et al., *La Sicilia nella resistenza,* 51–52; Miccichè, *Dopoguerra,* 189; *Il Tempo,* 16 January 1964; *Il Messaggero,* 16 January 1964.

22. For Finocchiaro Aprile's correspondence with Mussolini see ACS, *SPD/CO,* b. 184, f. 151851, "Andrea Finocchiaro Aprile."

23. Finocchiaro Aprile to Mussolini, 8 April 1936, ACS, *SPD/CO,* b. 184, f. 151851, "Andrea Finocchiaro Aprile"; from the same location see Finocchiaro Aprile to Osvaldo Sebastiani, 30 April 1934, 16 November 1937, and 9 April 1938; Ganci, *L'Italia antimoderata,* 270.

24. Finocchiaro Aprile to Mussolini, 8 April 1936, ACS, *SPD/CO,* b. 184, f. 151851, "Andrea Finocchiaro Aprile"; from the same location see Finocchiaro Aprile to Mussolini, 11 November 1938.

25. Finocchiaro Aprile wrote a letter and sent a telegram. Finocchiaro Aprile to Sebastiani, 16 April 1939, ACS, *SPD/CO,* b. 184, f. 151851, "Andrea Finocchiaro Aprile"; OSS, "Biographical Note on Finocchiaro Aprile," 23 February 1944, CIA. In April 1944, Concetto Battiato apologized for the telegram. He explained that the separatist leader approved of Fascist foreign policy only because it suited Italy's national interest at the time, but that he disapproved of Fascism's internal administration. "Appendix 'A' to Fortnightly Security Report for Period Ending 28 July 1944," 28 July 1944, NA, RG 331, 10100/143/275. According to the American consul in Palermo, news of the invasion of Albania was greeted in Palermo "without any apparent enthusiasm." Thomas McNelly to William Phillips, Rome, 11 April 1939, NA, RG 165, Entry 77, Box 2027, File-"Misc.-Italy Current Events."

26. Finocchiaro Aprile to Sebastiani, 21 October 1939, ACS, *SPD/CO,* b. 184, f. 151851, "Andrea Finocchiaro Aprile."

27. OSS, "Biographical Note on Finocchiaro Aprile," 23 February 1944, CIA; OSS, "Sicilian Separatist Leader Finocchiaro Aprile," 30 March 1944, CIA; "Political Information—Separatist Movement," 4 October 1943, NA, RG 165, Entry 77, Box 1904, File 3700.

28. Gaja, *L'esercito,* 126–127; Ganci, *L'Italia antimoderata,* 271; "Memo on Sicily Under Italian Rule," 1 December 1942, PRO, FO 371, 32351.

29. Those with whom Finocchiaro Aprile met included Salvatore Aldisio of the Christian Democrats, Francesco Musotto, the first high commissioner for Sicily, Franco Grasso of the Communist Party, and Augusto Martino of the Action Party. Ganci, *L'Italia antimoderata,* 271; de Antonellis, *Il sud,* 228; Gaja, *L'esercito,* 126.

30. Gaja, *L'esercito,* 126; Ganci, *L'Italia antimoderata,* 271.

31. Pantaleone, *Mafia and Politics,* 73; Mercuri, "Sicilia e alleati," 963–964.

32. Ganci, *L'Italia antimoderata,* 272.

33. The information on Finocchiaro Aprile's platform comes from the speeches he made during the separatist era. See the introduction by S. Massimo Ganci in Finocchiaro Aprile, *Il movimento indipendentista,* 7–40; Ganci, *L'Italia antimoderata,* 303–306; see also the preface Finocchiaro Aprile wrote for Trizzino, *Vento del sud,* 7–29.

34. Headquarters, 2677th Regiment OSS, "Separatists to Sponsor Volunteer Soldier Movement," 4 December 1944, CIA. This sentiment was similar to that of Croce, who felt no great desire to convince young men to fight for a flag which was repugnant to them. Degli Espinosa, *Il regno del sud,* 272.

35. His message of 4 October 1943 is an example of this anti-monarchist sentiment. "Al Re d'Italia Vittorio Emanuele III," 4 October 1943, NA, RG 331, 10100/143/277.

36. Gayre, *Italy in Transition,* 114; Nester to Secretary of State, "Separatist Movement: Appeal to Church Leaders," 15 November 1944, NA, RG 59, 865.00/ 11-1544. In general, Italian authorities reported that the clergy were either inactive, or loyal to the Christian Democrats. See ACS, *MI*, AG, 1944–1946, b. 81, f. 6910, 6911, 6916; b. 226, f. 23070; b. 234, f. 23540, 23541; Finocchiaro Aprile, *Il movimento indipendentista,* 60.

37. Marino, *Storia del separatismo,* 79.

38. Finocchiaro Aprile, *Il movimento indipendentista,* 83–89; Jacoviello, *La Sicilia,* 17.

39. Jacoviello, *La Sicilia,* 24–25.

40. Finocchiaro Aprile, *Il movimento indipendentista,* 66–67.

41. Ibid., 64–67.

42. As early as February 1944, the Allies reported that a good number of separatists were willing to opt for autonomy rather than struggle for independence. "Security Intelligence Report." 26 February 1944, ACS, *CAA,* Appendice, b.1, f.5.

43. Mercuri, "Sicilia e alleati," 952–953; "Separatism and Separatists," undated and unsigned, NA, RG 331, 10100/143/274.

44. Finocchiaro Aprile, *Il movimento indipendentista,* 58. For Fascist criticism of La Rosa see ACS, *CPC,* 2725, "Luigi La Rosa."

45. "Report on Sicilian Separatism and the Movimento per l'Indipendenza della Sicilia," 17 April 1946, PRO, FO 371, 67786. At least one author claims that the landowners wanted Sicily to fall under American control because it would be easier for them to retain their powers. Felice Chilanti, *Da Montelepre a Viterbo* (Rome: Croce, 1952), 2.

46. Giovanni Molè, *Studio-inchiesta sui latifondi siciliani* (Rome: Tipografia del Senato, 1929), 20; Alfredo De Polzer, *Statistiche agrarie* (Milan: A. Guiffre, 1942), 150, 160.

47. "Separatism and Separatists," unsigned and undated, NA, RG 331, 10100/143/274.

48. Nester to Secretary of State, "Summary of Statements Made by Finocchiaro Aprile to a PWB Officer on 29 January 1945," 16 February 1945, FBI, 51898-8; Nester to Secretary of State, "Maffia Leaders at Casteldaccia Inform Finocchiaro Aprile That They Do Not Approve of His Methods of Operation," 17 July 1945, NA, RG 59, 865.00/7-1745; Nester to Secretary of State, "Separatist Propaganda: Article by Finocchiaro Aprile in the Democrazia Internazionale," 29 March 1945, NA, RG 59, 865.00/3-2945. Separatists reportedly received financial support from many landowners, members of the island's aristocracy, and other leaders of local society. "Report on Sicilian Separatism and the Movimento per l'Indipendenza della Sicilia," 17 April 1946, PRO, FO 371, 67786; OSS, "The Separatist Party in Catania," 2 March 1944, NA, RG 165, Entry 77, Box 1950, File 3700; Finocchiaro Aprile, *Il movimento indipendentista,* 83–84; Renda, *Il movimento contadino,* 14.

49. Comando Generale dell'Arma dei Carabinieri Reali to the Presidenza del Consiglio dei Ministri, "Movimento separatista," 1 November 1944, ACS, *PCM,* 1944–1946, 8-2-10912; Office of Chief of Naval Operations, Intelligence Report, "Italy, Government, Political Parties in Sicily, Maffia and Separatist

Movement," 10 December 1943, NA, RG 38, Register No. 9632-H, C-10-f; Lupo, "Allies and mafia," 27.

50. *Time,* v. 44, no. 11, 11 September 1944, 33.

51. Office of Chief of Naval Operations, Intelligence Report, "Italy, Government, Political Parties in Sicily, Maffia and Separatist Movement," 10 December 1943, NA, RG 38, Register No. 9632-H, File C-10-f; OSS, "Survey of the Political Situation in Sicily," 23 February 1944, NA, RG 165, Entry 77, Box 1950, File 3700. Rennel fully expected that the mafia would be associated with the separatist movement, given its history of interference in Sicilian political affairs. Report by Rennel, August 1943, NA, RG 165, Entry 77, Box 1906, File 6960; Aldisio to MI, "Rapporto sulla situazione in Sicilia," 20 August 1944, ACS, *MI, AG,* 1944–1946, b. 24, f. 1878; Finocchiaro Aprile, *Il movimento indipendentista,* 19.

52. Office of Chief of Naval Operations, Intelligence Report, "Italy, Government, Political Parties in Sicily, Maffia and Separatist," 10 December 1943, NA, RG 38, Register No. 9632-H, File C-10-f; Experimental Detachment, G-3, X-2 Branch, Palermo, 5 October 1943, NA, RG 165, Entry 77, Box 1904, File 3700.

53. Provincial Public Safety Officer, Viterbo Province to Regional Public Safety Officer, Region 4 ACC, "Vito Genovese," 27 August 1944, Poletti Papers, AMG General File, S-9; on AMG, the mafia, and Vizzini see Report by Rennel, August 1943, PRO, FO 371, 37326; OSS, "Survey on the Political Situation in Sicily," 23 February 1944, NA, RG 165 Entry 77, Box 1950, File 3700; Experimental Detachment, G-3, X-2, Palermo, 5 October 1943, NA, RG 165, Entry 77, Box 1904, File 3700; Duggan, *Fascism and the Mafia,* 272–273; D'Este, *Bitter Victory,* 629–630; Mack Smith, *Modern Sicily,* 526; Nick Gentile, *Vita di capomafia* (Milan: Riuniti, 1963), 164; Pantaleone, *Mafia and Politics,* 54–66; 80–86; the same author claims that Vizzini had kept in contact with several American mafia chieftains. Michele Pantaleone, *Mafia e droga* (Turin: Einaudi, 1966), 23. Norman Lewis, *Honored Society,* 20–24; 51–66; Jacoviello, *La Sicilia,* 16. Recent scholarship has downplayed Vizzini's role as "head" of the Sicilian mafia. Lupo, "Allies and mafia," 25.

54. Rennel believed that mafia members did not warrant special favors or pardons because of their anti-Fascist attitude. Report by Rennel, August 1943, NA, RG 165, Entry 77, Box 1906, File 6960; OSS, "General Castellana Seeking Mafia Accord," 21 November 1944, NA, RG 226, 103050; Rosario Poma and Enzo Perrone, *Quelli della lupara: Rapporto sulla mafia di ieri e di oggi con prefazione del Senatore Simone Gatto* (Florence: Edizioni Casini, 1964), 51.

55. Rennel advised that the movement included a number of lawyers and doctors, but an Italian report suggested that the professional classes did not support the separatists. Report by Rennel, August 1943, PRO, FO 371, 37326; "Report on Sicilian Separatism and the Movimento per l'Indipendenza della Sicilia," 17 April 1946, PRO, FO 371, 67786; "Riassunti della Relazione del Prefetto di Palermo. Sunti della situazione generale della Sicilia (dal rapporto dell'Alto Commissario)," July 1944, ACS, *MI, AG,* 1944–1946, b. 24, f. 1878; Comando Generale dell'Arma dei Carabinieri Reali to the Presidenza del Consiglio dei Ministri, "Movimento separatista," 1 November 1944, ACS, *PCM,* 1944–1946, 8-2-10912; "Separatism and Separatists," unsigned and undated, NA, RG 331, 10100/143/274; Harris, *Military Administration,* 40; Finocchiaro Aprile, *Il movimento indipendentista,* 20; Jacoviello, *La Sicilia,* 34.

56. Mack Smith, *Modern Sicily,* 528; Legione Territoriale dei Carabinieri Reali di Catanzaro to Generale Commandante la 7 Armata, "Situazione politica

e economica della Sicilia in regime di occupazione," 29 October 1943, ACS, *MI*, AG, 1944–1946, b. 24, f. 1878.

57. "Report on Sicilian Separatism and the Movimento per l'Indipendenza della Sicilia," 17 April 1946, PRO, FO 371, 67786; Office of Chief of Naval Operations, Intelligence Report, "Interview With Italian Navy Technician (Enlisted) Giogiodi Antonio Modica," 9 December 1943, NA, RG 38, Register No. 9632-H, File C-10-f. In January 1945, students at the University of Catania elected a Permanent University Committee (Comitato Permanente Universitario). Out of the 21 members, 14 were labeled as separatist. Legione Territoriale dei Carabinieri Reali di Messina to the Commissione Alleata, "Comitato Permanente Universitario," 28 January 1945, NA, RG 331, 10103/143/28.

58. Renda, *Il movimento contadino,* 12. On the peasants, see Leonard W. Moss, "The Passing of Traditional Peasant Society in the South," in Edward Tannenbaum and Emiliana P. Noether, eds., *Modern Italy, A Topical History Since 1861* (New York: New York University Press, 1974); E. J. Hobsbawm, *Primitive Rebels: Studies in Archaic Forms of Social Movement in the Nineteenth and Twentieth Centuries* (New York: Frederick A. Praeger, 1959).

59. Trizzino, *Vento del sud* , 8–9; for the statistics see De Polzer, *Statistiche agrarie,* 150, 160.

60. Finocchiaro Aprile, *Il movimento indipendentista,* 87; Jacoviello, *La Sicilia,* 34.

61. Antonio Gramsci, *La questione meridionale,* eds. Franco De Felice and Valentino Parlato (Rome: Riuniti, 1957), 149–150; "Report on Sicilian Separatism and the Movimento per l'Indipendenza della Sicilia," 17 April 1946, PRO, FO 371, 67786.

62. Comando Generale dell'Arma dei Carabinieri Reali to MI, "Lega tra I lavoratori della terra," 19 November 1944, ACS, *MI*, AG, 1944–1946, b. 75, f. 6301; R. Prefettura di Palermo to MI, "Borgata-Roccella-Unione Siciliana Agricoltori Presidente Delano Roosevelt," 30 November 1944, ACS, *MI*, DGPS, AA.GG.RR., 1944, Cat. C-2-A, b. 39, f. "Movimento separatista Siciliana"; see also Sessa to Il Prefetto Palermo, "Borgata-Roccella-Unione Siciliana Agricoltori 'Presidente Delano Roosevelt'," 12 November 1944, NA, RG 331, 10100/143/272; in the same location see "From Fortnightly Security Report of 12 November 1944 of 51 Field Security Section."

63. For industrial conditions see ACS, *MI*, AG, 1944–1946, b. 10, f. 649; b. 34, f. 2588; ACS, *PCM,* 1944–1946, 3-1-7-14508; see also the documents in NA, RG 331, 10100/146/1; 10100/146/12; 10000/146/603; Maurizio Colonna, *L'industria zolfifera siciliana: Origini, sviluppo, declino* (Catania: Università di Catania, 1971), 225; Istituto Centrale di Statistica del Regno d'Italia, *Compendio statistico italiano 1939* (Rome: Istituto Poligrafico dello Stato, 1940), 43.

CHAPTER 3. THE STRUGGLE BEGINS

1. OSS, "Sicilian Separatist Leader Finocchiaro Aprile," prior to 16 March 1944, CIA. One American report characterized Lo Verde as "a rather uninteresting character, incapable." He was also said to have British affiliations; "Political Information, Separatist Movement," 4 October 1943, NA, RG 165, Entry 77, Box 1904, File 3700; OSS, "Conflict Between AMG and La Sicilia Liberata," 17 January 1944, NA, RG 165, Entry 77, Box 1909, File 6960.

2. "Development of the 'Partito d'Azione' in Sicily," 20 August 1943, NA, RG 226, Entry 115, Box 35, Folder 6; Gaja, *L'esercito,* 130–131; Giarrizzo, *Sicilia politica,* 12.

3. Cimino, et. al., *La Sicilia nella resistenza,* 51. Domenica Cigna, a separatist leader in Agrigento, might have suggested to Finocchiaro Aprile the plan for cooperating with the Communists. Finocchiaro Aprile might have rejected the move because he feared an increase in Communist prestige. Gaja; *L'esercito,* 130–131.

4. Report by Rennel, August 1943, NA, RG 165, Entry 77, Box 1906, File 6960. For a list of members see "Political Information, Separatist Movement," 4 October 1943, NA, RG 165, Entry 77, Box 1904, File 3700; Marino, *Storia del separatismo,* 18.

5. Marino, *Storia del separatismo,* 18–19; di Carcaci, *Memorie,* 22.

6. Finocchiaro Aprile, *Il movimento indipendentista,* 92. Rennel warned both Finocchiaro Aprile and Alessandro Tasca. Report by Rennel, August 1943, NA, RG 165, Entry 77, Box 1906, File 6960.

7. Matteo G. Tocco, *Libro nero di Sicilia: Dietro le quinte della politica degli affari e della cronaca della regione siciliano* (Milan: Sugar, 1972), 330–331; di Carcaci, *Memorie,* 22; Nicolosi, *Sicilia contro Italia,* 36.

8. "Il Comitato Per l'Indipendenza Siciliana," 28 July 1943, ACS, *MI,* DGPS, AA.GG.RR., 1944, Cat. C-2-A, b. 39, f. "Movimento separatista Siciliana"; "Political Information, Separatist Movement," 4 October 1943, NA, RG 165, Entry 77, Box 1904, File 3700.

9. Alto Commissario per la Sicilia to MI, "Relazione sul Movimento per l'Indipendenza Siciliana," 23 June 1945, ACS, *MI,* AG, 1944–1946, b. 8, f. 559, sf. 1; OSS, Research and Analysis Branch, "Sicilian Separatism with Particular Reference to the Report of Lord Rennel of Rodd," 19 November 1943, NA, RG 59, R&A Report 1521; "Separatism and Separatists," unsigned and undated, NA, RG 331, 10100/143/247; Key to Secretary of State, 12 March 1946, NA, RG 59, 865.00/3-1246. An American report noted that one of AMG's first measures was to raise the price of grain, a move that played into the hands of the landowners. It claimed that separatist elements who had gained the trust of the occupation authorities influenced the decision. "Separatism and Separatists," unsigned and undated, NA, RG 331, 10100/143/247.

10. "Separatism and Separatists," unsigned and undated, NA, RG 331, 10100/143/274. Gaja believes that the Americans and British might have supported separatism if Italy became socialist. Gaja, *L'esercito,* 149.

11. OSS, "Interview with Hon. Andrea Finocchiaro Aprile," 28 April 1944, CIA.

12. Mercuri, "Sicilia e alleati," 953.

13. "Separatism and Separatists," unsigned and undated, NA, RG 331, 10100/143/274; Gaja, *L'esercito,* 127; Finocchiaro Aprile, *Il movimento indipendentista,* 21.

14. Report by Rennel, August 1943, NA, RG 165, Entry 77, Box 1906, File 6960; Gayre, *Italy in Transition,* 141.

15. Gayre, *Italy in Transition,* 188; on Gayre's views see Ganci, *L'Italia antimoderata,* 286–294; Report by Rennel, August 1943, PRO, FO 371, 37326; Rennel to Mr. Bob Dixon, 11 November 1943, PRO, FO 371, 37328; for the Palermo administration see Experimental Detachment G-3, X-2 Branch, Palermo, 5 October 1943, NA 165, Entry 77, Box 1904, File 3700. The Allies appointed officials who represented landed interests to ninety percent of the

island's communal offices. This has been interpreted to mean that separatists controlled the island's administration. Anton Blok, *The Mafia of a Sicilian Village, 1860–1960: A Study of Violent Peasant Entrepreneurs* (New York: Harper & Row, 1974), 192; Gaja, *L'esercito*, 145. Giarrizzo disputes the ninety-percent figure. Giarrizzo, *Sicilia politica*, 11.

16. Finocchiaro Aprile, *Il movimento indipendentista*, 93; Nester to Secretary of State, "Summary of Statements Made by Finocchiaro Aprile to PWB Officer on 29 January 1945," 16 February 1945, FBI, 51898-8; Nester to Secretary of State, "Maffia Leaders at Casteldaccia Inform Finocchiaro Aprile That They Do Not Approve of His Methods of Operation," 17 July 1945, NA, RG 59, 865.00/7-1745; Report by Rennel, August 1943, NA, RG 165, Entry 77, Box 1906, File 6960. An American official in Catania agreed with Tasca's estimate. "Security Intelligence Summary—Period Ending 30 Oct. 44, Appendix B— Separatism in Eastern Sicily," undated, ACS, *CAA*, Appendice, b. 1, f. 5.

17. "Minutes of Meeting of SCAOs and AMGOT HQ Staff at AMGOT HQ, Palermo," 20–21 August 1943, PRO, FO 371, 37327; Report by Rennel, August 1943, NA, RG 165, Entry 77, Box 1906, File 6960; many of Rennel's observations were analyzed by the OSS. OSS, Research and Analysis Branch, "Sicilian Separatism with Particular Reference to the Report of Lord Rennel of Rodd," 19 November 1943, NA, RG 59, R&A Report 1521.

18. "Separatism and Separatists," unsigned and undated, NA, RG 331, 10100/143/274; Combined Civil Affairs Committee, "Operation of AMG in Sicily and Italy," 27 December 1943, NA, RG 165, Entry 77, Box 2013, File 6960.

19. OSS, Research and Analysis Branch, "Psychological Warfare Weekly Roundup No. 23," 22–28 August 1943, NA, RG 226, Entry 106, Box 1, Folder 10.

20. OSS, Research and Analysis Branch, "Psychological Warfare Weekly Roundup No. 24," 29 August–4 September 1943, NA, RG 226, Entry 106, Box 1, Folder 10; Territorial Legion of the Carabinieri Reali of Messina, Catania Group, "Sicilian Separatism," 8 February 1944, NA, RG 331, 10103/143/28.

21. OSS, "Development of Political Parties in Sicily; Political Personalities," 19 November 1943, CIA; OSS, "Notes on the Political Situation in Sicily After Its Occupation by Forces of the United Nations," 21 August 1943, NA, RG 165, Entry 77, Box 1909, File 6960; "Sicilian Separatist Movement," 23 October 1944, PRO, FO 371, 43918; Nester to Secretary of State, "Separatist Movement: Letter Addressed to the President of the United States and the Prime Minister of England as well as to All Responsible for the Allied Nations, Written by Lucio Tasca," 9 December 1944, NA, RG 59, 865.01.12-944; Giarrizzo, *Sicilia politica*, 14. The organizations that were created are in Ganci, *L'Italia anti-moderata*, 298–299.

22. Marino, *Storia del separatismo*, 66; Military Intelligence Division, "Weekly News Summary 5 to 11 February 1944," 12 February 1944, NA, RG 165, Entry 77, Box 1903, File 2400–2800.

23. Finocchiaro Aprile, *Il movimento indipendentista*, 49, 71, 94.

24. "Sicilian Separatist Movement," 23 October 1944, PRO, FO 371, 43918.

25. Garland and Smyth, *Sicily and the Surrender*, 2–7, 11, 24, 269; see also Trumbull Higgins, *Soft Underbelly: The Anglo-American Controversy Over the Italian Campaign, 1939–1945* (New York: The MacMillan Company, 1968), 5–131.

26. OSS, Research and Analysis Branch, "Sicilian Separatism with Particular Reference to the Report of Lord Rennel of Rodd," 19 November 1943, NA, RG 59, R&A Report 1521; in the same location see, "British Policy in Italy," 15

August 1944, R&A Report 2318; OSS, "British Authorities Provoked by *Time* Article 'Free Sicily' and Investigating Its Translation in Separatist Circles," 21 September 1944, CIA. The question of British support for the movement had been debated in Parliament as early as September 1943; degli Espinosa, *Il regno del sud,* 87–88.

27. Headquarters, 2677th Regiment, OSS, "Finocchiaro Aprile Confides of Letter from Churchill," 25 October 1944, CIA. It was reported that Finocchiaro Aprile had sent Churchill a copy of the separatist program and a facsimile of the separatist flag depicting an independent Sicily. Experimental Detachment G-3, X-2 Branch, Palermo, 5 October 1943, NA, RG 165, Entry 77, Box 1904, File 3700.

28. E.E. Conroy to J. Edgar Hoover, "Sicilian Separatist Movement; Autonomous Sicilian Republic," 7 October 1943, 5 January 1944; Hoover to Adolf A. Berle, Jr., "Sicilian Separatist Movement, Autonomous Sicilian Republic," 27 October 1943, FBI, 65-51898-X. The same charge is leveled in OSS, Research and Analysis Branch, "British Policy in Italy," 15 August 1944, NA, RG 59, R&A Report 2318. OSS officials also kept tabs on the British. Donald Downes, a close associate of Bill Donovan, head of the OSS, wrote Roosevelt that he thought Churchill was encouraging the separatist movement but with possible American involvement. Robin Winks, *Cloak and Gown: Scholars in the Secret War, 1939–1961* (William Morrow and Company, Inc: New York, 1987), 216.

29. In 1945, Finocchiaro Aprile related that the French government wanted Sicily in its sphere of influence, but called the proposal "extremely repugnant." Headquarters, 2677th Regiment, OSS, "France Wants Sicily In Its Sphere," 19 May 1945, CIA. In December 1943, the question of Soviet support for separatism ended after Andrei Vichinsky came to Palermo and declared that the Soviet Union was interested only in Italian unity and independence. Barbagallo, *Rivoluzione mancata,* 88; di Carcaci, *Memorie,* 39–40; Gaja, *L'esercito,* 154.

30. Allied Control Commission, Sicilia Region to Regional Public Safety Officer, Region I, "Political Meeting and Disturbance," 6 March 1944, NA, RG 331, 10100/143/276.

31. Nester to Secretary of State, "Present Organization of the Separatist Movement," 6 August 1945, NA, RG 59, 865.00/8-645; "Rapporto speciale sul 1 Congresso del Movimento Per La Indipendenza Siciliana," ACS, *MI*, DGPS, AA.GG.RR., 1944, Cat. C-2-A, b. 39, f. "Movimento separatista Siciliana." In the summer of 1943, the Committee had twenty-four members including Finocchiaro Aprile, Lucio and Alessandro Tasca, Antonino Varvaro, Vincenzo La Manna, and Sebastiano Lo Verde."Report on Sicilian Separatism and the Movimento per l'Indipendenza della Sicilia," 17 April 1946, PRO, FO 371, 67786. For a list of members see "Political Information: Separatist Movement," 4 October 1943, NA, RG 165, Entry 77, Box 1904, File 3700.

32. For copies of the message see "Al Re d'Italia Vittorio Emanuele III," 4 October 1943, NA, RG 331, 10100/143/277; Colonel (name illegible) from OSS, X-2, "Political Situation in Sicily," 2 March 1944, CIA.

33. "Confidential Report," unsigned and undated, NA, RG 331, 10100/143/ 82; Det. G. 3 ATT. to 7 Army Rear, "Confidential," 28 December 1943, NA, RG 331, 10100/142/414. At least one separatist opponent pointed out the existence of a secret executive committee. Among its members were Finocchiaro Aprile, Giovanni Guarino Amella, and Lucio Tasca; Enrico La Loggia to Bonomi, 6 June 1944, ACS, *PCM,* 1944–1946, 8-2-10912; "Rapporto speciale sul 1 Congresso del

Movimento Per l'Indipendenza Siciliana," ACS, *MI*, DGPS, AA.GG.RR., 1944, Cat. C-2-A, b. 39, f. "Movimento separatista Siciliana"; "Confidential Report," unsigned and undated, NA, RG 331, 10100/143/82; "Report on Sicilian Separatism and the Movimento per l'Indipendenza della Sicilia," 17 April 1946, PRO, FO 371, 67786.

34. Pantaleone, *Mafia and Politics*, 66, 75; Giarrizzo, *Sicilia politica*, 23; Marino, *Storia del separatismo*, 67–68; Alfonso Madeo, ed., *Testo integrale della relazione della Commissione Parlamentare d'inchiesta sul fenomeno della mafia* (Rome: Cooperative Scrittori, 1973), vol. II, 998. This source lists the meeting date as December 6.

35. Pantaleone, *Mafia and Politics*, 66.

·36. "With Reference to the Previous Memo Concerning the Separatist Movement," 14 January 1944, NA, RG 331, 10100/143/276.

37. There are two versions of the order. The signers common to both were Finocchiaro Aprile, Francesco Termini, Santi Rindone, Luigi La Rosa, Giuseppe Faranda, Girolamo Stancanelli, Domenico Cigna, Giovanni Guarino Amella, Edoardo Di Giovanni, and Mariano Costa. One version also contains the signature of Antonio Parlapiano Vella. "Il Comitato Centrale per l'Indipendenza Siciliana," 9 December 1943, NA, RG 331, 10100/101/146; "The Central Committee for the Independence of Sicily," 9 December 1943, NA, RG 331, 10100/143/278; in the same location see "Morning Bulletin," 7 January 1944.

38. Pantaleone, *Mafia and Politics*, 66.

39. OSS, "Program of the Sicilian Democratic Party of Order," 9 April 1944, NA, RG 165, Entry 77, Box 1950, File 3700; see also OSS, "Notes on Separatism: 1. Communist Leader 2. Aldisio's Attitude 3. Pro-American Maffia 4. Bagheria Meeting," 7–14 August 1944, FBI, 65-51898-3; Aga Rossi, "I governi Bonomi," 140–141.

40. Military Intelligence Division, "Stability Report 29 Jan. to 4 Feb. 1944, Sicily," 9 February 1944, NA, RG 165, Entry 77, Box 1903, File 2810–3020.

41. Pantaleone, *Mafia and politics*, 73.

42. "Seduta del Comitato Centrale-Giorno 8 Gennaio 1944," NA, RG 331, 10100/101/146. Some of the observers included Edoardo Milio Cangemi from Messina, Enrico Di Natale of Syracuse, and Michelangelo Cipolla. A special invitation had been extended to Vincenzo Vacirca. Committee members included Finocchiaro Aprile, Varvaro, Santi Rindone, Vincenzo La Manna and Giovanni Guarino Amella.

43. Ibid.

44. The Catania committee had been formed in October 1942, but did not join with the Palermo committee until 1944. The Catania committee was not "officially" formed until April 1944. Marino, *Storia del separatismo*, 114–115; di Carcaci, *Memorie*, 66; Barbagallo, *Rivoluzione mancata*, 69, 73.

45. Nester to Secretary of State, "Present Organization of the Separatist Movement," 6 August 1945, NA, RG 59, 865.00/8-645.

46. "Situazione dei partiti politici," August 1944, ACS, *MI*, AG, 1944–1946, b. 24, f. 1878; from the same location see "Situazione dei partiti politici-Mese di Dicembre 1944"; "Pro-Memoria," NA, RG 331, 10100/143/277.

47. Comando della 6 Brigata Carabinieri Reali to AMG Headquarters, "Segnalazione," 9 December 1943, NA, RG 331, 10100/143/277. Finocchiaro Aprile admitted that people were "easily attracted to separatism because it is simple and accessible to the masses, especially the agricultural classes." OSS, "Interview with Hon. Andrea Finocchiaro Aprile," 28 April 1944, CIA.

48. "Fascist Policeman's Ill Doings," March 1944, NA, RG 31, 10100/143/276.

49. The paper's editors were Finocchiaro Aprile, Michelangelo Cipolla, Sebastiano Lo Verde, Pietro Villasevaglios, Fausto Montesanti, Lucio Tasca, and Alessandro Tasca. Sirio Rossi compiled the paper's articles. R. Questore di Palermo to the Allied Military Government, undated, NA, RG 331, 10100/143/277. For copies see Allied Military Government, Sicily Region Headquarters to Chief, Public Safety Division, No. 1 Region Headquarters, "Political Propaganda," 7 January 1944, NA, RG 331, 10100/143/277.

50. R. Questore di Palermo to the Allied Military Government, undated, NA, RG 331, 10100/143/277; Nester to Secretary of State, "Clandestine Separatist Newspaper *L'Indipendenza,*" 17 October 1944, NA, RG 59, 865.00/10-1744. Publication of separatist literature also upset the Communists, who complained that freedom of the press had been granted the separatists because of their wealth and influence. Military Intelligence Division, "Weekly News Summary—5 to 11 February 1944," 12 February 1944, NA, RG 165, Entry 77, Box 1903, File 2400–2800.

51. OSS, "*The Sicilian Republic,* Pamphlet of the Sicilian Labor Party," 13 May 1944, CIA; from the same source, "*La Repubblica Siciliana,* a Pamphlet of the Sicilian Labor Party," 20 May 1944; "*La Repubblica di Sicilia* Ceases Publication," 15 June 1944; "Appendix 'A' to Fortnightly Security Report for Period Ending 28 July 1944," 28 July 1944, NA, RG 331, 10100/143/275.

52. For a copy see Military Intelligence Division, Military Attaché Report, Sicily, "Separatist Propaganda: *Catechismo del libero siciliano,*" 25 April 1944, NA, RG 165, Entry 77, Box 1950, File 3700.

53. Ibid.

54. References to Sicilian separatism in correspondence intercepted by the Allies made it the single most-written-about subject in Sicilian politics. At least two thirds of the letters were pro-separatist, and many rejected the belief that the English were behind the movement. Allied Force Headquarters, Information and Censorship Section to Chief, Communications Censorship Branch, "Sicilian Separatism," 1 April 1944, NA, RG 331, 10100/101/146; R. Questura di Palermo, "Pro-Memoria," 13 March 1944, NA, RG 331, 10100/143/278; OSS, "Andrea Finocchiaro Aprile's Visit to Catania," 15 April 1944, CIA; Communications Censorship Branch, "Sicilian Separatism," 1 April 1944, NA, RG 331, 10100/101/146.

55. R. Questura di Palermo, "Pro-Memoria," 13 March 1944, NA, RG 331, 10100/143/278; OSS, "Andrea Finocchiaro Aprile's Visit to Catania," 15 April 1944, CIA. On 2 March several high-level provincial officials in Trapani swore their allegiance to the separatist movement during a secret meeting. OSS, "Sicily, Separatist Party Meeting, Palermo," 18 February 1944, CIA.

56. Territorial Legion of the Royal Carabinieri of Messina to Major Gould, "Sicilian Separatism," 8 February 1944, NA, RG 331, 10100/273/278; Royal Questura of Palermo, "Memorandum," 2 February 1944, NA, RG, 331, 10100/273/278.

57. Finocchiaro Aprile addressed this question at a meeting held on 17 April 1944. He urged a more vigorous propaganda campaign by the movement's advocates. R. Questura of Palermo, "Memorandum," 17 April 1944, NA, RG 331, 10100/143/278.

58. Di Carcaci, *Memorie,* 45–46; R. Burks to Major Raffa, "Meeting Held by the Partito del Lavoro (Separatist) in the Teatro Bellini on 16 January 1944,"

19 January 1944, NA, RG 331, 10100/142/415. See Chapter 4 for the lifting of the ban on politics.

59. Giarrizzo, *Sicilia politica*, 30; Giuseppe Mammarella, *Italy After Fascism*, 1966), 65; degli Espinosa, *Il regno del sud*, 305–329. The Bari Congress increased support for Sicilian autonomy while weakening separatist strength. "Security Intelligence Report—5 Feb. 44," 5 February 1944, ACS, *CAA*, Appendice, b. 1, f. 5. The central committee decided not to send separatist representatives to the congress; Military Intelligence Division, "Stability Report 29 Jan. to 4 Feb. 1944, Sicily," 9 February 1944, NA, RG 165, Entry 77, Box 1903, File 2810–3020. The movement also issued a statement justifying its decision. Committee for Sicilian Independence, 28 January 1944, NA, RG 331, 10100/ 143/277.

60. On the meeting see R. Questura di Palermo, "Pro-Memoria," 14 February 1944 and "Summary of a Report on a Public Meeting Organized by the Independent Sicily Movement," NA, RG 331, 10100/142/14; OSS, "Sicily; Separatist Party Meeting, Palermo," 18 February 1944, CIA; Comando Arma Carabinieri Reali dell'Italia Liberata to MI, "Riunione in Palermo indetta dai separatisti. Echi nell'isola della restituzione del territorio al Governo Italiano," 3 March 1944, ACS, *MI*, AG, 1944–1946, b. 6, f. 426.

61. "Summary of a Report on a Public Meeting Organized by the Independent Sicily Movement," undated and unsigned, NA, RG 331, 10100/142/14; Territorial Legion of Carabinieri Reali of Palermo, "Relation on the Meeting of the Sicilian Independence Party," 13 February 1944, NA, RG 331, 10100/143/278; OSS, "Sicily, Separatist Party Meeting, Palermo, 18 February 1944, CIA.

62. Unsigned, undated, and untitled report on the meeting of 13 February 1944, NA, RG 331, 10100/142/14; "Summary of a Report on a Public Meeting Organized by the Independent Sicily Movement," unsigned and undated, NA, RG 331, 10100/142/14; Territorial Legion of the Carabinieri Reali of Palermo, "Relation on the Meeting of the Sicilian Independence Party," 13 February 1944, NA, RG 331, 10100/143/278. On the speech see di Carcaci, *Memorie*, 62–63; Giarrizzo, *Sicilia politica*, 30–31.

63. Territorial Legion of the Carabinieri Reali of Palermo, "Relation on the Meeting of the Sicilian Independence Party," 13 February 1944, NA, RG 331, 10100/143/278; "Summary of a Report of a Public Meeting Organized by the Independent Sicily Movement," unsigned and undated, NA, RG 331, 10100/ 142/14.

64. Territorial Legion of the Carabinieri Reali of Palermo, "Relation on the Meeting of the Sicilian Independence Party," 13 February 1944, NA, RG 331, 10100/143/278; Comando Arma Carabinieri Reali dell'Italia Liberata to MI, "Riunione in Palermo indetta dai separatisti. Echi nell'isola della restituzione del territorio al Governo Italiano," 3 March 1944, ACS, *MI*, AG, 1944–1946, b. 6, f. 426.

65. R. Questura of Palermo, "Pro-Memoria," 14 February 1944, NA, RG 331, 10100/142/14; Comando Arma Carabinieri Reali dell'Italia Liberata to MI, "Riunione in Palermo indetta dai separatisti. Echi nell'isola della restituzione del territorio al Governo Italiano," 3 March 1944, ACS, *MI*, AG, 1944–1946, b. 6, f. 426.

66. Di Carcaci, *Memorie*, 63, 87, 90–91; OSS, "Political Situation in Catania," 26 February, 1, 2 March, 6 April 1944, NA, RG 165, Entry 77, Box 1950, File 3700.

67. Nester to Secretary of State, "Clandestine Publication *Giallo Rosso,*" 18 November 1944, NA, RG 59, 865.911/11-1844. Other separatist publications included *La Voce Siciliana, La Repubblica Siciliana, Sicilia e Libertà-Partito Separatista Siciliano, Sicilia-Organo del Movimento per la Indipendenza della Sicilia, Sicilia Martire,* and *Sicilia Indipendente-Organo del Movimento per l'Indipendenza della Sicilia.* See Nicolosi, *Sicilia contro Italia,* 153–155; Trizzino, *Che vuole la Sicilia?,* 41.

68. OSS, "Political Situation in Catania," 26 February, 1, 2 March, 6 April 1944, NA, RG 165, Entry 77, Box 1950, File 3700. In late 1944, di Carcaci claimed that the Lega had 130,000 members. Guglielmo Carcaci to Bonomi, ACS, PCM, 1944–1946, 8-2, 10912.

69. OSS, "Meeting of the Lega Giovanile Separatista, Palermo, 23 April 1944; Speeches by Giganti and Aprile," 24, 25 April 1944, CIA; R. Questura of Palermo to his Excellency the Prefect, "Separatist Juvenile Union-Meeting," 24 April 1944, NA, RG 331, 10100/143/278.

70. OSS, "Weekly Political Bulletin from Sicily," 17 March 1944, NA, RG 165, Entry 77, Box 1949, File 3200–3300; di Carcaci, *Memorie,* 67. According to Nicolosi, the Catanese separatists adopted the official name first. Nicolosi, *Sicilia contro Italia,* 48.

CHAPTER 4. SEPARATISM AND ITS ENEMIES

1. Mario Missori, *Governi,* 156–161; Aga Rossi, "I governi Bonomi," 7–9.

2. Military Intelligence Division, Military Attache Report, "Stability Report," 19 April 1944, NA, RG 165, Entry 77, Box 1948, File 3000; ACC Monthly Report, Sicilia Region Headquarters, "Report for the Month of March 1944," undated, NA, RG 165, Entry 77, Box 1948, File 3000; OSS, "Attorney Vincenzo Purpura's Attitude on the High Commissioner for Sicily," 24 June 1944, NA, RG 226, 80525; Comando Arma Carabinieri Reali dell'Italia Liberata to Renato Morelli, Sottosegretario alla Presid. del Consiglio dei Ministri, "Movimento separatista in Sicilia," 28 May 1944, ACS, *PCM,* 1944–1946, 8-2-10912. "Security Intelligence Report-Period Ending 6 May 1944," 6 May 1944, ACS, *CAA,* Appendice, b. 1, f. 5; Comando Arma Carabinieri Reali dell'Italia Liberata to MI, "Relazione mensile riservatissima relativa al mese di Giugno 1944," 6 July 1944, ACS, *MI,* AG, 1944–1946, b. 24, f. 1878; Ganci, *L'Italia antimoderata,* 321.

3. Finocchiaro Aprile made this comment at a meeting of the Lega Giovanile on 23 April 1944 attended by approximately 1000 people in Palermo. Military Intelligence Division, Military Attache Report, "Speech of Honorable Finocchiaro Aprile," 1 May 1944, NA, RG 165, Entry 77, Box 1949, File 3200–3300; R. Questura of Palermo to Il Prefetto di Palermo, "Lega Giovanile Separatista-Comizio," 24 April 1944, NA, RG 331, 10100/143/27; Finocchiaro Aprile to Ivanoe Bonomi, 26 June 1944, NA, RG 331, 10100/143/275; OSS, "Events in Sicily During the Month of June 1944," 30 June 1944, CIA; Comando Arma Carabinieri Reali dell'Italia Liberata to Renato Morelli, Sottosegretario alla Presid. del Consiglio dei Ministri, "Movimento separatista in Sicilia," 28 May 1944, ACS, *PCM,* 1944–1946, 8-2-10912.

4. "Town Report Syracuse—Period Ending 1 June 1944," 1 June 1944, ACS, CAA, Appendice, b.1, f. 6.

5. For statistics on the work of one committee see R. Prefettura di Palermo to MI, "Defascistizazzione," 10 August 1944, ACS, *MI*, AG, 1944–1946, b. 8, f. 532; Coles and Weinberg, *Soldiers Become Governors,* 212.

6. Comando Arma Carabinieri Reali dell'Italia Liberata to Renato Morelli, Sottosegretario alla Presid. del Consiglio dei Ministri, "Movimento separatista in Sicilia," 28 May 1944, ACS, *PCM*, 1944–1946, 8-2-10912; "Town Report Syracuse-Period Ending 1 Jun. 1944," 1 June 1944, ACS, *CAA,* Appendice, b. 1, f. 6; "Town Report Syracuse—Period 15 Oct.-29 Oct. 44," 29 October 1944, ACS, *CAA,* Appendice, b. 1, f. 6; R. Prefetto di Enna to MI, 15 August 1944, ACS, *MI*, AG, 1944–1946, b. 12, f. 821. The OSS reported that out of 4,000,000 Sicilians, only 600,000 were actively participating in political affairs. OSS, "Political Parties and Organized Labor in Sicily," 26 April 1944, NA, RG 165, Entry 77, Box 1950, File 3100–3400; OSS, "Survey of the Political Situation in Sicily," 23 February 1944, NA, RG 165, Entry 77, Box 1950, File 3700; Surveys of Public Opinion Held in Sicily, November 1943-January 1944, Report 6, "Public Officials," December 1943, Sheets 1 and 3, NA, RG 165, Entry 77, Box 1909, File 6960.

7. "Town Report Syracuse-Period 15 Sept.-29 Sept. 44," dated 28 September 1944, ACS, *CAA,* Appendice, b. 1, f. 6; Comando Arma dei Carabinieri Reali dell'Italia Liberata to MI, "Relazione mensile riservatissima relativa al mese di Giugno 1944," 6 July 1944, ACS, *MI*, AG, 1944–1946, b. 6, f. 426.

8. Comando Arma Carabinieri Reali dell'Italia Liberata to MI, "Relazione mensile riservatisima relativa al mese di Giugno 1944," 6 July 1944, ACS, *MI,* AG, 1944–1946, b. 6, f. 426; Comando Arma Carabinieri Reali dell'Italia Liberata to MI, "Condizioni politico-economiche della Sicilia," 30 March 1944, ACS, *MI,* AG, 1944–1946, b. 24, f. 1878; Giarrizzo, *Sicilia politica,* 37–38.

9. See the order banning political activity in Allied Military Government of Occupied Territory, *Sicily Gazette,* July 1943; Report by Rennel, August 1943, PRO, FO 371, 37326; OSS, "Survey of the Political Situation in Sicily," 23 February 1944, NA, RG 165, Entry 77, Box 1950, File 3700; OSS, "Sicily: Political Parties in Palermo," 2 March 1944, NA, RG 165, Entry 77, Box 1904, File 3700. One report listed sixteen different political groups. Allied Military Government, Sicily Region to Chief, Public Safety Division, No. 1 Region, "Political Propaganda," 3 December 1943, NA, RG 331, 10100/143/1.

10. OSS, "Survey of the Political Situation in Sicily," 23 February 1944, NA, RG 165, Entry 77, Box 1950, File 3700.

11. Allied Military Government, Sicily Region to Chief, Public Safety Division, No. 1 Region, "Political Propaganda," 3 December 1943, NA, RG 331, 10100/143/1.

12. Degli Espinosa, *Il regno del sud,* 88; Comando Arma Carabinieri Reali dell'Italia Liberata to Ministro degli Interni, "Condizioni politico-economiche della Sicilia," 30 March 1944, ACS, *MI,* AG, 1944–1946, b. 24, f. 1878.

13. Allied Military Government, Sicily Region to Chief, Public Safety Division, No. 1 Region, "Political Propaganda," 3 December 1943, NA, RG 331, 10100/143/1; OSS, "Survey of the Political Situation in Sicily," 23 February 1944, NA, RG 165, Entry 77, Box 1950, File 3700.

14. Cable from AFHQ-Cinc, 9 January 1944, PRO, WO 204, 9741 F; Allied Military Government, Sicily Region Headquarters, "Official Order 17," 10 January 1944, NA, RG 331, 10000/132/308.

15. In many of the island's provinces, the members of the separatist movement outnumbered all the other political parties combined. "Security Intelli-

gence Summary-Period Ending 15 Jul. 44," undated, ACS, *CAA*, Appendice, b. 1, f. 6; Comitato Nazionale della Lega Giovanile, September 1944, ACS, *MI*, AG, 1944–1946, b. 8, f. 559, sf. 6.

16. Standard works on the Committee of National Liberation fail to mention the Sicilian branch. Roberto Battaglia, *Storia della resistenza italiana: 8 Settembre 1943–25 Aprile 1945* (Turin: Einaudi, 1964); Pietro Secchia and Filippo Frassati, *La resistenza e gli alleati* (Milan: Feltrinelli, 1962). On the formation of the Central Committee of the CLN see Enzo Piscitelli, *Storia della resistenza romana* (Bari: Laterza, 1965), 110–123. On the schism see OSS, "Survey of the Political Situation in Sicily," 23 February 1944, NA, RG 165, Entry 77, Box 1950, File 3700; OSS, "Weekly Political Bulletin From Sicily," 17 March 1944, NA, RG 165, Entry 77, Box 1949, File 3200–3300. On the Committee of National Liberation in Palermo, see "Gli Avvenimenti in Sicilia," *Nazioni Unite*, 1 November 1944.

17. In 1920, Finocchiaro Aprile supported a proposal by La Loggia to decentralize the administration of public works in Sicily. On La Loggia and the proposal see Enrico La Loggia, *Autonomia e rinascita della Sicilia* (Palermo: IRES, 1953), 23–35. On the *Fronte Unico* see "Preamble and Declaration of the Fronte Unico Unitaria," 21 October 1943, ACS, *PCM*, Governo di Salerno, 1943–1944, Cat. 4, f. 4/10; Partito Riformista Laburista Italiano—Comitato Centrale, "Quaderno 1," January 1944, ACS, *MI*, AG, 1944–1946, b. 24, f. 1878.

18. "Preamble and Declaration of the Fronte Unico Unitaria," 21 October 1943, ACS, *PCM*, Governo di Salerno, 1943–1944, Cat. 4, f. 4/10; La Loggia to Badoglio, 4 November 1943, ACS, *PCM*, Governo di Salerno, 1943–1944, Cat. 4, f. 4/10, sf. 6; La Loggia to Bonomi, June 1944, ACS, *PCM*, 1944–1946, 8-2-10912; La Loggia, *Autonomia e rinascita*, 58–63; Giarrizzo, *Sicilia politica*, 15–18.

19. Surveys of Public Opinion Held in Sicily, November 1943–January 1944, Report 1, "A Survey of Radio Listening Habits," December 1943, Sheet 11, NA, RG 165, Entry 77, Box 1909, Folder 6960; Luigi Sturzo to Salvatore Aldisio, 30 November 1943, NA, RG 331, 10103/143/28; R. Burks to Major Raffa, "Confidential Report on the Activities of the Various Political Parties in the Palermo Area as of 10 January 1944," 21 January 1944, NA, RG 331, 10100/131/415; OSS, "Political Situation in Catania," 26 February, 1, 2 March, 6 April 1944, NA, RG 165, Entry 77, Box 1950, File 3700; Miccichè, *Dopoguerra*, 20.

20. Sturzo knew of the party's reorganization and wished to send funds to help. Luigi Sturzo to Department of State, 24 February 1944, NA, RG 226, Entry 125, Box 42, Folder 534. In the same location see Sturzo to Mr. Earl Brennan, 24 February 1944. See also Sturzo to Aldisio, 30 November 1943, NA, RG 331, 10103/143/28. For his pre-war speeches see Luigi Sturzo, *I discorsi politici* (Rome: Istituto Luigi Sturzo, 1951). For Sturzo's program, see Luigi Sturzo, *La regione nella nazione* (Rome: Capriotti, 1949); "Partito Democratico Cristiano-Comitato per la Sicilia," 18 September 1943, ACS, *MI*, AG, 1944–1946, b. 24, f. 1878; Partito Democratico-Cristiano, Comitato Provinciale di Catania, "Memoriale a S.E. il Maresciallo Badoglio, Capo del Governo," 1 April 1944, ACS, *MI*, AG, 1944–1946, b. 24, f. 1878; from the same location, "Copia della Ordine d'Giorno della Congresso Regionale nella Caltanissetta," 16 December 1943.

21. Miccichè, *Dopoguerra*, 20, 179; Luigi La Rosa to Sturzo, 13 April 1944, in Sturzo, *Scritti inreditti*, Vol. 3, 254–257; Emanuele Macaluso, *I Comunisti e la Sicilia* (Rome: Riuniti, 1970), 31–32.

22. Miccichè, *Dopoguerra,* 54–89; Macaluso, *I Comunisti,* 24; Francesco Compagna and Vittorio De Caprariis, *Geografia delle elezioni italiane dal 1946 al 1953* (Bologna: Il Mulino, 1954), 38; Giarrizzo, *Sicilia politica,* 21, 24; Franco Grasso, ed., *Girolamo Li Causi e la sua azione politica per la Sicilia* (Palermo: Libri Siciliani, 1966), 51–52. For a general history see Paolo Spriano, *Storia del partito comunista italiano,* 5 vols. (Turin: Einaudi, 1967).

23. OSS, "Notes on Separatism," 7–14 August 1944, FBI, 65-51898-3; "Security Intelligence Report-17 Jun. 44," 17 June 1944, ACS, *CAA,* Appendice, b. 1, f. 5; Military Intelligence Division, "Weekly Stability Report," 14 November 1943, NA, RG 165, Entry 77, Box 1903, File 2810–3020; Luciano Salmi to Palmiro Togliatti, 17 April 1944, NA, RG 331, 10100/101/46.

24. "Partito Comunista di Sicilia-Palermo," ACS, *MI,* DGPS, AA.GG.RR., 1944, Cat. C-2-A, b. 39, f. "Movimento separatista Siciliana"; Nester to Secretary of State, "Communist Party: Restricted Pro-Separatist Manifesto," 15 November 1944, NA, RG 59, 865.008/11-1544; Spriano, *Partito comunista,* Vol. 5, 152.

25. Giarrizzo, *Sicilia politica,* 20; Harris, *Allied Military Administration,* 37; Report by Rennel, August 1943, PRO, FO 371, 37326; R. Burks to Major Raffa, "Confidential Report on the Activities of the Various Political Parties in the Palermo Area as of 10 January 1944," 21 January 1944, NA, RG 331, 10100/142/145; "Security Intelligence Report-8 Apl. 44," 8 April 1944, ACS, *CAA,* Appendice, b. 1, f. 5; OSS, "Development of Political Parties in Sicily, Political Personalities," 19 November 1943, CIA.

26. OSS, "Political Situation in Catania," 26 February, 1, 2 March, 6 April 1944," NA, RG 165, Entry 77, Box 1950, File 3700; "Security Intelligence Report-6 May 1944," 6 May 1994, ACS, *CAA,* Appendice, b.1, f. 5; Psychological Warfare Branch, Naples, "Conditions in Sicily," 1 July 1944, NA, RG 331, 10000/136/371; "Town Report Syracuse-Week Ending 6 Jul. 44," 6 July 1944, ACS, *CAA,* Appendice, b. 1, f. 6. In December 1943, Alessandro Tasca spread a rumor that there were 100,000 Communists in Palermo alone. Military Intelligence Division, "Stability of Government, Weekly Stability Report," 18 December 1943, NA, RG 165, Entry 77, Box 1903, Folder 2810–3020.

27. On Li Causi's work see Franco Grasso, ed., *Girolamo Li Causi;* Jacoviello, *La Sicilia,* 62–77.

28. Giarrizzo, *Sicilia politica,* 48–49; Grasso, *Girolamo Li Causi,* 57; Finocchiaro Aprile, *Il movimento indipendentista,* 28-29.

29. "Security Intelligence Report—20 May 44," 20 May 1944, ACS, *CAA,* Appendice, b. 1, f. 5; "Security Intelligence Report—8 Apl. 44," 8 April 1944, ACS, *CAA,* Appendice, b. 1, f. 5; *L'Unità,* 2 July 1944.

30. "Security Intelligence Summary—Period Ending 15 Nov. 44," undated, ACS, *CAA,* Appendice, b. 1, f. 5; "Town Report Syracuse—Period 15 Nov.-29 Nov. 44," dated 28 November 1944, ACS, *CAA,* Appendice, b. 1, f. 6.

31. The Fronte del Lavoro dissolved when the Communist party unified under Li Causi. In Palermo, the Republican-Social Party also belonged to the Fronte. "Declaration of the Fronte del Lavoro," 13 December 1943, NA, RG 331, 10100/101/146; OSS, Mr. A. E. Jolis to Arthur J. Goldberg, "Message from Len for Montana," 27 August 1943, NA, RG 226, Entry 106, Box 39, Folder 350.

32. "Distribution of Personnel—Italian—Section SI-Palermo," March 1944?, NA, RG 226, Entry 165, Box 30, Folder 258; "Interdepartmental Committee on Employee Investigations—Vincenzo Vacirca," 8 August 1944, FBI, 100-208-215-1; from the same source see SAC, New York, to Director, FBI, "Subject: Vincenzo Vacirca Passenger, SS Edward M. Crockett, Arrived New

York City 29 June 1944, Foreign Travel Control," 3 July 1944, 100-208-215-2; Alexander Kirk to J. Edgar Hoover, "Enclosure to 865.04417/5," 9 June 1926, 61-6107-1. On Vacirca's early career see Miccichè, *Dopoguerra,* 55–56, 85. In March 1944, many OSS personnel were removed from Sicily. Nester's OSS contacts after this date were probably native Sicilians. "Personnel to Be Returned to the United States," March 1944, NA, RG 226, Entry 165, Box 30, Folder 258; for a list of Vacirca's backers see Federazione Socialista Siciliana to Colonello Charles Poletti, 12 December 1943, NA, RG 331, 10100/101/146.

33. Federazione Socialista Siciliana to Colonello Charles Poletti, 12 December 1943, NA, RG 331, 10100/101/146; "Proposals for Sicilian Autonomy Prepared by the Italian Socialist Federation," 24 February 1944, NA, RG 331, 10000/132/152; Nester to Secretary of State, "Translation of a Pamphlet Recently Distributed in Palermo," 16 October 1944, NA, RG 59, 865.01/10-1644. In April 1944, Finocchiaro Aprile admitted that he counted "a great deal on the Sicilian Socialist Federation" led by Vacirca. "Interview With Hon. Andrea Finocchiaro Aprile," 28 April 1944, CIA. One American report labeled the followers of the Federazione as "die hard" separatists. Military Intelligence Division, "Schism in the Separatist Movement," 28 January 1944, NA, RG 165, Entry 77, Box 1904, File 3700. See Vacirca's article, "Gli Avvenimenti in Sicilia," in *Nazione Unite,* 1 November 1944; Giarrizzo, *Sicilia politica,* 31–33.

34. OSS, "Dissension in the Socialist Movement, Palermo, Sicily; Regulations for Youth Federation of the Socialist Party; Resolutions of the Italian Socialist Party," 21 April 1944, NA, RG 165, Entry 77, Box 1950, File 3700; Burks to Raffa, "Pamphlet Entitled Partito Socialista Circulated in Palermo on 15 January 1944," 17 January 1944, NA, RG 331, 10100/142/415.

35. "Town Report Syracuse—Week Ending 6 Jul. 44," 6 July 1944, ACS, *CAA,* Appendice, b. 1, f. 6; *Avanti!,* 30 June 1944.

36. F. Fancello, "Il Partito d'Azione nei suoi metodi e nei suoi fini," in *Quaderni del Partito d'Azione* (Tip. Ed. Sallustiana: Rome, 1944); Burks to Raffa, "Confidential Report on the Activities of the Various Political Parties in the Palermo Area as of 10 January 1944," 21 January 1944, NA, RG 331, 10100/142/415; OSS, "Political Situation in Catania," 26 February, 1, 2 March, 6 April 1944, NA, RG 165, Entry 77, Box 1950, File 3700; OSS, "Political Parties and Organized Labor in Sicily," 26 April 1944, NA, RG 165, Entry 77, Box 1950, File 3700.

37. *L'Italia Libera,* 1 April 1944; "Punti programmatici fondamentali del Partito d'Azione," 5–6, in *Quaderni del Partito d'Azione;* from the same source, Ugo La Malfa, "Per la rinascita dell'Italia"; OSS, "Political Situation in Catania," 26 February, 1, 2 March, 6 April 1944, NA, RG 165, Entry 77, Box 1950, File 3700.

38. Emilio Lussu, "La Ricostruzione dello stato," in *Quaderni del Partito d'Azione;* "Declaration of the Palermo Section of the Action Party," 12 December 1943, NA, RG 331, 10100/101/146; Burks to Raffa, "Meeting of the Party of Action on 19 January 1944," NA, RG 331, 10100/142/415.

39. Burks to Raffa, "Confidential Report on the Activities of the Various Political Parties in the Palermo Area as of 10 January 1944," NA, RG 331, 10100/142/215; Legione Territoriale dei Carabinieri Reali di Messina to Sig. Maggiore Gould, "Partiti liberale e repubblicano," 7 February 1944, NA, RG 331, 10100/143/28; in the same location, Legione Territoriale dei Carabinieri Reali di Messina to the Commissione Alleata di Controllo, "Passaggio della Sicilia al Governo Badoglio," 17 February 1944, NA, RG 331, 10103/143/28;

OSS, "Political Situation in Catania," 26 February, 1, 2 March, 6 April 1944, NA, RG 165, Entry 77, Box 1950, File 3700; OSS, "Political Parties and Organized Labor in Sicily," 26 April 1944, NA, RG 165, Entry 77, Box 1950, File 3700; Mammarella, *Italy After Fascism,* 58; see also Benedetto Croce, *Quando l'Italia era tagliata in due: Estratto di un diario, Luglio 1943–Giugno 1944* (Bari: Laterza, 1948).

40. "Security Intelligence Report-4 Mar. 1944," 4 March 1944, ACS, *CAA,* Appendice, b. 1, f. 5; Legione Territoriale dei Carabinieri Reali di Messina to Sig. Maggiore Gould, "Partito di Unione," undated, NA, RG 331, 10103/143/28; Comando Arma Carabinieri Reali dell'Italia Liberata to MI, "Riunioni in Palermo indetta dai separatisti. Echi nell'isola della restituzione del territorio al Governo Italiano," 3 March 1944, ACS, *MI,* AG, 1944–1946, b. 6, f. 426; Comando Arma Carabinieri Reali dell'Italia Liberata to Ministro degli Interni, "Condizioni politico-economiche della Sicilia," 30 March 1944, ACS, *MI,* AG, 1944–1946, b. 24, f. 1878.

41. Legione Territoriale dei Carabinieri Reali to Sig. Maggiore Gould, "Situazione dei partiti politici a Catania e in provincia," 6 February 1944, NA, RG 331, 10103/143/28; Military Intelligence Division, "Stability of Government; Proclamation of a New Party Partito Siciliano del Lavoro," 10 January 1944, NA, RG 165, Entry 77, Box 1904, File 3700.

42. OSS, "First Meeting of the Sicilian Labor Party in Palermo," 19 January 1944, CIA; from the same source, OSS, *"The Sicilian Republic,* Pamphlet of the Sicilian Labor Party," 13 May 1944. See the party's platform in Hoover to Berle, "Sicilian Separatist Movement," 4 May 1944, NA, RG 165, Entry 77, Box 2176, Folder 3840.

43. OSS, "Political Situation in Catania," 26 February, 1, 2 March, 6 April 1944, NA, RG 165, Entry 77, Box 1950, File 3700; Legione Territoriale dei Carabinieri Reali di Messina to Sig. Major Gould, "Partiti liberale e repubblicano," 7 February 1944, NA, RG 331, 10103/143/28.

44. Mr. Campbell, Lt. Burks, Ens. Roberts to Lt. Col. Fish, "Interview of Prof. Antonio Di Stefano, of the University of Palermo, head of the newly formed Party of Reconstruction, on 22 Dec. 1943," undated, NA, RG 331, 10100/142/414; the party was weakened by a division over policy between Di Stefano and the executive secretary, Tellaro. Military Intelligence Division, "Partito Siciliano della Ricostruzione," 17 February 1944, NA, RG 165, Entry 77, Box 1904, File 3700; from the same source see Military Intelligence Division, "Progress of Sicilian Party of Reconstruction," 11 February 1944, NA, RG 165, Entry 77, Box 1904, File 3700; Quaderno di Fronte del Lavoro, "Il separatismo," ACS, *MI,* AG, 1944–1946, b. 24, f. 1878. La Giovane Sicilia was another organization with a pro-American stance. For a brief time it suggested that Sicily could be economically independent if the United States actively supported it. OSS, "Proposals of the Sicilian Separatists to the U.S.A. and to Sicilians," 1 March 1944, NA, RG 165, Entry 77, Box 1904, File 3700.

45. On the *granai,* see the reports in ACS, *MI,* AG, 1944–1946, b. 7, f. 473 and b. 24, f. 1878; Alto Commissariato per la Sicilia to MI, "Rapporto sulla situazione in Sicilia," 28 August 1944, ACS, *MI,* AG, 1944–1946, b. 24, f. 1878.

46. Virgilio Nasi to Bonomi, 26 September 1944, ACS, *MI,* AG, 1944–1946, b. 46, f. 3724; Alto Commissariato per la Sicilia to MI, "Rapporto sulla situazione in Sicilia," 6 November 1944, ACS, *MI,* AG, 1944–1946, b. 24, f. 1878. OSS, "Events in Sicily During the Month of June 1944," 30 June 1944, CIA; "Security Intelligence Summary—Period Ending 15 Jul. 44," 15 July 1944, ACS, *CAA,*

Appendice, b. 1, f. 5; "Security Intelligence Summary—Period Ending 15 Aug. 44," undated, ACS, *CAA,* Appendice, b. 1, f. 5; Giarrizzo, *Sicilia politica,* 45.

47. Allied Force Headquarters, Information and Censorship Section, Psychological Warfare Branch, "Special Directive on *Granai del Popolo,*" undated, NA, RG 331, 10000/136/ 371.

48. Allied Control Commission, Public Relations Branch, 9 July 1944, NA, RG 331, 10000/136/371; in the same location see Psychological Warfare Branch, "Conditions in Sicily," 1 July 1944; Headquarters, Allied Control Commission, "Memorandum, Enforcement of Grain Collection in Sicily," 5 July 1944; Ralph J. Frantz to John Rayner, George Edman and James Minifle, 5 September 1944, NA, RG 331, 10000/132/152.

49. On these meetings see R. Questura di Palermo, "Memo," 24 April 1944, NA, RG 331, 10100/143/278; from the same source see R. Questura di Palermo to S.E. Alto Commissariato per la Sicilia, 15 May 1944; Charles Spofford to Headquarters, Allied Control Commission, "Publications—*Sicilia e Libertà* issue of 15 June," 2 July 1944, NA, RG 331, 10100/142/14.

50. *Sicilia—Organo del Movimento per la Indipendenza della Sicilia,* 14 May 1944; Charles Spofford to Headquarters, Allied Control Commission, "Publications—*Sicilia e Libertà* issue of 15 June," 2 July 1944, NA, RG 331, 10100/142/14. In May 1944, Sicilian prefects agreed that the amount paid to producers was too low, but asked that growers deliver their grain to the marketplace out of a "civic" duty and as a show of solidarity with the Sicilian people. "I Prefetti della Sicilia, Riuniti Presso l'Alto Commissariato di Palermo il Giorno 20 Maggio 1944," ACS, *MI,* AG, 1944–1946, b. 7, f. 473.

51. OSS, "Events in Sicily During the Month of June 1944," 30 June 1944, CIA; Finocchiaro Aprile to Generale Mariotti, 6 July 1944, ACS, PCM, 1944–1946, 8-2-10912.

52. "Town Report Syracuse—Period Ending 1 June 44," 1 June 1944, ACS, *CAA,* Appendice, b. 1, f. 6; OSS, "Interview with Hon. Finocchiaro Aprile," 28 April 1944, CIA.

53. "Appendix 'A' to Fortnightly Security Report for Period Ending 28 July 1944," 28 July 1944, NA, RG 331, 10100/143/275.

54. "Partito Comunista di Sicilia," undated, ACS, *MI,* AG, 1944–1946, b. 54, f. 4484.

55. "Town Report Syracuse—Period Ending 1 June 1944," 1 June 1944, ACS, *CAA,* Appendice, b. 1, f. 6.

56. Aldisio to the Comando Supremo, "Ordine Pubblico in Sicilia," 30 May 1944, ACS, *MI,* AG, 1944–1946, b. 24, f. 1878; "Town Report Syracuse—Period Ending 25 May 44," 25 May 1944, ACS, *CAA,* Appendice, b. 1, f. 6; "Security Intelligence Report—8 Apl. 44," 8 April 1944, ACS, *CAA,* Appendice, b. 1, f. 5; in the same location, "Security Intelligence Report—20 May 1944," 20 May 1944; Comando Arma Carabinieri Reali dell'Italia Liberata to Renato Morelli Sottosegretario alla Presid. del Consiglio dei Ministri, "Movimento separatista in Sicilia," 28 May 1944, ACS, *PCM,* 1944–1946, 8-2-10912; Allied Control Commission, Sicily Region Headquarters to Executive Commissioner, "Sicilian Separatism," 1 July 1944, NA, RG 331, 10100/143/275. In June, separatists decided to contact members of the armed forces in the hope of increasing support among those stationed on the island. In doing so, separatist leaders hoped that the army would not be "hostile" to them. OSS, "Separatist Propaganda Plans; Palermo, Sicily," 20 June 1944, CIA.

57. "Security Intelligence Report—1 Apl. 44," 1 April 1944, ACS, *CAA*, Appendice, b. 1, f. 5; from the same source, "Security Intelligence Report—20 May 44," 20 May 1944; "Town Report Syracuse—Period Ending 25 May 44," 25 May 1944, ACS, *CAA*, Appendice, b. 1, f. 6. The trial took place in Catania and was well attended. Finocchiaro Aprile defended himself and Raffaele Di Martino acted as the attorney for the other men. Comando Generale dell'Arma dei Carabinieri Reali to MI, "Sicilia—Propaganda separatista. Disordini," 6 January 1945, ACS, *MI*, AG, 1944–1946, b. 8, f. 559, sf.1.

58. "Town Report Syracuse—Period Ending 1 June 44," 1 June 1944, ACS, *CAA*, Appendice, b. 1, f. 6.

59. "Summary of Impressions Gained by J. A. Gengacelli on Tours of Sicily with PWB Sound Truck for the *Granai del Popolo* Campaign from 30 July to 30 August Inclusive," undated, NA, RG 331, 10000/132/152.

60. Comando 6 Brigata Carabinieri Reali to Allied Control Commission, Civil Police Section, "Fonogramma a mano," 29 May 1944, NA, RG 331, 10100/143/276; "Appendix 'A' to Fortnightly Security Report for Period Ending 28 July 1944," 28 July 1944, NA, RG 331, 10100/143/275; Psychological Warfare Branch, "Conditions in Sicily," 1 July 1944, NA, RG 331, 10000/136/371; di Carcaci, *Memorie*, 71.

61. *Sicilia e Libertà*, 15 June 1944.

62. Aldisio to the Comando Supremo, "Ordine pubblico in Sicilia," 30 May 1944, ACS, *MI*, AG, 1944-1946, b. 24, f. 1878.

63. Allied Control Commission, Sicilia Region Headquarters to Executive Commissioner, "Sicilian Separatism," 1 July 1944, NA, RG 331, 10100/143/275.

64. Nester to Secretary of State, "Separatist Movement in Sicily," 29 July 1944, NA, RG 59, 865.00/7-2944; "Town Report Syracuse—Week Ending 6 Jul. 44," 6 July 1944, ACS, *CAA*, Appendice, b. 1, f. 6; from the same source, see the report of 28 July to 15 August; "Movimento Per L' Indipendenza della Sicilia—Il Comitato per la Provincia di Messina," ACS, *MI*, DGPS, AA.GG.RR., 1944, b. 39, f. "Movimento separatista Siciliana"; from the same source, R. Prefettura di Palermo to MI, "Movimento separatista," 6 July 1944.

65. R. Prefettura di Ragusa to MI, "Apertura di sezione del Partito Separatista in Modica," 19 July 1944, ACS, *MI*, DGPS, AA.GG.RR., 1944, Cat. C-2-A, b. 39, f. "Movimento separatista Siciliana"; R. Prefetto di Ragusa to MI, "Apertura della sezione del partito separatista di Ragusa," 19 July 1944, ACS, *MI*, AG, 1944–1946, b. 13, f. 1014; "Estratto dalla relazione n.27 Ris. in data 30 Luglio 1944 del Prefetto di Messina," ACS, *MI*, AG, 1944–1946, b. 36, f. 2817; "Estratto dalla relazione n. 967 in data 30 Agosto 1944 del Prefetto di Caltanissetta," ACS, *MI*, AG, 1944–1946, b. 218, f. 22633; "Estratto dalla relazione n. 2694 in data 29 Luglio 1944 del Prefetto di Agrigento," ACS, *MI*, AG, 1944–1946, b. 42, f. 3299; "Riassunto della relazione del Prefetto di Palermo," July 1944, ACS, *MI*, AG, 1944–1946, b. 24, f. 1878; "Security Intelligence Report—13 May 44," 13 May 1944, ACS, *CAA*, Appendice, b. 1, f. 5; from the same source see the report for the week of 6 May; "Town Report Syracuse—Week Ending 6 Jul. 44," 6 July 1944, ACS, *CAA*, Appendice, b. 1, f. 6.

66. OSS, "Events in Sicily During the Month of June 1944," 30 June 1944, CIA.

67. Finocchiaro Aprile to General Mariotti, 6 July 1944, ACS, *PCM*, 1944–1946, 8-2-10912; in the same location, Comando Militare della Sicilia to Ministro della Guerra, "Movimento separatista in Sicilia," 17 July 1944; Legione Territoriale dei Carabinieri Reali di Messina, "Incident Between Underofficers

of the Sabauda Division and Members of the Sicilian Separatist Movement," 30 June 1944, NA, RG 331, 10100/143/28.

68. Office of the Chief of Naval Operations, Intelligence Report, "Italy, Sicilian Separatist Movement Reported in Tangier," 18 May 1944, NA, RG 38, Register No. 9632-H, File C-10-f; Comando Arma Carabinieri Reali dell'Italia Liberata to Renato Morelli, Sottosegretario alla Presid. del Consiglio dei Ministri,"Movimento separatista in Sicilia," 28 May 1944, ACS, *PCM*, 1944–1946, 8-2-10912.

69. Finocchiaro Aprile to Bonomi, 26 June 1944, ACS, *MI*, DGPS, AA.GG.RR., 1944, Cat. C-2-A, b. 39, f. "Movimento separatista Siciliana"; Marino, *Storia del separatismo,* 75.

70. "Movimento per la Indipendenza della Sicilia, Comitato Nazionale, Messaggio ai Siciliani di America," 10 July 1944, ACS, *MI*, DGPS, AA.GG.RR., 1944, Cat. C-2-A, b. 39, f. "Movimento separatista Siciliana"; Gaja, *L'esercito,* 166–167.

71. OSS, "Present State of Italian Politics in the United States," 1 December 1943, NA, RG 165, Entry 77, Box 1951, File 3800–3840.

72. "Separatist Plea to Allied Officials. On the Anniversary of Liberation— 10 July 1944—to Sicilians and Anglo-Americans," NA, RG 331, 10100/143/275; Nester to Secretary of State, "Separatist Movement in Sicily," 31 July 1944, NA, RG 59, 865.00/7-3144.

73. Nester to Secretary of State, "Separatist Movement in Sicily," 5 July 1944, NA, RG 59, 865.01/ 7–544.

74. Finocchiaro Aprile to Roosevelt, 20 July 1944, Franklin D. Roosevelt Library, File 233A. On 6 July the national committee sent a letter to Winston Churchill. It was signed by Finocchiaro Aprile and thanked the British leader for all the help given Sicily by Britain. It also claimed that the Sicilian people wanted their independence with the "concurrence and under the aegis of Great Britain." Movement for the Independence of Sicily, National Committee to Winston Churchill, 6 July 1944, PRO, FO 371, 43918. Finocchiaro Aprile wrote to a number of world leaders. For some of the letters see Marino, *Storia del separatismo,* 249–270.

75. Allied Force Headquarters, Information and Censorship Section, Psychological Warfare Branch to A. N. Hancock, "Separatist Propaganda Extracts," 11 July 1944, NA, RG 331, 10100/142/14.

76. *Times,* 15 July 1944; Nester to Secretary of State, "*London Times* Article on Conditions in Sicily," 19 July 1944, NA, RG 59, 865.00/7-1944.

77. Ministero degli Affari Esteri, Direzione Generale Affari Politici, "Appunto," see attached "Alcuni Cenni sul Separatismo Siciliano," 21 August 1944, Ministero Affari Esteri, Serie Affari Politici, 1931–1945, Italia, b. 95/2, f. 5; the movement also attracted the attention of Germany. In the same location see R. Ministero Esteri, Ufficio Stampa, "D'Radio Germania 7/9/44," 8 September 1944. In 1946, officials of the Turkish government requested an assessment of the separatist movement. R. Ambasciata d'Italia, Ankara to R. Ministero degli Affari Esteri, "Oggetto: Separatismo siciliano," ACS, *MI*, AG, 1950–1951, b. 35, f. 11436.

78. "Movement for the Independence of Sicily, National Committee, to the United States Secretary of State for Foreign Affairs, the British Minister for Foreign Affairs, General DeGaulle, Chiang Kai-shek, the Cardinal Secretary of State for His Holiness, the Ministers for Foreign Affairs of Belgium, Czechoslovakia, Denmark, Greece, Yugoslavia, Norway, Holland, Poland, and Sweden," 20 July 1944, NA, RG 331, 10000/132/152; the same document can be found in ACS, *PCM*, 1944–1946, 8-2-10912. Finocchiaro Aprile sent a copy of the proclamation to Nester in case he wished to send it to the government: Nester to Secretary of State, "Separatist Movement in Sicily. Letter from Finocchiaro

Aprile." Enclosures No. 1 and No. 2, 18 August 1944, NA, RG 59, 865.01/8-1844; Nicolosi, *Sicilia contro Italia*, 188–189; Jacoviello, *La Sicilia*, 101–104.

79. Aldisio to MI, "Rapporto sulla Situazione in Sicilia," 28 August 1944, ACS, *MI*, AG, 1944–1946, b. 24, f. 1878.

80. Allied Control Commission, Sicily Region Headquarters to Executive Commissioner, "Sicily and Separatism," 9 August 1944, NA, RG 331, 10100/101/47.

81. Headquarters, Allied Control Commission to Sir Noel Charles, 29 August 1944, NA, RG 331, 10000/132/152.

82. "Appendix 'A' to Fortnightly Security Report for Period Ending 28 July 1944," 28 July 1944, NA, RG 331, 10100/143/275.

83. OSS, "Disagreement Between Musotto and D'Antoni, Prefect of Palermo," 23 June 1944, CIA. Musotto complained to Poletti about his difficulties but Poletti's superiors told him to refrain from interfering. Lush to Poletti, 20 April 1944, Poletti Papers, AMG General File, S-6.

84. Nester to Secretary of State, "Change of High Commissioner for Sicily," 31 July 1944, NA, RG 59, 865.01/7-3144; Giarrizzo, *Sicilia politica*, 46–47; Marino, *Storia del separatismo*, 92; Di Matteo *Anni roventi*, 238–239.

85. Alto Commissariato per la Sicilia to MI, "Rapporto sulla Situazione in Sicilia," 28 August 1944, ACS, *MI*, AG, 1944–1946, b. 24, f. 1878; *Il Tempo*, 4 October 1944.

86. OSS, "Notes on Separatism: 1. Communist Leader, 2. Aldisio's Attitude, 3. Pro-American Maffia, 4. Bagheria Meeting," 7–14 August 1944, FBI, 65-51898-3; Alto Commissariato per la Sicilia to MI, "Rapporto sulla Situazione in Sicilia," 28 August 1944, ACS, *MI*, AG, 1944–1946, b. 24, f. 1878.

87. Aldisio admitted having spoken with Finocchiaro Aprile but declined an invitation to join the Committee for Sicilian Independence. Marino, *Storia del separatismo*, 92–93; Finocchiaro Aprile, *Il movimento indipendentista*, 95; di Carcaci, *Memorie*, 24.

88. OSS, "Notes on Separatism: 1. Communist Leader, 2. Aldisio's Attitude, 3. Pro-American Maffia, 4. Bagheria Meeting," 7–14 August 1944, FBI, 65-51898-3; OSS, "Statement of Vizzini, Maffia Member on Separatism, Grain Problem and Orlando," 10 August 1944, CIA.

89. Giarrizzo, *Sicilia politica*, 52; on Aldisio's methods see Ganci, *L'Italia antimoderata*, 324–325.

90. Separatists no longer held any public offices in the provinces of Ragusa, Syracuse, Caltanissetta, Agrigento and Trapani. Comando Arma Carabinieri Reali del'Italia Liberata to Renato Morelli, Sottosegretario alla Presid. del Consiglio dei Ministri, "Movimento Separatista in Sicilia," 28 May 1944, ACS, *PCM*, 1944–1946, 8-2-10912; Alto Commissariato per la Sicilia to MI, "Rapporto sulla Situazione in Sicilia," 28 August 1944, ACS, *MI*, AG, 1944–1946, b. 24, f. 1878; in the same location see Comando Generale dell 'Arma dei Carabinieri Reali to MI, "Relazione mensile riservatissima relativa al mese di Agosto 1944 sulla situazione politica-economica e sulle condizioni dell'ordine, spirito pubblico, ecc., della Sicilia," 15 September 1944; Marino, *Storia del separatismo*, 97.

91. Giarrizzo, *Sicilia politica*, 38. He held another meeting on the issue on June 4. Di Carcaci, *Memorie*, 84–86.

92. Comando Generale del Arma dei Carabinieri Reali to Presidenza del Consiglio dei Ministri, "Manifesto a firma del Sindicato uscente della città di Palermo." See the attached manifesto, "Città di Palermo," 26 September 1944, ACS, *PCM*, 1944–1946, 8-2-10912. Di Carcaci, *Memorie*, 95–98.

93. Lucio Tasca to Charles Poletti, 31 August 1944, Poletti Papers, AMG General File, S-9.

94. R. Prefettura di Palermo to MI, "Attività svolta dal partito separatista," 7 August 1944, ACS, *MI*, DGPS, AA.GG.RR., 1944, Cat. C-2-A, b. 39, f. "Movimento separatista Siciliana"; Legione Territoriale dei Carabinieri Reali di Palermo—Gruppo di Caltanissetta to MI, "Movimento separatista," 17 August 1944, ACS, *MI*, AG, 1944–1946, b. 209, f. 22222.

95. Nester to Secretary of State, "Separatist Movement in Sicily," 5 July 1944, NA, RG 59, 865.01/7-544; OSS, "Notes on Separatism: 1. Communist Leader, 2. Aldisio's Attitude, 3. Pro-American Maffia, 4. Bagheria Meeting," 7–14 August 1944, FBI, 65-51898-3; R. Prefettura di Palermo to MI, "Comizio separatista a Bagheria," 9 August 1944, ACS, *MI*, DGPS, AA.GG.RR., 1944, Cat. C-2-A, b. 39, f. "Movimento separatista Siciliana."

96. OSS, "Notes on Separatism: 1. Communist Leader, 2. Aldisio's Attitude, 3. Pro-American Maffia, 4. Bagheria Meeting," 7–14 August 1944, FBI, 65-51898-3.

97. Ibid.

98. OSS, "Events in Sicily During the Month of June 1944," 30 June 1944, CIA.

99. Nester to Secretary of State, "Certain Elements Within the Separatist Party Which are Known as the Pro-American Group Organized Under the Name 'Fronte Democratico d'Ordine Siciliano'," 22 August 1944, NA, RG 59, 865.01/ 8-2244; Nester to Secretary of State, "Separatist Movement in Sicily," NA, RG 59, 865.01/ 8-2244; Prefetto di Palermo to MI, "Movimento per l'Indipendenza Siciliana," 3 October 1944, ACS, *MI*, DGPS, AA.GG.RR., 1944, Cat. C-2-A, b. 39, f. "Movimento separatista Siciliana." At the same time a section of the Agrarian Party formed in Villalba. It was a separatist organization whose followers carried a representation of Sicily and the American flag. Alto Commissariato per la Sicilia to MI, "Villalba—Caltanissetta—Partito Agrario Costituzione," 13 September 1944, ACS, *MI*, AG, 1944–1946, b. 46, f. 3670.

100. OSS, "Notes on Separatism: 1. Communist Leader, 2. Aldisio's Attitude, 3. Pro-American Maffia, 4. Bagheria Meeting," 7–14 August 1944, FBI, 65-51898-3; see also OSS, "Program of the Sicilian Democratic Party of Order," 9 April 1944, NA, RG 165, Entry 77, Box 1950, File 3700. Stato Maggiore Generale to Ministero degli Interni, "Stralcio di letttera censurata," 20 October 1944, ACS, *MI*, AG, 1944–1946, b. 57, f. 4729.

101. Finocchiaro Aprile to Direttore del Giornale "La Parola" (Valenti), 23 July 1944, Girolamo Valenti Papers, Tamiment Library, New York University, Box 1, Folder, "Valenti Correspondence, 1930–1950." Valenti opposed independence for Sicily, believing that it would weaken Italy and make the island an easy target for another nation. See his arguments in the above collection, Box 1, Folder, "Valenti Manuscripts."

102. For details on the meeting see Regia Questura di Catania to Commissione Alleata di Controllo, Catania, 15 August 1944, NA, RG 331, 10103/143/28; Comandante Compagnia Interna to MI, 13 August 1944, ACS, *MI*, AG, 1944–1946, b. 23, f. 1809; from the same location, Comando Generale dell'Arma dei Carabinieri Reali to MI, "Catania-Movimento per l'Indipendenza della Sicilia," 28 August 1944.

103. Di Carcaci, *Memorie,* 90–91.

CHAPTER 5. ON THE RISE

1. "Appendix 'C' to SR for Period Ending 28 September 1944," 28 September 1944, NA, RG 331, 10100/143/275.

2. "Town Report Syracuse—15 Sept.–29 Sept. 44," dated 28 September 1944, ACS, *CAA,* Appendice, b. 1, f. 6; *L'Unità,* 20 September 1944.

3. Alto Commissariato per la Sicilia to Ministero Interni, "Rapporto sulla situazione in Sicilia," 7 October 1944, ACS, *MI,* AG, 1944–1946, b. 24, f. 1878.

4. Sir Noel Charles to Foreign Office, 8 September 1944, PRO, FO 371, 43918; for press comment see *Il Tempo,* 13, 22 September 1944; *L'Italia Libera,* 13 October 1944; *Italia Nuova,* 21 September 1944; *L'Unione Sardo,* 23 September 1944.

5. OSS, "Miscellaneous Items on Separatist Movement in Sicily," 1, 4, 11, 16 September 1944, NA, RG 226, 95923.

6. R. Prefettura di Palermo to MI, "Comitato Nazionale per l'Indipendenza della Sicilia," 16 September 1944, ACS, *MI,* DGPS, AA.GG.RR., 1944, Cat. C-2-A, b. 39, f. "Movimento separatista Siciliana"; see also "Movimento per l'Indipendenza della Sicilia," 1 September 1944, ACS, *MI,* AG, 1944–1946, b. 8, f. 559, sf. 1; see the same document in b. 36, f. 2817.

7. Comando Generale dell'Arma dei Carabinieri Reali to MI, "Messina—Diffusione di manifestini a carattere separatista," 3 October 1944, ACS, *MI,* AG, 1944–1946, b. 36, f. 2817. Included in the attachments to this report is the national anthem of the separatist movement.

8. Ibid; for the reaction of the Catanese Lega Giovanile see Comando Generale dell'Arma dei Carabinieri Reali to MI, "Catania—Movimento separatista," ACS, *MI,* AG, 1944–1946, b. 23, f. 1809; Guglielmo Carcaci to Bonomi, 3 September 1944, ACS, PCM, 1944–1946, 8-2-10912.

9. "Appendix 'C' to SR for Period Ending 28 September 1944," 28 September 1944, NA, RG 331, 10100/143/275.

10. "Appendix 'C' to SR for Period Ending 28 September 1944," 28 September 1944, NA, RG 331, 10100/143/275; Comando Generale dell'Arma dei Carabinieri Reali to Presidenza del Consiglio dei Ministri, "Palermo—Lancio di manifestini di propaganda separatista," 26 September 1944, ACS, *PCM,* 1944–1946, 8-2-10912; Nester to Secretary of State, "Confidential Police Report on Labor Democracy Meeting Broken Up By Separatists," 27 September 1944, NA, RG 59, 865.00/9-2744.

11. Nester to Secretary of State, "Speech of Finocchiaro Aprile to the Separatists," 30 September 1944, NA, RG 59, 865.00/9-3044.

12. Ibid.; "Appendix 'C' to SR for Period Ending 28 September 1944," 28 September 1944, NA, RG 331, 10100/143/275. "Movimento per l'Indipendenza della Sicilia—Comitato Nazionale," undated, ACS, *MI,* AG, 1944–1946, b. 8, f. 559, sf. 1.

13. OSS, "Cianca Hesitates to Speak at Press Congress in Sicily," 24 October 1944, CIA; Nester to Secretary of State, "Removal of Prefect D'Antoni and Questore Garbo," 16 October 1944, NA, RG 59, 865.00/10-1644.

14. OSS, "Minister Ruini and Prefect D'Antoni Meet Secretly with Tasca Brothers on Sicilian Autonomy," 15 September 1944, CIA; Headquarters, 2677th Regiment OSS, SI Branch, Italian Section, "Report for Period 16–30 September 1944," 6 October 1944, NA, RG 226, Entry 99, Box 20, Folder 106. According to di Carcaci, Finocchiaro Aprile knew of Tasca's meeting and approved of his work. Di Carcaci, *Memorie,* 103–104.

15. OSS, "Questore's Monthly Report: Family Feud Officially Blamed in Communist-Separatist Clash at Villalba," 2 October 1944, NA, RG 226, 100643; OSS, "I. Communist-Socialist Version of the Attack on Girolamo Li Causi. II. Vizzini's (Separatist) Version of the Same Attack," 20, 22 September 1944, CIA.

16. "Villalba—Perturbation of the Public Order," NA, RG 331, 10100/143/276.

17. Ibid.; "Appendix 'C' to SR for Period Ending 28 September 1944," 28 September 1944, NA, RG 331, 10100/143/275; Grasso, *Li Causi*, 59.

18. "Villalba—Perturbation of the Public Order," NA, RG 331, 10100/143/276; on the judicial proceedings see Jacoviello, *La Sicilia*, 76–77; Sansone and Ingrasci, *Sei anni*, 63–64.

19. Nester to Secretary of State, "Separatist Activity in Sicily, September 15–30," 30 September 1944, NA, RG 59, 865.00/3044; Earl Brennan, Chief, Italian Section, S. I. Washington from Vincent J. Scamporino, "La Verità sui Fatti di Villalba," 19 October 1944, CIA. The OSS blamed Pantaleone. According to its informants, Pantaleone had persuaded Li Causi to mention the property which had been at the center of the two families' dispute. After Li Causi mentioned the property, the shooting started. OSS, "Questore's Monthly Report: Family Feud Officially Blamed in Communist-Separatist Clash at Villalba," 2 October 1944, NA, RG 226, 100643.

20. Nester to Secretary of State, "Separatist Activity in Sicily, September 15–30," 30 September 1944, NA, RG 59, 865.00/9-3044. The OSS urged that the incident not be seen as a political protest against the Communists, who were generally approved by the population. OSS, "Questore's Monthly Report: Family Feud Officially Blamed in Communist-Separatist Clash at Villalba," 2 October 1944, NA, RG 226, 100643.

21. "Appendix 'C' to SR for Period Ending 28 September 1944," 28 September 1944, NA, RG 331, 10100/143/275; *L'Unità*, 20 September 1944.

22. *L'Indipendente*, undated; OSS, "I. Communist-Socialist Version of the Attack on Girolamo Li Causi. II. Vizzini's (Separatist) Version of the Same Attack," 20, 22 September 1944, CIA.

23. Carr to ACC HQ, "Outgoing Message," 18 September 1944, NA, RG 331, 10100/143/276; in the same location, Regia Questura di Palermo, "Sicilian Independence Meeting," 17 September 1944; R. Prefettura di Palermo to MI, "Movimento Indipendenza Siciliana-Comizio," 24 September 1944, ACS, *MI*, DGPS, AA.GG.RR., 1944, Cat. C-2-A, b. 39, f. "Movimento separatista Siciliana."

24. Il Generale di Corpo d'Armata Comandante Generale to MI, "Valdese-Partanna-Mondello—Partito Separatista—Denunzia On. Finocchiaro Aprile," 27 November 1944, ACS, *MI*, AG, 1944–1946, b. 50, f. 4071; Regia Questura di Palermo, "Sicilian Independence Meeting," 17 September 1944, NA, RG 331, 10100/143/276; Bonomi to Aldisio, 4 October 1944, ACS, *MI*, DGPS, AA.GG.RR., 1944, Cat. C-2-A, b. 39, f. "Movimento separatista Siciliana." On 26 September 1944, Roosevelt and Churchill announced a "New Deal" for Italy. Under this proposal, the Rome government would gradually gain more control over Italian affairs, provided it could demonstrate the ability to maintain stability. Coles and Weinberg, *Soldiers Become Governors*, 492–499.

25. Nester to Secretary of State, "Separatist Activity During the First Two Weeks of October 1944," 16 October 1944, NA, RG 59, 865.00/10-1644; Alto Commissariato per la Sicilia to MI, "Messina-Separatismo," 14 October 1944, ACS, *MI*, AG, 1944–1946, b. 36, f. 2817; from the same location see Bonomi to Ministero di Grazia e Giustizia, "Messina-Processo a carico de Edouardo Milio Cangemi," 8 October 1944; from the same location Comando Generale dell'Arma dei Carabinieri Reali to Presidente del Consiglio dei Ministri, "Messina-Movimento separatista siciliano," 28 September 1944; Procura Generale del Regno Presso la Corte d'Appello di Messina to Sig. Ufficiale Legale

Regionale della Commissione Alleata, "Procedimento penale contro il separatista Cangemi Milio," 25 October 1944, NA, RG 331, 10100/142/14; in the same location see Allied Commission, Sicilia Region Headquarters to Headquarters, Allied Control Commission, "Sicilian Separatists-Finocchiaro Aprile," 18 November 1944; "Security Intelligence Summary-Period Ending 30 Sep. 44," 30 September 1944, ACS, *CAA*, Appendice, b. 1, f. 5; *L'Unità*, 3 October 1944; *La Voce Communista*, 30 September 1944.

26. Procura Generale del Regno Presso la Corte d'Appello di Messina to Sig. Ufficiale Legale Regionale della Commissione Alleata, "Procedimento penale contro il separatista Cangemi Milio 25 Ottobre 1944," NA, RG 331, 10100/142/14; Alto Commissariato per la Sicilia to MI, "Messina—Separatismo," 14 October 1944, ACS, *MI*, AG, 1944–1946, b. 36, f. 2817; in the same location, Emanuele Conti to Bonomi, 19 September 1944; "Security Intelligence Summary—Period Ending 30 Sep. 44," undated, ACS, *CAA*, Appendice, b. 1, f. 5; *La Voce Communista*, 30 September 1944.

27. Di Natale was regarded as a leader of the separatist movement in Syracuse and a staunch anti-Fascist, and was well respected by his opponents. Extract from 314 PS Section Report, no. 31, "Sicilian Independence Movement," NA, RG 331, 10100/143/ 33; Procura Generale della Legge di Catania to Ufficio Legale della ACC, 24 April 1944, NA, RG 331, 10100/142/14; Nicolosi, *Sicilia contro Italia*, 167.

28. Finocchiaro Aprile to Signor Colonnello Hancock, 15 April 1944, NA, RG 331, 10100/142/14; from the same location see Rear Headquarters, Allied Control Commission, Legal Sub-Commission to RC, Region I, "Freedom of Political Parties," 17 March 1944; Extract from 314 PS Section Report, no. 35, "Subversive Movements: Free Sicily Movement," undated, NA, RG 331, 10100/143/33.

29. Headquarters, Allied Commission, Civil Affairs Section to Regional Commissioner, Sicilia Region, "Freedom of Political Parties: Prosecution of Professor Di Natale Enrico," 5 November 1944, NA, RG 331, 10100/142/14; from the same location see Aldisio to Carr, 27 November 1944; "In Nome di S.A. Reale Umberto di Savoia Lungotenente Generale del Regno," undated.

30. Frantz to Rayner, Edman and Minifie, 25 September 1944, NA, RG 331, 10000/132/152; in the same location, "Draft-Memorandum to Allied Force Headquarters," 1 October 1944; "Sicily's Political Future," PRO, FO 371, 43918; Giarrizzo, *Sicilia politica*, 59–60; *L'Italia Libera*, 10 October 1944.

31. Frantz to Rayner, et al., 25 September 1944, RG 331, 10000/132/152.

32. Nester to Secretary of State, 12 October 1944, NA, RG 59, 865.01/10-1244; Nester to Secretary of State, 8 October 1944, NA, RG 59, 865.01/10-844.

33. Ellery W. Stone to Bonomi, 16 October 1944, ACS, *PCM,* 1944–1946, 8-2-10912; telegram, Rome to Washington, 12 October 1944, NA, RG 59, 865.01/10-1244; in a broadcast from the United States, Sturzo claimed that the American denunciation of separatism was proof of America's respect for Italy's territorial integrity. Rome to Foreign Office, 8 October 1944, PRO, FO 371, 43918.

34. OSS, "Churchill-Umberto Talk in Rome," 20 September 1944, NA, RG 226, L46775.

35. Kirk to Secretary of State, 11 October 1944, NA, RG 59, 865.00/10-1144; *L'Italia Libera*, 10 October 1944.

36. "Report on Sicilian Separatism and the Movimento per l'Indipendenza della Sicilia," 17 April 1946, PRO, FO 371, 67786; Foreign Office to Washington,

26 October 1944, PRO, FO 371, 43918; *Risorgimento Liberale,* 19 October 1944.

37. Nester to Secretary of State, "British and American Statements Refuting Reports of Cooperation with Separatism," 16 October 1944, NA, RG 59, 865.00/10-1644; Alto Commissariato per la Sicilia to MI, "Rapporto sulla situazione in Sicilia," 6 November 1944, ACS, *MI,* AG, 1944–1946, b. 24, f. 1878; *L'Italia Libera,* 4 October 1944.

38. "Separatist Activity in Palermo," November 1944, NA, RG 331, 10100/ 143/275; Headquarters, 2677th Regiment OSS, "Finocchiaro Aprile Confides of Letter from Churchill," 25 October 1944, CIA. On separatist reaction see Il Capo della Polizia to MI, "Movimento Separatista siciliano," 21 November 1944, ACS, *MI,* AG, 1944–1946, b. 8, f. 559, sf. 7. Sansone and Ingrasci believe that Soviet pressure played a heavy role in forcing the Americans and British to renounce the movement. Sansone and Ingrasci, *Sei anni,* 69.

39. Nester to Secretary of State, "Separatist Movement: Letter Addressed to the President of the United States and the Prime Minister of England, as well as to all Responsible for the Allied Nations, Written by Lucio Tasca," 9 December 1944, NA, RG 59, 865.01/12-944; Nester to Secretary of State, "Open Letter to President Roosevelt and Prime Minister Churchill, Written by Cav. Lucio Tasca," 15 December 1944, NA, RG 59, 865.01/12-1544.

40. Alto Commissariato per la Sicilia to MI, "Rapporto sulla situazione in Sicilia," 14 December 1944, ACS, *MI,* AG, 1944–1946, b. 24, f. 1878; "Stralcio della relazione sulla situazione generale della provincia di Palermo nell'ultimo quadrimestre del 1944," ACS, *MI,* AG, 1944–1946, b. 122, f. 10646; "Security Intelligence Summary—Period Ending 15 Sep. 1944," undated, ACS, *CAA,* Appendice, b. 1, f. 5; from the same source see "Town Report Syracuse—15 Oct.–29 Oct. 1944," 29 October 1944, ACS, CAA, Appendix, b. 1, f. 6; "Report on Sicilian Separatism and the Movimento per l'Indipendenza della Sicilia," 17 April 1946, PRO, FO 371, 67786; for all the disturbances see Regional Public Safety Director for Sicily to the High Commissioner, "Public Order and Public Security—Monthly Report," 4 October 1944, NA, RG 331, 10100/143/272; Prefetto di Catania to MI, "Provvedimenti per la Sicilia e la situazione della pubblico spirito," 29 December 1944, ACS, *MI,* AG, 1944–1946, b. 81, f. 6871; *L'Italia Libera,* 4 October 1944.

41. Alto Commissariato to MI, "Palermo—Sciopero Impiegati—Agitazione popolare—luttuosi," 20 October 1944, ACS, *MI,* AG, 1944–1946, b. 54, f. 4484; from the same source see R. Prefetto di Palermo to MI, 20 October 1944; L'Ispettore Generale di PS to Procuratore Militare Presso il Tribunale Militare, "Inchiesta sul luttuosi fatti del 19 Ottobre a Palermo," 3 November 1944; Pampillonia to MI, 20 October 1944; "Civil Disturbances in Palermo," 23 October 1944, NA, RG 331, 10000/136/349; Allied Control Commission, Sicily Region Headquarters to Headquarters, Allied Control Commission, "Report of Incident in Palermo, 19 October 1944," 25 October 1944, attached to Kirk to Secretary of State, "October 19th Incident at Palermo," 6 November 1944, NA, RG 59, 865.00/11-644; Sansone and Ingrasci, *Sei anni,* 57–61.

42. L'Ispettore Generale di PS to Procuratore Militare Presso il Tribunale Militare, "Inchiesta sul luttuosi fatti del 19 Ottobre a Palermo," 3 November 1944, ACS, *MI,* AG, 1944–1946, b. 54, f. 4484.

43. Alto Commissariato per la Sicilia to MI, "Palermo—Sciopero Impiegati—Agitazione popolare—luttuosi," 20 October 1944, ACS, *MI,* AG, 1944–1946, b. 54, f. 4484; in the same location, "Urgente per il Presidente," 24

October 1944; Harold MacMillan, the head of the Allied Commission, believed that the troops had been called out "somewhat precipitately." Coles and Weinberg, *Soldiers Become Governors,* 510.

44. L'Ispettore Generale di PS to Procuratore Militare Presso il Tribunale Militare, "Inchiesta sul luttuosi fatti del 19 Ottobre a Palermo," 3 November 1944, ACS, *MI,* AG, 1944–1946, b. 54, f. 4484; OSS, "Local Statements as to Responsibility for Palermo Riot of 19 October," 23, 25, 28 October 1944, CIA.

45. Allied Control Commission, Sicily Region Headquarters to Headquarters, Allied Control Commission, "Report of Incident in Palermo, 19 October 1944," 25 October 1944, attached to Kirk to Secretary of State, "October 19th Incident at Palermo," 6 November 1944, NA, RG 59, 865.00/11-644.

46. Alto Commissariato per la Sicilia to Bonomi, "Riservatissima confidenziale," 23 November 1944, ACS, *MI,* AG, 1944–1946, b. 8, f. 559, sf. 1; Giarrizzo, *Sicilia politica,* 60.

47. Aldisio disputed the conclusions reached at the gathering. Alto Commissariato per la Sicilia to Bonomi, "Riservatissima confidenziale," 23 November 1944, ACS, *MI,* AG, 1944–1946, b. 8, f. 559, sf. 1. In the United States, the Mazzini Society criticized Aldisio's reactionary methods and warned of "sad days" in the future for Sicily and Italy. *Nazioni Unite,* 1 November 1944.

48. Aldisio to MI, "Relazione," 28 October 1944, ACS, *MI,* AG, 1944–1946, b. 54, f. 4484; *L'Unità,* 21 October 1944.

49. Finocchiaro Aprile to Bonomi, 23 October 1944, NA, RG 331, 10100/143/275; in the same location, "Copia telegramma spedito da Catania alle ore 21.15 del 23.10.1944," 23 October 1944.

50. Nester to Secretary of State, "Copy and Translation of Telegram from Comitato Nazionale of Indipendenza Sicilia." Enclosure to Despatch No. 294, 24 October 1944, NA, RG 59, 865.01/10-2444.

51. Nester to Secretary of State, "Separatist Movement. Letter from Finocchiaro Aprile." See Enclosure No. 2 to Despatch No. 324, 3 November 1944, NA, RG 59, 865.01/11-344; Marino, *Storia del separatismo,* 124.

52. *Giallo Rosso,* undated; Legione Territoriale dei Carabinieri Reali di Palermo, Compagnia di Palermo-Messina to MI, "Rivenimento di Manifestini," 20 October 1944, ACS, *MI,* DGPS, AA.GG.RR., 1944, Cat. C-2-A, b. 39, f. "Movimento separatista Siciliana"; Comando Generale dell'Arma dei Carabinieri Reali to Presidente del Consiglio dei Ministri, "Palermo-Propaganda separatista," 6 November 1944, ACS, *MI,* AG, 1944–1946, b. 210, f. 22269.

CHAPTER 6. AT THE HEIGHT

1. "Security Intelligence Summary-Period Ending 30 Oct. 44," undated, ACS, *CAA,* Appendice, b. 1, f. 5; "Separatist Activity in Palermo—A Summary of Separatist Activity in Palermo from 23–31 October 1944," NA, RG 331, 10100/143/275.

2. See "Following is an Account of the First Congress of the Separatist Movement Held in Taormina on 20, 21, and 22 October 1944," NA, RG 331, 10000/132/152; "First Separatist Congress, Taormina, 20–22 October 1944," 23 October 1944, NA, RG 331, 10100/143/278; 21 Port Security Section to GSO, No. 3 District, "Political Movements," 23 October 1944, NA, RG 331, 10100/143/275; Aldisio to MI, 22 October 1944, ACS, *MI,* DGPS, AA.GG. RR., 1944, Cat. C-2-A, b. 39, f. "Movimento separatista Siciliana"; from the same location,

"Rapporto speciale sul 1 Congresso del Movimento per la Indipendenza Siciliana," undated; Comando Generale dell'Arma dei Carabinieri Reali to Emilio Canevari, Sottosegretario di Stato per l'Interno, "Primo Congresso Nazionale Separatista," 16 November 1944, ACS, *MI*, AG, 1944–1946, b. 8, f. 559, sf. 6.

3. "Rapporto speciale sul 1 Congresso del Movimento per l'Indipendenza Siciliana," undated, ACS, *PCM*, 1944–1946, 8-2-10912; "Following is an Account of the First Congress of the Separatist Movement Held in Taormina on 20, 21, 22 Oct. 44," NA, RG 331, 10000/143/278; Nester to Secretary of State, "Separatist Movement: Congress at Taormina," 4 November 1944, NA, RG 59, 865.01/11-444.

4. "Rapporto speciale sul 1 Congresso del Movimento per l'Indipendenza Siciliana," undated, ACS, *MI*, DGPS, AA.GG.RR., 1944, Cat. C-2-A, b. 39, f. "Movimento separatista Siciliana"; Nester to Secretary of State, "Separatist Movement: Congress at Taormina," 4 November 1944, NA, RG 59, 865.01/11-444.

5. "Following is an Account of the First Congress of the Separatist Movement Held in Taormina on 20, 21, 22 Oct. 44," NA, RG 331, 10000/143/278; Comando Generale dell'Arma dei Carabinieri Reali to Emilio Canevari, Sottogegretario di Stato per l'Interno, "Primo Congresso Nazionale Separatista," 16 November 1944, ACS, *MI*, AG, 1944–1946, b. 8, f. 559, sf. 6; "Rapporto speciale sul 1 Congresso del Movimento per l'Indipendenza Siciliana," undated, ACS, *PCM*, 1944–1946, 8-2-10912. The American consul noted that "it was not clear what compensation the separatist leader intended to offer France in exchange for Tunisia." Nester to Secretary of State, "Separatist Movement: Congress at Taormina," 4 November 1944, NA, RG 59, 865.01/11-444.

6. "Rapporto speciale sul 1 Congresso del Movimento per l'Indipendenza Siciliana," undated, ACS, *PCM*, 1944–1946, 8-2-10912; "Following is an Account of the First Congress of the Separatist Movement Held in Taormina on 20, 21, 22, Oct. 44," NA, RG 331, 10000/132/152.

7. Finocchiaro Aprile would be president. The other four posts would be minister of interior, minister of press and propaganda, minister of finance, and minister of foreign affairs. Comando Generale dell'Arma dei Carabinieri Reali to Emilio Canevari, Sottosegretario di Stato per l'Interno, "Primo Congresso Nazionale Separatista," 16 November 1944, ACS, *MI*, AG, 1944–1946, b. 8, f. 559, sf. 6; "Rapporto speciale sul 1 Congresso del Movimento per la Indipendenza Siciliana," ACS, *MI*, DGPS, AA.GG.RR., 1944, Cat. C-2-A, b. 39, f. "Movimento separatista Siciliana."

8. Comando Generale dell'Arma dei Carabinieri Reali to Emilio Canevari, Sottosegretario di Stato per l'Interno, "Primo Congresso Nazionale Separatista," 16 November 1944, ACS, *MI*, AG, 1944–1946, b. 8, f. 559, sf. 6; "First Separatist Congress, Taormina, 20–22 Oct. 44," 23 October 1944, NA, RG 331, 10100/143/274.

9. "First Separatist Congress, Taormina, 20–22 Oct. 44," NA, RG 331, 10100/143/274; "Rapporto speciale sul 1 Congresso del Movimento per la Indipendenza Siciliana," undated, ACS, *MI*, DGPS, AA.GG.RR., 1944, Cat. C-2-A, b. 39, f. "Movimento separatista Siciliana."

10. Comando Generale dell'Arma dei Carabinieri Reali to Emilio Canevari, Sottosegretario di Stato per l'Interno, "Primo Congresso Nazionale Separatista," 16 November 1944, ACS, *MI*, AG, 1944–1946, b. 8, f. 559, sf. 6; "First Separatist Congress, Taormina, 20–22 Oct. 44," 23 October 1944, NA, RG 331, 10100/143/274.

11. "Copia della Relazione del Comando Generale dell'Arma dei Carabinieri in Data 16 Novembre 1944 sul Primo Congresso 'Nazionale' per l'Indipendenza della Sicilia Tenutosi A Taormina Durante i Giorni 20-21-22 Agosto 1944," ACS, *MI*, AG, 1944–1946, b. 8, f. 559, sf. 1.

12. On this day the members of the secret executive committee were probably selected."Rapporto speciale sul 1 Congresso del Movimento per l'Indipendenza Siciliana," undated, ACS, *MI*, DGPS, AA.GG.RR., Cat. C-2-A, b. 39, f. "Movimento separatista Siciliana"; "First Separatist Congress, Taormina, 20–22 Oct. 44," 23 October 1944, NA, RG 331, 10100/143/274.

13. "Security Intelligence Summary—Period Ending 30 Oct. 44," undated, ACS, *CAA,* Appendice, b. 1, f. 5.

14. Alto Commissariato per la Sicilia, "Attività del Movimento Separatista," 29 October 1944, ACS, *MI*, DGPS, AA.GG.RR., 1944, Cat. C-2-A, b. 39, f. "Movimento separatista Siciliana"; "Appendix," undated, NA, RG 331, 10100/143/275.

15. "Copia Del Promemoria In Data 14 Luglio 1945 Del Generale Attilio Lazzarini Comandante La Divisione J. I. Sabauda sull'Organizzazione della Bande Armate del Movimento Separatista Siciliano (EVIS)," 14 July 1945, ACS, *MI*, AG, 1944–1946, b. 8, f. 559, sf. 1. The formation of the committee seems to have created more internal chaos since the members of the executive committee were not known by the national committee. Rie and Switzer, "Separatist Activity in Palermo," undated, NA, RG 331, 10100/143/275.

16. Nester to Secretary of State, "Separatist Movement in Sicily: Capt. Rie of JICA Visited by Leaders of Movement," 28 November 1944, NA, RG 59, 865.01/11-2844.

17. "Rapporto sulla attività del Movimento per l'Indipendenza Siciliana dal Congresso di Taormina al 31 Ottobre 1944," ACS, *MI*, AG, 1944–1946, b. 8, f. 559, sf. 2; Rie and Switzer "Separatist Activity in Palermo," undated, NA, RG 331, 10100/143/ 275; "Appendix C," undated, NA, RG 331, 10100/143/275; Report by Rie and Switzer, undated, NA, RG 331, 10100/143/275; Office of Chief of Naval Operations, Intelligence Report, "Sicily-Algeria-Tunisia, Sicilian Republic (Separatist) Proposed Organization Of," 6 November 1944, NA, RG 38, Register No. 9632-I, File C-10-f. Nester believed that the action squads had already been formed. Nester to Secretary of State, "Separatist Movement: Congress at Taormina," 4 November 1944, NA, RG 59, 865.01/11-444.

18. Report of Rie and Switzer, undated, NA, RG 331, 10100/143/275; Nester to Secretary of State, "Separatist Movement: Appeal to Church Leaders," 15 November 1944, NA, RG 59, 865.00/11-1544; Office of the Chief of Naval Operations, Intelligence Report, "Sicily-Algeria-Tunisia, Sicilian Republic (Separatist) Proposed Creation of," 6 November 1944, NA, RG 38, Register No. 9632-I, File C-10-f. In a telegram to the ambassador at Rome, Nester indicated that separatists would press for the opening of a Russian consulate in Catania. Nester to Kirk, 15 November 1944, NA, RG 331, 10000/132/152.

19. Stone to Bonomi, 3 November 1944, ACS, *PCM*, 1944–1946, 8-2-10912; Sottosegretario di Stato to Direzione Generale della PS, "Movimento separatista in Sicilia," 18 November 1944, ACS, *MI*, DGPS, AA.GG.RR., 1944, Cat. C-2-A, b. 39, f. "Movimento separatista Siciliana"; "Separatist Plans for Action," 27 October 1944, NA, RG 331, 10100/143/275; Office of the Chief of Naval Operations, Intelligence Report, "Sicily—Algeria—Tunisia, Sicilian Republic (Separatist) Proposed Organization Of," 6 November 1944, NA, RG 38, Register No. 9632-I, File C-10-f; from the same source, "Italy—Sicily—Separatists, Plan for Action By," 3 November 1944.

20. Alto Commissariato per la Sicilia to Presidenza del Consiglio Ministri, "Movimento Separatista," 24 October 1944, ACS, *MI*, DGPS, AA.GG.RR., 1944, C-2-A, b. 39, f. "Movimento separatista Siciliana."

21. Rie and Switzer "Separatist Activity in Palermo," undated, NA, RG 331, 10100/143/275; Alto Commissariato per la Sicilia, "Attività del Movimento Separatista," 29 October 1944, ACS, *MI*, DGPS, AA.GG.RR., 1944, C-2-A, b. 39, f. "Movimento separatista Siciliana"; OSS, "Counter Espionage and Political Investigations of Italian SIM in Sicily and Calabria," 5 September 1944, NA, RG 226, XL1967; Direttore Capo Divisione Affari Generali e Riservati to Divisione FAP, "Personale della Questure della Sicilia," 6 November 1944, ACS, *MI*, DGPS, AA.GG.RR., 1944, Cat. C-2-A, b. 39, f. "Movimento separatista Siciliana." Early in 1945, it was reported that separatists were using "attractive women" to try to influence ACC officers and members of "information services" to support separatism. It was noted that the "experiment has already had excellent results." Office of Chief of Naval Operations, Intelligence Report, "Italy—Sicily—Separatist Movement, Information Concerning," 15 February 1945, NA, RG 38, Register No. 9632-I, File C-10-f.

22. "Interview: Colonel Jordan, Lt. Colonel Snook, High Commissioner, Prefect of Palermo," 30 October 1944, NA, RG 331, 10100/143/275; in the same location see Rie and Switzer, "Separatist Activity in Palermo," undated; Nester to Secretary of State, "Separatist Movement-Congress at Taormina," 4 November 1944, NA, RG 59, 865.01/11-444.

23. Rie and Switzer, "Separatist Activity in Palermo," undated, NA, RG 331, 10100/143/275; in the same location see "Separatist Plan for Action," 27 October 1944.

24. Presidente del Consiglio dei Ministri to Capo della Polizia, "SICILIA—Movimento Separatista," 4 October 1944, ACS, *MI*, DGPS, AA.GG.RR., 1944, Cat. C-2-A, b. 39, f. "Movimento separatista Siciliana"; from the same location see Il Capo della Polizia to Presidente del Consiglio dei Ministri, "Sicilia—Movimento Separatista," 8 October 1944.

25. The article is found in the post-Palermo riot issue of *Giallo Rosso;* Alto Commissariato per la Sicilia to Presidenza del Consiglio Ministri, "Movimento separatista," 24 October 1944, ACS, *MI*, DGPS, AA.GG.RR., 1944, Cat. C-2-A, b. 39, f. "Movimento separatista Siciliana"; from the same location, Aldisio to Bonomi, 22 October 1944 and R. Prefettura di Palermo to MI, "Palermo-Ordine Pubblico," 23 October 1944; see also *Italia Nuova*, 24 October 1944.

26. Nester to Secretary of State, "Separatist Movement—Swing of Communism Toward Separatism," 14 November 1944, NA, RG 59, 865.00/11-1444.

27. "Town Report Syracuse—Period 15 Oct.–29 Oct. 44," 29 October 1944, ACS, *CAA*, Appendice, b. 1, f. 6; Alto Commissariato per la Sicilia to Presidenza del Consiglio Ministri, "Movimento separatista," 24 October 1944, ACS, *MI*, DGPS, AA.GG.RR., 1944, Cat. C-2-A, b. 39, f. "Movimento separatista Siciliana"; Rie and Switzer, "Separatist Activity in Palermo," undated, NA, RG 331, 10100/143/275; "Rapporto sulla attività del Movimento per l'Indipendenza Siciliana dal Congresso di Taormina al 31 Ottobre 1944," ACS, *MI*, AG, 1944–1946, b. 8, f. 559, sf. 2.

28. R. Questura di Palermo to Procuratore del Regno, "Oggetto: Arresto di Carruba Gaspare di Gioacchino, Trifiro Emerico di Antonino e Vecchioni Marcello fu Enrico, responsabili dei delitti di cui agli articoli 278 e 279 C.P. in relazione all'art. 58 C.P. Denunzia a carico di: Finocchiaro Aprile Andrea fu Camillo, Varvaro, Antonino di Gaspare, Mastrogiovanni Tasca Lucio fu Giu-

seppe, Mastrogiovanni Tasca Alessandro fu Giuseppe, Lo Verde Sebastiani fu Antonino, Villasevaglios Pietro fu Gaspare, Sanfilippo Filippo fu Rosolino, Montesanti Fausto fu Emanuele, responsabili del delitto previsto dall'art. 241 C.P.," 28 October 1944, ACS, *MI*, DGPS, AA.GG.RR., 1944, Cat. C-2-A, b. 39, f. "Movimento separatista Siciliana."

29. On the differences among the three see R. Prefettura di Palermo to MI, "Questore di Palermo-Dott. Anselmo Sessa," 26 November 1944, ACS, *MI*, DGPS, AA.GG. RR., 1944, Cat. C-2-A, b. 39, f. "Movimento separatista Siciliana"; in the same location see R. Questura di Palermo to Il Capo della Polizia, "Movimento per l'Indipendenza della Sicilia," 27 November 1944; Alto Commissariato per la Sicilia to Bonomi, Presidente del Consiglio Ministri, "Situazione locale," 23 November 1944. Also see Alto Commissariato per la Sicilia to Ministero Interni, "Situazione politica della Sicilia," 23 November 1944, ACS, *MI*, AG, 1944–1946, b. 8, f. 559, sf. 1.

30. After the keys to the office had been given to Varvaro, D'Antoni signed an order allowing the separatists to meet there. Sessa countermanded the decree, further antagonizing the prefect. R. Prefettura di Palermo to MI, "Questore di Palermo-Dott. Anselmo Sessa," 26 November 1944, ACS, *MI*, DGPS, AA.GG.RR., 1944, Cat. C-2-A, b. 39, f. "Movimento separatista Siciliana"; in the same location R. Questura di Palermo to Il Capo della Polizia, "Movimento per l'Indipendenza della Sicilia," 27 November 1944.

31. Barone to Alto Commissario per la Sicilia, 23 November 1944, ACS, *MI*, AG, 1944–1946, b. 8, f. 559, sf. 1; R. Questura di Palermo to Il Capo della Polizia, "Movimento per l'Indipendenza della Sicilia," 27 November 1944, ACS, *MI*, DGPS, AA.GG.RR., 1944, Cat. C-2-A, b. 39, f. "Movimento separatista Siciliana"; see Sessa's report of 20 December 1944 in the same file.

32. Nester to Secretary of State, "Separatist Movement: Speech by Finocchiaro Aprile Upon the Reopening of Separatist Headquarters in Palermo," 18 November 1944, NA, RG 59, 865.01/11-1844; "Discorso Pronunciato Dall'On. Le Finocchiaro Aprile il 13 Novembre 1944 Dinanzi Alla Assemblea Generale Del Movimento," ACS, *MI*, AG, 1944–1946, b. 8, f. 559, sf. 1.

33. Alto Commissario per la Sicilia to Presidente del Consiglio Ministri, "Situazione politica della Sicilia," 23 November 1944, ACS, *MI*, AG, 1944–1946, b. 8, f. 559, sf. 1; from the same location see Aldisio to MI, "Situazione politica della Sicilia," 23 November 1944.

34. "Rapporto sulla attività del Movimento per l'Indipendenza Siciliana dal Congresso di Taormina al 31 Ottobre 1944," ACS, *MI*, AG, 1944–1946, b. 8, f. 559, sf. 2; Alto Commissariato per la Sicilia, "Attività del Movimento Separatista," 29 October 1944, ACS, *MI*, DGPS, AA.GG.RR., 1944, Cat. C-2-A, b. 39, f. "Movimento separatista Siciliana."

35. OSS, "Counter Espionage and Political Investigations of Italian SIM in Sicily and Calabria," 5 September 1944, NA, RG 226, XL1967.

36. JICANA, Sicily, "Sicily—Weekly News Summary—4–10 November 1944," 10 November 1944, NA, RG 38, Register No. 21279, File C-10-f.

37. Nester to Secretary of State, "Separatist Movement: Demonstration in Alcamo," 5 December 1944, NA, RG 59, 865.01/12-544; Nester to Secretary of State, "Separatist Movement: Speech by Finocchiaro Aprile Upon the Reopening of Separatist Headquarters in Palermo," 18 November 1944, NA, RG 59, 865.01/11-1844.

38. Legione Territoriale dei Carabinieri Reali di Palermo to MI, "Rinvenimento di manifestini," 20 October 1944, ACS, *MI*, DGPS, AA.GG.RR., 1944, Cat.

C-2-A, b. 39, f. "Movimento separatista Siciliana"; Nester to Secretary of State, "Communist Party: Restricted Pro-Separatist Manifest," 15 November 1944, NA, RG 59, 865.008/11-1544. Aldisio credited Finocchiaro Aprile with the creation of the separatist-Communist faction. Alto Commissariato per la Sicilia, "Attività del Movimento Separatista," 29 October 1944, ACS, *MI*, DGPS, AA.GG.RR., 1944, Cat. C-2-A, b. 39, f. "Movimento separatista Siciliana."

39. Nester to Secretary of State, "Statement of Communist Leader Regarding Possible Russian Influence in Sicily," NA, RG 59, 865.01/8-2244; OSS, "Notes on Separatism: 1. Communist Leader 2. Aldisio's Attitude 3. Pro-American Maffia 4. Bagheria Meeting," 6 September 1944, FBI, 65-51898-3.

40. "Rapporto Sull'Attività del Movimento per l'Indipendenza Siciliana," undated, ACS, *MI*, AG, 1944–1946, b. 8, f. 559, sf. 2; "Aspects of the Fight Against Separatism," undated, NA, RG 331, 10100/143/275. There were also talks between separatists and other left-wing or moderate groups. Separatists attempted to gain the allegiance of the Partito dei Lavoratori in Catania, the Partito Socialista Rivoluzionario, the Action and the Republican parties. From JICA AFHQ at Sicily, "Subject-Sicily," 27 December the 1944, NA, RG 226, 111215.

41. Nester to Secretary of State, "Separatist Movement: Swing of Communism Toward Separatism," 14 November 1944, NA, RG 59, 865.00/11-1444; OSS, "1. Sforza Possible New Premier, 2. Separatists Plot Life of Togliatti," 21 October 1944, NA, RG 226, 98273; OSS, "Communist Leader Disavows Separatists," 16 December 1944, CIA.

42. OSS, "Communist Leader Says Monarchists Attempting to Create a New Crisis," 5 February 1945, NA, RG 226, L53676.

43. Overseas News Agency by Pat Frank, "Palermo Plebiscite," 27 October 1944, FBI, 65-51898-4.

44. Nester to Secretary of State, "Separatist Movement in Sicily," 4 September 1944, NA, RG 59, 865.01/9-444; Nester to Secretary of State, "Separatist Movement in Sicily: Capt. Rie of JICA Visited by Leaders of Movement," 28 November 1944, NA, RG 59, 865.01/11-2844; Nester to Secretary of State, "Reorganization of Fronte Democratico d'Ordine Siciliano," 14 October 1944, NA, RG 59, 865.01/10-1444; OSS, "Miscellaneous Items on Separatist Movement in Sicily," 1, 4, 11, 16 September 1944, NA, RG 226, 95923.

45. OSS, "Notes on Separatism: 1. Communist Leader 2. Aldisio's Attitude 3. Pro-American Maffia 4. Bagheria Meeting," 6 September 1944, FBI, 65-51898-3; Nester to Secretary of State, "Separatist Movement in Sicily, Enclosure No. 2," 4 September 1944, NA, RG 59, 865.01/9-444.

46. OSS, "Maffia-Separatist Infiltration in Christian-Democratic Party," 5 October 1944, CIA; Headquarters, 2677th Regiment OSS, SI Branch-Italian Section, "Report for Period 1–15 September 1944," 16 September 1944, NA, RG 226, Entry 99, Box 20, Folder 106.

47. OSS, "Maffia-Separatist Infiltration in Christian-Democrat Party," 5 October 1944, CIA; OSS, "Democratic Front of Order to Become an Open Political Party," 11 September 1944, CIA; Headquarters 2677th Regiment OSS-SI Branch-Italian Section, "Report for Period 16–30 September 1944," 6 October 1944, NA, RG 226, Entry 99, Box 20, Folder 106.

48. OSS, "Democratic Front of Order to Become an Open Political Party," 11 September 1944, CIA.

49. OSS, "Separatists Try to Penetrate Democratic Front of Order," 19 September 1944, CIA.

50. Nester to Secretary of State, "Separatist Movement in Sicily, Proposed Congress to be Held at Catania on October 18, 1944," 8 October 1944, NA, RG 59, 865.00/10-844.

51. Nester to Secretary of State, "Reorganization of Fronte Democratico d'Ordine Siciliano," 14 October 1944, NA, RG 59, 865.01/10-1444.

52. Ibid.

53. Nester to Secretary of State, "Reorganization of the Fronte Democratico d'Ordine Siciliano," 7 November 1944, NA, RG 59, 865.01/11-744

54. Ibid.

55. Ibid.

56. Ibid.

57. Nester to Secretary of State, "Sicilian Democratic Front of Order—Excerpts From Speech Made by Attorney Francesco Di Pietra at the Taormina Congress. Speech of Giovanni La Cara," 7 November 1944, NA, RG 59, 865.01/11-744.

58. Ibid.

59. R. Prefettura di Palermo to MI, "Movimento per l'Indipendenza Siciliana," 3 October 1944, ACS, *MI*, DGPS, 1944, Cat. C-2-A, b. 39, f. "Movimento separatista Siciliana."

60. Nester to Secretary of State, "Attempt of Prince Castel Cicala to Bring the Separatists Over to the Monarchy," 5 December 1944, NA, RG 59, 865.01/12-544.

61. OSS, "General Castellana Insists Separatists Must Have Their Own Newspaper," 25 October 1944, NA, RG 226, 102466.

62. OSS, "General Castellano Seeking Maffia Accord," 13 October 1944, NA, RG 226, 103050.

63. Nester to Secretary of State, "Statements Made by General Castellano Regarding Sicilian Situation and Possible Solution Thereof," 18 January 1945, NA, RG 59, 865.00/1-1845.

64. OSS, "Confirmation of Vizzini-Aldisio Split," 5 October 1944, CIA; from the same source see "Vizzini and the Democratic Front of Order in Sicily," 7 October 1944.

65. Nester to Secretary of State, "Excerpts From a Secret Report by General Castellano to Count Sforza and Carondini," 4 November 1944, NA, RG 59, 865.01/11-444.

66. Nester to Secretary of State, "Leaders of the Maffia Meet at a Number of Secret Meetings in Palermo," 18 November 1944, NA, RG 59, 865.01/11-1844; Nester to Secretary of State, "Meeting of Maffia Leaders with General Giuseppe Castellano and Formation of Group Favoring Autonomy," 21 November 1944, NA, RG 59, 865.00/11-2144; Nester to Secretary of State, "Formation of Group Favoring Autonomy Under Direction of Maffia," 27 November 1944, NA, RG 59, 865.01/11-2744; Mario Tedeschi, "I Tabù dell'anti-mafia," *Il Borghese,* 4 June 1972, 327–328, 367–368. It is possible that Nasi had some connection with a wartime autonomist movement. According to Italian documentation, the supporters of the *Movimento autonomo siciliano* were called "Nasisti" after Nasi, a pre-war politician. For information see ACS, *MI*, DGPS, AA.GG. RR., 1943, Cat-K-4, b. 88, f. "Sicilia movimento autonomista."

67. Nester to Secretary of State, "Meeting of Maffia Leaders with General Giuseppe Castellano and Formation of Group Favoring Autonomy," 21 November 1944, NA, RG 59, 865.00/11-2144; Nester to Secretary of State, "Formation of Group Favoring Autonomy Under Direction of Maffia," 27 November 1944,

NA, RG 59, 865.01/11-2744; on the peasant leagues headed by Alessandro and Lucio Tasca see Alto Commissariato per la Sicilia to MI, "Partito Agrario aderente al movimento separatisti," 14 October 1944, ACS, *MI*, AG, 1944–1946, b. 40, f. 3150.

68. Nester to Secretary of State, "Formation of Group Favoring Autonomy Under Direction of Maffia," 27 November 1944, NA, RG 59, 865.01/11-2744.

69. Ibid.

70. Nester to Secretary of State, "Meeting of Maffia Leaders with General Giuseppe Castellano and Formation of Group Favoring Autonomy," 21 November 1944, NA, RG 59, 865.01/11-2144.

71. Nester to Secretary of State, "Statements Made by General Castellano Regarding Sicilian Situation and Possible Solution Thereof," 18 January 1945, NA, RG 59, 865.00/1-1845.

72. Nester to Secretary of State, "Interview Between General Giuseppe Castellano and Alessandro, Lucio, and Paolo Tasca, Separatist Leaders," 11 December 1944, NA, RG 59, 865.01/12-1144.

73. Nester to Secretary of State, "Statements Made by General Castellano Regarding Sicilian Situation and Possible Solution Thereof," 18 January 1945, NA, RG 59, 865.00/1-1845.

74. Nester to Secretary of State, "Possible Fusion of Maffia and Separatists Under Leadership of Vittorio Emanuele Orlando," 10 April 1945, NA, RG 59, 865.00/4-1045; Nester to Secretary of State, "Further Developments in General Castellano's Solution to the Sicilian Problem," 23 January 1945, NA, RG 59, 865.00/1-2345. Lucio Tasca had written to Orlando concerning the island's situation. Tasca understood clearly that Orlando was not a separatist. Lucio Tasca to V. E. Orlando, 18 October 1944, ACS, Carte del Vittorio Emanuele Orlando, Carteggio, b. 12.

75. JICA, AFHQ, "Italy-Interview With Vittorio Emanuele Orlando," 18 September 1944, NA, RG 226, L46271; OSS, "Federalistic Movement," 18 November 1944, NA, RG 226, L49973.

76. Nester to Secretary of State, "Further Developments in General Castellano's Solution to the Sicilian Problem," 23 January 1945, NA, RG 59, 865.00/1-2345.

77. Nester to Secretary of State, "Statements Made by General Castellano Regarding Sicilian Situation and Possible Solution Thereof," 18 January 1945, NA, RG 59, 865.00/1-1845.

78. Ibid.

79. Nester to Secretary of State, "Possible Fusion of Maffia and Separatists Under Leadership of Vittorio Emanuele Orlando," 10 April 1945, NA, RG 59, 865.00/4-1045.

80. OSS, Italian Division, SI, MEDTO, Headquarters, 2677 Regiment (Prov), Joint Intelligence Collection Agency, "Discussion of the Possibility of an Agreement Between Separatists and Unitarians," 28 March 1945, NA, RG 226, 122735; Office of the Chief of Naval Operations, Intelligence Report, "Italy—Sicily—Separatist Movement, Trends Of," 28 March 1945, NA, RG 38, Register No. 9632-I, File C-10-f.

81. OSS, "Interview with V.E. Orlando," 3 February 1945, NA, RG 226, L 537290. The two men met again in March but could not make any sort of agreement. Nester to Secretary of State, "Finocchiaro Aprile Alleges That Orlando Desires to Become President of the Italian Republic and to Represent Italy at the Peace Conference," 17 March 1945, NA, RG 59, 865.00/3-1745.

82. Nester to Secretary of State, "Possible Fusion of Maffia and Separatists Under Leadership of Vittorio Emanuele Orlando," 10 April 1945, NA, RG 59, 865.00/4-1045; Office of Chief of Naval Operations, Intelligence Report, "Italy—Sicily—Separatist Movement, Trends Of," 28 March 1945, NA, RG 38, Register No. 9632-I, File C-10-f.

83. Ibid.

84. OSS, Italian Division, SI, MEDTO, Headquarters, 2677 Regiment (Prov), Joint Intelligence Collection Agency, "Discussion of the Possibility of an Agreement Between Separatists and Unitarians," 28 March 1945, NA, RG 226, 122735; from the same OSS detachment, "Dissension Among the Separatists," 25 January 1945, CIA; Nester to Secretary of State, "Finocchiaro Aprile Alleges that Orlando Desires to Become President of the Italian Republic and to Represent Italy at the Peace Conference," 17 March 1945, NA, RG 59, 865.00/3-1745.

85. Nester to Secretary of State, "Statements Made by General Castellano Regarding Sicilian Situation and Possible Solution Thereof," 18 January 1945, NA, RG 59, 865.00/1-1845.

CHAPTER 7. IN THE BALANCE

1. Alto Commisariato per la Sicilia to MI, "Rapporto sulla situazione in Sicilia," 7 October 1944, ACS, *MI*, AG, 1944–1946, b. 24, f. 1878; Comando Generale dell'Arma dei Carabinieri Reali to Presidenza del Consiglio dei Ministri, "Movimento separatista," 1 November 1944, ACS, *PCM*, 1944–1946, 8-2-10912.

2. "Bollettino D'Informazioni Siciliane di Salvatore Aponte," 18 September 1944, ACS, *MI*, DGPS, AA.GG.RR., 1944, Cat. C-2-A, b. 39, f. "Movimento separatista Siciliana."

3. Ibid.; "Movimento per l'Indipendenza della Sicilia, Lega Giovanile Separatista, Comitato Nazionale," ACS, *MI*, AG, 1944–1946, b. 8, f. 559, sf. 1; JICA, AFHQ, "Sicily, Estimate of Separatism," 27 December 1944, NA, RG 226, 111215; the same report stated that the movement was viable and growing. See also "Town Report Syracuse—15 Oct.–29 Oct. 1944," 29 October 1944, ACS, CAA, Appendice, b. 1, f. 6.

4. Even as these figures appeared, Rome recognized that separatist sympathizers existed throughout the island and had organized unofficial sections. Nester to Secretary of State, "Summary of Statements Made by Finocchiaro Aprile to a PWB Officer on 29 January 1945," 16 February 1945, FBI, 51898-8; Comando Generale dell'Arma dei Carabinieri Reali to Presidenza del Consiglio dei Ministri, "Movimento separatista," 1 November 1944, ACS, *PCM,* 1944–1946, 8-2-10912.

5. Specific numbers can be located in "Situazione dei partiti politici," September 1944, ACS, *MI*, AG, 1944–1946, b. 24, f. 1878.

6. For these statistics see the "Relazioni Mensile" for January, February, and March 1945 and "Situazione dei partiti politici in Sicilia" for these months. ACS, *MI*, AG, 1944–1946, b. 24, f. 1878.

7. "Situazione dei partiti politici in Sicilia" in the "Relazioni Mensile" for October, November, December 1944, and March 1945, ACS, *MI*, AG, 1944–1946, b. 24, f. 1878; "Estratto dalla relazione n. 8517 R. del Prefetto di Palermo in data 7 VIII 944," ACS, *MI*, AG, 1944–1946, b. 210, f. 22269; Comando Generale

dell'Arma dei Carabinieri Reali to Presidenza del Consiglio dei Ministri, "Movimento separatista," 1 November 1944, ACS, *PCM,* 1944–1946, 8-2-10912.

8. "Security Intelligence Summary—Period Ending 30 Oct. 44, Appendix B—Separatism in Eastern Sicily," undated, ACS, *CAA,* Appendice, b. 1, f. 5; "Estratto della relazione mensile dei CCRR del 16/12/44," ACS, *MI,* AG, 1944–1946, b. 113, f. 9774; "Situazione dei partiti politici in Sicilia," attached to the "Relazione Mensile" for August 1944, ACS, *MI,* AG, 1944–1946, b. 24, f. 1878; from the same location, "Riassunti della relazione del Prefetto di Messina"; Comando Generale dell'Arma dei Carabinieri Reali to Presidenza del Consiglio dei Ministri, "Messina—Movimento separatista della Sicilia," 30 September 1944, ACS, *PCM,* 1944–1946, 8-2-10912.

9. "Security Intelligence Summary—Period Ending 30 Oct. 44, Appendix B—Separatism in Eastern Sicily," undated, ACS, *CAA,* Appendice, b. 1, f. 5; "Riassunti della relazione del Prefetto di Catania," July 1944, ACS, *MI,* AG, 1944–1946, b. 24, f. 1878; Comando Generale dell'Arma dei Carabinieri Reali to Presidenza del Consiglio dei Ministri, "Movimento separatista," 1 November 1944, ACS, *PCM,* 1944–1946, 8-2-10912.

10. "Town Report Syracuse—Period Ending 25 May 44," 25 May 1944, ACS, *CAA,* Appendice, b. 1, f. 6; "Security Intelligence Summary—Period Ending 30 Oct. 44, Appendix B—Separatism in Eastern Sicily," undated, ACS, *CAA,* Appendice, b. 1, f. 5; Comando Generale dell'Arma dei Carabinieri Reali to Presidenza del Consiglio dei Ministri, "Movimento separatista," 1 November 1944, ACS, *PCM,* 1944–1946, 8-2-10912. See the "Situazione dei Partiti Politici in Sicilia" attached to the "Relazione Mensile" for August and November 1944, ACS, *MI,* AG, 1944–1946, b. 24, f. 1878.

11. "Estratto dalla relazione 1 Agosto 1944 del Prefetto di Enna," ACS, *MI,* AG, 1944–1946, b. 41, f. 3259; Comando Generale dell Arma dei Carabinieri Reali to Presidenza del Consiglio dei Ministri, "Movimento separatista," 1 November 1944, ACS, *PCM,* 1944–1946, 8-2-10912.

12. Comando Generale dell' Arma dei Carabinieri Reali to Presidenza del Consiglio dei Ministri, "Movimento separatista," 1 November 1944, ACS, *PCM,* 1944–1946, 8-2-10912; "Situazione dei partiti nella provincia di Caltanissetta relativa al mese di Novembre 1944," ACS, *MI,* AG, 1944–1946, b. 113, f. 9778; "Estratto dalla relazione in data 13 Agosto 1944 del Prefetto di Caltanissetta," ACS, *MI,* AG, 1944–1946, b. 218, f. 22633.

13. Regia Prefettura di Agrigento to MI, "Movimento Separatista in Sicilia," 22 September 1944, ACS, *MI,* DGPS, AA.GG.RR., 1944, Cat. C-2-A, b. 39, f. "Movimento separatista Siciliana." Compare the "Relazione mensile" for the months of October 1944 through March 1945 in ACS, *MI,* AG, 1944–1946, b. 24, f. 1878. Comando Generale dell'Arma dei Carabinieri Reali to Presidenza del Consiglio dei Ministri, "Movimento separatista," 1 November 1944, ACS, *PCM,* 1944–1946, 8-2-10912.

14. Mammarella, *Italy After Fascism,* 78–79; Missori, *Governi,* 162–164.

15. On the Gullo decrees see Paul Ginsborg, *A History of Contemporary Italy: Society and Politics, 1943–1988* (New York: Penguin Books, 1990), 60–63, 106–108; Renda, *Il movimento contadino,* 37–57; Renato Zangheri, *Agricoltura e contadini nella storia d'Italia* (Turin: Einaudi, 1977), 10–12; Giarrizzo, *Sicilia politica,* 104–107; Ganci, *L'Italia antimoderata,* 327.

16. "Security Intelligence Summary—Period Ending 31 Dec. 44," undated, ACS, *CAA,* Appendice, b. 1, f. 5. From the same location see "Security Intelligence Summary—Period Ending 15 Dec. 44," undated; Headquarters, Allied

Commission—Office of the Chief Commissioner to Supreme Allied Commander—Allied Force Headquarters, "Food Ration—Italy," 12 December 1944, NA, RG 331, 10000/132/189; Prefetto di Trapani to MI, "Provincia di Trapani—Ordine Pubblico," 17 December 1944, ACS, *MI*, AG, 1944–1946, b. 46, f. 3724.

17. Nester to Secretary of State, "Sicilian Crisis," 20 December 1944, NA, RG 59, 865.00/12-2044; Office of the Chief of Naval Operations, Intelligence Report, "Italy—Sicily—Mobilization Results," NA, RG 38, Register No. 24844, File F-6-e. Bonomi warned Allied officials that grain shortages in Palermo, Messina, and Catania had created a dangerous situation. Bonomi to Ammiraglio Ellery Stone, Commissario Capo Commissione Alleata, 9 December 1944, ACS, *MI*, AG, 1944–1946, b. 7, f. 473.

18. Joint Intelligence Collection Agency Report, "Sicily—Interview With Salvatore Aldisio—High Commissioner for Sicily," 27 January 1945, NA, RG 226, 114564; Headquarters, Allied Commission, Civil Affairs Section to COS, "Demonstrations Against Military Call-Up in Sicily," 28 December 1944, NA, RG 331, 10000/136/344; Comando Generale dell'Arma dei Carabinieri Reali to MI, "Relazione mensile riservatissima relativa al mese di Dicembre 1944," 5 January 1944, ACS, *MI*, AG, 1944–1946, b. 24, f. 1878; Il Capo della Polizia, Direzione Generale PS to MI, "Richiamo alle arme classi 1922–23–24," 18 January 1945, ACS, *MI*, AG, 1944–1946, b. 41, f. 3192; Allied Commission, Eastern Sicily, "Causes of Recent Civil Disturbances in Eastern Sicily," 27 December 1944, NA, RG 331, 10100/143/294. At least one writer argued that Sicilians had always resisted the draft: Trizzino, *Vento del sud,* 75–76.

19. Comando Generale dell'Arma dei Carabinieri Reali to MI, "Relazione mensile riservatissima relativa al mese di Dicembre 1944," 5 January 1945, ACS, *MI*, AG, 1944–1946, b. 24, f. 1878; Allied Control Commission—Palermo Province to Regional Commissioner, Sicilia Region HQ, "Political Activity in Sicily," 22 February 1944, NA, RG 331, 10100/101/46; No. 21 Port Security Section to GSI, No. 3 District, "Separatism—Messina," 20 December 1944, NA, RG 331, 10100/101/38; "Security Intelligence Summary—Period Ending 15 Dec. 44," undated, ACS, *CAA,* Appendice, b. 1, f. 5; "Town Report Syracuse—29 Nov.-15 Dec. 44," dated 14 December 1944, ACS, *CAA,* Appendice, b. 1, f. 6; JICA, AFHQ, "Sicily, Estimate of Separatism," 27 December 1944, NA, RG 226, 111215.

20. "Relazione stralciata della lettera della PS—Provincia—Messina," September 1944, ACS, *MI*, AG, 1944-1946, b. 24, f. 1878; "Security Intelligence Summary—Period Ending 15 Aug. 44," undated, ACS, *CAA* Appendice, b. 1, f. 5. From the same source, "Security Intelligence Summary—Period Ending 15 Dec. 44," undated.

21. Aldisio to MI, "Relazione," 15 December 1944, ACS, *MI*, AG, 1944–1946, b. 8, f. 559, sf.1; R. Prefettura di Catania to MI, "Disordini di Catania," 30 December 1944, ACS, *MI*, AG, 1944–1946, b. 307, f. 29149; from the same location, Comando dell'Arma dei Carabinieri Reali to MI, "Catania—Disordini," 18 December 1944; Nester to Secretary of State, "Riots in Catania," 19 December 1944, NA, RG 59, 865.2222/12-1944; Allied Commission, Eastern Sicily, "Causes of Recent Civil Disturbances in Eastern Sicily," 27 December 1944, NA, RG 331, 10100/143/294; Headquarters, Allied Commission, Civil Affairs Section to COS, "Demonstrations Against Military Call-Up in Sicily," 28 December 1944, NA, RG 331, 10000/136/344.

22. On the disturbances see R. Prefettura di Catania to MI, "Disordini di Catania," 30 December 1944, ACS, *MI*, AG, 1944–1946, b. 307, f. 29149; in

the same location, Comando dell'Arma dei Carabinieri Reali to MI, "Catania—Disordini," 18 December 1944; "Statistica del reati verificatisi durante il mese di Dicembre 1944 nella Sicilia," ACS, *MI*, AG, 1944–1946, b. 24, f. 1878; Aldisio to MI, "Relazione," 15 December 1944, ACS, *MI*, AG, 1944–1946, b. 8, f. 559, sf. 1; Allied Commission, Sicilia Region Headquarters to Regional Commissioner, 27 December 1944, NA, RG 331, 10100/101/38; No. 21 Port Security Section, "Civil Disturbances—Catania," 16 December 1944, NA, RG 331, 10100/143/294; Allied Commission, Eastern Sicily to G 3 HQ 204 Sub Area, "Causes of Recent Civil Disturbances in Eastern Sicily," 27 December 1944, NA, RG 331, 10000/136/344; "Security Intelligence Summary—Period Ending 15 Dec. 1944," undated, ACS, *CAA*, Appendice, b. 1, f. 5; Nester to Secretary of State, "Sicilian Crisis: Demonstrations and Disorders Continue," 22 December 1944, NA, RG 59, 865.00/12-2244; Nester to Secretary of State, "Riots Occurring Over Calling Up of Youth for Military Service," 19 December 1944, NA, RG 59, 865.2222/12-2244.

23. Comando Generale dell'Arma dei Carabinieri Reali to MI, "Catania—Disordini," 18 December 1944, ACS, *MI*, AG, 1944–1946, B. 307, f. 29149. Other separatists denounced as accomplices in the disturbances included Concetto Gallo and Isidoro Piazza; see Marino, *Storia del separatismo,* 128–129. Police chief Sessa had no doubt as to separatist responsibility for the disturbances. Sessa to Capo della Polizia,"Movimento per l'Indipendenza della Sicilia," 20 December 1944, ACS, *MI*, DGPS, AA.GG.RR., 1944, Cat. C-2-A, b. 39, f. Movimento separatista Siciliana."

24. Nester to Secretary of State, "Sicilian Crisis: Telegram from General Branca, Commanding Carabinieri," 21 December 1944, NA, RG 59, 865.00/12-2144.

25. Allied Commission, Sicilia Region Headquarters to Headquarters, Allied Commission, Rome, "Unrest in Sicily," 20 December 1944, NA, RG 331, 10000/136/444; No. 21 Port Security Section, "Civil Disturbances—Catania," 16 December 1944, NA, RG 331, 10100/143/294; from the same location, Allied Commission, Eastern Sicily to G3, HQ, "Causes of Recent Civil Disturbances in Eastern Sicily," 27 December 1944.

26. Movimento per L'Indipendenza Della Sicilia—Comitato Nazionale, ACS, *MI*, AG, 1944–1946, b. 218, f. 22633; Movimento per l'Indipendenza della Sicilia, Comitato Nazionale to Alto Commissario per la Sicilia, 13 December 1944, NA, RG 331, 10100/143/276; Nester to Secretary of State, "Summary of Statements Made by Finocchiaro Aprile to a PWB Officer on 29 January 1945," 16 February 1945, FBI, 51898-8; *Avanti!,* 14 January 1945.

27. Gaja, *L'esercito,* 180–181; Ganci, *L'Italia antimoderata,* 328–329.

28. Alto Commissariato per la Sicilia to Presidente del Consiglio, "Situazione generale dell'Isola," 14 December 1944, ACS, *MI*, DGPS, AA.GG.RR., 1944, Cat. C-2-A, b. 39, f. "Movimento separatista Siciliana"; in the same location, Alto Commissariato per la Sicilia to Presidente del Consiglio, "Relazione sui fatti di Catania," 15 December 1944; Aldisio to MI, "Relazione," 22 December 1944, ACS, *MI*, AG, 1944–1946, b. 2, f. 149; *Il Popolo,* 16 December 1944.

29. Nester to Secretary of State, "Sicilian Crisis: Summary of Address by High Commissioner," 22 December 1944, NA, RG 59, 865.00/12-2244.

30. OSS, "Interview with V. E. Orlando," 3 February 1945, NA, RG 226, L53720.

31. Nester to Secretary of State, "Statements Made by General Castellano Regarding Sicilian Situation and Possible Solution Thereof," 18 January 1945, NA, RG 59, 865.00/1-1845.

32. Nester to Secretary of State, "Official Call Paid to his Excellency Francesco Battiati, New Prefect of the Province of Palermo," 15 December 1944, NA, RG 59, 865.5018/12-1544. Battiati had become prefect on 8 December 1944. Missori, *Governi,* 425.

33. 51 Field Security Section to CSI, HQ 3 District, "Disorders in Western Sicily, 17 to 24 December 1944," NA, RG 331, 10100/143/294; Joint Intelligence Collection Agency, "Interview with Salvatore Aldisio—High Commissioner for Sicily," 27 January 1945, NA, RG 226, 114564; Nester to Secretary of State, "Results of Draft in Sicily," 20 December 1944, NA, RG 59, 865.2222/12-2044; Nester to Secretary of State, "Translation of One of the Many Leaflets Being Circulated Throughout Sicily Urging Men Not to Respond to the Call for Military Service," 19 December 1944, NA, RG 59, 865.01/12-1944; Office of Chief of Naval Operations, Intelligence Report, "Italy—Sicily—Mobilization Results," 8 February 1945, NA, RG 38, Register No. 24844, File F-6-e.

34. Bonomi to Comandante Generale dell'Arma dei CCRR, 28 December 1944, ACS, *MI,* AG, 1944–1946, b. 2, f. 149; Headquarters, Allied Commission, Civil Affairs Section to COS, "Demonstrations Against Military Call-Up in Sicily," 28 December 1944, NA, RG 331, 10000/136/344.

35. R. Questura di Palermo to Capo della Polizia, "Movimento per l'indipendenza della Sicilia," 20 December 1944, ACS, *MI,* DGPS, AA.GG.RR., 1944, C-2-A, b. 39, f. "Movimento separatista Siciliana"; Presidente del Consiglio Ministro per l'Interno to Alto Commissario per la Sicilia, "Movimento separatista," 28 December 1944, ACS, *MI,* AG, 1944–1946, b. 8, f. 559, sf. 2; in the same location see Alto Commissariato per la Sicilia to Presidente Consiglio dei Ministri, 17 December 1944.

36. The declaration also broadened the powers of the Sardinian High Commissioner. "Dichiarazione Sul Separatismo," undated, ACS, *MI,* AG, 1944–1946, b. 8, f. 559, sf. 2; Giarrizzo, *Sicilia politica,* 69–71; Di Matteo, *Anni roventi,* 328–332.

37. Presidente del Consiglio Ministro per l'Interno to Alto Commissario per la Sicilia, "Movimento separatista," 28 December 1944, ACS, *MI,* AG, 1944–1946, b. 8, f. 559, sf. 2.

38. "Sviluppi dell'Alto Commissariato per la Sicilia," ACS, *PCM,* 1944–1946, 8-2-3001.

39. *Sicilia Indipendente—Organo del Movimento per l'Indipendenza della Sicilia,* 1 January 1945.

40. Nester to Secretary of State, "Separatist Movement: Recent Manifesto Distributed," 27 December 1944, NA, RG 59, 865.01/12-2744.

41. "Movimento per l'Indipendenza della Sicilia," 22 December 1944, ACS, *MI,* AG, 1944–1946, b. 8, f. 559, sf. 4; "Aspects of the Fight Against Separatism," 28 December 1944, NA, RG 331, 10100/143/275; Nester to Secretary of State, "Separatist Movement: Recent Manifesto Distributed." Enclosure No. 2 to Despatch No.482, 27 December 1944, NA, RG 59, 865.01/12-2744.

42. Prefettura di Catania to MI, "Provvedimenti per la Sicilia e situazione dello spirito pubblico," 29 December 1944, ACS, *MI,* AG, 1944–1946, b. 81, f. 6871.

43. No. 21 Port Security Section to GSI, "Separatism—Messina," 20 December 1944, NA, RG 331, 10100/101/38.

44. Comando dell VI Brigata Carabinieri Reali to Allied Commission, Public Safety Division, "Riunione degli aderenti al movimento per l'indipendenza siciliana," 27 December 1944, NA, RG 331, 10100/143/275; Nester to Secretary

of State, "Finocchiaro's Speech Given December 24th on the Occasion of the Blessing of the Separatist Youth League Banner," 27 December 1944, NA, RG 59, 865.01/12-2744; Office of the Chief of Naval Operations, Intelligence Report, "Italy—Sicily—Separatist Movement Tendencies and Reaction to Autonomy Measures," 3 January 1945, NA, RG 38, Register No. 9632-I, File C-10-f.

45. R. Questura di Palermo to Capo della Polizia, "Movimento per l'indipendenza della Sicilia," 20 December 1944, ACS, *MI*, DGPS, AA.GG.RR., 1944, Cat. C-2-A, b. 39, f. "Movimento separatista Siciliana"; Allied Commission, Sicilia Region Headquarters, Public Safety Division to Regional Commissioner, "Demonstrations-Sicily," 27 December 1944, NA, RG 331, 10100/101/38.

46. 21 Port Security Section to GSI, "Separatism—Messina," 20 December 1944, NA, RG 331, 10100/101/38; Nester to Secretary of State, "Sicilian Crisis: Separatists About to Occupy Messina and Other Cities, According to Italian Admiral," 27 December 1944, NA, RG 59, 865.01/12-2744.

47. 21 Port Security Section to GSI, "Separatism—Messina," 20 December 1944, NA, RG 331, 10100/101/38.

48. Nester to Secretary of State, "Sicilian Crisis: Separatists About to Occupy Messina and Other Cities, According to Italian Admiral," 27 December 1944, NA, RG 59, 865.01/12-2744; Kirk to Secretary of State, 24 January 1945, NA, RG 59, 865.00/1-2445.

49. "Aspects in the Fight Against Separatism," 28 December 1944, NA, RG 331, 10100/143/275; 51 Field Security Section to GSI, "Disorders in Western Sicily—17–24 December," 24 December 1944, NA, RG 331, 10100/13/294; Office of the Chief of Naval Operations, Intelligence Report, "Italy—Sicily—Separatist Movement Tendencies and Reaction to Autonomy Measures," 3 January 1945, NA, RG 38, Register No. 9632-I, File C-10-f.

50. There is debate about whether this was actually a separatist uprising. To Rear Admiral Stone, "Classification: Secret," 9 January 1945, NA, RG 331, 10000/136/344. In the same location, "Memorandum to Chief Commissioner," 8 January 1945; "Subject: Disturbances—-Sicily," 8 January 1945; see also Ganci, *L'Italia antimoderata*, 328; Gaja, *L'esercito*, 172–179; Di Matteo, *Anni roventi*, 333–334.

Chapter 8. The Radical Phase

1. R. Prefettura di Catania to MI, "Movimento indipendenza Sicilia," 20 January 1945, ACS, *MI*, AG, 1944–1946, b. 8, f. 559, sf. 8.

2. Comando Generale dell'Arma dei Carabinieri Reali to MI, "Relazione mensile riservatissima relativa al mese di Gennaio 1945," 11 February 1945, ACS, *MI*, AG, 1944–1946, b. 24, f. 1878.

3. Comando Generale dell'Arma dei Carabinieri Reali to MI, "Relazione mensile riservatissima relativa al mese di Febbraio 1945," 10 March 1945, ACS, *MI*, AG, 1944–1946, b. 24, f. 1878; Giarrizzo, *Sicilia politica*, 77–78.

4. Nester to Secretary of State, "Separatist Propaganda," 19 January 1945, NA, RG 59, 865.00/1-1945; R. Prefettura di Catania to MI, "Movimento indipendenza Sicilia," 20 January 1945, ACS, *MI*, AG, 1944–1946, b. 8, f. 559, sf. 8.

5. Nester to Secretary of State, "Statements Made by General Castellano Regarding Sicilian Situation and Possible Solution Thereof," 18 January 1945, NA, RG 59, 865.00/1-1845; OSS, "Separatist Leader Warns Allied Officials," 14

February 1945, CIA; HDS. Det. 2677th Regt. OSS to Hon. Alfred T. Nester, "Separatist Activity," 12 April 1945, CIA.

6. Office of Chief of Naval Operations, Intelligence Report, "Italy—Sicily—Separatist Movement, Plans Of," 23 January 1945, NA, RG 226, 115698. For a speech given at the meeting see Office of Chief of Naval Operations, Intelligence Report, "Italy—Sicily—Separatist Movement, Speech Concerning," 8 February 1945, NA, RG 38, Register No. 9632-I, File C-10-f. See also "Special Report on the Separatist Movement," 19 January 1945, NA, RG 331, 10100/101/38; Nester to Secretary of State, "Separatist Movement: Resolution Adopted at Meeting of National Committee 15 January 1945." Enclosure No. 1 to Despatch No. 534, 19 January 1945, NA, RG 59, 865.00/1-1945.

7. Nester to Secretary of State, "Separatist Movement: Intensification of Propaganda." Enclosures No. 1 and No. 2 to Despatch No. 539, 24 January 1945, NA, RG 59, 865.00/1-2445; Giarrizzo, *Sicilia politica,* 76.

8. R. Prefettura di Catania to MI, "Movimento indipendenza Sicilia," 20 January 1945, ACS, *MI,* AG, 1944–1946, b. 8, f. 559, sf. 8.

9. Office of Chief of Naval Operations, Intelligence Report, "Italy—Sicily—Separatist Movement, Information Concerning," 23 February 1945, NA, RG 38, Register No. 9632-I, File C-10-f.

10. Comando Generale dell'Arma dei Carabinieri Reali to MI, "Messina—Diffusione di manifestini separatisti," 14 April 1945, ACS, *MI,* AG, 1944–1946, b. 36, f. 2817; Nester to Secretary of State, "Separatist Movement: Propaganda Pamphlets Distributed." Enclosures No. 1–4 to Despatch No. 517, 13 January 1945, NA, RG 59, 865.00/1-1345; Office, Chief of Naval Operations, Intelligence Report, "Italy—Sicily—Separatist Movement, Plans Of," 23 January 1945, NA, RG 226, 115698.

11. Comando Generale dell'Arma dei Carabinieri Reali to MI, "Messina—Diffusione volantini separatista," 2 February 1945, ACS, *MI,* AG, 1944–1946, b. 36, f. 2817; Il Capo della Polizia to MI, "Diffusione di manifestini relativi al movimento per l'indipendenza della Sicilia," 29 March 1945, ACS, *MI,* AG, 1944–1946, b. 218, f. 22633; "Security Intelligence Summary—Period Ending 27 Feb. 45," undated, ACS, *CAA,* Appendice, b. 1, f. 5; OSS, "Aldisio's Attempt to Confer with Separatist Leader is Rebuffed," 20 February 1945, CIA; Marino, *Storia del separatismo,* 97.

12. *Avanti!* 20 February 1945; "Security Intelligence Summary—Period Ending 27 Feb. 45," undated, ACS, *CAA,* Appendice, b. 1, f. 5.

13. Nester to Secretary of State, "Italian Republican Party Speech Delivered by Randolfo Pacciardi, editor of *La Voce Repubblicana,*" 6 March 1945, NA, RG 59, 865.00/3-645; Alto Commissariato per la Sicilia to MI, "Rapporto sulla Situazione in Sicilia," 11 April 1945, ACS, *MI,* AG, 1944–1946, b. 24, b. 1878.

14. Pacciardi's efforts coincided with those of other political leaders who proposed a federalist approach to the separatist problem. OSS, "Federalistic Movement," 18 November 1944, NA, RG 226, L49973. "Town Report Syracuse-Period 28 Feb.-12 Mar. 45," 12 March 1945, ACS, *CAA,* Appendice, b. 1, f. 6; Nester to Secretary of State, "Italian Republican Party Speech Delivered by Randolfo Pacciardi, editor of *La Voce Repubblicana,*" 6 March 1945, NA, RG 59, 865.00/3-645; Finocchiaro Aprile had written Pacciardi explaining that a federation of regions was unacceptable unless both Italy and Sicily were independent states. Di Carcaci, *Memorie,* 144; Tocco, *Libro nero,* 134–135.

15. Prefettura di Catania to MI, "Attività separatista," 8 March 1945, ACS, *MI*, AG, 1944–1946, b. 23, f. 1809; Italian Division, SI, Headquarters, 2677th Regiment, "Italy—Political," 18 May 1945, CIA; EVIS drew some followers from the Lega Giovanile. Barbagallo, *Rivoluzione mancata,* 102–103, 110–112; di Carcaci implied that the Guardia was not the military arm of the movement. He also did not list Gallo or di Carcaci as its leaders. Di Carcaci, *Memorie,* 67, 92–93. Gaja claims that the Corpo became an "instrument and tool" of the di Carcaci family. Gaja, *L'esercito,* 184–185.

16. Canalis, *Alcuni aspetti,* 114–122; Ganci, *L'Italia antimoderata,* 333.

17. After Canepa's arrival, *Sicilia Indipendente* began publication. Di Carcaci, *Memorie,* 172–173, 372. At the same time, Canepa met with Communists but decided to stay within the separatist movement. Gaja, *L'esercito,* 201–203; Marino, *Storia del separatismo,* 143–144.

18. Di Carcaci, *Memorie,* 175.

19. "Palermo, 14/1/1944," NA, RG 331, 10100/143/276; Canalis, *Alcuni aspetti,* 127; di Carcaci, *Memorie,* 372.

20. "Report on Sicilian Separatism and the Movimento per l'Indipendenza della Sicilia," 17 April 1946, PRO, FO 371, 67786; Barbagallo, *Rivoluzione mancata,* 109.

21. "Report on Sicilian Separatism and the Movimento per l'Indipendenza della Sicilia," 17 April 1946, PRO, FO 371, 67786; Alto Commissariato per la Sicilia to MI, "Rapporto sulla situazione in Sicilia," 28 August 1944, ACS, *MI,* AG, 1944–1946, b. 24, f. 1878. For a discussion of bandits as socially conscious soldiers see E. J. Hobsbawm, *Primitive Rebels,* (New York: W. W. Norton & Co., 1959).

22. Nester to Secretary of State, "Increasing Power of the Maffia Which is Endeavoring to Eliminate Uncontrolled Delinquent Elements," 12 April 1945, NA, RG 59, 865.00/4-1245; Nester to Secretary of State, "Alleged Volunteer Army for the Independence of Sicily," 22 June 1945, NA, RG 59, 865.00/6-2245; "Untitled," undated, NA, RG 331, 10000/109/482. Di Carcaci confirms that Vizzini wanted the Lega Giovanile and EVIS to adhere to legal means. Di Carcaci, *Memorie,* 168. Romano claims that Vizzini supported an alliance with the bandits and was backed by the di Carcacis, Stefano La Motta, and Giuseppe Tasca. Salvatore Romano, *Storia del mafia* (Milan: Sugar, 1963), 236–237. According to testimony during the mafia hearings in Italy, the idea of an alliance came from Lucio Tasca. Alfonso Madeo ed. *Testo integrale della relazione della Commissione Parlamentare d'inchiesta sul fenomeno della mafia,* 3 vols. (Rome: Cooperativa Scrittori, 1973), vol. II, 66.

23. Nester to Secretary of State, "Increasing Power of the Maffia Which is Endeavoring to Eliminate Uncontrolled Delinquent Elements," 12 April 1945, NA, RG 59, 865.00/4-1245.

24. The name "EVIS" was reported to have been given the organization by one of its members from Syracuse. Nester to Secretary of State, "Alleged Volunteer Army for the Independence of Sicily," 22 June 1945, NA, RG 59, 865.00/6-2245; "Security Intelligence Summary—Period Ending 15 Jan. 45," undated, ACS, *CAA,* Appendice, b. 1, f. 5; "Report on Sicilian Separatism and the Movimento per l'Indipendenza della Sicilia," 17 April 1946, PRO, FO 371, 67786; Gaja, *L'esercito,* 204.

25. The information about EVIS and its structure comes from the following document unless otherwise noted. Based on the study of Canepa, the author is assuming that these are his plans of organization. "Copia del Promemoria

in Data 14 Luglio 1945 del Generale Attilio Lazzarini, Comandante la Divisione, J.I. Sabauda, sulla Organizzazione delle Bande Armate del Movimento Separatista Siciliano (EVIS)," Allegato 1, 14 July 1945, ACS, *MI*, AG, 1944–1946, b. 8, f. 559, sf. 1.

26. Ibid; see also di Carcaci, *Memorie,* 371.

27. "Report on Sicilian Separatism and the Movimento per l'Indipendenza della Sicilia," 17 April 1946, PRO, FO, 371, 67786.

28. "Copia del Promemoria in Data 14 Luglio 1945 del Generale Attilio Lazzarini, Comandante la Divisione J. I. Sabauda, sulla Organizzazione delle Bande Armate del Movimento Separatista Siciliano (EVIS)," Allegato No. 1, 14 July 1945, ACS, *MI*, AG, 1944–1946, b. 8, f. 559, sf. 1. Separatists tried to use international accords to give EVIS legal status. See "L'EVIS nel Diritto Internazionale," in *Sicilia Indipendente,* 1 September 1945.

29. "Untitled," undated, NA, RG 331, 10000/109/482. At least one Italian official believed that EVIS was never a real threat and that its importance was exaggerated by the public. Comando Generale dell'Arma dei Carabinieri Reali to MI, "Sedicente esercito di indipendenza siciliana (EVIS)," 12 December 1945, ACS, *MI*, AG, 1950–1951, b. 35, f. 11436; Jacoviello agrees that EVIS was not a real threat to the Italian state. Jacoviello, *La Sicilia,* 137.

30. Nester to Secretary of State, "Rindone, Separatist Leader in Catania Expresses Assurances of American Sympathy with Movement," 24 April 1945, NA, RG 59, 865.00/4-2445.

31. One of these controversies stemmed from the reported pro-separatist activities of a Captain Nichols who was stationed at the American naval base in Palermo. Bonomi was scolded by Ellery Stone, the Chief Commissioner of the Allied commission, for his allegations, and reminded that Nichols was providing free food to the needy in Palermo regardless of political affiliation, work for which Stone said he should be complimented. Bonomi to Stone, 24 January 1945, ACS, *MI*, AG, 1944–1946, b. 8, f. 559, sf. 7. From the same location see Castellano to Bonomi, undated; Headquarters, Allied Commission, Office of the Chief Commissioner to Bonomi, 13 February 1945.

32. Nester to Secretary of State, "Report on Vincenzo d'Asta, an Active Exponent of Separatism, Who is Used by the Movement Actively to Spread Their Propaganda," 3 April 1945, NA, RG 59, 865.00/4-345.

33. Winant to Secretary of State, 17 March 1945, NA, RG 59, 865.00/3-1745. Reportedly the movement had contracted with an agency in Rome to translate and disseminate its propaganda. It was also believed that five mainland papers were prepared to endorse separatism. Office of Chief of Naval Operations, Intelligence Report, "Italy—Sicily—Separatist Propaganda: Information Concerning," 26 January 1945, NA, RG 38, Register No. 9632-I, File C-10-f.

34. *New York Times,* 12 February 1945; Ganci, *L'Italia antimoderata,* 313.

35. Nester to Secretary of State, "Alleged Meeting Between Finocchiaro Aprile and a Senior British Officer," 10 February 1945, NA, RG 59, 865.00/2-1045; Chairman, Reporting Board SI to Mr. Frederick B. Lyon, "British and Separatist Movement in Sicily," 8 March 1945, CIA.

36. Nester to Secretary of State, "Alleged Meeting Between Finocchiaro Aprile and a Senior British Official," 10 February 1945, NA, RG 59, 865.00/2-1045.

37. "Town Report Syracuse—Period 28 Feb.–12 Mar. 45," 12 Mar. 1945, ACS, *CAA,* Appendice, b. 1, f. 6; Nester to Secretary of State, "Separatist Move-

ment: Visit of Lucio Tasca, Separatist Leader," 31 March 1945, NA, RG 59, 865.00/3-3145; Vincent J. Scamporino to Whitney H. Shepardson, Chief, SI, "Separatist Movement," 13 April 1945, CIA. The San Francisco Conference was officially known as the United Nations Conference on International Organization.

38. For the text of the proclamation see Nester to Secretary of State, "Separatist Movement: Visit of Lucio Tasca, Separatist Leader." Enclosure No. 1 to Despatch No. 780, 31 March 1945, NA, RG 59, 865.00/3-3145; "Movimento per l'Indipendenza della Sicilia," 31 March 1945, ACS, *MI*, AG, 1944–1946, b. 8, f. 559, sf. 1; Legione Territoriale dei Carabinieri Reali di Messina, Compagnia Interna di Messina to MI, "Movimento per l'Indipendenza Sicilia," 13 April 1945, ACS, *MI*, AG, 1944–1946, b. 36, f. 2817; Finocchiaro Aprile, *Il movimento indipendentista,* 116–121; Jacoviello, *La Sicilia,* 107–112.

39. Nester to Secretary of State, "Separatist Movement: Visit of Lucio Tasca, Separatist Leader." Enclosure No. 1 to Despatch No. 780, 31 March 1945, NA, RG 59, 865.00/3-3145

40. Ibid.

41. "Stralcio Dall'Intervista Concessa dall'Avv. Andrea Finocchiaro Aprile ai Giornalista Anselmo Crisafulli, Pubblicata Sul Giornale 'Il Risveglio' del 22 Agosto 1945," ACS, *MI*, AG, 1944–1946, b. 8, f. 559, sf. 1; Comando Generale dell'Arma dei Carabinieri Reali to MI, "Inaugurazione delle sede separatista ad Uditore (Palermo)," 22 January 1945, ACS, *MI*, AG, 1944–1946, b. 210, f. 22269; Nester to Secretary of State, "Separatists Distribute Typewritten Circular to Members of Their Movement Regarding Separatism and the San Francisco Conference," 10 July 1945, NA, RG 59, 500 CC /7-1045; Finocchiaro Aprile, *Il movimento indipendentista,* 140–142; di Carcaci, *Memorie,* 198.

42. Finocchiaro Aprile to Winston Churchill, 11 June 1945, PRO, FO 371, 49767; di Carcaci, *Memorie,* 198–199.

43. Rome Chancery to Foreign Office, "Position Concerning Sicilian Independence," 23 June 1945, PRO, FO 371, 49767; A. C. E. Malcolm to Finocchiaro Aprile, 14 June 1945, PRO, FO 371, 49767.

44. *Avanti!,* 24 August 1945; Kirk to Secretary of State, 25 August 1945, NA, RG 59, 865.00/8-2545.

45. *Avanti!,* 20 April 1945.

46. Comitato di Liberazione Nazionale, Palermo to Presidente del Consiglio dei Ministri, 2 May 1945, ACS, *MI*, AG, 1944–1946, b. 8, f. 559, sf. 6; Nester to Secretary of State, "Committee of National Liberation Requests Italian Government to Take Action Against Separatist Movement," 12 May 1945, NA, RG 59, 865.00/5-1245.

47. Alto Commissario per la Sicilia to MI, "Relazione sul Movimento per l'Indipendenza Siciliana," 23 June 1945, ACS, *MI*, AG, 1944-1946, b. 8, f. 559, sf. 1.

CHAPTER 9. DECLINE

1. *Il Popolo,* 16 December 1944; 21 January 1945.
2. *Il Popolo,* 18 April 1945.
3. *Il Popolo,* 6 March 1945.
4. On these groups see Comando Generale dell'Arma dei Carabinieri Reali to Presidenza del Consiglio dei Ministri, "Movimento Antiseparatista Siciliana,"

29 March 1945, ACS, *PCM,* 1944–1946, 8-2-10912; Comando Generale dell'Arma dei Carabinieri Reali to Parri, "Movimento Anti-Separatista Siciliano," 29 April 1945, ACS, *PCM,* 1944–1946, 8-2-30001. At this time, the *Comitato Siciliano d'Azione* (Sicilian Committee of Action) was formed in Rome. It called for broad autonomy and acted as a support group for the separatists. See Nester to Secretary of State, "Sicilian Action Committee in Rome Alleged to be Pro-Separatist," 2 March 1945, NA, RG 59, 865.00/3-245; di Carcaci, *Memorie,* 140–142.

5. Office of Chief of Naval Operations, Intelligence Report, "Italy—Sicily—Separatist Movement, Reports On," 27 April 1945, NA, RG 226, 129115; "AC Weekly Bulletin, vol. II, no. 3," 22 April 1945, NA, RG 331, 10000/136/545.

6. Alto Commissariato per la Sicilia to Presidenza del Consiglio dei Ministri, "Secondo Congresso movimento separatista," 24 April 1945, ACS, *PCM,* 1944–1946, 8-2-10912; Comando Generale dell'Arma dei Carabinieri Reali to MI, "Secondo congresso nazionale per l'indipendenza della Sicilia," 2 May 1945, ACS, *MI,* AG, 1944–1946, b. 8, f. 559, sf. 6; di Carcaci, *Memorie,* 151–152.

7. See the various reports cited above for the details.

8. "Stralcio Dalla Relazione Mensile Riservatissima Del Comando Generale dell 'Arma dei CCRR in Data 5 Maggio 1945, Relativa al Mese di Aprile 1945 Sulla Situazione Politico-Economica, Sulla Condizioni Dell'Ordine, Spirito Pubblico, ecc., Nella Sicilia," ACS, *MI,* AG, 1944–1946, b. 8, f. 559, sf. 1.

9. See the speech in Finocchiaro Aprile, *Il movimento indipendentista,* 122–135; Giarrizzo, *Sicilia politica,* 87–88.

10. Finocchiaro Aprile, *Il movimento indipendentista,* 122–123. This is probably the speech that the separatist press reported to have been printed in northern Africa in French, English, and Spanish and sent to the San Francisco Conference. The translations were supposed to be sold in bookstores in major cities. "Movimento per l'Indipendenza della Sicilia-Ufficio Stampa," ACS, *MI,* AG, 1944–1946, b. 8, f. 559, sf. 1.

11. Office of Chief of Naval Operations, Intelligence Report, "Italy—Sicily—Separatist Movement, Reports On," 27 April 1945, NA, RG 38, Register No. 9632-I, File C-10-f.

12. R. Ministero degli Affari Esteri to Ambasciate Italiane, 16 January 1945, NA, RG 331, 10000/132/361.

13. Aldisio to Bonomi, 21 April 1945, ACS, *MI,* AG, 1944–1946, b. 119, f. 10271. From the same source, Battiati to Interno Gabinetto, 22 April 1945; R. Questura di Palermo to Alto Commissario per la Sicilia, "Manifestazione studentesca per l'italianità di Trieste, Chiusura dei locali del movimento per l'indipendenza siciliana," 19 September 1945, ACS, *PCM,* 1944–1946, 8-2-10912; Nester to Secretary of State, "Clash Between Separatists and Youth Movement of the Action Party. Separatist Headquarters Destroyed," 24 April 1945, NA, RG 59, 865.00/4-2445; di Carcaci, *Memorie,* 154–155. The Allies had some doubts about the spontaneity of the Palermo demonstration. See Office of Chief of Naval Operations, Intelligence Report, "Italy—Sicily—Separatist Movement, Reports On," 27 April 1945, NA, RG 38, Register No. 9632-I, File C-10-f. There were smaller disturbances both before and after the 21 April incident. R. Prefettura di Palermo to MI, "Manifestazione di giubilo da parte di studenti per la liberazaione dell'Italia del Nord," 28 April 1945, ACS, *MI,* AG, 1944–1946, b. 119, f. 10271. In the same location see R. Prefettura di Palermo to MI, "Incidenti fra elementi dei Partiti d'Azione e Repubblicano ed elementi del movimento per l'indipendenza Siciliana," 21 April 1945.

14. Aldisio to Bonomi, 21 April 1945, ACS, *MI*, AG, 1944–1946, b. 119, f. 10271.

15. Nester to Secretary of State, "Clash Between Separatists and Youth Movement of the Action Party. Separatist Headquarters Destroyed," 24 April 1945, NA, RG 59, 865.00/4-2445.

16. Nester to Secretary of State, "Absence of Retaliation on the Part of the Separatists Subsequent to the Destruction of Their Headquarters," 28 April 1945, NA, RG 59, 865.00/4-2845.

17. He was soon released. Stella to MI, 27 April 1945, ACS, *MI*, AG, 1944–1946, b. 121, f. 10554.

18. Vitelli to MI, 3 May 1945, ACS, *MI*, AG, 1944–1946, b. 119, f. 10288; from the same source, Aldisio to MI, 2 May 1945; Carabinieri General Command to AC, S/C Rome, "Demonstration for the Liberation of Northern Italy and the Italianization of Trieste," 5 May 1945, NA, RG 331, 10000/143/1417; di Carcaci, *Memorie,* 156–157.

19. Vitelli to Alto Commissario Sicilia, 4 May 1945, ACS, *MI*, AG, 1944–1946, b. 8, f. 559, sf. 1; Vitelli to MI, 10 May 1945, ACS, *MI*, AG, 1944–1946, b. 119, f. 10288; Il Capo della Gabinetto to Direzione Generale di PS, "Catania—Movimento Separatista," 8 August 1945, ACS, *MI*, AG, 1944–1946, b. 23, f. 1809.

20. Alto Commissariato per la Sicilia to MI, "Separatismo," 20 April 1945, ACS, *MI*, AG, 1944–1946, b. 119, f. 10271. See Alto Commissariato per la Sicilia to Presidenza del Consiglio dei Ministri, "Chiusura sedi separatista Catania ed Acireale," 8 May 1945, ACS, *MI*, AG, 1944–1946, b. 8, f. 559, sf. 1. See also Nester to Secretary of State, "Statements Made By High Commissioner Aldisio on Separatism in His Report for the Month of April Do Not Express the Same Sentiment as His Recent Speeches," 6 June 1945, NA, RG 59, 865.00/6-645.

21. Comando Militare Territoriale di Palermo to Alessandro Casati, Ministro della Guerra, 26 April 1945, ACS, *MI*, AG, 1944–1946, b. 8, f. 559, sf. 2.

22. "Movimento per l'Indipendenza della Sicilia—Comitato Nazionale," ACS, *MI*, AG, 1944–1946, b. 8, f. 559, sf. 4. The National Committee also sent a note to Admiral Stone. "Movimento per l'Indipendenza Siciliana, Comitato Nazionale to Admiral Stone," July 1945, ACS, *MI*, AG, 1944–1946, b. 8, f. 559, sf. 2. The Allied Commission felt that separatist complaints should be dealt with by the Italian government. Headquarters Allied Commission, Civil Affairs Section to Ministry of Interior, "Forwarding of Correspondence," 12 July 1945, ACS, *MI*, AG, 1944–1946, b. 8, f. 559, sf. 2;

23. "Comitato Nazionale per l'Indipendenza della Sicilia," ACS, *MI*, AG, 1944–1946, b. 8, f. 559, sf. 4.

24. Nester to Secretary of State, "Separatist Movement: Regarding Destruction of Their Headquarters," 25 April 1945, NA, RG 59, 865.00/4-2545; Office of Chief of Naval Operations, Intelligence Report, "Italy—Sicily—Separatist Messages to Allied Officials," 1 May 1945, NA, RG 38, Register No. 9632-I, File C-10-f.

25. Ibid.

26. Nester to Secretary of State, "Letter from Provincial Secretary of Catania of the Movement for the Independence of Sicily." Enclosure No. 1 to Despatch No. 886, 25 April 1945, NA, RG 59, 865.00/4-2545.

27. Nester to Secretary of State, "Statements Made by High Commissioner Aldisio on Separatism in His Report for the Month of April Do Not Express the Same Sentiment as His Recent Speeches," 6 June 1945, NA, RG 59, 865.00/6-645.

28. "Movimento per l'Indipendenza della Sicilia—Comitato Nazionale to Alto Commissario per la Sicilia," 9 May 1945, ACS, *MI*, AG, 1944–1946, b. 8, f. 559, sf. 2; the complaint sought compensation from Aldisio for the damages done to the headquarters. The court eventually decided for the separatists and ordered Aldisio to pay. "Tribunale Di Palermo Atto di Citazione," 17 July 1945, ACS, *MI*, AG, 1944–1946, b. 8, f. 559, sf. 1; in the same location see Alto Commissariato per la Sicilia to MI, "Movimento separatista. Atto di Citazione dell'On. Finocchiaro Aprile," 19 September 1945.

29. Alto Commissariato per la Sicilia to MI, "Movimento per l'indipendenza siciliana," 7 May 1945, ACS, *MI*, AG, 1944–1946, b. 8, f. 559, sf. 1.

30. Ibid.

31. "Security Intelligence Summary—Period Ending 14 Feb. 45," undated, ACS, *CAA*, Appendice, b. 1, f. 5; "Town Report Syracuse-Period 28 Feb.–12 Mar. 45," 12 March 1945, ACS, *CAA*, Appendice, b. 1, f. 6; "Security Intelligence Summary-Period Ending 14 Mar. 45", undated, ACS, *CAA*, Appendice, b. 1, f. 5; Prefetto di Ragusa to MI, "Trasmissione ordine del giorno dal Comitato del Liberazione Nazionale del Modica 24 April 1945," 11 May 1945, ACS, *MI*, AG, 1944–1946, b. 12, f. 871; "Stralcio dalla Relazione del Prefetto di Trapani sulla situazione politico-economica, sull'ordine e spirito pubblico e sulle condizioni della PS," 4 July 1945, ACS, *MI*, AG, 1944–1946, b. 42, f. 3287; Nester to Secretary of State, "Present Organization of the Separatist Movement," 6 August 1945, NA, RG 59, 865.00/8-645; *New York Times,* 27 May 1945. The Christian Democrats benefited the most from the defections of moderate separatists. Giarrizzo, *Sicilia politica,* 89–90.

32. Nester to Secretary of State, "Finocchiaro Aprile Telegraphs Congratulations to the Lieutenant General of the Realm, Prince Umberto," 3 May 1945, NA, RG 59, 740.00119 EW/5-345; Office of AC, Liaison Office, Report for 5 July, "The Separatist Movement in Sicily," 21 September 1945, PRO, FO 371, 49767; di Carcaci, *Memorie,* 165.

33. Nester to Secretary of State, 6 June 1945, NA, RG 59, 865.00/6-645; Italian Division, SI, MEDTO, Headquarters, Detachment 2677th Regiment, OSS, "Political," 17 May 1945, CIA; Alto Commissario per la Sicilia to MI, "Relazione sul Movimento per l'Indipendenza Siciliana," 23 June 1945, ACS, *MI*, AG, 1944–1946, b. 8, f. 559, sf. 1.

34. Comando Generale dell'Arma dei Carabinieri Reali to MI, "Propaganda per l'Indipendenza della Sicilia, Distribuzione dei Volantini," 28 May 1945, ACS, *MI*, AG, 1944–1946, b. 36, f. 2817; di Carcaci, *Memorie,* 165–166.

35. Nester to Secretary of State, "Finocchiaro Aprile's Answer to Criticism Regarding Telegram to Lieutenant General Extending Congratulations on the Liberation of Northern Italy," 19 May 1945, NA, RG 59, 740.00119 EW/5-1945; "Stralcio dalla Relazione del Comando Generale dell'Arma dei CCRR sulla Situazione in Generale della Sicilia," 11 June 1945, ACS, *MI*, AG, 1944–1946, b. 8, f. 559, sf. 1.

36. Di Carcaci, *Memorie,* 165–166. As early as February 1945, Finocchiaro Aprile had mentioned the possibility of an alliance with the monarchy in the event Italy went Communist. See Office of Chief of Naval Operations, Intelligence Report, "Italy—Sicily—Separatist Movement, Information Concerning," 15 February 1945, NA, RG 38, Register No. 9632-I, File C-10-f.

37. "Stralcio dalla Relazione del Comando Generale del Arma dei CCRR sulla Situazione in Generale della Sicilia," 11 June 1945, ACS, *MI*, AG, 1944–1946, b. 8, f. 559, sf. 1; Italian Division, SI, MEDTO, Headquarters, Detachment

2677th Regiment, OSS, "Political," 17 May 1945, CIA; Office of Chief of Naval Operations, Intelligence Report, "Sicily—Political—Separatist Movement, Monarchist Trends In," 3 July 1945, NA, RG 38, Register No. 9632-I, File C-10-f.

38. Office of Chief of Naval Operations, Intelligence Report, "Sicily—Political—Separatist Movement, Monarchist Trends In," 3 July 1945, NA, RG 38, Register No. 9632-I, File C-10-f; di Carcaci, *Memorie*, 148–149. Marino confirms that Tasca was trying to formulate a monarchist compromise. Marino, *Storia del separatismo*, 140.

39. Nester to Secretary of State, "Split in the Separatist Ranks," 16 May 1945, NA, RG 59, 865.00/5-1645; Nester to Secretary of State, "Agents of Monarchy Are Alleged to Have Approached Separatist Leaders with a View to Obtaining their Support," 8 May 1945, NA, RG 59, 865.00/5-845; Nester to Secretary of State, "Excerpts from a Report Prepared by the Intelligence Section of the Royal Carabinieri Regarding Friction Which Exists Between High Commissioner Aldisio and General Berardi, Commander of the Troops in Sicily," 28 May 1945, NA, RG 59, 865.00/5-2845; OSS, "Events Preceding Change in Separatist Movement," 3–22 May 1945, CIA; Office of Chief of Naval Operations, Intelligence Report, "Sicily—Political—Separatist Movement, Monarchist Trends In," 3 July 1945, NA, RG 38, Register No. 9632-I, File C-10-f.

40. Nester to Secretary of State, "Finocchiaro Aprile Alleges that Orlando Desires to Become President of the Italian Republic and to Represent Italy at the Peace Conference," 17 March 1945, NA, RG 59, 865.00/3-1745; Nester to Secretary of State, "Possible Fusion of Maffia and Separatists Under Leadership of Vittorio Emanuele Orlando," 10 April 1945, NA, RG 59, 865.00/4-1045; di Carcaci, *Memorie*, 156–164.

41. Nester to Secretary of State, 6 June 1945, NA, RG 59, 765.00/6-645.

42. Nester to Secretary of State, "Possible Fusion of Maffia and Separatists Under Leadership of Vittorio Emanuele Orlando," 10 April 1945, NA, RG 59, 865.00/4-1045; Nester to Secretary of State, "Finocchiaro Aprile Telegraphs Congratulations to the Lieutenant Governor of the Realm, Prince Umberto," 3 May 1945, NA, RG 59, 740.00119 EW/5-345.

43. "Report on Sicilian Separatism and the Movimento per l'Indipendenza della Sicilia," 17 April 1946, PRO, FO 371, 67786; "Stralcio dalla Relazione Riservatissima del Comando dell'Arma dei CCRR sulla Situazione Generale della Sicilia nel Giugno 1945," ACS, *MI*, AG, 1944–1946, b. 8, f. 559, sf. 2; Office of Chief of Naval Operations, Intelligence Report, "Sicily—Political—Separatist Merger, Report Of," 19 June 1945, NA, RG 38, Register No. 9632-I, File C-10-f. Restuccia led a squad of Messinese separatists. Marino, *Storia del separatismo*, 145.

44. Nester to Secretary of State, "Present Organization of the Separatist Movement," 6 August 1945, NA, RG 59, 865.00/8-645.

45. Alto Commissario per la Sicilia to MI, "Relazione sul Movimento per l'Indipendenza Siciliana," 23 June 1945, ACS, *MI*, AG, 1944-1946, b. 8, f. 559, sf. 1; Nester to Secretary of State, "Secretary of the Separatist Party Approaches High Commissioner with Request for Permission to Re-Open Separatist Headquarters," 3 July 1945, NA, RG 59, 865.00/7-345.

46. Nester to Secretary of State, "Present Organization of the Separatist Movement," 6 August 1945, NA, RG 59, 865.00/8-645.

47. Ibid; Italian Division, SI, MEDTO, Headquarters, Detachment 2677th Regiment, "Political," 9 May 1945, CIA. Di Carcaci mentions the formation of a national executive or secret executive at this time. Di Carcaci, *Memorie*, 166.

48. Nester to Secretary of State, "Present Organization of the Separatist Movement," 6 August 1945, NA, RG 59, 865.00/8-645. Earlier, Catanese separatists wanted to move separatist headquarters to their city in order to balance the influence of the Tasca family. Office of Chief of Naval Operations, Intelligence Report, "Italy—Sicily—Separatist Movement, Trends Of," 28 March 1945, NA, RG 38, Register No. 9632-I, File C-10-f.

49. Nester to Secretary of State, "Present Organization of the Separatist Movement," 6 August 1945, NA, RG 59, 865.00/8-645.

CHAPTER 10. THE STATE ACTS

1. On 21 June 1945, the first Parri government came to power. It remained in power until 10 December 1945, when Alcide De Gasperi replaced Parri. Missori, *Governi,* 165–170.

2. Alto Commissariato per la Sicilia to MI, "Sedicente Esercito volontario Indipendenza Siciliana (EVIS)," 23 June 1945, ACS, *MI,* AG, 1944–1946, b. 8, f. 559, sf. 2; Legione Territoriale dei CCRR di Messina to Alto Commissario per la Sicilia, "Movimento separatista," 3 June 1945, ACS, *MI,* AG, 1944–1946, b. 140, f. 12464; in the same location, Ispettorato Generale di PS per la Sicilia to MI, "Movimento separatisti," 5 June 1945; di Carcaci, *Memorie,* 174.

3. Legione Territoriale dei CCRR di Messina to Alto Commissario per la Sicilia, "Movimento separatista," 3 June 1945, ACS, *MI,* AG, 1944–1946, b. 140, f. 12464; in the same location, Ispettorato Generale di PS per a Sicilia to MI, "Movimento separatisti," 5 June 1945; Ispettorato Generale di PS per la Sicilia to MI, "Movimento separatista," 31 May 1945. Castrogiovanni and another sympathizer warned separatists in the area of the impending operation. Alto Commissariato per la Sicilia to MI, "Sedicente Esercito volontario Indipendenza Siciliana (EVIS)," 22 June 1945, ACS, *MI,* AG, 1944–1946, b. 8, f. 559, sf. 2; for a list of the captured materials see Nester to Secretary of State, "Raid on Separatist Ammunition Dump," 13 June 1945, NA, RG 59, 865.00/6-1345.

4. Alto Commissariato per la Sicilia to MI, "Sedicente Esercito volontario Indipendenza Siciliana (EVIS)," 22 June 1945, ACS, *MI,* AG, 1944–1946, b. 143, f. 12751; for the same report see b. 8, f. 559, sf. 2.

5. Ibid.

6. Canalis, *Alcuni aspetti,* 135–136; di Carcaci, *Memorie,* 184–186.

7. Alto Commissariato per la Sicilia to MI, "Sedicente Esercito volontario Indipendenza Siciliana (EVIS)," 22 June 1945, ACS, *MI,* AG, 1944–1946, b. 143, f. 12751.

8. Canalis, *Alcuni aspetti,* 137–140.

9. *Sicilia Indipendente,* 1 July 1945; those killed with Canepa seemed to have been relatively unknown although Rosano may have been elected in January 1945 to the Permanent University Committee at the University of Catania. Legione Territoriale dei Carabinieri Reali di Messina to the Commissione Alleata, 28 January 1945, NA, RG 331, 10103/143/28; di Carcaci, *Memorie,* 190.

10. Comando Generale dell'Arma dei Carabinieri Reali to MI, "Catania—Diffusione di manifesti del Movimento per l'Indipendenza della Sicilia," 12 July 1945, ACS, *MI,* AG, 1944–1946, b. 140, f. 12421; R. Prefettura di Palermo to MI, "Propaganda separatista," 22 August 1945, ACS, *MI,* AG, 1944–1946, b. 210, f. 22269; Movimento per l'Indipendenza della Sicilia, "In Memoria dei

Martiri—Antonio Canepa (Mario Turri), Carmelo Rosano e Vincenzo Giudice—
Nel Trigesimo 17 Giugno-17 Luglio 1945," ACS, *MI*, AG, 1944–1946, b. 8, f.
559, sf. 1; R. Prefettura di Palermo to MI, "Rito religioso," 20 July 1945, ACS,
MI, AG, 1944–1946, b. 210, f. 22269; *Sicilia Indipendente,* 1 July 1945.

11. Salvo Barbagallo argues that Canepa's death was a murder. Barbagallo,
Rivoluzione mancata, 125–132; by the same author see *Randazzo 17 Giugno
1945: Anatomia di una strage* (Catania: Piscator, 1946). In his testimony to the
Parliamentary Commission on the mafia, Varvaro confirmed that conservative
separatists arranged Canepa's death. See Madeo, ed., *Testo integrale,* vol. II,
741; Sansone and Ingrasci, *Sei anni,* 81–82.

12. Nester to Secretary of State, "Alleged Volunteer Army for the Independence of Sicily," 22 June 1945, NA, RG 59, 865.00/6-2245.

13. "Copia del Promemoria in Data 14 Luglio 1945 del Generale Attilio
Lazzarini, Comandante la Divisione J.I. Sabauda sulla Organizzazione delle
Bande Armate del Movimento Separatista Siciliano (EVIS)," 14 July 1945, ACS,
MI, AG, 1944–1946, b. 8, f. 559, sf. 1.

14. Il Capo della Polizia to MI, "Militello—Rosmarino—banda armata," 19
July 1945, ACS, *MI*, AG, 1944–1946, b. 143, f. 12751; Il Capo della Polizia to
MI, "Cesarò—banda di separatisti armati," 25 July 1945, ACS, *MI*, AG, 1944–
1946, b. 143, f. 12751.

15. Comando Generale dell'Arma dei Carabinieri Reali to MI, "Sedicente
Esercito volontario per l'Indipendenza della Sicilia," 24 July 1945, ACS, *MI*,
AG, 1944–1946, b. 143, f. 12751; in the same location, Il Capo della Polizia to
MI, "Cesarò—banda di separatisti armati," 25 July 1945.

16. Prefetto di Catania to MI, 6 July 1945, ACS, *MI*, AG, 1944–1946, b. 140,
f. 12421; from the same location, Prefetto Vitelli to Ministero Interno Gabinetto, 7 July 1945; Aldisio to Ministero Interno Sicurezza, 10 July 1945.

17. Comando Generale dell'Arma dei Carabinieri Reali to MI, "Movimento
per l'indipendenza della Sicilia," 4 August 1945, ACS, *MI*, AG, 1944-1946, b.
36, f. 2817.

18. Di Carcaci, *Memorie,* 189–190.

19. R. Prefettura di Trapani to MI, "Movimento separatista," 10 August
1945, ACS, *MI*, AG, 1944–1946, b. 42, f. 3287.

20. On Giuliano see Gavin Maxwell, *God Protect Me From My Friends*
(London: Longmans, Green, 1957); Billy Jaynes Chandler, *King of the Moun-
tain: The Life and Death of Giuliano the Bandit* (Dekalb: Northern Illinois
University Press, 1988); Felice Chilanti, *Da Montelepre a Viterbo* (Rome: Croce,
1952); Pantaleone, *Mafia and Politics,* 155; Lewis, *Honored Society,* 147–157.
An OSS report characterized Giuliano as dangerous and labeled him a member
of the mafia. OSS, "Mafia Activities in Montelepre, Sicily," 2 January 1944, NA,
RG 165, Entry 77, Box 1903, File 2700.

21. Di Carcaci, *Memorie,* 168–170. One of Giuliano's cohorts, Pasquale Sciortino, claimed that Charles Poletti attended one meeting in 1945 when Giuliano was promised arms and weapons. Madeo, ed., *Testo integrale,* vol. II, 617.

22. Di Carcaci, *Memorie,* 208–209.

23. Ibid., 208–210; Gaja, *L'esercito,* 236; Chandler, *King of the Mountain,*
51–52.

24. Joint Intelligence Collection Agency, "Sicily—Separatists Reported
Willing to Negotiate with Italian Govt.," 13 July 1945, NA, RG 226, 138574.

25. Joint Intelligence Collection Agency, "Sicily—Separatists Planning Negotiations with Italian Government," 5 August 1945, NA, RG 226, 142223;

Nester to Secretary of State, "Separatist Movement Plans to Start Negotiations With the Italian Government with a View to Official Recognition," 6 August 1945, NA, RG 59, 865.00/8-645.

26. Il Capo della Polizia to MI, "Manifestini del movimento separatista," 27 August 1945, ACS, *MI*, AG, 1944–1946, b. 210, f. 22269; R. Prefettura di Catania to MI, 13 September 1945, ACS, *MI*, AG, 1944–1946, b. 23, f. 1809; "EVIS-Esercito Volontario Indipendenza Siciliana—Comando Generale—Secondo Turri," 7 August 1945, ACS, *MI*, AG, 1944–1946, b. 8, f. 559, sf. 1; di Carcaci, *Memorie,* 211–212.

27. Sansone and Ingrasci, *Sei anni,* 77–80; Chandler, *King of the Mountain,* 51–53; Maxwell, *God Protect Me,* 60–62; Lewis, *Honored Society,* 159–162. In his testimony to the mafia commission, Varvaro claimed that he opposed bringing Giuliano into EVIS and that Lucio Tasca and Concetto Gallo proposed the idea. Madeo, ed., *Testo integrale,* vol. II, 492. Discussions with the bandit did upset some separatist followers. Di Carcaci, *Memorie,* 212–215.

28. Nester to Secretary of State, "Separatist Activity," 21 August 1945, NA, RG 59, 865.00/8-2145.

29. "Extracts from the Rome Press on the Question of Sicilian Separatism—Finocchiaro Aprile's Allegations on Sicilian Separatism and the Allies," 30 August 1945, PRO, FO 371, 49767; Nester to Secretary of State, 20 August 1945, NA, RG 59, 865.00/8-2045.

30. Kirk to Secretary of State, 15 August 1945, NA, RG 59, 865.00/8-1545; Nester to Secretary of State, "Separatist Propaganda: Americans to Administer Sicily," 14 August 1945, NA, RG 59, 865.00/8-1445; Rome to Foreign Office, 19 August 1945, PRO, FO 371, 49767.

31. The London Declaration was signed by fifty one members of the National Committee. Movimento per l'Indipendenza della Sicilia, "Appello del Comitato Nazionale alla Conferenza di Londra," 1 September 1945, ACS, *MI*, AG, 1944–1946, b. 8, f. 559, sf. 1.

32. Alto Commissariato per la Sicilia to MI, "Movimento separatista," 14 September 1945, ACS, *MI*, AG, 1944–1946, b. 8, f. 559, sf. 1. Word of the declaration reached London. According to testimony at the mafia commission, De Gasperi, who was at the conference, was embarrassed by the London Declaration and informed Parri of it. Madeo, *Testo integrale,* vol. II, 26; Ganci, *L'Italia antimoderata,* 334–335.

33. Questura di Palermo to Alto Commissariato per la Sicilia "La Manna Salvatore di Vincenzo e Castrogiovanni Attilio di Francesco," 14 September 1945, ACS, *MI*, AG, 1944–1946, b. 210, f. 22269; see also the questura's report of the next day in the same location; R. Prefettura di Palermo to MI, "La Manna Salvatore di Vincenzo e Castrogiovanni Attilio di Francesco—Movimento Separatista," 14 September 1945, ACS, *MI*, AG, 1944–1946, b. 8, f. 559, sf. 1; in the same location, Alto Commissariato per la Sicilia to Presidenza Consiglio Ministri, "Movimento separatista," 14 September 1945; di Carcaci, *Memorie,* 227.

34. Castrogiovanni was not released from prison until July 1946. Di Carcaci, *Memorie,* 324.

35. Di Carcaci, *Memorie,* 226–227.

36. MI to Comando Generale Arma CCRR, "Congedamento carabinieri classi anziane," 19 August 1945, ACS, *MI*, AG, 1944–1946, b. 2, f. 149; see also Il Capo della Polizia to Gabinetto del Signor Ministro, "Movimento Insurrezionale in Sicilia," 15 October 1945, ACS, *MI*, AG, 1944–1946, b. 167, f. 15886; Aldisio to MI, 11 October 1945, ACS, *MI*, AG, 1944–1946, b. 143, f. 12751; MI

to Stato Maggiore R. Esercito, "Sicilia-Radio clandestina separatista," 31 October 1945, ACS, *PCM,* 1944–1946, 8-2-10912; *Il Lavoro,* 25 December 1945.

37. Alto Commissariato per la Sicilia to MI, "Tutela dell'ordine pubblico—situazione della forza pubblica in Sicilia," 22 September 1945, ACS, *MI,* AG, 1944–1946, b. 2, f. 149; from the same source, Ministero della Guerra to MI, "Impiego forze in Sicilia," 27 September 1945.

38. Comando Generale dell'Arma dei Carabinieri Reali to MI, "Situazione del movimento separatista siciliano," 8 August 1945, ACS, *MI,* AG, 1944–1946, b. 8, f. 559, sf. 2.

39. Comando Generale dell'Arma dei Carabinieri Reali to MI, "Sicilia—movimento separatista," 17 September 1945, ACS, *MI,* AG, 1944–1946, b. 8, f. 559, sf. 2.

40. Separatists in Tunisia were to supply arms for the revolt. "Stralcio dalla Relazione del Comando Generale dell'Arma dei CCRR Riguardante la Sicilia Relativa al Mese di Agosto 1945," ACS, *MI,* AG, 1944–1946, b. 8, f. 559, sf. 2; Prefetto di Catania to MI, 21 September 1945, ACS, *MI,* AG, 1944–1946, b. 167, f. 15886; Alto Commissariato per la Sicilia to Presidenza del Consiglio dei Ministri, "Movimento per l'Indipendenza Siciliana-insurrezioni armate," 21 September 1945, ACS, *PCM,* 1944–1946, 8-2-10912.

41. *Avanti!,* 23 August 1945; "Stralcio dal Rapporto dell'Alto Commissariato per la Sicilia Sulla Situazione in Sicilia nel Mese di Luglio," 14 August 1945, ACS, *MI,* AG, 1944–1946, b. 8, f. 559, sf. 2.

42. Parri to Aldisio, 25 September 1945, ACS, *MI,* AG, 1944–1946, b. 8, f. 559, sf. 1; William Peck to Secretary of State, 27 September 1945, NA, RG 59, 865.00/9-2745.

43. Giovanni Mira to Aldisio, 25 September 1945, ACS, *MI,* AG, 1944–1946, b. 8, f. 559, sf. 1.

44. Alto Commissariato per la Sicilia to MI, "Movimento separatista," 26 September 1945, ACS, *MI,* AG, 1944–1946, b. 8, f. 559, sf. 2.

45. Carabinieri Compagnia Interna to MI, 1 October 1945, ACS, *PCM,* 1944–1946, 8-2-10912; L'Ispettore Generale di PS to Il Capo della Polizia, "All. N. 6," 3 October 1945, ACS, *MI,* AG, 1944–1946, b. 8, f. 559, sf. 1; Questore Guglielmi to Capo Polizia Ministero Interno, 3 October 1945, ACS, *MI,* AG, 1944–1946, b. 8, f. 559, sf. 2; *Il Popolo,* 4 October 1945.

46. A separate order was signed for each man. For Parri's orders, see Il MI, 4 October 1945, ACS, *MI,* AG, 1944–1946, b. 8, f. 559, sf. 1; for Parri's explanation see Parri to Palmiro Togliatti, 26 November 1945, ACS, *MI,* AG, 1950–1951, b. 35, f. 11436.

47. Kirk to Secretary of State, 2 October 1945, NA, RG 59, 865.00/10-245; Aldisio to Prefetti Isola, 1 October 1945, ACS, *PCM,* 1944–1946, 8-2-10912, sf. 2.

48. Questore Guglielmi to Capo Polizia Ministero Interno, 3 October 1945, ACS, *MI,* AG, 1944–1946, b. 8, f. 559, sf. 2; from the same source, Alto Commissariato per la Sicilia to Presidenza Consiglio Ministri, 4 October 1945. Alto Commissariato per la Sicilia to MI, "Movimento separatista," 8 October 1945, ACS, *MI,* AG, 1944–1946, b. 8, f. 559, sf. 2. See also Aldisio to Parri, 4 October 1945, ACS, *PCM,* 1944–1946, 8-2-10912, sf. 2.

49. Rome to Foreign Office, 10 October 1945, PRO, FO 371, 49767; see also Kirk to Secretary of State, 3 October 1945, FBI, 109-12-233-111.

CHAPTER 11. THE END

1. Comando Generale dell'Arma dei Carabinieri Reali to MI, "Provincia di Palermo—Affissione manifestini di propaganda separatista," 24 November

1945, ACS, *MI*, AG, 1944–1946, b. 210, f. 22269; from the same location, Il Esecutivo, "Movimento per l'Indipendenza della Sicilia," 3 October 1945; Comandante Compagnia Carabinieri to MI, 12 November 1945, ACS, *MI*, AG, 1944–1946, b. 42, f. 3287.

2. Comando Generale dell'Arma dei Carabinieri Reali to Presidenza del Consiglio dei Ministri, "Fermo dei capi del movimento indipendenza Sicilia," 18 October 1945, ACS, *PCM*, 1944–1946, 8-2-10912, sf. 2; William Peck to Kirk, See Enclosure, 9 October 1945, NA, RG 59, 865.00/10-945; *Avanti!*, 3 October 1945.

3. Comando Generale dell'Arma dei Carabinieri Reali to Presidenza del Consiglio dei Ministri, "Fermo dei capi del movimento indipendenza Sicilia," 18 October 1945, ACS, *PCM,* 1944–1946, 8-2-10912, sf. 2.

4. Nester to Kirk, 5 December 1945, NA, RG 59, 865.00/12-545.

5. George R. Gayre to Sir Percy, 20 January 1946, PRO, FO 371, 60655.

6. Nester had been asked to attend the meeting but declined. Nester to Kirk, 23 November 1945, NA, RG 59, 865.00/11-2345. The possibility of a mafia rift was mentioned in a 19 November 1945 message. It implied that Vizzini was losing power and influence. Nester to Kirk, 19 November 1945, NA, RG 59, 865.00/11-1945.

7. Nester to Kirk, 23 November 1945, NA, RG 59, 865.00/11-2345.

8. Ibid.

9. Nester to Kirk, 5 December 1945, NA, RG 59, 865.00/12-545.

10. Nester to Kirk, 12 January 1946, NA, RG 59, 865.00/1-1246.

11. Nester to Kirk, 5 December 1945, NA, RG 59, 865.00/12-545.

12. Ibid.

13. On the Movimento per l'Autonomia, see Nester to Kirk, 19 November 1945, NA, RG 59, 865.00/11-1945; Nester to David Key, 3 December 1945, NA, RG 59, 865.00/12-345; Peck to Kirk, 19 November 1945, NA, RG 59, 865.00/ 11-1945; Comando Generale dell'Arma dei Carabinieri Reali to MI, "Movimento per l'autonomia della Sicilia," 13 November 1945, ACS, *MI*, AG, 1944–1946, b. 235, f. 23607; from the same location, Aldisio to MI, "Movimento siciliano di autonomia Antiseparatista," 1 December 1945; "Movimento per l'Autonomia della Sicilia—Programma," September 1945.

14. Gayre, *Italy in Transition,* 153.

15. Di Carcaci, *Memorie,* 222–225; Pantaleone, *Mafia and Politics,* 136; Gaja, *L'esercito,* 240; Di Matteo, *Anni roventi,* 418–422.

16. Gaja, *L'esercito,* 242–243; di Carcaci, *Memorie,* 251–252.

17. On GRIS see *Giornale di Sicilia,* 31 July 1965; di Carcaci, *Memorie,* 237; Ispettorato Generale della Polizia, "Formazioni EVIS e bande armate," 17 February 1946, ACS, *PCM,* 1944–1946, 8-2-10457. Nicolosi claims that GRIS was more an intention than reality and implies that the two organizations were basically one and the same. Nicolosi, *Sicilia contro Italia,* 314–336. Gaja asserts that GRIS was the body through which the bandits joined the movement. Gaja, *L'esercito,* 234–238, 315–317. Testimony before the mafia commission seems to have supported that view. Madeo, ed., *Testo integrale,* vol. II, 64–66, 741; Sansone and Ingrasci, *Sei anni,* 75–77; Di Matteo, *Anni roventi,* 446–447.

18. Gaja, *L'esercito,* 255.

19. Comando Generale dell'Arma dei Carabinieri Reali to MI, "Provincia di Messina—Disordini," 15 October 1945, ACS, *MI*, AG, 1944–1946, b. 143, f. 12751; in the same location see a similar report dated 18 October 1945; see

also in the same location Alto Commissario per la Sicilia to MI, "Messina—Situazione politica," 19 October 1945; Prefetto di Messina to MI, 13 October 1945; Comando Generale dell'Arma dei Carabinieri Reali to MI, "Provincia di Messina—Ordine pubblico," 23 October 1945.

20. Gallo's presence was never certified. Gaja, *L'esercito*, 244–245; Sansone and Ingrasci, *Sei anni*, 84.

21. Gaja, *L'esercito*, 257, 260; Maxwell, *God Protect Me*, 66; Sansone and Ingrasci, *Sei anni*, 85; Chandler, *King of the Mountain*, 58.

22. A number of these bandits supposedly followed Communist ideas and were inscribed in the Communist Party. Comando Generale dell'Arma dei Carabinieri Reali to Presidenza del Consiglio dei Ministri, "Formazione armata dell' EVIS," 2 February 1946, ACS, *PCM*, 1944–1946, 8-2-10457; di Carcaci, *Memorie*, 238; Gaja, *L'esercito*, 245–247; Lewis, *Honored Society*, 162–169.

23. Nester to Kirk, 10 January 1946, NA, RG 59, 865.00/1-1046.

24. Di Carcaci, *Memorie*, 239; Gaja, *L'esercito*, 253.

25. British authorities reported that Gallo had been killed. "Report on Sicilian Separatism and the Movimento per l'Indipendenza della Sicilia," 17 April 1946, PRO, FO 371, 67786; Alto Commissario to Presidenza Consiglio Ministri, 31 December 1945, ACS, *PCM*, 1944–1946, 8-2-10457; Nester to Kirk, 2 January 1946, NA, RG 59, 865.00/1-246; *Giornale di Sicilia*, 31 July 1965; Chandler, *King of the Mountain*, 58–59; Lewis, *Honored Society*, 169–173.

26. Gallo's account can be found in di Carcaci, *Memorie*, 240-246; for other accounts of the battle see Gaja, *L'esercito*, 261-263; *Giornale di Sicilia*, 31 July 1965.

27. For events following the battle see Comando Generale dell'Arma dei Carabinieri Reali to Presidenza del Consiglio dei Ministri, "Formazione armata dell' EVIS," 2 February 1946, ACS, *PCM*, 1944–1946, 8-2-10457; R. Prefettura di Enna to MI, "Relazione settimanale della situazione politica, economica, sull'ordine e lo spirito pubblico e sulle condizioni della pubblica sicurezza," 31 January 1946, ACS, *MI*, AG, 1944–1946, b. 216, f. 22539; di Carcaci, *Memorie*, 247–250, 259.

28. For a partial list of those arrested and denounced for EVIS activities see Ispettore Generale di PS per la Sicilia to Capo della Polizia, "EVIS e bande armate-Denunzia all'Autorità Militare," 20 March 1946, ACS, *PCM*, 1944–1946, 8-2-10457.

29. On Giuliano's campaign, see "Report on Sicilian Separatism and the Movimento per l'Indipendenza della Sicilia," 17 April 1946, PRO, FO 371, 67786; CCRR General Command to Allied Commission, Sub Commission of PS, "Pioppo di Monreale (Palermo District)—Barracks of the Arma Assaulted by a Gang of Evildoers," 4 January 1946, NA, RG 331, 10000/143/1420; Comando Generale dell'Arma dei Carabinieri Reali to Presidenza del Consiglio dei Ministri, "Sicilia-situazione politica," 23 April 1946, ACS, *PCM*, 1944–1946, 8-2-10457; from the same source, Alto Commissariato per la Sicilia to Presidenza del Consiglio dei Ministri, "Formazione armate-ordine pubblico," 9 January 1946; Nester to Kirk, 8 January 1946, NA, RG 59, 865.00/1-846; in the same record group, Nester's dispatches to Kirk dated 9 and 10 January; Nester to Secretary of State, 15 January 1946, NA, RG 59, 865.00/1-1546; Gaja, *L'esercito*, 279–289; Gayre, *Italy in Transition*, 152–153; Maxwell, *God Protect Me*, 68–69; *New York Times*, 10 January 1946; *Giornale di Sicilia*, 25 July 1965; Chandler, *King of the Mountain*, 64–105.

30. Palermo to Secretary of State, 4 May 1947, NA, RG 59, 865.00/5-447; Dunn to Secretary of State, 24 June 1947, NA, RG 59, 865.00/6-2447; Chubb, *The Mafia and Politics,* 16–17; Chandler, *King of the Mountain,* 82–105; *Il Nuovo Giornale l'Italia,* 24 June 1947; *Italia Nuova,* 1 July 1947; *La Voce Repubblicana,* 24 June 1947; Maxwell, *God Protect Me,* 101–125.

31. One American translator labeled Giuliano "a very famous bandit chief, probably the most famous living criminal in Italy." No letters of reply exist in the Truman Library. Department of State, "Translator's Summary of Communication, Giuliano to Truman." 12 May 1947 and 13 April 1948, Harry S Truman Library, Papers of Harry S Truman, General File; Maxwell, *God Protect Me,* 80; Sansone and Ingrasci, *Sei anni,* 148. Giuliano's career did not end with the demise of the separatist movement. In fact his later activities gained him much more fame and attention. See Chandler, *King of the Mountain,* 123–224; Maxwell, *God Protect Me,* 80–255; Felice Chilanti, *Da Montelepre a Viterbo*; in the archival collections, see the documents in the ACS, *MI*, AG, 1947, b. 19, f. 827.

32. For reports on the government's actions against the bands see L'Ispettore Generale di PS to Capo della Polizia, "Formazioni EVIS e bande armate," 17 February 1946, ACS, *PCM,* 1944–1946, 8-2-10457; from the same location see Messana's report dated 8 March; see also "Pro-Memoria per Il Capo della Polizia," 14 July 1947, ACS, *MI*, AG, 1947, b. 19, f. 827; Il Capo della Polizia to the Gabinetto del Ministro, "Movimento separatista," 25 February 1946, ACS, *MI*, AG, 1950–1951, b. 35, f. 11436; *Avanti!*, 16 March 1946.

33. Di Carcaci, *Memorie,* 260; "Report of Major A. E. Heath," 21 January 1946, PRO, FO 371, 60655, 07938.

34. Peck to Kirk, 23 October 1945, NA, RG 59, 865.00/10-2345.

35. Nester to Secretary of State, 18 January 1946, NA, RG 59, 865.00/1-1846; also see Nester's message of the 19th in the same location.

36. R. Prefetto di Messina to MI, "Relazione mensile della situazione generale," 12 March 1946, ACS, *MI*, AG, 1944–1946, b. 215, f. 22528; Kirk to Secretary of State, 8 February 1946, NA, RG 59, 865.00/2-846; Nester to Kirk, 12 January 1946, NA, RG 59, 865.00/1-1246; di Carcaci, *Memorie*, 253–254; Maxwell, *God Protect Me,* 67; Giarrizzo, *Sicilia politica,* 130; Sansone and Ingrasci, *Sei anni,* 100.

37. "Istruzioni per il Funzionario cui sono affidati in Ponza in nominati avv. Finocchiaro Aprile Andrea, avv. Varvaro, Antonino, e prof. Restuccia Francesco," 2 October 1945, ACS, *MI*, AG, 1944–1946, b. 8, f. 559, sf. 1; Il Capo della Polizia to Gabinetto del MI, "Avvocati Finocchiaro Aprile Andrea, Varvaro, Antonino, e Restuccia, Francesco. Internati a Ponza," 25 February 1946, ACS, *MI*, AG, 1950–1951, b. 35, f. 11436; in the same location, Il Capo della Polizia to Gabinetto del Sig. Ministro, "Avvocato Finocchiaro Aprile, Andrea già internato a Ponza," 27 March 1946; Procura Generale Presso la Corte d'Appello di Roma to Ministro di Grazia e Giustizia, "Denunzia di Finocchiaro Aprile Andrea, Varvaro Antonino e Restuccia Francesco," 14 November 1945; "Copia di Telegramma diretto al Procuratore Generale della Corte d'Appello di Roma," 24 October ACS, *PCM,* 1944–1946, 8-2-10912; *La Voce Repubblicana,* 12 March 1946.

38. See the "confessions," untitled and undated, ACS, *MI*, AG, 1944–1946, b. 8, f. 559, sf. 1.

39. Ibid.

40. "Memoria Difensiva per Andrea Finocchiaro Aprile, Varvaro e Restuccia," 16 October 1945, ACS, *MI*, AG, 1950–1951, b. 35, f. 11436; Peck to Kirk,

23 October 1945, NA, RG 59, 865.00/10-2345; they also wrote to Admiral Stone. American Embassy, Rome to Secretary of State, 5 December 1945, NA, RG 59, 865.00/12-545. On the legitimacy of Finocchiaro Aprile's arrest and imprisonment see *La Voce Repubblicana,* 12 March 1946.

41. William Peck to Secretary of State, 23 October 1945, NA, RG 59, 865.00/10-2345.

42. Ibid.

43. Kirk to Secretary of State, 14 March 1946, NA, RG 59, 865.00/3-1446; Il Capo della Polizia to Gabinetto del MI, "Finocchiaro Aprile Andrea, Varvaro Antonino e Restuccia Francesco—Internati a Ponza—Revoca del provvedimento," 18 March 1946, ACS, *MI*, AG, 1950–1951, b. 35, f. 11436; di Carcaci, *Memorie,* 282.

44. Kirk to Secretary of State, 19 March 1946, NA, RG 59, 865.00/3-1946; Comando Generale dell'Arma dei Carabinieri Reali to Presidenza del Consiglio dei Ministri, "Sicilia—situazione politica," 24 April 1946, ACS, *PCM,* 1944–1946, 8-2-10457.

45. Those in attendance included Bruno di Belmonte, Rosario Cacopardo, Francesco Restuccia, Edoardo Milio Cangemi, Raffaele Di Martino, Lucio Tasca, and Antonino Varvaro. Di Carcaci, *Memorie,* 286. At an earlier meeting with Romita, Finocchiaro Aprile had rejected separatism and asked for an amnesty for all those who had belonged to EVIS. Key to Secretary of State, 19 March 1946, NA, RG 59, 865.00/3-1946.

46. "Sunto del Discorso Pronunziato dall'On. Finocchiaro Aprile al Suo Arrivo all'Aeroporto di Bocca di Falco," ACS, *PCM,* 1944–1946, 8-2-10912; *L'Indipendente,* 27 March 1946; *La Voce della Sicilia,* 28 March 1945; di Carcaci, *Memorie,* 288.

47. Comando Generale dell'Arma dei Carabinieri Reali to Presidenza del Consiglio dei Ministri, "Sicilia—Situazione politica," 23 April 1946, ACS, *PCM,* 1944–1946, 8-2-10457; Comando Generale dell'Arma dei Carabinieri Reali to MI, "Messina—Movimento indipendentista siciliano," 14 April 1946, ACS, *MI*, AG, 1944–1946, b. 195, f. 21310; "Stralcio dalle relazione delle Prefetture sulle situazione delle rispettive provincie," undated, ACS, *MI*, AG, 1950–1951, b. 35, f. 11436.

EPILOGUE

1. Giarrizzo, *Sicilia politica,* 131; di Carcaci, *Memorie,* 284–285; Di Matteo, *Anni roventi,* 452–454; *Avanti!,* 12 March 1946. For list of the candidates see ACS, *MI*, AG, 1944–1946, b. 224, f. 22974.

2. File No 997/B, 26 March 1946, "Sicilian Separatism," 19 April 1946, CIA.

3. Ispettorato Generale di PS per la Sicilia to Capo della Polizia, "Formazioni EVIS e bande armate," 17 February 1946, ACS, *PCM,* 1944–1946, 8-2-10457.

4. Ibid.; Counter Intelligence Corps, Naples Detachment, "Lucania, Salvatore (alias Charles 'Lucky' Luciano)," 13 August 1946, FBI, 39-2141-62.

5. Comando Generale dell'Arma dei Carabinieri Reali to Presidenza del Consiglio dei Ministri, "Sicilia—situazione politica," 20 April 1946, ACS, *PCM,* 1944–1946, 8-2-10457.

6. R. Prefettura di Messina to MI, "Movimento separatista," 29 March 1946, ACS, *MI*, AG, 1950–1951, b. 35, f. 11436; Il Capo della Polizia to Gabinetto del

Ministero dell'Interno, "Movimento indipendentista," 15 April 1946, ACS, *MI, AG*, 1994–1946, b. 195, f. 21310; in the same location, R. Prefettura di Messina to MI, "Movimento indipendentista," 2 April 1946.

7. Comando Generale dell'Arma dei Carabinieri Reali to Presidenza del Consiglio dei Ministri, "Messina—Movimento indipendentista siciliano," 14 April 1946, ACS, *PCM*, 1944–1946, 8-2-10912; Comando Generale dell'Arma dei Carabinieri Reali to Presidenza del Consiglio dei Ministri, "Sicilia—situazione politica," 20 April 1946, ACS, *PCM*, 1944–1946, 8-2-10457; Ispettorato Generale di PS per la Sicilia to MI, "Movimento Indipendenza Siciliana," 6 June 1946, ACS, *MI, AG*, 1950–1951, b. 35, f. 11436; di Carcaci, *Memorie*, 287; Marino, *Storia del separatismo*, 226–227.

8. R. Prefettura di Enna to MI, "Relazione settimanale della situazione politica, economica, sull'ordine e lo spirito pubblico e sulle condizioni della PS," 19 June 1946, ACS, *MI, AG*, 1944–1946, b. 216, f. 22539; see the Prefect's report of 15 April 1946 in the same location; Ispettorato Generale di PS della Sicilia to MI, "Movimento Indipendenza Siciliana (MIS)," 6 June 1946, ACS, *MI, AG*, 1950–1951, b. 35, f. 11436.

9. Allied Commission, Sicily Liaison Group to Executive Commissioner, "DO Report," 27 May 1946, NA, RG 331, 10000/109/77; from the same location, "Second Do Letter" from the same source dated 31 May 1946; on May 9 Victor Emmanuel III abdicated the throne and Umberto II immediately filled it.

10. Field HQ, File No. JRX-3138, "Sicilian Separatism," 15 May 1946, CIA. By this time Aldisio, who had decided to run for the Constituent as a Christian Democrat, had been replaced as high commissioner by Igino Coffari. Coffari served only a short time and was replaced in November 1946 by Giovanni Selvaggi. Di Matteo, *Anni roventi*, 457, 471–472, 481–482.

11. Raffaele Di Martino to Romita, 3 May 1946, ACS, *MI, AG*, 1944–1946, b. 263, f. 25516; Finocchiaro Aprile to Romita, 12 April 1946, ACS, *MI, AG*, 1944–1946, b. 195, f. 21310; in the same location, Varvaro to Romita, 5 April 1946; di Carcaci, *Memorie*, 307, 314.

12. Comando Generale dell'Arma dei Carabinieri to MI, "Autonomia della Regione Siciliana," 24 September 1946, ACS, *MI, AG*, 1944–1946, b. 235, f. 23607; Key to Secretary of State, 13 March 1946, NA, RG 59, 865.00/3-1346. For the statute, see "Lo Statuto della Regione Siciliana e le leggi relative," *Mediterranea: Almanacco dai Sicilia* (1949), 273–287. Sturzo considered the announcement of autonomy an act of pacification while Gaetano Salvemini argued that the formation of a region should be decided by a popular vote, not by the deputies in the Constituent. Luigi Sturzo, *La regione nella nazione* (Rome: Capriotti, 1959), 102; Gaetano Salvemini, *L'Italia vista dall'America* (Milan: Feltrinelli, 1969), 713; further debate on whether the separatist movement influenced the decision to grant Sicily autonomy is found in Di Matteo, *Anni roventi*, 460–461. For a detailed discussion concerning the plan for autonomy see Jacoviello, *La Sicilia*, 159–183; see also Giarrizzo, *Sicilia politica*.

13. Both Gallo and Castrogiovanni were still imprisoned at the time of the election, but were released in July to serve in the Constituent. Gallo was exonerated of most criminal charges in March 1947, but was still facing trial for the murder of three carabinieri. Dunn to Secretary of State, 21 April 1947, NA, RG 59, 865.00/4-2147; Comando Generale dell'Arma dei Carabinieri to Presidenza del Consiglio dei Ministri, "Deputato della Costituente Gallo Concetto-Comandante della EVIS-già detenuto presso le carceri giudiziarie di

Palermo," 22 July 1946, ACS, *PCM,* 1944–1946, 8-2-10912, sf. 2; di Carcaci, *Memorie,* 322–323, 328; Presidenza della Regione Siciliana, *Elezioni in Sicilia: Dati e grafici dal 1946 al 1956* (Milan: A. Giuffre, 1956); Di Matteo, *Anni roventi,* 475–478.

14. Comando Generale dell'Arma dei Carabinieri Reali to Parri, "Situazione politica in Sicilia," 10 June 1946, ACS, *PCM,* 1944–1946, 8-2-10457; di Carcaci, *Memorie,* 320, 329; *New York Times,* 6 and 8 June 1946.

15. Comando Generale dell'Arma dei Carabinieri Reali to MI, "Enna—Convegno indipendentista," 11 June 1946, ACS, *MI,* AG, 1944–1946, b. 218, f. 22633; in the same location, "Movimento Per L'Indipendenza Della Sicilia—Il Comitato Regionale del MIS"; R. Prefettura di Enna to MI, "Riunione degli esponenti del MIS—Movimento per l'Indipendenza della Sicilia," 15 June 1946; Alto Commissariato per la Sicilia to MI, "Movimento Indipendenza Siciliana," see the attached "Elenco dei Partiipanti Al Congresso Degli Indipendentisti Tenutosi ad Enna il 9 e il 10 Giugno 1946," 15 June 1946; Prefetto Biancorosso to Ministero Interno Gabinetto e Direzione Sicurezza, 12 June 1946.

16. Comando Generale dell'Arma dei Carabinieri to MI, "Movimento indipendentista siciliano," 27 June 1946, ACS, *MI,* AG, 1944–1946, b. 195, f. 21310; in the same location, Prefetto di Messina to MI, "Movimento separatista siciliano. Servizio informativo speciale," 6 July 1946.

17. Ispettorato Generale di PS per la Sicilia to MI, "Movimento Indipendenza Siciliana (MIS)," 6 June 1946, ACS, *MI,* AG, 1950–1951, b. 35, f. 11436.

18. Jack Ward to Hoyer Millar, Foreign Office, 20 December 1946, PRO, FO 371, 67786; Finocchiaro Aprile, *Il movimento indipendentista,* 155–193.

19. Finocchiaro Aprile, *Il movimento indipendentista,* 177–178; di Carcaci, *Memorie,* 331–333, 348–349. Marino claims that Finocchiaro Aprile fought for southern Italy as well as Sicily. Marino, *Storia del separatismo,* 231–233. Finocchiaro Aprile also caused a national uproar by accusing government officials of corruption. Dunn to Secretary of State, 19 February 1947, NA, RG 59, 865.00/2-1947; also see the dispatches of 21 February and 12 March in the same record group. Mario Tedeschi, *Roma democristiana* (Longanesi e Co., Milan, 1956), 188–203.

20. Ispettorato Generale di PS to MI, "Movimento Indipendenza Siciliana (MIS)," 6 June 1946, ACS, *MI,* AG, 1950–1951, b. 35, f. 11436; Comando Generale dell'Arma dei Carabinieri Reali to MI, "Catania—Dimissioni di dirigenti provinciali del MIS," 27 August 1946, ACS, *MI,* AG, 1944–1946, b. 263, f. 25516.

21. Prefetto di Palermo to MI, "Relazione mensile sulla situazione politico-economico e sulle condizioni della sicurezza pubblica nella Provincia di Palermo durante il mese di Dicembre 1946," 12 January 1947, ACS, *MI,* AG, 1947, b. 34, f. 2003; R. Prefetto di Messina to MI, "Relazione mensile sulla situazione generale della Provincia durante il mese di Luglio," 1 August 1946, ACS, *MI,* AG, 1944–1946, b. 215, f. 22528; di Carcaci, *Memorie,* 340–341.

22. Comando Generale dell'Arma dei Carabinieri to MI, "Dimissioni dell'On. Antonino Varvaro, Segretario del MIS," 29 September 1946, ACS, *MI,* AG, 1950–1951, b. 35, f. 11436; Finocchiaro Aprile, *Il movimento indipendentista,* 36; di Carcaci, *Memorie,* 332–333; Madeo, ed., *Testo integrale,* vol. II, 1716.

23. Prefettura di Palermo to MI, "Movimento per l'indipendenza Siciliana," 20 January 1947, ACS, *MI,* AG, 1947, b. 3, f. 53; from the same location, Prefettura di Messina to MI, "Movimento Indipendentista Siciliano"; di Carcaci, *Memorie,* 335–336.

24. Comando Generale dell'Arma dei Carabinieri to MI, "Taormina (Messina)—Congresso Separatista," 8 February 1947, ACS, *MI*, AG, 1947, b. 3, f. 53; di Carcaci, *Memorie*, 343–345; *L'Umanità*, 2 February 1947; *Avanti!*, 2 February 1947; *L'Unità*, 2 February 1947; Madeo, *Testo integrale*, vol. II, 1716–1717; Marino, *Storia del separatismo*, 240–244.

25. Comando Generale dell'Arma dei Carabinieri to MI, "Taormina (Messina)—Congresso Separatista," 9 February 1947, ACS, *MI*, AG, 1947, b. 3, f. 53.

26. Ibid.

27. Comando Generale dell'Arma dei Carabinieri to MI, "Taormina (Messina)—Congresso Separatista," 13 February 1947, ACS, *MI*, AG, 1947, b. 3, f. 53; in the same location, Movimento per l'Indipendenza della Sicilia, Segretaria Nazionale, "III Congresso Nazionale, Taormina, 31 Gennaio, 1, 2, 3, Febbraio 1947"; Finocchiaro Aprile, *Il movimento indipendentista*, 148–154.

28. Prefettura di Messina to MI, "Taormina—Congresso del movimento indipendentista siciliano," 11 February 1947, ACS, *MI*, AG, 1947, b. 3, f. 53; Prefettura di Palermo to MI, "Partinico-Sezione del Movimento Indipendenza Siciliana Democratico Repubblicano," 9 June 1947, ACS, *MI*, DGPS, AA.GG.RR., 1944, C-2-A, b. 39, f. "Movimento separatista Siciliana"; *Il Giornale di Sicilia*, 9 February 1947; *Il Risorgimento Liberale*, 5 February 1947; di Carcaci, *Memorie*, 345.

29. "Carissimo Sig. Ferarri, Capo della Polizia Italiana," undated, ACS, *MI*, AG, 1947, b. 19, f. 827. Varvaro denied having received any support from Giuliano. Other testimony before the mafia commission disputed his claim. Madeo, ed., *Testo integrale*, vol. II, 1558, 1720–1721, 1725, 1006. There was talk of postponing the elections, but several political leaders argued that doing so would make it appear that the government was reneging on its pledge of autonomy. Dunn to Secretary of State, 26 February 1947, NA, RG 59, 865.00/2-2647; in the same location see the dispatch of 28 February.

30. Scott to Secretary of State, 24 April 1947, NA, RG 59, 865.00/4-2447; Dunn to Secretary of State, 26 April 1947, NA, RG 59, 865.00/4-2647; also see Dunn's dispatch of 2 May 1947; Presidenza della Regione Siciliana, *Le elezioni in Sicilia*, 451–473; Presidenza della Regione Siciliana, *L'Assemblea regionale siciliana: Gli uomini e le opere* (Palermo: OSEP, 1951), 7–100; Finocchiaro Aprile, *Il movimento indipendentista*, 36; di Carcaci, *Memorie*, 351; Zingali, *L'invasione*, 402–403; *L'Unità*, 22, 23 April 1947; di Matteo, *Anni roventi*, 512–514.

31. Di Carcaci, *Memorie*, 359–360. Finocchiaro Aprile surrendered his seat in the Regional Assembly on 2 March 1948. Vincenzo Bongiorno replaced him. Presidenza della Regione Siciliana, *Le elezioni in Sicilia*, 471.

32. Di Carcaci, *Memorie*, 360–361.

33. Prefettura di Palermo to MI, "Dimissioni dell'ex deputato Andrea Finocchiaro Aprile dalla Presidenza dell'Movimento d'Indipendenza della Sicilia," 8 June 1948, ACS, *MI*, AG, 1950–1951, b. 35, f. 11436.

34. Prefettura di Palermo to MI, "Movimento per la Indipendenza della Sicilia," 7 August 1948, ACS, *MI*, AG, 1950–1951, b. 35, f. 11436; from the same location, Prefettura di Messina to MI, "Attività MIS," 16 June 1948. Many conservative separatists became Christian Democrats. For those with leftist sympathies, the transition to new parties was more difficult. Marino, *Storia del separatismo*, 212.

35. Prefettura di Messina to MI, "Taormina—IV Congresso MIS," 31 July 1950, ACS, *MI*, AG, 1950–1951, b. 35, f. 11436. Tasca became disillusioned

with autonomy in the 1950s. In one of his works he called for the separation of Italy and Sicily, and characterized the two nations as "incompatible, like members of a bad family unit." He also complained that Sicily did not have enough control over its agriculture. Lucio Tasca Bordonaro, *Le gioie della riforma: Hanno trasformato il latifondo? O rovinato l'agricoltura?* (Palermo: S. F. Flaccovio, 1951), 55–56.

36. On the postwar mafia see Chubb, *Mafia and Politics;* the quotation is from page 45. On the struggle between the mafia and the state in 1980s and 1990s see Alexander Stille, *Excellent Cadavers: The Mafia and the Death of the First Italian Republic* (New York: Pantheon Books, 1995). For an earlier attack on autonomy and Sicily's political leadership, see Giuseppe Garretto, *Realtà siciliana* (Edizioni Gianape: Palermo, 1967), 96–109.

37. On Bossi and the Northern League see Douglas A. Wertman, "Italy: The Right Break with the Past," *Current History* November 1994: 369–374; John Torpey, "Affluent Secessionists: Italy's Northern League," *Dissent* Summer 1994: 311–315; Angelo Codevilla, "No, Italy Is Not Going Fascist," *Commentary* August 1994: 45–48; by the same author, "A Second Italian Republic," *Foreign Affairs* Summer 1992: 147–162; W. V. Harris, "Italy: Purgatorio," *The New York Review of Books* 3 March 1994: 38–41; Frederika Randall, "The Italians Cry Basta!" *The Nation* 16 March 1992: 337–340; Larry Garner and Roberta Garner, "Italy: Richer and Unhappier," *Current History* November 1990: 369–372, 386–388; "A League of Their Own," *The Economist* 21 July 1990:51.

38. Orazio Vasta, *Quale Sicilia per I siciliani?*, (Ragusa: Sicilia Punto L, 1985); "Appellu a lu populu sicilanu," 20 December 1971; "Statu di Sicilia." These documents were obtained in Italy and are in the author's possession.

Bibliography

Primary Unpublished Sources

A. Archivio Centrale dello Stato, Rome, Italy.
   1. Carte Vittorio Emanuele Orlando, Carteggio.
   2. Casellario Politico Centrale.
   3. Comando Anglo-Americano, Appendice.
   4. Governo del Sud, Ministero dell'Interno, Direzione Generale Pubblica Sicurezza, 1943–1944.
   5. Ministero dell'Interno, Atti del Gabinetto, 1944–1946.
   6. Ministero dell'Interno, Atti del Gabinetto, 1947.
   7. Ministero dell'Interno, Atti del Gabinetto, 1950–1951.
   8. Ministero dell'Interno, Direzione Generale Pubblica Sicurezza, Affari Generali e Riservati, 1920.
   9. Ministero dell'Interno, Direzione Generale Pubblica Sicurezza, Affari Generali e Riservati, 1943.
   10. Ministero dell'Interno, Direzione Generale Pubblica Sicurezza, Affari Generali e Riservati, 1944–1945.
   11. Ministero dell'Interno, Direzione Generale Pubblica Sicurezza, Divisione Polizia Politica, 1927–1944.
   12. Presidenza del Consiglio dei Ministri, Governo di Salerno, 1943–1944.
   13. Presidenza del Consiglio dei Ministri, 1944–1946.
   14. Segretaria Particolare del Duce, Carteggio Ordinario.

B. Central Intelligence Agency, Washington, D.C.

C. Department of Justice, Federal Bureau of Investigation.

D. Franklin Delano Roosevelt Library.

E. Ministero Affari Esteri, Rome, Italy.
   Affari Serie Politici, 1931–1945.

F. National Archives and Records Administration, Washington, D.C.
   1. RG 38: Records of the Office of the Chief of Naval Operations.
   2. RG 59: General Records of the Department of State.
   3. RG 165: Records of the War Department and Special Staffs.
   4. RG 226: Records of the Office of Strategic Services
   5. RG 331: Records of Allied Operational and Occupational Headquarters, World War II.

G. Poletti Papers, Herbert H. Lehman Collection, Columbia University.

H. Public Records Office, London.
   1. Foreign Office 371: General Political Correspondence.
   2. War Office 204: Military Headquarters Papers, Allied Force Headquarters.

I. Harry S Truman Library.

J. Girolamo Valenti Papers, Tamiment Library, New York University.

PUBLISHED

Allied Military Government of Occupied Territory. *AMGOT Plan, Proclamations and Instructions.* Palermo: IRES, 1943.

Allied Military Government of Occupied Territory. *Sicily Gazette,* No. 1, July 1943; No. 2, 17 September 1943; No. 3, 20 October 1943.

Badoglio, Pietro. *L'Italia nella seconda guerra mondiale.* Verona: Mondadori, 1946.

Bonomi, Ivanoe. *Diario di un anno: 2 Giugno 1943–10 Giugno 1944.* Milan: Garzanti, 1947.

Bordonaro, Lucio Tasca. *Le gioie della riforma: Hanno trasformato il latifondo? O rovinato l'agricoltura?* Palermo: S. F. Flaccovio, 1951.

———. *Elogio del latifondo siciliano: La riforma della fame-II.* Palermo: S. F. Flaccovio, 1950.

Canepa, Antonio. *L'organizzazione del P.N.F.* Palermo: F. Ciuni Libraio Editore, 1939.

Caristia, Carmelo. *La Sicilia d'oggi e di ieri: Breve saggio-documentario su alcune grandi verità rivelate dall'istoriografia separatista.* Turin: Società Editrice Internazionale, 1944.

Cascino, Giovanni. *Il movimento separatista e la questione siciliana.* Rome: Edizione Il Commento, 1945.

Corvo, Max. *The OSS in Italy: 1942–1945: A Personal Memoir.* New York: Praeger, 1990.

Croce, Benedetto. *Quando l'Italia era tagliata in due: Estratto di un diario, Luglio 1943-Giugno 1944.* Bari: Laterza, 1948.

Damilano, Andrea, ed., *Atti e documenti della Democrazia Cristiana, 1943–1967.* Vol. 1. Rome: Edizione Cinque Lune, 1968.

Di Carcaci, Francesco Castello di Paterno. *Il movimento per l'indipendenza della Sicilia: Memorie del Duca di Carcaci.* Palermo: S. F. Flaccovio, 1977.

Faldella, Emilio. *Lo sbarco e la difesa della Sicilia.* Rome: L'Aniene, 1956.

Finocchiaro Aprile, Andrea. *Il movimento indipendentista siciliano.* Edited by Massimo S. Ganci. Palermo: Libri Siciliani, 1966.

Gayre, George R. *Italy in Transition: Extracts from the Private Journal of G. R. Gayre.* London: Faber & Faber Limited, 1946.

Gennuso, Giuseppe. *La questione siciliana.* Rome: O.E.T. Edizioni del Secolo, 1945.

Gentile, Nick. *Vita di capomafia.* Milan: Riuniti, 1963.

La Loggia, Enrico. *Autonomia e rinascita della Sicilia.* Palermo: IRES, 1953.

Madeo, Alfonso, ed. *Testo integrale della relazione della Commissione Parlamentare d' inchiesta sul fenomeno della mafia.* Vol. 2. Rome: Cooperativa Scrittori, 1973.

Mori, Cesare. *The Last Struggle with the Mafia.* Translated by Orlo Williams. London and New York: Putnam, 1933.

Ragusa, Pippo. *Storia dello squadrismo fascista palermitano.* Palermo: G. Di Bella, 1934.

Simili, Massimo. *I siciliani vogliono il re.* Milan: Riunite, 1946.

Salvemini, Gaetano. *L'Italia vista dall'America.* Edited by Enzo Tagliacozzo. Milan: Feltrinelli, 1969.

Sturzo, Luigi. *La mia battaglia da New York.* Rome: Garzanti, 1949.

———. *La regione nella nazione.* Rome: Capriotti, 1949.

———. *Le autonomie regionali e il mezzogiorno.* Rome: Edizioni Il Commento, 1944.

———. *Scritti ineditti.* Edited by Francesco Malgeri. 3 vols. Rome: Cinque Lune, 1974–1976.

Susmel, Edoardo and Duilio, eds. *Opera omnia di Benito Mussolini.* 36 Vols. Florence: La Fenice, 1951–1963.

Togliatti, Palmiro. *La questione siciliana.* Edited by Francesco Renda. Palermo: Libri Siciliani, 1965.

Trizzino, Antonnio. *Che vuole la Sicilia?* Rome: STEI, 1944.

———. *Vento del sud.* Rome: Editrice Faro, 1945.

Turri, Mario [Antonio Canepa]. *La Sicilia ai siciliani!.* Catania?: 1942.

NEWSPAPERS

Avanti!, 1945–47.

Giallo-Rosso, 1945.

Giornale di Sicilia, 1945; 1965.

Il Messaggero di Roma, 1964.

Il Popolo, 1944–45.

Il Tempo, 1944; 1964.

Italia Nuova, 1944.

La Voce Comunista, 1944.

La Voce della Sicilia, 1945.

La Voce Repubblicana, 1947.

L'Indipendente, 1946.

L'Indipendenza Siciliana, 1944.

L'Italia Libera, 1944.

Nazioni Unite, 1944.

The New York Times, 1943–46.

Popolo e Libertà, 1944.

Risorgimento Liberale, 1944; 1947.

Sicilia, 1944.

Sicilia e Libertà, 1944.

Sicilia Indipendente, 1945.

Sicilia Martire, 1945.

L'Unità, 1944.

SECONDARY SOURCES: BOOKS

Alatri, Paolo. *Lotte politiche in Sicilia sotto il governo della destra*. Turin: Einaudi, 1954.

Arena, Paolo. *La Sicilia nella sua storia e nei suoi problemi*. Palermo: F. Agate, 1949.

Arlacchi, Pino. *Mafia Business: The Mafia Ethic and Spirit of Capitalism*. Translated by Martin Pyle. London: Verso, 1986.

———. *Mafia, Peasants, and Great Estates: Society in Traditional Calabria*. Translated by Jonathan Steinberg. Cambridge: Cambridge University Press, 1983.

Attanasio, Sandro. *Sicilia senza Italia, Luglio-Augusto 1943*. Milan: Mursia, 1976.

Barbagallo, Corrado. *La questione meridionale*. Cernusco sul Naviglio: Garzanti, 1948.

Barbagallo, Salvo. *Randazzo 17 Giugno 1945: Anatomia di una strage*. Catania: Erwin Piscator, 1976.

———. *Una rivoluzione mancata*. Catania: Bonanno, 1974.

Battaglia, Giuseppe Ganci. *L'ordinamento della regione siciliana: Storia dei parlamenti e dell'autonomia*. Palermo: G. Denaro, 1961.

Battaglia, Roberto. *Storia della resistenza italiana: 8 Settembre 1943–25 Aprile 1945*. Turin: Einaudi, 1964.

Blok, Anton. *The Mafia of a Sicilian Village, 1860–1960: A Study of Violent Peasant Entrepreneurs*. New York: Harper & Row, 1974.

Brancato, Francesco. *Storia della Sicilia post-unificazione: La Sicilia nel primo ventennio del Regno d' Italia*. Bologna: Cesare Zuffi, 1956.

Caizzi, Bruno. *Antologia della questione meridionale*. Milan: Edizioni di Comunità, 1955.

Campbell, Rodney. *The Luciano Project: The Secret Wartime Collaboration of the Mafia and the United States Navy*. New York: McGraw-Hill, 1977.

Canalis, Ettore. "*Alcuni aspetti del movimento per l'indipendenza siciliana ed una breve ricerca sulla figura di Antonio Canepa.*" Thesis, University of Rome, 1974.

Candida, Renato. *Questa mafia*. Caltanissetta: Salvatore Sciascia, 1964.

Catalano, Franco. *L'Italia dalla dittatura alla democrazia, 1919–1948*. Milan: Feltrinelli, 1962.

Catanzaro, Raimondo. *Men of Respect: A Social History of the Sicilian Mafia*. Translated by Raymond Rosenthal. New York: The Free Press, 1988.

Chandler, Billy Jaynes. *King of the Mountain: The Life and Death of Giuliano the Bandit*. Dekalb, Illinois: Northern Illinois University Press, 1988.

Chilanti, Felice. *Chi e Milazzo? Mezzo barone e mezzo villano*. Florence: Parenti Editore, 1959.

———. *Da Montelepre a Viterbo*. Rome: Croce, 1952.

Chubb, Judith. *The Mafia and Politics: The Italian State Under Siege*. Cornell University Press, 1989.

———. *Patronage, Power and Poverty in Southern Italy: A Tale of Two Cities*. Cambridge: Cambridge University Press, 1982.

Cimino, Marcello, Ettore Serio, and Giuseppe Cardaci, eds. *La Sicilia nella resistenza*. Palermo: Quaderno di Cronache Parlamentari Siciliane, 1975.

Cimino, Marcello. *Fine di una nazione: Che cosa non è, che cosa può essere la Sicilia dopo il '43*. Palermo: S. F. Flaccovio, 1977.

Coles, Harry L. and Albert K. Weinberg. *Civil Affairs: Soldiers Become Governors*. The United States Army in World War II, Special Studies. Washington, D.C.: Department of the Army, 1964.

Colonna, Maurizio. *L'industria zolfifera siciliana: Origini, sviluppo, declino*. Catania: Università di Catania, 1971.

Compagna, Francesco and Vittorio De Caprariis, *Geografia delle elezioni italiane dal 1946 al 1953*. Bari: Il Mulino, 1954.

Compagna, Francesco. *La lotta politica italiana nel secondo dopoguerra e il mezzogiorno*. Bari: Laterza, 1950.

Cortese, Nino. *La prima rivoluzione separatista siciliana, 1820–1821*. Naples: Libreria Scientifica, 1951.

De Antonellis, Giacomo. *Il sud durante il fascismo*. Manduria: Lacaita Editore, 1977.

De Felice, Renzo. *Mussolini il fascista*. Vol. 1. Turin: Einaudi, 1966.

Degli Espinosa, Agostino. *Il regno del sud*. Rome: Riuniti, 1973.

Delzell, Charles F. *Mussolini's Enemies: The Italian Anti-Fascist Resistance*. Princeton: Princeton University Press, 1961.

De Polzer, Alfredo. *Statistiche agrarie*. Milan: A. Guiffre, 1942.

D'Este, Carlo. *Bitter Victory: The Battle for Sicily, July–August 1943*. New York: Harper Collins, 1991.

Di Fresco, Antonio Maria. *Sicilia: 30 anni di regione*. Palermo: Vittorietti Editore, 1976.

Di Matteo, Salvo. *Anni roventi: La Sicilia dal 1943 al 1947, cronache di un quinquennio*. Palermo: G. Denaro, 1967.

Dorso, Guido. *La rivoluzione meridionale*. Turin: Einaudi, 1955.

Duggan, Christopher. *Fascism and the Mafia*. New Haven: Yale University Press, 1989.

Finley, M. I., *A History of Sicily: Ancient Sicily To the Arab Conquest*. New York: Viking Press, 1968.

Finley, M. I., Denis Mack Smith, and Christopher Duggan. *A History of Sicily*. London: Chatto & Windus, 1986.

Gaja, Filippo. *L'esercito della lupara*. Milan: Area Editore, 1962.

Gambetta, Diego. *The Sicilian Mafia: The Business of Private Protection*. Cambridge: Harvard University, 1993.

Ganci, Massimo S. *I fasci dei lavoratori*. Caltanissetta-Rome: Sciascia, 1977.

———. *L'Italia antimoderata: radicali, repubblicani, socialisti, autonomisti dall'unità a oggi*. Parma: Edizioni Guanda, 1968.

Garland, Albert N. and Howard McGaw Smyth. *Sicily and the Surrender of Italy.* The United States Army in World War II, Mediterranean Theatre of Operations, Washington, D.C.: Office of Chief of Military History, 1965.

Garretto, Giuseppe. *Realtà siciliana.* Palermo: Gianape, 1967.

Giarrizzo, Giuseppe. *Sicilia politica, 1943–1945: La genesi dello statuto regionale.* Catania: Istituto Universitario, 1970.

Ginsborg, Paul. *A History of Contemporary Italy: Society and Politics, 1943–1988.* New York: Penguin Books, 1990.

Gosch, Martin and Richard Hammer. *The Last Testament of Lucky Luciano.* Boston: Little, Brown and Company, 1974.

Gramsci, Antonio. *La questione meridionale.* Edited by Franco De Felice and Valentino Parlato. Rome: Riuniti, 1957.

Grasso, Franco, ed. *Girolamo Li Causi e la sua azione politica per la Sicilia.* Palermo: Libri Siciliani, 1966.

Harris, Charles R. S. *Allied Military Administration of Italy: 1943–1945.* History of the Second World War. United Kingdom Military Series. Edited by Sir James Butler. London: Her Majesty's Stationery Office, 1957.

Hess, Henner. *Mafia and Mafiosi: The Structure of Power.* Westread, England: Saxon House, 1973.

Higgins, Trumbull. *Soft Underbelly: The Anglo-American Controversy Over the Italian Campaign, 1939–1945.* New York: The MacMillan Company, 1968.

Hobsbawm, Eric J. *Primitive Rebels: Studies in Archaic Forms of Social Movement in the Nineteenth and Twentieth Centuries.* New York: W. W. Norton, Inc., 1959.

Howard, Michael. *Grand Strategy, August 1942–September 1943.* Vol. 4. History of the Second World War. United Kingdom Military Series. Edited by Sir James Butler. London: Her Majesty's Stationery Office, 1972.

Hughes, H. Stuart. *The United States and Italy.* Cambridge, Mass: Harvard University Press, 1953.

Istituto Centrale di Statistica del Regno d'Italia. *Compendio statistico italiano, 1939.* Rome: Istituto Poligrafico dello Stato, 1940.

Jacoviello, Michele. *La Sicilia dalle lotte per l'indipendenza dall'Italia all'autonomia regionale: 1943–1948.* Naples: Simone Editore, 1978.

Kefauver, Estes. *Crime in America.* Edited by Sidney Shalett. Garden City, New York: Doubleday and Company, Inc., 1951.

Kogan, Norman. *Italy and the Allies.* Cambridge, Mass.: Harvard University Press, 1956.

Lanza, Rosario. *L'esperienza regionale siciliana.* Palermo: S. F. Flaccovio, 1971.

Lepre, Aurelio. *Storia del mezzogiorno nel Risorgimento.* Rome: Riuniti, 1969.

Lessa, William. *Spearhead Governatore: Remembrances of the Campaign in Italy.* Malibu: Undena Publications, 1985.

Lewis, Norman. *The Honored Society: A Searching Look at the Mafia.* New York: G. P. Putnam's Sons, 1964.

Lupo, Salvatore. *Storia della mafia dalle origini ai giorni nostri.* Rome: Donzelli, 1993.

Macaluso, Emanuele. *I Comunisti e la Sicilia*. Rome: Riuniti, 1970.

——. *La mafia e lo stato*. Rome: Riuniti, 1972.

Mack Smith, Denis. *A History of Sicily: Medieval Sicily, 800–1713*. New York: Viking Press, 1968.

——. *A History of Sicily: Modern Sicily After 1713*. New York: Viking Press, 1968.

Mammarella, Giuseppe. *Italy After Fascism: A Political History, 1943–1965*. Notre Dame, Indiana: University of Notre Dame Press, 1966.

Marino, Giuseppe Carlo. *Partiti e lotta di classe in Sicilia*. Bari: De Donato, 1976.

——. *Storia del separatismo siciliano*. Rome: Riuniti, 1979.

Maxwell, Gavin. *God Protect Me From My Friends*. London: Longmans, Green, 1956.

Miccichè, Giuseppe. *Dopoguerra e fascismo in Sicilia*. Rome: Riuniti, 1976.

Missori, Mario. *Governi, alte cariche dello stato e prefetti del regno d'Italia*. Rome: Ministero dell'Interno, 1973.

Mitcham, Jr., Samuel and Friedrich von Stauffenberg. *The Battle of Sicily: How the Allies Lost Their Chance for Total Victory*. New York: Orion, 1991.

Molè, Giovanni. *Studio-inchiesta sui latifondi siciliani*. Rome: Tipografia del Senato, 1929.

Molony, C. J. C., et al., *The Mediterranean and Middle East*. Vol. 5. History of the Second World War. United Kingdom Military Series. Edited by Sir James Butler. London: Her Majesty's Stationery Office, 1973.

Moore Jr., Barrington. *Social Origins of Dictatorship and Democracy: Lord and Peasant in the Making of the Modern World*. Boston: Beacon Press, 1966.

Nicholson, Gerald W. L. *The Canadians in Italy: 1943–1945*. Official History of the Canadian Army in the Second World War, Vol. 2. United Kingdom Military Series. Edited by Sir James Butler. London: Her Majesty's Stationery Office, 1973.

Nicolosi, Pietro. *Gli "antemarcia" di Sicilia, 23 Marzo 1919–28 Ottobre 1922*. Catania: Niccolo Giannotta, 1972.

Nicolosi, Salvatore. *Il bandito Giuliano*. Milan: Longanesi, 1977.

——. *Sicilia contro Italia*. Catania: Carmelo Tringale, 1981.

Novacco, Domenico. *Inchiesta sulla mafia*. Milan: Feltrinelli, 1963.

Pantaleone, Michele. *Mafia e droga*. Turin: Einaudi, 1966.

——. *The Mafia and Politics*. New York: Coward McCann, Inc., 1966.

Piscitelli, Enzo. *Storia della resistenza romana*. Bari: Laterza, 1965.

Poma, Rosario and Enzo Perrone. *Quelli della lupara: Rapporto sulla mafia di ieri e di oggi*. Florence: Edizioni Casini, 1964.

Presidenza della Regione Siciliana. *L'Assemblea regionale siciliana: Gli uomini e le opere*. Palermo: OSEP, 1951.

——. *Le elezioni in Sicilia: Dati e grafici dal 1946 al 1956*. Milan: A. Giuffre, 1956.

Quazza, Guido, Leo Valiani, and Edoardo Volterra. *Il governo dei CLN*. Turin: G. Giappichelli, 1966.

Renda, Francesco. *Il movimento contadino in Sicilia e la fine del blocco agrario nel mezzogiorno.* Bari: De Donato, 1976.

———. *Storia della questione meridionale.* Palermo: Pantea, 1945.

Romeo, Rosario. *Il Risorgimento in Sicilia.* Bari: Laterza, 1950.

Romano, Salvatore Francesco. *Storia della mafia.* Milan: Sugar, 1963.

———. *Storia della questione meridionale.* Palermo: Edizioni Pantea, 1945.

Roselli, John. *Lord William Bentinck and the British Occupation of Sicily, 1811–1814.* Cambridge: Cambridge University Press, 1956.

Ruini, Carlo. *Le vicende del latifondo siciliano.* Florence: G.C. Sansoni, 1946.

Runciman, Steven. *The Sicilian Vespers: A History of the Mediterranean World in the Later Thirteenth Century.* Cambridge: Cambridge University Press, 1958.

Saija, Marcello. *Un "Soldino"contro il fascismo: Istituzioni ed elites politiche nella Sicilia del 1923.* Catania: Cooperativa Universitaria Libraria Catanese, 1981.

Sansone, Vito and G. Ingrasci. *Sei anni di banditismo in Sicilia.* Milan: Le Edizioni Sociali, 1950.

Savarese, Nino. *Chronachetta siciliana.* Rome: Sandron, 1944.

Schneider, Jane and Peter Schneider. *Culture and Political Economy in Western Sicily.* New York: Academic Press, 1976.

Secchia, Pietro and Filippo Frassati. *La resistenza e gli alleati.* Milan: Feltrinelli, 1962.

Spriano, Paolo. *Storia del partito comunista italiano.* Vol. 5. Turin: Einaudi, 1967.

Stille, Alexander. *Excellent Cadavers: The Mafia and the Death of the First Italian Republic.* New York: Pantheon, 1995.

Tedeschi, Mario. *Roma democristiana.* Milan: Longanesi & Co., 1956.

Titone, Virgilio. *La costituzione del 1812 e l'occupazione Inglese della Sicilia, con un saggio sul concetto di rivoluzione.* Bologna: Licinio Cappelli, 1936.

Tocco, Matteo G. *Libro nero di Sicilia: Dietro le quinte della politica degli affari e della cronaca della regione siciliano.* Milan: Sugar Editore, 1972.

Vasta, Orazio. *Quale Sicilia per I siciliani?* Ragusa: Sicilia Punto L, 1985.

Vella, Giuseppe. *Gli orizzonti scientifici della cosidetta "questione meridionale.* Catania: Moderno, 1934.

Villari, Luigi. *The Liberation of Italy: 1943–1947.* Appleton, Wisconsin: C. C. Nelson Publishing Co., 1959.

Villari, Rosario, ed. *Il sud nella storia d'Italia.* Bari: Laterza, 1963.

Williams, Mary H., comp. *Chronology 1941–1945.* The United States Army in World War II, Special Studies. Washington, D.C.: Department of the Army, 1962.

Winks, Robin. *Cloak and Gown: Scholars in the Secret War, 1939–1961.* New York: William Morrow and Company, 1987.

Zangheri, Renato. *Agricoltura e contadini nella storia d'Italia.* Turin: Einaudi, 1977.

Zingali, Gaetano. *L'invasione della Sicilia, 1943: Avvenimenti militari e responsabilità politiche.* Catania: Università di Catania, 1962.

ARTICLES

Aga Rossi, Elena. "La politica degli alleati verso l'Italia nel 1943." *Storia Contemporanea* 4 (December 1972): 847–895.

———. "La situazione politica ed economica nell'Italia nel periodo 1944–1945: I governi Bonomi." *Quaderni dell'Istituto Romano per la Storia d'Italia dal Fascismo alla Resistenza* 2 (1971): 5–151.

"A League of Their Own," *The Economist* 21 July 1990, 51.

Alosco, Antonio. "Il Partito d'Azione dell'Italia liberata e la svòlta di Salerno." *Storia Contemporanea* 2 (April 1979): 359–375.

"Barbarians at the Gates of Rome." *The Economist,* 10 July 1993, 41.

Berti, Giuseppe. "La Situazione in Sicilia e I compiti nostri." *Rinascita* (November 1948): 381–388.

Benson, George C.S., and Maurice Neufeld. "American Military Government in Italy." In Carl J. Friedrich et. al., *American Experiences in Military Government in World War II,* 111–147. New York: Rinehart & Company, Inc., 1948.

Codevilla, Angelo M. "A Second Italian Republic." *Foreign Affairs* 71 (Summer 1992): 146–162.

———. "No, Italy Is Not Going Fascist." *Commentary,* August 1994, 45–48.

———. "Rome Wasn't Burned in a Day." *National Review,* 26 September 1994, 42–43.

Dafferi, Giulio. "La questione siciliana." *Il Ponte* 1 (September 1945): 480–487.

Di Gualtieri, Carol Avarna. "La questione siciliana," *Nuova Antologia* 439 (January–April 1947): 68–75.

Drozdiak, William, "Federalist Movement in Italy Faces Crisis." *The Washington Post,* 16 December 1994, A44.

Garner, Larry and Roberta Garner. "Italy: Richer and Unhappier." *Current History* 89 (November 1990): 369–372, 386–388.

Harris, W. V. "Italy: Purgatorio." *The New York Review of Books,* 3 March 1994, 38–41.

"Lo Statuto della regione siciliana e le leggi relative." *Mediterranea; Almanacco di Sicilia* (1949): 273–287.

Lupo, Salvatore. "The Allies and the mafia." *Journal of Modern Italian Studies* 2 (Spring 1997): 21–33.

Mercuri, Lamberto. "La Sicilia e gli alleati." *Storia Contemporanea* 4 (December 1972): 897–968.

Moss, Leonard W. "The Passing of Traditional Peasant Society in the South." In *Modern Italy, A Topical History Since 1861.* Edited by Edward R. Tannenbaum and Emiliana P. Noether, 147–170. New York: New York University Press, 1974.

Neufield, Maurice. "The Failure of Allied Military Government in Italy." *Public Administration Review* 6 (Spring 1946): 137–148.

"Now, Govern Italy." *The Economist,* 2 April 1994, 45.

Randall, Frederika. "The Italians Cry Basta!" *The Nation,* 16 March 1992, 337–340.

Reece, Jack E. "Fascism, the Mafia, and the Emergence of Sicilian Separatism: 1919–1943." *Journal of Modern History* 45 (1973): 261–276.

Renda, Francesco. "Sicilia: tra separatismo e avvio di una politica di massa." *Rinàscita* 13 (March 29, 1974): 30–32.

Rosenberger, Chandler. "Italy's Capitalist Crusaders." *National Review,* 7 March 1994, 25–26.

Russo, Ferdinando. "La lotta politica in Sicilia dalla liberazione alle elezioni regionale, Luglio 1943–Aprile 1947." *Società* (March–April 1947): 110–121.

Salvatorelli, Luigi. "Il mezzogiorno nella storia d'Italia." *Il Ponte* 2 (October 1946): 846–860.

Singer, Daniel. "Fiddling While Rome Smolders." *The Nation,* 29 July–5 August 1991, 152–154.

———. "Italy's Summer of Discontent." *The Nation,* 31 August–7 September 1992, 203–208.

Sturzo, Luigi. "Autogoverno e suoi limiti." *Il Ponte* 2 (October 1946): 839–845.

Tedeschi, Mario. "I tabù dell'anti-mafia." *Il Borghese* 7 (June 4 1972): 327–328; 367–368.

Torpey, John. "Affluent Secessionists: Italy's Northern League." *Dissent,* Summer 1994, 311–315.

Wertman, Douglas A. "Italy: The Right Break With the Past?" *Current History* 93 (November 1994): 369–373.

Wollemborg, Leo J. "A Shaky Coalition: How Far to the Right?" *Commonweal,* 3 June 1994, 8–9.

Index

Aci Sant Antonio, 154

Action Party, 71, 85, 131, 140, 156, 162; cooperation with OSS, 25–26; cooperation with separatists, 53, 238 n. 40; origins 76–77; views on separatism and autonomy, 76–77

Action Squads, 135, 142, 235 n. 17; in Algiers and Tunisia, 110; in Palermo area, 61

Administrative Elections, 186

Agrarian Party, 228 n. 99

Agricultural League, 122

Agricultural Leagues (Separatist), 52

Agrigento: separatist movement in, 83, 127, 128, 174

Aldisio, Salvatore, 98, 123, 126, 131, 143, 168, 233 n. 47, 238 n. 38, 253 n. 28; appointed as high commissioner, 88–90; arrests separatist leaders, 172–74; asks for autonomy for Sicily, 93; assesses separatist movement, 157; begins anti-separatist campaign, 88–90; blames Allies for Sicilian crisis, 104; and Catania disturbances, 130–31; convenes regional council, 138; court decision against, 253 n. 28; criticized by Nester, 156; discusses arrest of separatist leaders, 174; fears American support for separatists, 170; as leader of Christian Democrats, 73; linked to Mussolini, 139–40; meets with Finocchiaro-Aprile, 208 n. 29, 227 n. 87; as member of Musotto's consultative committee, 69–70; as minister of the interior, 69; negotiates with Varvaro, 160–61; orders suppression of separatist movement, 174; plans to arrest separatist leaders, 111, 154; powers as high commissioner expanded, 133; proposes closing separatist head-

quarters, 113; replaced as high commissioner, 263 n. 10; requests government action against separatists, 133, 155; takes anti-separatist measures, 111–12; requests troops for Sicily, 82, 111, 172; and San Francisco Declaration, 148; views on separatism, 88; and Vizzini, 120–21

Alexander, Harold, 28, 54

Allied Control Commission (ACC), 204 n. 73, 233 n. 43, 236 n. 21, 252 n. 22; formation, 33; and granai del popolo, 78–79; rejects Finocchiaro Aprile's request for help, 82, 85; supports Musotto as high commissioner, 34, 205 n. 79

Allied Military Government of Occupied Territory (AMG), 144, 203 n. 54; aims and objectives, 27–28; bans political activity in Sicily, 71; British desire to control, 29; development, 27; food supplies in Sicily under, 30–31, 203 n. 60; in north Africa, 27; in Sicily, 27–32; lifts ban on political activities in Sicily, 71; raises grain prices, 212 n. 9; rebirth of Sicilian politics under, 70–78; transfers control of Sicily to Italian government, 32–33

Allied Powers, 43, 45, 85, 54, 77, 86, 89, 90, 99, 106, 130, 209 n. 42, 251–52 n.13; accused of supporting separatism, 144; attitudes toward Finocchiaro Aprile, 87, 100, 109; and Communists in Sicily, 74; criticize separatists, 81; denial of support for separatists, 184; and food supply in Sicily, 129; formally denounce separatism 100–102; invasion of Sicily, 22–24; pre-invasion contacts with separatists, 55; recommend arrest of separatists, 79, 82; relations with separatist movement 54–59; and separatist revolt, 94, 110, 135; and sulphur miners, 52. *See also* Allied Military Government of Occupied Territory; Great Britain; United States

Amassi, 31

Ameduri, Pasquale, 109, 161

Amendola, Giovanni, 41

Anti-Fascist Resistance, in Sicily, 19, 20, 201 n. 28; *See also* Canepa, Antonio; Gerbini airport; Soldino Movement

Armistice, 27

Armed Bands, 31–32, 144

Arrigo, Salvatore, 109

Associazione Agraria, 52

Autonomy, 13, 32, 35, 93, 137, 150; as consequence of separatist movement, 193; failure of, 193–94; granted to Sicily, 187–88; promised to Sicily by Bonomi government, 133. *See also*

Bonomi government; (Sicilian) Constituent Assembly

Aventine Secession, 41

Badoglio, Pietro: forms second government, 69; government accused on mistreating Sicilians, 30; government gains control of Sicily, 32–33; installs Musotto as high commissioner, 35; labeled as enemy of separatism, 44; replaces Mussolini, 26; selection of high commissioner for Sicily, 33–35; and separatism, 66

Bagheria, as site of separatist meeting, 90

Bandits, 29, 172, 180, 204 n. 68; alliance with EVIS, 167; Communist sympathies of, 260 n. 22; as EVIS recruits, 142–43; and GRIS, 179. *See also* Giuliano, Salvatore

Bari Congress, 66, 217 n. 59

Barone, Vito, 156; dismisses indictment against separatists, 113. *See also* Sessa, Anselmo

Battiati, Francesco, 132

Battiato, Concetto, 40, defends Finocchiaro Aprile, 208 n. 25; as Fronte

leader, 117; and *La Repubblica Siciliana,* 64; leader of Sicilian Labor Party, 77; as separatist propagandist, 64–65, 207 n. 18

Bellolampo, 179

Berardi, Paolo, 159; links to monarchy, 159; urges government action against separatists, 155

Berle, Adolph A., 58–59

Black Market: under Allied Military Government of Occupied Territory, 30–31; mafia control of, 50

Blok, Anton, 212–13 n. 15

Bongiorno, Vincenzo, 265 n. 31

Bonomi government, 137; appoints Aldisio high commissioner, 88; authorizes legal measures against separatist movement, 98; orders surveillance on Finocchiaro Aprile, 98; promises autonomy for Sicily, 133; promises to combat separatism, 133; removes Musotto as high commissioner, 87–88

Bonomi, Ivanoe, 84, 138, 144, 157, 249 n. 31; formation of first government, 69;

formation of second government, 128; receives letter from Finocchiaro Aprile, 93; warns Allies of possible violence, 243 n. 17

Bossi, Umberto, 7; compared to Finocchiaro Aprile, 194, 207 n. 19; program, 194. *See also* Northern League

Bourbons, 14

Brandaleone, Carlo, 61

Bruno, Giuseppe, 192

Bruno, Mazzaro del Vallo, 176

Buongiorno, Michele, 117

Cacopardo, Rosario, 192, 262 n. 45.

Caltabiano, Giuseppe, 106, 192

Caltagirone: separatists in, 37

Caltanissetta: separatist movement in, 83, 127, 128

Canepa, Antonio, 17, 44, 109, 159, 160, 162, 248 n. 25; attacks promise of autonomy, 133; connections with British Secret Service, 22, 206 n. 6, contacts with Giuliano, 168; death of, 164–66, 256 n. 11; EVIS activities 163–64; imprisoned by Fascist government, 21; in Italian resistance, 39–40, 141; leads separatists in Catania, 37; meets with Communists, 248 n. 17; opposed by conservative separatists, 141; organizes EVIS, 141–44; organizes Giustizia e Libertà in Sicily, 21–22; and raid on San Marino, 21; program for Sicilian independence, 39–40; role in separatist revolution, 110; writes *L'organizzazione del partito nazionale Fascista*, 21; writes *La Sicilia ai siciliani*, 22; writes *Sistema della dottrina del fascismo*, 21; writes *Vent'anni di malgoverno fascista*, 22

Cangemi, Edoardo Milio, 107, 151, 215 n. 42, 262 n. 45; trial of, 98–99

Carabinieri, 132–33; role in Canepa's death, 164–65; separatist sympathizers in ranks, 111

Cardamone, Luigi, 96

Carr, M., 129; and Palermo riot, 104; refuses to aid separatists, 112

Cascino, Giovanni, 151

Castellano, Giuseppe, 50, 131, 137, 138, 205 n. 79; criticizes Italian government on draft, 132; attempts to end separatist crisis, 120–25; plans to appease separatists, 120; and mafla, 120; 121–25; as possible high commissioner for Sicily, 34, 205 n. 79. *See also* Finocchiaro Aprile, Andrea; Fronte Democratico d' Ordine Siciliano; Mafla (Sicilian); Orlando, Vittorio Emanuele; Tasca, Lucio

Castrogiovanni, Attilio, 37, 151, 161, 189, 190; arrest of, 171; elected to Constituent Assembly, 188, 264 n. 13; elected to Regional Assembly, 192; as EVIS supporter, 164, 255 n. 3; meets with Giuliano, 168, 169; protests destruction of separatist headquarters in Catania, 156; as Secretary General of the Movement, 160; supports formation of EVIS, 141; at Third National Congress, 190–91; and Varvaro's expulsion from the movement, 190–91

Catania, 13; anti draft riots in, 129, 130–31; anti-separatist demonstrations in, 154; separatist movement in, 80, 83, 127, 158, 161, 218 n. 70, 255 n. 48; separatist provincial committee in, 63;

"Catechism of the Free Sicilian", 64. *See also* Battiato, Concetto

Central Committee: make up and organization of, 60–63; 8 January 1944 meeting, 62–63; 9 December 1943 meeting, 60–62. *See also* Sicilian Separatist Movement

Coffari, Igino, 263 n. 10

Cesarò, 163, 164. *See also* Canepa, Antonio; Esercito Volontario per l'Indipendenza Sicilian

Charles, Noel, 101

Chilanti, Felice, 209 n. 45

Christian Democrats, 71, 110, 126, 128, 139, 150, 253 n. 31, 265 n. 34; and administrative elections, 186; blamed by separatists for destruction of Palermo headquarters, 156; criticized by Finocchiaro Aprile, 45; defections to separatist movement, 114; and mafla, 193; platform on autonomy and separatism, 73; post invasion reorganization, 72–73; separatist support in, 73; and Vizzini, 120–21. *See also* Aldisio, Salvatore; La Rosa, Luigi; Milazzo, Silvio

Chubb, Judith, 193

Churchill, Winston, 102, 146, 230 n. 24; meets with Umberto, 101; possible support for separatism, 58–59; receives letter from Finocchiaro Aprile, 148, 214 n. 27; receives letter from National Committee. 226 n. 74; wants British to control AMG, 29

Cianca, Alberto, 95

Cicala, Castel Prince, 120

Cigna, Domenico, 75, 212 n. 3, 215 n. 37

Cipolla, Michelangelo, 215 n. 42, 216 n. 49

Circolo per l'Indipendenza Siciliana, 206 n. 2

Civil Affairs Officers (CAOs), 28. *See*

also Allied Military Government of Occupied Territory (AMG)

Clergy: Finocchiaro Aprile on, 45; political activity of, 209 n. 36; separatists seek support of, 110

Comiso uprising, 136, 246 n. 50

Nazionale Movimento Antiseparatista ed Unitaria, 151

Comitato Siciliano Anti-Fascista Brigate Volontari della Libertà, 172

Comitato Siciliano d'Azione, 251 n. 4

Committee for Sicilian Independence, 143, 227 n. 87; criticizes Finocchiaro Aprile's leadership, 83; formation, 54; 4 October 1943 declaration, 60; operation of, 59–60; organization of, 59–60; proclamation of 22 July 1943, 36; 10 July 1943 proclamation, 54; 28 July 1943 declaration, 54. *See also* National Committee; Separatist Movement

Committee of National Liberation (CLN), 121, 168–69; and Bari Congress, 66; and Castellano initiative, 123; contacts with mafia, 123; creation in Rome, 72; criticized by separatists, 85, 95; opposition to Badoglio government, 26–27; opposition to separatism, 72, 89, 148; supports Aldisio as high commissioner, 88

Communist Party, 49, 71, 126, 152, 193, 216 n. 50; blamed for Catania disturbances, 131; denounces Italian government, 112; during constituent campaign, 186; and Gullo Decrees, 128; faces hostility from Allied powers, 74; incident with separatists, 67–68; negotiations with separatists, 114–16; and Palermo riot, 104; plan of cooperation with separatists, 53; possible shift toward separatist movement, 111–12; post-invasion reorganization, 73–75; reaction to arrest of separatist leaders, 175; at Regalbuto, 81–82; separatist support in, 73–74; in Villalba incident, 230 n. 20. *See also* dell'Aria, Ignazio; Li Causi, Girolamo; Montalbano, Giuseppe; Togliatti, Palmiro

Communist Party, of Catania, 153

Constituent Assembly, 66, 183, 184, 185, 190; campaign for, 186–88; election results, 188; given power to approve autonomy, 93; plan for autonomy debated, 189

Constituent Assembly (Sicilian): separatists request formation of, 138–39

Corpo della Guardia alla Bandiera, 141, 248 n. 15

Corvo, Max, 201 n. 36

Costa, Mariano, 47, 75, 215 n. 37

Costello, Frank, 23

Cottone, Giuseppe Jr., 176

Cottone, Giuseppe Sr. 176, 177

Crisafulli, Anselmo, 190

Crisafulli, Michele, 191

Croce, Benedetto, 77, 208 n. 34

D'Antoni, Paolo, 94–95; criticized by Finocchiaro Aprile, 84; feud with Musotto, 88; feuds with Aldisio and Sessa, 113, 237 n. 30; meets with Tasca brothers, 95; meets with Tasca and Varvaro, 167

Defascistization: 28, 70

DeGasperi, Alcide, 257 n. 32

Dell'Aria, Ignazio, 106; forms Partito Comunista di Sicilia, 73, 81

Democratic Liberals, 71

Demoliberal party (separatist), 77–78

De Stefano, Antonio, 207 n. 14

Di Belmonte, Bruno, 37, 107, 151, 161, 262 n. 45; and monarchists, 159; possible arrest of, 79; threatens violence, 152

Di Carcaci Family, 37, 106; and Corpo della Guardia alla Bandiera, 248 n. 15

Di Carcaci, Francesco Paternò, 151, 229 n. 14, 248 nn. 15 and 22, 254 n. 47, 257 n. 27

Di Carcaci, Guglielmo, 49, 109, 130, 151, 165, 166, 180; and Castellano initiative, 121–22; connections to GRIS, 179; contacts with Giuliano, 168, 169; and Corpo della Guardia alla Bandiera, 141, 248 n. 15; elected as president of Lega Giovanile,

67; rejects government offer of amnesty, 167; threatens violence, 92; tries to rebuild EVIS, 167, 168
Di Giovanni, Edoardo, 215 n. 37
Di Martino, Raffaele, 161, 188, 225 n. 57, 262 n. 45; possible arrest of, 79
Di Matteo, Salvo, 161
Di Natale, Enrico, 156, 215 n. 42, 231 n. 27; criminal proceedings against, 99; as separatist leader in Syracuse, 231 n. 27
Di Pietra, Francesco, 118, 119
Di Stefano, Antonio, 78, 223 n. 44. See also Party of Reconstruction
Donovan, Bill, 214 n. 28
D'Orso, Guido, 42
Downes, Donald, 214 n. 28
Draft, 125; anti draft demonstrations in Catania, 130–31; protests against, 130–32; results of , 132; Sicilian resistance to, 129–32
Drago, Gaetano, 192

Enna: separatist movement in, 127
Esercito Volontario per l'Indipendenza Siciliana (EVIS), 174, 189, 248 n. 24, 249 n. 28, 262 n. 45; activities of, 144, 163, 179–82; alliance with bandits, 248 n. 22, 257 n. 27; assessment of strength, 144, 249 n. 29; encampment at San Mauro, 180; destruction of, 181–82; formation of, 141–43; government campaign against, 166–67; plan for revolt, 172; planned March on Palermo, 163; potential recruits for, 142; rejected by Executive Committee, 166; structure of, 143–44, 248–49 n. 25. See also Canepa, Antonio; Di Carcaci, Guglielmo; Gallo, Concetto; Giuliano, Salvatore
Executive Committee (separatist), 235 nn. 12 and 15; plans for revolution, 109–10, 139

Falcone, 179
Faranda, Giuseppe, 215 n. 37
Farina, Beniamino, 96
Fasci Siciliani, 14
Fascism, 31; anti-mafia campaign, 19–20; in Sicily, 14–15, 18–21; assessment of strength in Sicily, 132,

198 n. 2; comparison to separatist movement, 16. See also Anti-Fascist Resistance; Mori, Cesare; Mussolini, Benito
Fascist Grand Council, 26
Federal Bureau of Investigation (FBI), 58–59
Finocchiaro Aprile, Andrea, 7, 78, 83, 90, 92, 95, 116, 128, 130, 133, 135; 150, 154, 161, 188, 208 n. 29, 215 nn. 37 and 42, 216 n. 49, 57, 222 n. 33, 229 n. 14, 265 n. 31; accused of pro-British sympathies, 117; activities during Fascist period, 41–43; alliance with monarchists, 159–60, 253 n. 36; and Allied denunciations of the movement, 100–102; and antimonarchical position, 44, 60; appeals to Allies for help, 82, 156; arrest of, 172, 173, 174; at First National Congress, 106–9; at Second National Congress, 151–53; at Third National Congress, 190–91; and Badoglio government, 44; and campaign for Constituent Assembly, 186–88; and campaign for foreign assistance, 84, 226–27 n. 78; and Canepa's death, 165; and Cangemi case, 98–99; and Castellano initiative, 123–25; on Central Committee, 60; centrist policies of, 16; claims Americans to re-occupy Sicily, 169–70; and clergy, 45; and Communists, 45, 53, 114–15, 131; conspires with Yugoslavs, 83–84; correspondence with Mussolini, 41–42; as deputy in Constituent, 189, 264 n. 19; and Di Natale case, 99; elected to Constituent Assembly, 188; elected to Regional Assembly, 192; and election for Senate, 192; and EVIS, 141–42, 143, 168, 262 n. 45; estimates separatist strength, 56; exploits Allied fears about Communism, 55, 80, 131; and extremists, 138; and federation with Italy, 46, 66; and Fronte Democratico, 90–92, 116; and granai del popolo, 79–80, 85–86, 90; as head of Sicilia e Libertà, 42; helps Jews

in Italy, 41; imprisonment of, 183–84; indictment against, 112–13; and landowners, 48–49; loses support, 157, 158, 160; and mafia, 62, 90–91, 159–60, 176, 177; meets with Aldisio, 227n. 87; message to Umberto, 157–58; and monarchist-republican schism in movement, 189–91; and Musotto, 34–35, 69, 218n. 3; opposes Aldisio as high commissioner, 88, 139; opposes conscription, 129–30; and Pacciardi, 247n. 14; and Palermo riot, 104–5; and Papacy, 45; and peasants, 45, 215n. 47; planned cooperation with Action Party, 53; plans for revolution, 80–81, 234n. 7; and Poletti, 57, possible arrest of, 79; possible assassination of, 83, in pre-Fascist Italy, 41, 220n. 17; pre invasion contacts with the Allies, 55; program of, 43–46, 65; receives letter from Churchill, 214n. 27; Regalbuto incident, 81–82; rejects American or British rule, 59; rejects French rule, 214n. 29; rejects government promise of autonomy, 93; rejects violence, 166–67; refusal of OSS to support, 25; release from prison, 184–85; Rennel's attitude toward, 207n. 19, 212n. 6; resigns as president of the movement, 192; and San Francisco Declaration, 146, 147–48; seeks British support, 146; as separatist leader, 52, 214nn. 31 and 33; and Soviet Republic in Sicily, 114–15; supports Mussolini's land reform program, 42; and supporters of movement, 47; surrenders seat in Regional Assembly, 265n. 31; threatens violence, 93–94, 110, 113–14, 134, 138; trial of, 81, 225n. 57; Valdese incident, 98; writes to Churchill, 148, 214n. 27, 226n. 74; writes to Cordell Hull, 104–5; writes to Alexander Kirk, 156; writes to Roosevelt, 85; writes to Ellery Stone, 156

Fronte del Lavoro (Labor Front), 75, 221n. 31

Fronte Democratico d'Ordine Sicili-ano (Sicilian Democratic Front of Order), 100; anti-British sentiments of, 117; breaks with Finocchiaro Aprile, 118, 119; and Castellano initiative, 120–21; formation and platform, 90–92, 116–19; at First National Congress, 106, 118–19; popularity, 116; pro-American attitudes, 117–19; welcomed by Finocchiaro Aprile, 90–92. See also Castellano, Giuseppe; Mafia (Sicilian); Vizzini, Calogero

Fronte Unico Siciliano, 72. See also La Loggia, Enrico

Gaja, Filippo, 248n. 15, 259n. 17

Gallo, Concetto, 151, 161, 165, 182, 192; alliance with Giuliano, 169, 257n. 27; at Battle of San Mauro, 180–81, 260n. 25; at Third National Congress, 191; breaks with Finocchiaro Aprile, 160; and Catania disturbances, 244n. 23; in Constituent Assembly, 189; and Corpo della Guardia, 141; elected to Constituent Assembly, 188, 263–64n. 13; and EVIS, 166, 167, 168, 169, 178–79; heads Catania committee, 190; as head of separatist intelligence service, 161; in separatist press bureau, 107

Gambino, Baldassone, 151

Gasparotto, Luigi, 151

Gattucio, Gaspare, 49

Gayre, George R.: assesses separatist strength, 55–56; condemns arrest of Finocchiaro Aprile, 175–76; on condition of the mafia, 199n. 9; meets with Finocchiaro Aprile, 146; warns of separatist strength, 176

Genovese, Vito, 50

Gerbini airport: attack on, 20, 22. See also Anti-Fascist Resistance; Canepa, Antonio

Germanà, Gioacchino, 192

Giallo-Rosso, 67, 105

Giganti, Pietro, 152

Giornale di Sicilia, 101

Giovane Sicilia, La, 223n. 44

Giudice, Giuseppe, 164. See also Canepa, Antonio: death of

Giuliano, Salvatore, 166, 256n. 20; accused of supporting Varvaro, 189, 265n. 29; alliance with separatists, 167–69, 257n. 27; attack on Bellolampo, 179; as EVIS commander, 178–80; contacts with Canepa, 168; early career, 167; meets with Gallo at San Mauro, 180; post-separatist activities, 181, 261n. 31; rumored support for the monarchy, 187; writes to Truman, 182

Giustizia e Libertà, 25, 76

Giustizia e Libertà (Sicily), 21

Granai del popolo, 78–80

Grasso, Franco, 41; meets with Finocchiaro Aprile, 208n. 29

Great Britain: attitudes toward separatists, 85, 87, 94, 145, 213–14n. 26, 28; Finocchiaro Aprile claims support of, 146; policy in Mediterranean, 29, 58, reaction to arrest of separatist

leaders, 175; reaction to San Francisco Declaration, 148; suspect American support for separatism, 57–58. See also Allied Military Government of Occupied Territories; Allied powers; Churchill, Winston

Great Meadows Prison, 24

Gruppi Rivoluzionari Indipendenza Siciliana (GRIS): creation of, 179; at San Mauro, 180; relationship to EVIS, 179, 259n. 17

Guarino Amella, Giovanni, 47; as candidate for high commissioner, 33; as member of central committee, 215nn. 37 and 42; as member of secret executive committee, 214n. 33

Gullo Decrees, 128

Gullo, Fausto, 78. See also Gullo Decrees

Hall, George, 101

Hancock, A. N.: counsels against arrest of separatists, 87; and Musotto nomination, 34;

recommends arrest of separatists, 82

High Commissioner, Sicily, 205n. 78; See also Aldisio, Salvatore; Coffari, Igino; Musotto, Francesco; Selvaggi, Giovanni

Hoover, J. Edgar: investigates British support for separatism, 58–59

Hull, Cordell, 104–5

Iantaffi, Michele, 29

Indipendente, L', 97

Indipendenza Siciliana, L', 64

Ingrasci, Gastone, 231n. 28

Ionia, 154

Italian-American Labor Committee, 145

Italian-Americans: affect on American policy toward Sicily, 28–29, 203n. 49; fears concerning separatism, 84–85

Italian Republican Movement in Sicily, 124. See also Mafia (Sicily)

Italian Social Republic (Republic of Salò), 27

Kefauver Committee, investigates Luciano role in invasion, 200n. 22

Kingdom of the South, 27

Kirk, Alexander, 100–101, 156

Kingdom of Two Sicilies, 187

La Cara, Giovanni, 118, 119

La Guardia, Fiorello, 90

La Loggia, Enrico, 220n. 17; and CLN, 72; views on separatism, 72; rebuffed by Poletti, 72; on Musotto's advisory council, 69, 70; supports Aldisio as high commissioner, 88

La Manna, Salvatore, 171

La Manna, Vincenzo, 53, 214n. 31, 215n. 42

La Motta, Stefano, 21, 37, 49, 168, 248n. 22; arrest of, 181; and GRIS, 179; meets with

Giuliano, 169

land seizures, 128. See also Gullo Decrees

Landolina, Pietro, 192

Lansky, Meyer, 23

Lanza, Joe "Socks," 23

La Rosa, Luigi, 47, 106, 107, 109–10, 151, 161, 215n. 37; and armed bands, 166; breaks with Christian Democrats 73; leads separatists in Caltagirone, 37; as head of Sicilian Christian Democratic Party, 114 latifondi, 74, 107; defended by Lucio Tasca, 38–39; and Fascism, 20; Finocchiaro Aprile supports reform of, 42, 46; in Sicily, 48

Latifondisti, 209 nn. 45 and 48; and Fascism, 18, 20; support separatism, 16, 48–49, 212–13 n. 15

Leanza, Nino, 121

Lega Giovanile Separatista, 49, 83, 90, 138, 141, 171, 188, 248 n. 22; creation of, 67; and GRIS, 179; issues call for violence, 92, 94, 134; loses support, 160; 23 April meeting of, 67–68; participation in Catania riots, 130–31. See also Guglielmo di Carcaci; Giganti, Pietro

Liberal Party, 77

Li Causi, Girolamo, 137; as communist leader, 74; on latifondi and latifondisti, 74; talks with Mafia, 123; views on separatism and autonomy, 74–75; and Villalba incident, 95–98, 230 n. 19

London Conference, 170

London Times, 86

Lo Verde, Sebastiano, 47, 53, 211 n.1, 214 n. 31, 216 n. 49

Luciano, Charles "Lucky": campaign for Constituent Assembly, 186; cooperation with Naval Intelligence, 23–24, 201 n. 30, 31. See also Mafia (American)

Lupo, Antonio, 117

MacMillan, Harold, 233 n. 43

Mafia (American): cooperation with Naval Intelligence, 23–24; See also Lansky, Meyer; Luciano, Charles "Lucky"

Mafia (Sicilian), 8–9, 17, 137, 141, 153, 201–2 nn. 36 and 37; Aldisio talks with, 88–89; and AMG, 210 n.54; anti-Communist stance and support for autonomy, 176–78; campaign for Constituent Assembly, 186; and control of bandits, 142–43; cooperates with Castellano, 120–25; demands Aldisio's removal, 121; and Fascist regime, 19–20; and Finocchiaro Aprile, 49, 121, 122, 123; as force of stability, 125; internal schism, 176–78; and Ital-

ian Republican Movement in Sicily, 124; and latifondisti, 49; and Musotto, 34, 35; and Orlando, 124, 160; and OSS, 24–26; in post-war Italy, 193–94; role in Canepa's death, 165; support for separatism, 49–50, 156, 210 n. 51; ; talks with monarchists, 159–60; traditions and practices of, 15–16, 197 n. 7. See also Castellano, Giuseppe; Fronte Democratico d'Ordine Siciliano; Mori, Cesare; Partito Democratico d'Ordine; Vizzini, Calogero

Mafiosi, 122; Allied assessment of, 49; in AMG, 50; and black market, 26; character of, 15; and latifondisti, 49

March on Rome, 18

Martino, Augusto, 208 n. 29

Marino, Giuseppe Carlo, 215 n. 44, 254 n. 38

Mattarella, Bernardo, 73

Matteoti Brigade, 141

Mazzini Society, 233 n. 47

McSherry, Frank, 28

Messina: antiseparatist demonstrations in, 154; separatist movement in, 127, 174

Milazzo, Silvio, 73

Millemaggi, Edoardo, 161

Millemaggi, Giovanni, 106, 107; and Cangemi case, 98

Ministry of the Interior, 126

Monarchists: and possible cooperation with separatists, 187, 188. See also Savoy Dynasty; Kingdom of Two Sicilies; Tasca, Lucio; Umberto; Victor Emmanuel III

Mondini, Enrico, 191

Montalbano, Francesco, 151

Montalbano, Giuseppe: blames separatists for draft riots, 132; talks with separatists, 115–16

Montana, Vanni, 145

Montedoro, Battle of, 181

Montesanti, Fausto, 47, 53, 60, 75, 112, 216 n. 49

Mori, Cesare, 125; anti-Mafia campaign, 19–20

Movement for the Annexation of Sicily to the American Confederation, 182. See also Giuliano, Salvatore

Movimento Antiseparatista della Sicilia per l'Unita, 151
Movimento per l'Autonomia Siciliana, 178
Movimento per l'Indipendenza della Sicilia, 68. See also Sicilian Separatist Movement
Movimento per l'Indipendenza Siciliana Democratico Repubblicano, 190; congress in Taormina, 191. See also Varvaro, Antonino
Musotto, Francesco, 38, 41, 89, 208 n. 29; appointment as high commissioner, 33–35; as high commissioner, 69–70, removal as high commissioner, 87–88, 227 n. 83; and separatists, 67, 68, 69; views on separatism, 34–35
Mussolini, Benito, 18, 44, 125, 147, 150; and land reform; 20–21; linked to Aldisio, 140; and Mafia, 19–20; overthrow, 26–27; visits Sicily, 199 n. 12. See also Anti-Fascism; Fascism; Mori, Cesare

Nasi, Virgilio, 121, 122–23, 239 n. 66
National Committee, 182; and antiseparatist demonstrations, 156; appeals to United Nations for control of Sicily, 138; declines in importance, 161; and EVIS, 235 n. 15; letter to Churchill, 226 n. 74; and London Declaration, 257 n. 31; and possible Communist coup, 153; rejects autonomy, 93, 134
Nenni, Pietro, 76, 140, 148
Nester, Alfred T., 8, 118, 235 nn. 17 and 18, 259 n. 6; and Castellano plan, 122–23; and death of Canepa, 166; denies vote on San Francisco Declaration, 148; estimates Fascist strength, 132; on Finocchiaro Aprile, 124–25, 175; on Fronte Democratico, 116; estimates separatist strength, 56; and mafia, 176, 177; on Movimento per l'Autonomia Siciliana, 178; on possibility of separatist revolt, 110, 111, 135; rejects separatist protest, 156; takes favorable attitude toward mafia, 154; on Tasca, 38; urges rejection of

separatist movement, 100–101; and Villalba incident, 96
New York Times, 145
Nicolosi, Salvatore, 218 n. 70, 259 n. 17
Nicosia, 37
Nitti, Francesco 184
Northern League, 7, 194–95. See also Bossi, Umberto

Oddo, Antonio, 166
Oddo, Giuseppe Amilcare, 151
Oddo, Vincenzo, 166
Office of Naval Intelligence, 23–24. See also Mafia (American)
Office of Strategic Services (OSS), 31, 56, 118, 129, 221–22, 32; and Finocchiaro Aprile, 42; and invasion of Sicily, 24–26; view of Castellano plan, 122; and Villalba incident, 230 n. 20
Omertà, 8
Orlando, Vittorio Emanuele, 184, 186, 240 n. 74; and Castellano plan, 123–25; on draft riots, 131–32; and Fascism, 19; and mafia, 159–60, 177; meets with Finocchiaro Aprile, 124; view of separatism, 123

Pacciardi, Randolfo, 77, 247 n. 14; and possible coalition with separatists and party of Action, 140. See also Republican Party
Palermo: American naval base in, 101; disturbance in, 102–5, 107; separatist movement in, 83, 127, 174
Palermo, Vincenzo, 121
Pantaleone, Michele, 95–96, 210 n. 53, 230 n. 19.
Parri, Ferruccio, 162, 257 n. 32; and arrest of separatists, 172–74; government plans to recognize separatists, 168–69
Partito Comunista di Sicilia, 73–74, 81, 106. See also Dell'Aria, Ignazio
Partito dei Lavoratori: in Catania, 238 n. 40
Partito dei Lavoratori, 39, 141. See also Canepa, Antonio
Partito del Lavoro, 65, 40
Partito Democratico d'Ordine, 90,

platform, 62. *See also* Mafia (Sicilian)
Partito Democratico Siciliano (Sicilian Democratic Party), 106
Partito Laburista Siciliano, 40, 77
Partito Sociale Communista, 106
Partito Socialista Rivoluzionario, 238 n. 40
Party of Union, 77
Pearson, Drew, 145
Peasants, 16; Finocchiaro Aprile views on, 45; as separatist supporters, 51–52
Pellegrino, Ettore, 36
Pentarchy, 161
Piazza, Isidoro, 244 n. 23
Pirrone, Giuseppe, 118
Pliny, 75. *See also* Vacirca, Vincenzo
Polakoff, Moses, 23
Poletti, Charles, 53, 256 n, 21; and appointment of high commissioner, 33, 34, 57, 205 n. 78; criticized by Rennel, 205 n. 75; criticizes AMG, 30; criticizes Rennel, 29; and Finocchiaro Aprile, 57; and Musotto, 227 n. 83; and separatists, 57; and Tasca, Lucio, 38, 57, 90
Poma, Francesco 127
Ponza, 173
Popolo, Il , 150–51
Popular Party, 72–73. *See also* Christian Democrats; Sturzo, Luigi
Prefects, Sicilian, 32, 70, 224 n. 50
Progresso Italo-Americano, Il , 100
Press Office (separatist) 107
Purpura, Vincenzo, 25, 76. *See also* Action Party

Ragusa, separatist movement in, 127, 174
Ramirez, Antonio, 103
Randazzo, 154; Canepa's death in, 164; EVIS formation in, 166; separatist-communist incident in, 81
Regalbuto, 80; separatist-communist incident in, 81–82
Regional Assembly, 193; campaign for, 191–92
Regional Council, 137–38
Rennel, Lord of Rodd, 127; 213 n. 17; in AMG, 28, 30, 204 n. 73; and

mafia, 198–99 n. 9; 210 nn. 51 and 54; and Poletti, 205 n. 75; and separatists, 55, 210 n. 55; 212 n. 6
Republican Party, 77, 238 n. 40. *See also* Pacciardi, Randolfo
Restuccia, Francesco, 47, 107, 151, 152, 188, 190, 252 n. 17, 254 n. 43, 262 n. 45; arrest of, 154, 173–74; and EVIS, 142; imprisonment and release of, 183, 184; splits with Finocchiaro Aprile, 160
Riesi, 36
Rindone, Santi, 37, 107, 108, 144, 161, 167, 181, 215 nn. 37 and 42
Romano, Salvatore, 248 n. 22
Romita, Giuseppe, 184, 187, 262 n. 45
Roosevelt, Franklin, 90, 146, 230 n. 24; and AMG, 28–29; and letter from Finocchiaro Aprile, 85; and Mediterranean policy, 58
Rosa, Giovanni, 36–37
Rosano, Carmelo, 255 n. 9; death of, 164, 165. *See also* Canepa, Antonio
Rossi, Sirio, 168, 179, 216 n. 49
Ruini, Meuccio, 94, 95, 120
Russo, Giuseppe, 121
Russo, Sciacca, 176

Sabauda Division, 103
Salamone, Gioacchino, 192
Salvemini, Gaetano, 263 n. 12
SanFilippo, Filippo, 152, 158
San Francisco Conference, 146, 147, 148, 156, 250 n. 37
San Mauro, Battle of, 232 n. 38. *See also* Concetto Gallo
Sansone, Vito, 232 n. 38
Savoy Dynasty, 36, 43, 49, 54, 63, 120, 187
Scardino, Arturo, 73, 106
Schifani, Salvatore, 164
Scialabba, Giuseppe, 76
Sciortino, Pasquale, 256 n. 21
Secondo Turri, 169. *See also* Gallo, Concetto
Selvaggi, Giovanni, 263 n. 10
Seminara, Mauro, 121
Separatist Movement of 1920, 36
Separatist movements, contemporary, 194–95
Sessa, Anselmo, 111–13, 135, 237 n. 30, 244 n. 23. *See also* Aldisio, Sal-

vatore; D'Antoni, Paolo; Barone, Vito
Sforza, Carlo, 66–67, 203 n. 49
La Sicilia ai siciliani!, 39–40. *See also* Canepa, Antonio
Sicilian Association of Rome, 151
Sicilian Christian Democratic Party, 81
Sicilian Party of Reconstruction, 78
Sicilian Regional Assembly, 192
Sicilian Separatist Movement (Movimento per l'Indipendenza della Sicilia): alliance with the mafia, 61–62; and Allied powers, 109, 144; Appeal to Anglo-Americans, 85; Appeal to Sicilian Americans, 84–85; arrest of leaders, 171–76; and autonomy, 133–34; British support for, 57–58, 100, 101–2, 145–46, and Catania disturbances, 130–31; and clergy, 110; and campaign for Constituent Assembly, 186–88; communal committees, formation of, 63; and Communists, 114–16, 152; and plebiscite, 36, 46, 54, 84, 85, 93, 94, 170; and draft, 129–30; federalists in, 137; First National Congress (Taormina), 106–9; Fourth National Congress (Taormina), 192–93; and granai del popolo, 79–80, 86; leadership of and support for, 15, 46–52; 56, 66, 126–28, 157, 215 n. 47, 216 n. 54, 219–20 n. 15, 241 n. 4; London Declaration, 170–71, 174, 257 n. 31; and monarchists, 157–60, 188; monarchist-republican split, 188–90; name given to, 68; newspapers of, 64, 67, 218 n. 67; origins of, 37–52; and Palermo riot, 108; Palermo headquarters closed, 153–54; possible revolution by, 80–81, 94, 106, 109–11, 134–36, 138–39, 152, 172, 179; propaganda by, 63–65, 139–40, 155–56; protests against, 153–55; provincial committee, Catania, 215 n. 44; provincial committee, Messina, 93; provincial committee, Palermo, 53, 63; provincial committees, formation of, 63; radio station of, 172; San Francisco Declaration,

146–49; Second National Congress (Palermo), 151–53; 16 January meeting of, 65; Statute of Sicilian Independence, 108–9; Third National Congress (Taormina), 190–91; 13 February meeting of, 65–67; and Togliatti, 110; 20 July appeal, 86–87; and United States, 58–59, 144–45. *See also* Central Committee; Finocchiaro Aprile, Andrea; National Committee; Tasca, Lucio
Sicilian Socialist Federation, 152, 222 n. 33; platform, 75–76. *See also* Vacirca, Vincenzo
Sicilian Socialist Party, 81
Sicilian Vespers, 14, 64, 94, 146, 147
Simili, Massimo, 197 n. 4
Socialist Party, 71, 75–76, 186
Soldino Movement, 19, 36
Southern Question, 14
Soviet Union: and Italian territorial integrity, 214 n. 29; interest concerning separatism, 86; and San Francisco Declaration, 147
Squadrismo, 18
Stampinato, Antonio, 130
Stancanelli, Girolamo, 215 n. 37
Stone, Ellery, 156, 249 n. 31
Students, 48, 51, 142, 211 n. 57
Sturzo, Luigi, 72–73, 220 n. 20, 263 n. 12, 231 n. 33. *See also* Christian Democrats
Sulphur miners, 52
Syracuse: Communists in, 127; separatist movement in, 82–83, 127, 174

Tangiers: separatists in, 84
Taormina. See Sicilian Separatist Movement
Tasca family, 58, 255 n. 48
Tasca, Alessandro, 49, 112, 120, 213 n. 16, 214 n. 3, 216 n. 49, 221 n. 26; and antimonarchical declaration, 60; and Castellano initiative, 122, 123, 124; estimates separatist strength, 56; meets with Ruini, 95; supports Movimento per l'Autonomia Siciliana, 178
Tasca, Giuseppe, 134, 137, 151, 165, 168, and EVIS, 141–42, 182, 248 n..

22; and GRIS, 179; warns of separatist violence, 156

Tasca, Lucio, 17, 21, 34, 106, 107, 112, 128, 135, 146, 192, 212 n. 6; 214 nn. 31 and 33; 216 n. 49, 229 n. 14, 240 n. 74, 262 n. 45; alliance with Giuliano, 257 n. 27; and Constituent Assembly campaign, 186, and Castellano initiative, 120, 122, 123, 124; criticizes autonomy, 266 n. 35; decides against violence, 136, 137, 167, 206–7 n. 9, 10; and EVIS, 142, 168, 177, 182–83, 187, 248 n. 22; feud with Musotto, 69; and GRIS, 179; leads separatist movement, 182; leads separatists in Palermo, 37; letter to Roosevelt, 85; as mayor of Palermo, 57; meets with Ruini, 95; monarchist sentiments of, 158–59, 189; negotiates with monarchists, 120, 158–60, 254 n. 38; as member of Pentarchy, 161; plans revolution, 109, 110, 111; pre-separatist background, 38, 206–7 n. 9, 10; and Poletti, 57, 90; program, 38–39, 48; protests arrest of separatist leaders, 184; removal as mayor of Palermo, 89–90; supports 1920 separatist movement, 36; ties to mafia, 49–50; visits Gallo at San Mauro, 180

Tasca, Paolo, 123

Termini, Francesco, 47, 215 n. 37

Tito, Josef, 153

Togliatti, Palmiro, 69, 116, 153

Tolu, 141. See also Canepa, Antonio

Trapani, separatist movement in, 127, 128, 174

Trieste, 154

Tunisia, 110, 234 n. 5, 258 n. 40. See also Action squads; Rosa, Giovanni

Turkish government, 226 n. 77

Turri, Mario, 22, 133. See also Canepa, Antonio

Umberto, 187, 189; contacts with separatists, 158–60

Unione Siciliana dell'Ordine, 106

Unione Siciliana Lavoro Giustizia e Libertà, 151

Unione Siciliani Agricoltori-Presidente Roosevelt, 52

Unità, L', 74, 97

Unità Proletaria, 74

United States, 94; and AMG, 28–29; denies support for separatist movement, 100–101, 170; and Palermo disturbance, 104; policy in Mediterranean, 58; policy toward separatists, 111; reaction to arrest of separatist leaders, 175; rumors of annexation of Sicily, 145; and San Francisco Declaration, 147–48; suspects British support for separatism, 58–59. See also Allied Powers; Allied Military Government of Occupied Territory; Poletti, Charles

Vacirca, Vincenzo, 40, 47, 161, 215 n. 42, 222 n. 33; and OSS, 75; and plan for autonomy, 75–76. See also Sicilian Socialist Federation

Valdese incident, 98

Valenti, Girolamo, 91, 228 n. 101

Varvaro, Antonino, 17, 40, 47, 60, 90, 106, 108, 112, 128, 135, 152, 162, 207 n. 17; 214 n. 31; 215 n. 42; 237 n. 30; 262 n. 45; arrest of, 173; and campaign for Constituent Assembly, 186, 189; and Catania disturbance, 130, 13; and death of Canepa, 256 n. 11; elected to the Constituent Assembly, 188; election for Regional Assembly, 192; expelled from movement, 190–91; and Giuliano, 257 n. 27, 265 n. 29; imprisonment and release, 183–84; as member of Pentarchy, 161; and Movimento per l'Indipendenza Siciliana Democratico Repubblicano, 190, 191; negotiates with Aldisio, 160–61; negotiates with Parri government, 168–69; plans separatist revolution, 109, rejects use of violence, 167; resigns as secretary-general, 190; supports violence, 134–35

Vella, Antonio Parlapiano, 215 n. 37

Venezia-Giulia, 153

Verax, 64. See also Finocchiaro Aprile, Andrea

"Verità sui fatti di Villalba, La," 96. See also Villalba; Vizzini, Calogero

Vichinsky, Andrei, 214 n. 29

Victor Emmanuel II, 188
Victor Emmanuel III, 60, 69
Villalba, confrontation between Communists and separatists, 95–98. *See also* Li Causi, Girolamo; Vizzini, Calogero
Villasevaglios, Pietro, 216 n. 49
Vinciguerra, Pietro, 121
Virzi, Paolo, 61, 176
Vizzini, Calogero, 182; and Aldisio, 88–89, 120–21; aligns with separatists, 60–61; as AMG appointed mayor of Villalba, 50; and Castellano initiative, 120, 121, 122, 137; and EVIS, 142–43, 248 n. 22; and Giuliano, 168; as head of Sicilian mafia, 154, 210 n. 53; leads Fronte Democratico d'Ordine Siciliano, 106, 116, 120; and Lucio Tasca, 37, 60–61; and Movimento per l'Autonomia Siciliana, 178; negotiates with monarchists, 159; and schism in the mafia, 176–77, 259 n. 6; supports Finocchiaro Aprile, 160; and Villalba incident, 95–97
Voce Comunista, La, 99
Volpe, Calogero, 89, 118, 121

Women's Committee, separatist, 112

Yugoslavia, 153